HITCHCOCK
AND SELZNICK

Also by Leonard J. Leff

FILM PLOTS: Scene-by-Scene Narrative Outlines
for Feature Film Study (1983)

HITCHCOCK
AND SELZNICK

•

THE RICH AND STRANGE COLLABORATION
OF ALFRED HITCHCOCK AND DAVID O. SELZNICK
IN HOLLYWOOD

•

LEONARD J. LEFF

Weidenfeld & Nicolson
New York

Published by Weidenfeld & Nicolson, New York
A Division of Wheatland Corporation
10 East 53rd Street
New York, NY 10022

Published in Canada by General Publishing Company, Ltd.

Portions of this book originally appeared in *Premiere*.

Illustrations have been supplied and are reproduced by kind permission of the following:
Marc Wanamaker/Bison Archives: pp. 7, 14, 17 (top and bottom), 32, 61 (top), 65, 138 (top),
147, 150 (top and bottom), 153, 212 (top);
Cinema Collectors: pp. 22, 41, 50, 219 (bottom), 242, 246;
The Kobal Collection: p. 58 (top);
The Museum of Modern Art/Film Stills Archive: pp. 58 (bottom), 68 (top), 73 (top), 83, 89,
96, 103, 113 (top), 121, 138 (bottom), 158 (top and bottom), 178, 183 (top and bottom), 188, 204,
219 (top), 253, 274 (top);
Selznick Properties, Ltd./David O. Selznick Archive, Theatre Arts Library, Harry Ransom
Humanities Research Center, The University of Texas at Austin: pp. 61 (bottom), 141, 212
(bottom), 214;
Film Favorites: pp. 68 (bottom), 73 (bottom), 76 (top and bottom), 131, 171, 186, 202, 234 (top
and bottom), 274 (bottom);
Carol Stevens Shourds: pp. 106, 108 (top, middle, bottom), 113 (bottom), 226, 267;
IMP/GEH Still Collection: p. 249;
Lord Bernstein, LL.D.: p. 257.

Library of Congress Cataloging-in-Publication Data

Leff, Leonard J.
Hitchcock and Selznick.

Bibliography: p.
Includes index.
1. Hitchcock, Alfred, 1899-1980
2. Selznick, David O., 1902–1965. 3. Moving-picture
producers and directors—United States—Biography.
I. Title.
PN1998.A3H5484   1987   792'.023'0922   87-8185
ISBN 1-55584-057-4

Manufactured in the United States of America
Designed by Irving Perkins Associates
First Edition

10 9 8 7 6 5 4 3 2 1

for my parents

ACKNOWLEDGMENTS

The research and writing of *Hitchcock and Selznick* involved numerous persons who generously offered their assistance. At the Humanities Research Center, The University of Texas at Austin, W. H. Crain and Raymond Daum welcomed me to the Selznick Collection; Paul Bailey pulled files with tireless efficiency. Daniel Selznick not only granted permission to cite from the collection but also carefully read my manuscript and made suggestions that contributed to its accuracy.

At the Margaret Herrick Library of the Academy of Motion Picture Arts and Sciences, which houses the Hitchcock Collection, archivist Samuel Gill and his assistant Barbara Hall lent their intelligence and good humor to the project. I am equally grateful to John Hall of RKO Pictures; Robert Knudson, Leith Adams, and Ned Comstock of Special Collections at the University of Southern California; Ron Davis and the Oral History Collection at Southern Methodist University; Warner Bros., Inc.; and the staffs of the Humanities and Interlibrary Loan Divisions, Oklahoma State University; the Margaret Herrick Library;

ACKNOWLEDGMENTS

the Billy Rose Theatre Collection, Lincoln Center Library for the Performing Arts, New York; the American Film Institute, Los Angeles; and the British Film Institute, London.

Laird International Studios historian Walter O'Connor graciously showed me through the Culver City studio complex that David Selznick leased in the 1930s and 1940s, the same facility where Selznick and Hitchcock made *Rebecca*. Ronald Haver led me to several former Selznick staff members, and Caroline Moorehead answered questions about Sidney Bernstein. Mary Corliss, Film Stills Archivist of the Museum of Modern Art; Alexandra Lascelles of the Kobal Collection; Jenny Sussex of the British Film Institute; Marc Wanamaker of the Bison Archives; and Jan-Christopher Horak of the George Eastman House offered their expertise to the project.

Men and women who worked with Selznick or Hitchcock shared with me their memories of the two filmmakers: Judith Anderson, Pandro Berman, Robert Boyle, Niven Busch, William Dozier, Joan Fontaine, Olivia de Havilland, John Michael Hayes, Raymond Klune, Arthur Laurents, Ernest Lehman, Marcella Rabwin, Peggy Robertson, Robert Saunders, Lydia Schiller, Leonard South, and Ann Todd. Irene Mayer Selznick and Patricia Hitchcock O'Connell also granted interviews. Carol Stevens Shourds provided abundant insight into the man whom she served as secretary and business manager from 1939 to the mid-sixties, Alfred Hitchcock. I am indebted to her and all of the others for their assistance.

My agent, Nat Sobel, believed in the book; my editor, Mark Polizzotti, improved it. Richard Jewell of the University of Southern California and Leland Poague of Iowa State University read the manuscript and supplied constructive criticism. At Oklahoma State University, Dean Smith Holt and Associate Dean Neil Hackett, as well as Gordon Weaver and John Crane, offered considerable support. My thanks to them all.

Along with my son, Jonathan, my wife, Linda Kay, brought some much-needed perspective to the years of research and writing. *Hitchcock and Selznick* owes much to her. And so do I.

CONTENTS

PREFACE

Fred Astaire
with Ginger Rogers.
Josef von Sternberg
with Marlene Dietrich.
David Selznick
with Alfred Hitchcock.

The elegant dancer and his willing partner. The autocratic director and his pliant subject. The independent filmmaker and . . . the independent filmmaker. Terrific marquee value, a press agent might have remarked about this last pair, but volatile chemistry.

Producer Selznick withheld little. "I snore loudly, drink exuberantly, cuddle (i.e., snuggle) expansively, work excessively," he once confessed to his wife. When he formed Selznick International in the mid-1930s, he proclaimed that the industry rewarded those who made "either the very cheap pictures or the expensive pictures"; he intended to release "topnotch product." Thereafter he spent freely and refused to delegate responsibility for major and even minor artistic decisions. He ruled his studio less by threat or menace—the weapon of several fellow moguls—than by the thoroughness and heat of his commitment, manifest daily through his eruptive "notes." Words came easily to Selznick. Chronically disorganized but relentlessly verbal, he threw long-winded memoranda at a chaos he sometimes helped to create. Certain pictures might have fared better without his dictation and close supervision, yet the point was moot: As Irene Selznick observed about her husband, "Containment wasn't his."

In contrast to Selznick's raggedy motion, director Hitchcock strove for Nirvana. He drank but not exuberantly, he worked but not excessively (he asked *Life* magazine to characterize him as "a fundamentally lazy man"), and he probably neither cuddled nor snuggled. More than once, Hitchcock confessed that sex had never much interested him. He preferred sleep to exertion, spectatorship to participation. According to Walter Wanger, for whom Hitchcock directed *Foreign Correspondent,* the bourgeois grocer's son would "never reveal fatigue or worry"; in fact, Hitchcock often said, his elaborate planning left him bored during the period of principal photography.

Photographer Sanford Roth captured the essential Hitchcock. Holding his briefcase, expressionless, the English director posed for a publicity shot outside an American studio, much of the left half of his face and body hidden behind the wall of a soundstage. The composition implies order, stillness, and a fair share of enigma. For a director who gave dozens of interviews, Hitchcock gave away very little. Though generous with his wit, he seemed to use it as both weapon and shield; like his dark suits, it kept others at a distance. He commented at length on the mechanics of his films—the lighting, the special effects, the problems with actors—but he rarely spoke of their essence: guilt, passion, and repression. Containment was his.

Hitchcock spent nearly a decade with Selznick, beginning in 1938. More than either acknowledged, they joined forces primarily to extend their independence as filmmakers. A director of "little British thrillers," Hitchcock lacked the wherewithal to attain international status. Selznick not only brought Hitchcock to Hollywood but offered him stories and actors commensurate with his presumed talent. Their collaboration bore fruit: Hitchcock added bite to Selznick's style, Selznick added American gloss to Hitchcock's. Though the temporal and logistical constraints of motion picture production forced compromises upon both men, they scored some very real achievements, from their triumphant first film—*Rebecca*—through *Spellbound, Notorious,* and the troubled *Paradine Case.*

Yet Selznick and Hitchcock never meshed. Their personalities and their aesthetics clashed. Their mutual exploitation, their conflicting managerial styles, their long periods apart, their increasingly tense periods together, and their negotiation and near continual renegotiation of employment agreements also buffeted their relationship. The friction ultimately claimed its toll. As the various option dates on his Selznick contracts matured throughout the 1940s, Hitchcock desperately pursued the freedom that other independent producer-directors had achieved, just as Selznick energetically tried to re-sign him. English exhibitor Sidney Bernstein finally enabled Hitchcock to break away, but their coproductions of *Rope* and *Under Capricorn* hardly rivaled the popular or critical acclaim of the director's best Selznick films. History subsequently proved that Selznick needed Hitchcock more than Hitchcock needed Selznick, yet Hitchcock did not succeed *despite* Selznick any more than Selznick succeeded *because of* Hitchcock. The dynamics of the relationship served both men, not only as artists but—of equal importance to them—as Hollywood professionals.

HITCHCOCK
AND SELZNICK

1

TRANSATLANTIC OVERTURES

In a small gift shop on palm-lined Vine Street, between the Plaza Hotel and the bowling alley, a tourist visiting southern California in the late 1930s could buy postcards of Los Angeles. Street scenes of "World Famous Hollywood and Vine" and the "Famed Sunset Strip" sold best, but pictures of the studios were also popular. Since most movie companies had closed their gates to the public, only through photographs could the curious peek into studio fortresses. Often these commercial snapshots revealed the dream factories for what they actually were: a motley collection of buildings that resembled warehouses, airplane hangars, and government office buildings. A postcard of Carl Laemmle's "Universal City, California: 'The Capital of Filmland' " featured a mishmash of nondescript structures, a colony more penal than movie. Metro-Goldwyn-Mayer's Thalberg Building, all stone and concrete, seemed cold and inaccessible. Aerial postcard shots of Warner Bros., Paramount, and Fox positioned the viewer still farther from studios

3

that suggested barracks, not workshops. How, a tourist might have wondered, could those who labored inside such drab facilities generate such rich fantasies?

That question might not have occurred to someone motoring past Culver City's Selznick International Pictures, one of the few studios with a public facade. Separated from Washington Boulevard by an expanse of verdant lawn and manicured hedge, Selznick International's colonnaded administration building resembled a wealthy Southern planter's home: the windows had shutters; the roof, dormer windows. While the tall stages rising up behind this mansion compromised the image of placid if elegant domesticity, they also reminded tourists that motion pictures were produced there. Among the five major motion picture companies, the sheer number of annual releases militated against a chief executive's interesting himself in each film. At Selznick International, however, David Selznick influenced everything that he touched, and he touched almost everything, from the acquisition of the literary property to screenplay development, cast selection, pre-production, production, post-production, distribution, exhibition, rerelease, and, near the end of his life, the recutting for television. This plantation owner knew cotton from the seed to the shirt.

Selznick's teacher had been his father. Moving from Russia to America, where he became a retail jeweler, Lewis J. Selznick quickly realized the immigrant's dream of opportunity. By 1912, though, this larger-than-life entrepreneur had apparently tired of selling paste and precious gems, for he had closed "The World's Largest Jewelry Store" and entered motion picture making, a nascent industry with plenty of room for shrewd, genially aggressive men like himself. Selznick's company involved his wife, Florence, as well as his sons David and Myron. For David, born in 1902, the organization's motto—"Selznick Pictures Make Happy Hours"—had a personal meaning. "I remember at the age of ten or eleven being dragged down to a big Long Island estate where I sat on the porch while my father organized the World Film Company—with my father occasionally directing questions at me." David eagerly began finding answers. While his schoolmates played, David read voluminously and prepared evaluative reports of characterization, plot, and themes in the classics. "The trouble with you," screenwriter Ben Hecht later told Selznick, "is that you did all your reading before you were twelve." Selznick's affinity for the verbal, encouraged by his father, later manifested itself not only in his prodigious memoranda but in his preference for strongly plotted, rationally motivated, dialogue-bound scripts, a nineteenth-century aesthetic flouted by some of his directors. No matter. David had trust in his ability, and so did "Pop." Other moguls' children began their careers in the mailroom; Lewis J. turned Myron into a director and David into a story editor. Both were still in their teens.

Like their father, whom they adored, Myron and David worked hard but spent extravagantly. Louis B. Mayer witnessed firsthand the Diony-sian lifestyle of the Selznicks. One night, when Mayer was visiting the Selznicks' Park Avenue apartment, young David asked his father for pocket money to go to the movies. To Mayer's astonishment, L. J. gave his son a ten-dollar bill. The conservative Mayer later told his family, "Mark my words, no good will ever come of either of those boys." Just as David reached his majority in 1923, his father went broke, partially the victim of the big companies that edged him out. "Everything we owned personally was taken away from us," David wrote. Some men would have been permanently scarred by failure, but Lewis Selznick's ambition and optimism, both of which his sons inherited, remained intact. With little more than his opinions—dozens of them, many un-conventional—and a sense of destiny beneath an inveterate tardiness, David followed his brother Myron to Hollywood in the mid-1920s.

David was "precociously mature, more sophisticated than I was," recalled Niven Busch, who grew up with the Selznick boys. "He was going to bed with girls when I was buggering off." Irene Mayer seemed his antithesis. Although Louis B. had taught his shy but curious daugh-ter to observe the amenities that David so cheerfully scorned, she found herself somehow attracted to him; his brashness at once frightened and excited her. The intelligence behind her stutter likewise engaged him. With poems and books and flowers, a sentimentality more characteris-tic of his personal life than his pictures, David Selznick courted the dark-haired Hollywood princess. In 1930, they married.

In the five years that followed, Myron became an agent and David's productions of *What Price Hollywood?, A Bill of Divorcement* (both RKO, 1932), *Dinner at Eight* (MGM, 1933), and *David Copperfield* (MGM, 1935) made him one of the film capital's most esteemed pro-

5

ducers. Still, he lacked the refinement and fluidity of his pictures. He ate like a trencherman (when she first met him, Ingrid Bergman later recalled, he was "shoveling food into his mouth") and dressed with bemusement, dumping his six-foot-one frame into hand-tailored but wrinkled suits. Journalist Susan Myrick thought his clothes looked "like they'd been slept in"; frequently, given Selznick's erratic work habits, they had. No athlete, he once struck himself in the eye with his own tennis racket. One morning he broke his toe getting out of bed and on another occasion, standing naked before a mirror, he absentmindedly slammed shut a bureau drawer on his penis. "Knowing how mechanically minded you are," Columbia Broadcasting head William Paley wrote him, recommending a new advance in shaving, "I would have a servant sharpen a blade every day and put it in your razor." But however maladroit the man, the producer had a remarkable aptitude for filmmaking. When in the mid-1930s millionaire sportsman John Hay Whitney offered to assume the risks of independent production and back David's founding of Selznick International Pictures, no one could have been much surprised: Selznick had earned the privilege of running his own company.

As a mogul, Selznick was no more venturesome than the Warner brothers, Darryl F. Zanuck, or Harry Cohn. "It never has been nor ever should be the function of motion picture producers consciously to educate," he told reporters in 1935; "our mission is to discover the nature of the demand and meet it as best we can." *Little Lord Fauntleroy* and *The Garden of Allah,* the first Selznick International releases to manifest his philosophy, wrapped conventional narratives in classic Hollywood gift paper. Unlike his peers in the major studios, though, Selznick produced films as medieval architects built cathedrals: one by one. In the course of a day, Selznick might collaborate with writers about a treatment, confer with executives about proposed contracts, haggle with department heads about budgets, or visit the set of a film in production; in the evening, after supper in the private dining room adjacent to his office, Selznick might screen rushes, then dictate alterations far into the morning. "Work was only real work," Irene later said, "if it was done at ungodly hours or under intense pressure." His slogan might have been "Selznick Pictures Make Long Hours."

The Culver City studio operated on Whitney dollars and Selznick

6

Selznick International Studios in 1936. Built in 1919, the facility was leased in 1936 to Selznick, who used the colonnaded façade as his trademark.

words. The producer communicated in writing—at length—with almost everyone in his organization, from the board chairman to makeup artists, cameramen, publicists, and actors. "I dictate easily," Selznick said; "the memos flow right along." Most ran three or more pages, single-spaced, elite type. These now legendary "notes" (as his staff called them) began in self-defense. In his teens, whenever David conferred with his father, he competed with interruptions from the telephone and from executives who flowed in and out of the office. He found that typewritten memoranda not only countered the immaturity of his round, fresh face and presumably callow point of view but received more serious consideration from "Pop." At RKO and MGM, he honed the stream-of-consciousness style that bloomed at Selznick International.

Selznick used memoranda to lend permanence to his opinions. Though chatter with screenwriters and production supervisors could evanesce, black characters on yellow paper endured. He also used them to control his small operation. A conference between a producer and a subordinate encouraged discussion; a memorandum—Selznick believed—forestalled objections and constituted a directive. Finally, these "notes" functioned as the middle management that Selznick International lacked. Selznick could not regularly and personally confer with every scenarist, floor man, and department head on the payroll, but his memoranda could shape their work. They addressed mountain and molehill with equal fervor. "Would you *please* speak to Marlene [Dietrich] about the fact that her hair is getting so much attention, and is being coiffed to such a degree that all reality is lost," Selznick directed the director of *The Garden of Allah* in 1936. The producer expected his answer in the forthcoming footage.

Selznick generally dictated very late at night, sometimes with two or three secretaries beside his desk. He paced, often mumbled, but "never changed the volume of his voice," recalled Lydia Schiller, one of his assistants. Afterward, the women would compare notes to reconstruct a completed memorandum. Selznick rarely proofed the result.

Typical memoranda snaked toward closure, exhausting first the reader and then the topic. They defined problems no less than they defined their author, for they embodied Selznick's doubts and convictions, his hopes and decisions. Some of the memos were hortatory, others blunt. Some were reasoned, others overheated. Selznick had "a peculiar kind of temper," his executive secretary Marcella Rabwin recalled, "very explosive and then very quiet."

> I was shocked by the very tepid, if not actually damning review of *Nothing Sacred* in this week's *Time* [Selznick wrote Henry Luce in December 1937]. I was particularly surprised because the reviewer seemed to miss the whole point of the picture. . . . When I made inquiries concerning the review I found that the picture had been covered on the coast by an old friend, who, as I have previously advised you, has the ax to grind of my having refused repeatedly over a period of years to give him a job.

When distemper or ego tainted a memorandum, Rabwin ordered it typed but left it on her desk for several days. "Hey, I didn't send this one," she would later tell Selznick. "You think you still want it to go?" The producer usually asked her to stamp it NOT SENT and file it. The *Time* memo never reached Luce.

Seasoned staff members recognized many of the "notes" for what they were—so much thinking aloud. Clever staffers could even anticipate them. Hours after a projection room fire, production manager Raymond Klune wrote his boss, "This is in answer to your memo of tomorrow. . . ." Paradoxically, the memoranda often preached decentralization of authority. Though Selznick repeatedly urged his subordinates to make routine decisions for themselves, the producer whose supervision extended to choice of hair lacquer never convinced those under him (much less himself) that he wished to share control. And the more "notes" he dictated, the more concentrated his power became. None could dispute his painstaking craftsmanship, though. Such 1937 releases as *The Prisoner of Zenda* and *A Star Is Born* demonstrated that he lived by his company motto, "In the Tradition of Quality." Likewise, many talented filmmakers associated with him came to believe that he valued their uniqueness, accorded their work special recognition within the industry, and advanced their careers.

Pursuing the world's best writers, actors, and directors, Selznick maintained contacts both in New York and Europe. Many of the artists whom his London office scouted, including directors Gustaf Molander and Carol Reed, were not well known in their own countries, much less abroad. But one filmmaker sold himself almost as well as his pictures.

By the late 1930s, *Blackmail*, *The Man Who Knew Too Much*, and *The 39 Steps* had become synonymous with the name Alfred Hitchcock.

Behind the name stood a man with a narrow worldview. His Jesuit teachers had demanded discipline; his father, William, had insisted upon order; and his mother, Emma, had regularly called him to account. Well into old age, Hitchcock could vividly recall "the evening confession": each night, young Alfred stood before his mother's bed to detail the events of the day. If by the conduct of their lives Florence and Lewis Selznick expanded the world for their sons, Emma and William Hitchcock restricted it for theirs. Perhaps the director's most famous anecdote concerns not his films but rather himself and his father. "I must have been about four or five years old," Hitchcock told François Truffaut in 1962. "My father sent me to the police station with a note. The chief of police read it and locked me in a cell for five or ten minutes, saying, 'This is what we do to naughty boys.'" Why had Alfred been punished? He hadn't "the faintest idea." Whether or not apocryphal, Hitchcock's recollections of his parents' treatment of him suggest the formation of boundaries, the abridgment of freedom, and the limits of opportunity, all anathema to Selznick but the essence of Hitchcock's best work.

Originally a draftsman, the young Hitchcock fell under the spell of German film expressionism in the 1920s. "I've always believed that you can tell as much visually as you can with words," the director later recalled. "That's what I learned from the Germans." Though his first two pictures, *The Pleasure Garden* and *The Mountain Eagle,* impressed neither the distributor nor the public, the slanted shadows and perverse angles of *The Lodger* brought the twenty-seven-year-old director considerable fame. Hitchcock sent friends an unusual Christmas card in 1927, the year all three films appeared: a jigsaw puzzle of his caricature profile. The greeting implied an aesthetic. "Cinema is simply pieces of film put together in a manner that creates ideas and emotions," Hitchcock believed. The director soon added "pieces of sound." In *Blackmail,* the first notable "talkie" in England, Alice White stabs an artist who attempts to rape her; her detective boyfriend protects her not only from a blackmailer but ultimately from prison. Hitchcock photographed the story with keen attention to sound and image. Over breakfast, Mother and Father White discuss the unsolved murder of the artist Crewe. Hitchcock muffles the dialogue of a busybody neighbor, yet one word constantly surfaces—*knife*. The word jabs at Alice, who slices bread until one final *knife* drives the utensil from her hand. In the infancy of sound pictures, when audiences applauded the clarity of human speech, Hitchcock had muddied the soundtrack to create the aural point-of-view shot.

A man of consuming appetite, Hitchcock borrowed from the Russians as well as the Germans. The mythology of Soviet cinema included a famous experiment in montage, a film style that shapes meaning through the arrangement of shots. Revolutionary theorist Lev Kulshov discovered some stock footage of an actor with a fixed expression on his face. Having cut the filmstrip into three pieces, Kulshov juxtaposed each with shots of a steaming bowl of soup, a woman in a casket, and a child playing with a stuffed animal. Viewers who saw the edited sequence insisted that the man seemed hungry, then sad, then joyful. Like the Soviets, Hitchcock believed that the camera and the cut powered the film. "Actors are cattle," he sneered. In *Blackmail* he enlarged upon the Kulshov experiment by substituting stretched canvas for the face of a performer. Crewe has painted a jester with open mouth and pointing finger. Through dynamic editing, Hitchcock animated the static portrait. When Alice enters the studio, the jester seems festive. When Crewe seduces her, the jester seems leering. When Crewe dies, the jester seems censorious. Alice later sees the portrait, en route to a Scotland Yard storage room. Though the police have failed to charge her, her empty laughter suggests that the reproachful jester has laughed last and laughed best. Hitchcockian montage had drawn suspense and terror as well as passion and guilt from "pieces of film." The result fascinated moviegoers and critics.

While the thriller already seemed his métier, Hitchcock had little control over story selection for the works that immediately followed *Blackmail*. He directed an Irish folk drama *(Juno and the Paycock)*, a romance *(Rich and Strange)*, a musical *(Waltzes from Vienna)*, and several other forgettable works whose weaknesses ranged from trite stories to poor casting and indifferent production. Hitchcock was celebrated for his camera flourishes, his realistic detail, his provocative motifs—from staircases to women's legs. But when the "touches" mattered more than the picture, they became meaningless. Hitchcock needed a breakthrough. A solid script. A talented cast. A commercial producer who shared his wit and taste. Michael Balcon came forward.

As mentor and novice, producer Balcon and director Hitchcock had worked together a decade before. Now they would make English film history.

Under his five-film contract with Balcon and Gaumont-British, Hitchcock directed the pictures that won the attention of Hollywood scouts. Both *The Man Who Knew Too Much* and *The 39 Steps* explored the horrific beneath the normal. Early in *The Man Who Knew Too Much,* Bob Lawrence attaches the loose end of his wife's knitting to a man's coat button. As the man dances with Betty, the Lawrences' young daughter, he becomes entangled in the yarn, notices what has happened, and smiles. Suddenly his face drains of expression: he has been shot. Now the Lawrences are entangled. This melodrama about espionage pulses to a close in the Albert Hall. Anarchists responsible for the earlier murder plan to assassinate a visiting diplomat during a concert, the fatal shot to coincide with a crash of cymbals. Jill Lawrence must choose whether to interfere and jeopardize the life of her kidnapped daughter or to remain mute and betray her country. Montage heightens the suspense. Hitchcock cuts from the assassin to the intended victim, the mother, the conductor, and the cymbals, faster and faster. The love-versus-duty theme suddenly had renewed ginger.

Hitchcock claimed that Balcon gave him considerable freedom from supervision on *The Man Who Knew Too Much,* and claimed further that he worked best when left alone. Yet talented collaborators always made Hitchcock perform—and look—better. Though Balcon and his associate, Ivor Montague, may have offered minimal advice or assistance, they provided ballasts that enhanced the first Hitchcock picture for Gaumont-British. The reviews must have pleased the producers. "I am very happy about *The Man Who Knew Too Much,* " C. A. Lejeune wrote in *The Observer.* "It seems to me, because of its very recklessness, its blank refusal to indulge in subtleties, to be the most promising work that Hitchcock has produced since *Blackmail.* " The notices certainly pleased Hitchcock, for he made pictures especially for the press. He told Montague that reviewers were his primary audience,

the reason for "the Hitchcock touches"—novel shots that the critics would pick out and comment upon—as well as the trademark he later made his own (picked up admittedly from Chaplin's [cameo appearance as a] porter shouldering the trunk in *A Woman of Paris*) of a momentary flash appearance in every film he directed. If we had thought there was charlatanry about this we would have found it odious. But we were all friends who understood him and knew exactly what he meant.

Speed lent *The Man Who Knew Too Much* its recklessness, its absence of subtleties, its critical appeal. Hitchcock made not *pretty* but *moving* pictures. He shaded the villains, mixed comedy with melodrama, and sometimes abandoned logic on the cutting room floor. Not every Hollywood mogul appreciated such derring-do, but Hitchcock was undeniably an original.

"I don't seek out publicity," Hitchcock maintained, "it seeks me." During his early days with Gaumont-British, however, the director ardently wooed the press, which in turn helped bring Hollywood to his door. Throughout the Gaumont-British period, Hitchcock entertained journalists one by one in his Cromwell Road walk-up. With one person, Hitchcock said, he could charm and persuade; with a group, he became lost and uncommunicative. A reporter who climbed the four flights to Hitchcock's flat probably expected to see the director in his business clothes, a plain blue serge suit, bagged at the knees. Instead, the five-foot-eight Hitchcock wore a dressing gown over a pair of deep-dyed Chinese silk pajamas, no doubt exaggerating his weight yet also lending an air of informality, perhaps even conspiracy and intimacy, to the meeting of writer and subject. He seduced journalists not only with his pithy opinions on cinematic style but his manner—the snapping black eyes, drawling voice, and expressive hands, surprisingly gentle and soft. By the mid-1930s in Great Britain's trade and fan publications, the Hitchcock film and the Hitchcock persona had begun to reinforce and promote each other.

The 39 Steps added heft to the bandwagon. Charles Bennett, who had worked on *Blackmail* and *The Man Who Knew Too Much,* transformed the John Buchan novel into the exemplar of Hitchcockian man-on-the-run stories. In the picture, police accuse Richard Hannay of murdering a woman, actually a government agent. (Hitchcock experimented not only within shots but *between* them. When a landlady discovers the corpse, the director bleeds her scream into the diesel whistle of a locomotive carrying the hero north.) Hannay eludes the authorities and pursues the real killers. He encounters a yearning country wife, a villainous country squire, and a cool blonde named Pamela, but it is

Hitchcock dressed in his interview attire.

finally a vaudevillian with a photographic memory who unlocks the secret of "the 39 steps." To the raw energy that drove *The Man Who Knew Too Much* Hitchcock added tongue-in-cheek sexuality. Adversaries rather than lovers, Hannay and Pamela are handcuffed together and forced to spend the night at a country inn. Hannay gallantly offers to help Pamela remove her wet stockings. She declines, but as her handcuffed hand pulls off the hose, his own limply dangles down her leg. Another director might have rendered the bedroom scene wanton or perverse. Hitchcock leavened eros and bondage with humor. Even the censor smiled.

Handcuffs intrigued Hitchcock. "There's a special terror," he told an interviewer, "a sort of 'thing' about being tied up." Dull stories, capricious producers, and tyrannical distributors had tied up Hitchcock throughout the early thirties. Had Michael Balcon been overbearing or even meddlesome, Hitchcock might have bridled under his five-year contract with Gaumont-British. Yet Balcon supervised from afar. Moreover, he supplied Hitchcock with superb collaborators, especially screenwriter Bennett and cinematographer Bernard Knowles. Much of the repartee belonged to Bennett, many of the lighting effects to Knowles. The press attention belonged to Hitchcock alone. His droll humor, ranging from tart comments about actors to recountings of his practical jokes, seemed to confirm the source of his films' high spirits. American reporters now joined their British counterparts in covering Hitchcock.

Having begun to contemplate a transatlantic move, the director welcomed the attention. Little compelled him to remain at home. In the late 1930s, English film production approached a cul-de-sac. The companies' inefficient management as well as the instability of personnel, financing, and budgets severely limited growth, which Hitchcock surely perceived. The big salaries paid to imported actors (often American stars who shone only dimly in British pictures) and the high cost of domestic distribution militated against many pictures ever showing a profit, much less sharing that profit with contractual participants. Furthermore, throughout the 1930s, accounting methods penalized successful filmmakers like Hitchcock, whose box office receipts were used to offset the commercial failures of his more prodigal associates. Around Hollywood, it was said, a director was only as good as his last picture; in England, a director's last picture guaranteed him nothing.

Since American moguls were generally unfamiliar with his pictures, Hitchcock used his persona to attract the Yankee press and its Hollywood readership. Journalists from abroad knew Hitchcock first by reputation, not appearance. According to Caroline Lejeune (one of the rotund director's best friends on Fleet Street), American reporters expected "a lean, tough, saturnine fellow," yet discovered a Falstaffian figure whom one writer compared to a Macy's float. Hitchcock inherited his "cottage loaf figure" from his mother, he said, and throughout his adult life, his weight fluctuated from 190 to 300 pounds. If his size embarrassed or distressed him, he nonetheless cannily exploited it. Announcements of his constant dieting bouts fed the Hitchcock publicity mill. Having sharply cut his calorie intake, he quipped to one newspaperman that the sequel to *The Lady Vanishes* might be called *The Gentleman Famishes.*

"Three unique and valuable institutions the British have that we in America have not," observed a *New York Times* feature writer: "Magna Charta, the Tower Bridge and Alfred Hitchcock, the greatest director of screen melodramas in the world." Like American filmmakers Cecil B. De Mille and Frank Capra, Hitchcock became "a name above the title." By 1937, the foreign representatives of Selznick International, as well as RKO, Metro-Goldwyn-Mayer, and Samuel Goldwyn, had furnished Hollywood with press clippings and reports about the director whom *Picturegoer* magazine had dubbed "Alfred the Great." The studios, especially Selznick International, were interested.

Though David Selznick had seen not one Hitchcock picture, the clippings impressed him. Certain moguls read "great" as "difficult." They noted that Hitchcock rarely mentioned Balcon and that he seemed director *and* producer of his pictures. Lieutenants they wanted, generals they had. But Selznick respected talent. He also desperately needed director-producers, men whom he could trust to assume the daily supervisory tasks on a film. By serving as both unit and executive producer on every release, Selznick jeopardized his health and damaged his family life. At home, his long, unpredictable hours left meals cold and servants exasperated. His young sons, Jeffrey and Danny, were an ornament and a pleasure, Irene said, asleep when he arrived from the studio, gone when he awoke. Selznick International treasurer John Wharton urged David to become more the executive producer, but Selznick feared the results. "Ninety-nine directors out of a hundred are

Selznick at work and Hitchcock at home, the 1930s.

worthless as producers, particularly for themselves," he observed in April 1937. "The director-producer system has been proven terribly costly and fruitless of good results many, many times and is being proven wrong again right now at Paramount." If he continued to personally produce each of his company's films, however, he would never generate enough of them to absorb studio overhead and thus increase profits. Solutions existed. Independent filmmakers like De Mille and Capra earned enormous salaries, he said, yet their dual roles as producer-directors justified them. Perhaps Hitchcock would be Selznick International's one-in-a-hundred.

When the overtures from America first began, Hitchcock had only a business agent. He recognized the bearing that an American contract would have on his financial and artistic future, however, and requested assistance from Harry Ham, an affiliate of Myron Selznick's London office. In late spring 1937, with the expectation of receiving numerous offers, Hitchcock asked his agent to negotiate a two-film, $100,000-a-year contract. In return for an escalating price-per-picture clause (an advantage to Hitchcock), the director would consent to a series of long-term options whereby his American employer could secure—if he wished—Hitchcock's services for three successive years (potentially an advantage to both Hitchcock and the studio). During the option periods, Hitchcock boldly added, he would make not two but three pictures annually. Hitchcock moved with remarkable dispatch on a soundstage, where he shot pictures as the Swiss made watches, but he would not be rushed. "My chassis is built for comfort," he said in 1936, "not for speed." Looking for work in an industry that demanded speed, however, the director may have heedlessly promised three pictures annually in order to assure American producers of his efficiency and thus his worth.

By early June, though, Hitchcock's terms—including a relatively high salary and an accelerated demand for at least two years' work guaranteed in America—forced Selznick to retreat. Neither RKO, MGM, Goldwyn, nor Selznick wanted to lose a major talent to a competitor, yet none would have been eager to commit beyond one or at most two pictures. After all, Hitchcock's ability to direct commercial films in America remained problematic. Metro, aware of the risk, planned to offer Hitchcock $1,500 a week (roughly equivalent to $2,000 a week in America) to direct films under Michael Balcon's supervision at England's new MGM-Denham studio. Exempt from the restrictions that Great Britain placed upon MGM's American-produced pictures, these works would circulate freely in Hollywood's most lucrative foreign market; at the same time, the studio could stage a well-paid audition for Hitchcock, whom it might later import. Would Hitchcock accept such a proposal? However attractive by British standards, working for MGM-Denham would deny him the superior facilities, range of potential assignments, and international exposure of working in America. Moreover, control would remain in Culver City, where the scenarios would be prepared and the leading actor cast; the director would merely connect the dots. From Hitchcock's point of view, then, negotiations had cooled practically before they had begun. Perhaps an Atlantic crossing would heat them up.

2

SIGNING HITCHCOCK

While still under contract to Gaumont-British, Hitchcock sailed to America in August 1937. The rhythms of life aboard the *Queen Mary*—eating and sleeping, sleeping and eating—suited Hitchcock, a sybarite at heart. He defined happiness as "a clear horizon"; and for a week at sea, happiness was his. Joining Hitchcock at dinner each night were his nine-year-old daughter, Pat; his wife, Alma Reville; and his assistant, Joan Harrison. Alma, a head shorter than her husband and a third his weight, had met "Hitch" at Islington Studios, where she had worked as a film editor in the early 1920s. Their collaboration on several pictures had strengthened their mutual respect and led to a more personal relationship. They had married on December 2, 1926. Over the next decade, "Kitty" (as Hitchcock sometimes called Alma) had earned writing or supervisory credit on many of her husband's films. More than that of anyone else, Hitchcock trusted—and feared—Alma's opinion of his work. A new member of the Hitchcock entourage, Joan Harrison had studied literature at the university and criminal behavior with her Uncle Harold, an official at London's Old Bailey; over their lunches together, she later recalled, he told her the grisly details of one shocking crime after another. Hitchcock, whose appetite extended beyond food to murder stories, had hired Joan in 1935 as a fifteen-dollar-a-week secretary and quickly advanced her to continuity assistant, then script consultant. To some, he appeared smitten. But if Alma objected to his schoolboy infatuation with Joan Harrison, she concealed her feelings well.

From base camp at Manhattan's St. Regis Hotel, Hitchcock and company went sight-seeing and restaurant-hopping. Yet no activity overshadowed the purpose of the director's visit: he had come to America not for the ice cream (which he could spoon down in pints), but for the contacts. While abroad, he intended to discuss terms with all interested parties. Between indulgences at "21" and other New York restaurants, Hitchcock made time for Selznick International, RKO, and MGM. The press had conditioned studio representatives to expect a little British god. The director of *The 39 Steps* "uses his camera the way a painter uses his brush," *The New York Times* had noted, "stylizing his story and giving it values which the scenarists could hardly have suspected." The separation of genius from donkeywork must have annoyed cinematographer Bernard Knowles, screenwriter Charles Bennett, and producers Michael Balcon and Ivor Montague. By stepping aside, the mammoth Hitchcock could have revealed these and other collaborators clustered behind him, but he stood his ground. He would sell himself as *Variety* had billed him, "probably the best native director in England."

Selznick International and the other companies knew that Hitchcock had a small but loyal American audience. Along the Manhattan art-theater circuit, *The Man Who Knew Too Much* and *The 39 Steps* generated brisk business. Since revivals of the latter picture always cured box office doldrums, small exhibitors called it a mortgage lifter. But the American companies also knew that Hitchcock wanted something more than a cult following. During a Hollywood fishing expedition, Michael Balcon had landed American actors Robert Young and Sylvia Sydney for Hitchcock's *Secret Agent* and *Sabotage.* Though not stars, they were intended to enlarge his American audience; but neither brought Hitchcock wider notice across the Atlantic. *Secret Agent* and *Sabotage* were darker, more downbeat than the earlier Gaumont-Brit-

Hitchcock dictates script revisions to his wife, Alma Lucy Reville.

ish releases. They also betrayed the relative poverty of British film production in 1936. A prominent American critic found *Secret Agent* "marred by inexpert camera technique, film editing whose incorrectness hits one between the eyes, and strangely uneven sound recording which, at one point, simply causes the screen to go dead with an effect as though novocaine had just been administered to the ear-drums." *Variety* conceded that *Sabotage* improved matters but "just misses being great." Longing for American studios, American craftsmen, and American audiences, Hitchcock dangled his own line in the watering holes around Manhattan.

Hitchcock leaned toward Selznick International. *Little Lord Fauntleroy, The Garden of Allah,* and *A Star Is Born* could not have differed more from *The Man Who Knew Too Much* or *The 39 Steps.* They had neither the invention nor the speed, the rawness nor the sensibility of British Hitchcock. They also lacked the realism and the irony. They were nonetheless superior picturemaking. *Fauntleroy* had inaugurated Selznick International, against odds that the producer would have refused at the Santa Anita racetrack. Selznick poured his enormous creative energy into the fusty Victorian tale, promoted it aggressively, and won critical and popular success for his studio. A director raked for his "inexpert camera technique" and "incorrect" film editing must have admired the gloss. Yet more than craftsmanship drew Hitchcock to Selznick, for any major American studio could have given him technical support. Selznick offered Hitchcock an environment that fostered quality. The workplace should be called a factory, Hitchcock often grumbled, not a studio. Selznick International seemed both.

Hitchcock met the Selznick organization on the social and business fronts. Debonair Jock Whitney took the Hitchcocks to Saratoga for the races, and Kay Brown, the studio's quick-witted New York representative, met Hitchcock for lunch. Discover his salary demands and the status of his negotiations with MGM, Selznick directed Kay Brown, but offer Hitchcock nothing. The Englishman also dined with RKO's Lillie Messinger. Though she mentioned a couple of possible stories and Hitchcock indicated that he wished to make "a few pictures a year in Hollywood," RKO likewise offered the director nothing. Only MGM nibbled. Eager to staff its Denham studio near London with competent directors, Metro tentatively proposed $165,000 for four pictures spread over two years, an arrangement that MGM's new British supervisor,

Michael Balcon, hoped his good friend would accept. Hitchcock stalled: MGM-Culver City appealed, MGM-Denham did not. Seeking a compromise without appearing anxious, he asked Selznick's representative to explore the possibility of offering him a tandem contract shared by MGM and Selznick International.

While Hitchcock returned to England to edit *Young and Innocent*, another of his man-on-the-run pictures, Selznick contemplated the future of Hitchcock with Selznick International. Like the previous generation's moguls, Selznick negotiated the way street fighters rumbled. For *Gone With the Wind*, he opened discussions on Leslie Howard by bluntly pointing out to agent Mike Levee that "Howard has been a box-office failure in all of his pictures in recent years without exception." Selznick wanted Oliver H. P. Garrett to script the film, yet invoked the writer's recently failed play in order to "buy him cheaply." Though not cattle, actors, writers, and directors were commodities; no producer wished to pay more than a fair market price. Selznick nevertheless considered bending on Hitchcock.

Like German director Fritz Lang, whom Selznick had brought to America several years before, Hitchcock was an original, someone capable of lending distinction to a company's releases; he was also a producer. Certainly Hitchcock remained eager. In the November 1937 *Film Weekly,* the director argued that motion picture production demanded "one man at the helm . . . the producer," generous, instinctive, perceptive; as an example, he named David Selznick. By late fall 1937, believing that Hitchcock had "a number of deals pending," Selznick appeared ready to offer the director not only a handsome per-picture fee but a guaranteed two-picture arrangement. At Thanksgiving, however, MGM suddenly withdrew from the Hitchcock sweepstakes. According to Louis Mayer's confidant Benjamin Thau, the studio did not want Hitchcock "under any circumstances or at any price"; furthermore, it regarded its own George Seitz as "a much better director than Hitchcock."

There are several possible reasons for the reversal. When a 1937 recession hurt the film business, even Mayer must have been haunted by memories of the Depression. HOLLYWOOD SITS ON A POWDER-KEG, read one headline on Halloween 1937. Hitchcock might have been swept away in a momentary wave of conservatism. The tottering relationship between Mayer and Michael Balcon may also explain the change. Though Mayer demanded that Balcon complete a long intern-ship in Culver City before sailing home to operate MGM abroad, he apparently never trusted the Englishman. Mayer closely supervised the stories, the budgets, and the schedules emanating from Denham. When he visited the studio in summer 1937, he publicly lectured Balcon on company policy. By terminating negotiations with a Balcon protégé, Mayer could further chasten his production supervisor. He would have considered the loss of Hitchcock small. The "best native director in England" resembled the "best native steak-and-kidney pie in America": Who cared? The comparison to George Seitz explains precisely how Metro—and perhaps much of Hollywood—perceived Hitchcock.

"Up the street," as Selznick, also located on Washington Boulevard, referred to Metro, filmmakers like George Seitz epitomized the MGM director. Accomplished yet pedestrian, Seitz made films the way Ford made cars. Screen goddesses Joan Crawford and Greta Garbo called Metro home, but the studio had earned its bread and butter through jungle adventures, sentimental family fare, and the robust comedies of Marie Dressler and Wallace Beery. Seitz could direct them all, with speed substituting for imagination. His record of five films in 1934, six in 1935, and five in 1936, so impressive to a company that relied on a steady flow of product to feed its distribution mechanism, shamed Hitchcock's, both in number and range of subject matter. Between 1929 and 1937, Hitchcock had averaged just over one film per year, the only successful ones thrillers. According to *The Saturday Evening Post,* "Hollywood regarded him [Hitchcock] as merely a good cops-and-robbers man." Yet rather than too slow or too narrow, Mayer may have found Hitchcock too venturesome. Hitchcock liked to experiment. He tended to cut against, rather than with, the grain of the narrative; and by suddenly altering point of view, revealing the storyteller's power, and thus forcing the audience to confront its own vulnerability, he elicited his most authentic thrills. British critics hailed the "psychologi-cal reactions of [his] leading characters" and called Hitchcock a genius. The notorious Erich von Stroheim may have been one artiste too many for MGM. Preferring Seitz's arithmetic to Hitchcock's algebra, Metro finally withdrew.

MGM's retreat concerned Selznick. Although he asked Daniel O'Shea to determine what American assignments Hitchcock might want, he also suspended all negotiations until he could see another

Hitchcock picture with the Metro decision in mind. *Young and Innocent,* which the British trade paper *Film Weekly* called "typically English," arrived in New York at Christmas 1937. In it, a young woman (Nova Pilbeam) becomes the unwitting accomplice of a man falsely accused of murder. Their flight from the police takes them to a roadside café, a children's birthday party (an amusing sequence initially eliminated from prints in American distribution), and an abandoned mine. At the end, in a notably long moving-camera shot set in a ballroom, Hitchcock tracks from the heroine to a close-up of the actual murderer's twitching eyes. After the visceral excitement of the Balcon-produced films—*The Man Who Knew Too Much, The 39 Steps, Sabotage*—*Young and Innocent* may have seemed tame. "It is lacking in its technical aspect," Kay Brown reported to Selznick; "the miniatures look as though they had been done by a child." Jock Whitney yawned, then urged Selznick to follow the MGM lead. "If I am right about the picture," Whitney concluded, Hitchcock "could save himself a trip across the ocean to have me direct his next picture—and you can get me cheaper!"

With at least half a million dollars at stake on most films, the risks of employing untried artists were enormous. MGM's size and output permitted it to absorb at least some of its mistakes, but because Selznick produced so few films a year—and none of them inexpensive programmers (the bottom half of a double feature)—he could not afford a $100,000 liability. The imponderables mounted. He and Hitchcock had never even met: Could they work together? If not, could the director be loaned out? If so, who would want him? Whitney's and MGM's apathy about this "cops-and-robbers man" left the already doubtful Selznick at a crossroads familiar to his Hollywood peers. If he did nothing, Hitchcock would probably languish in England. If he hired the director and his first picture succeeded, Selznick would reap the rewards and, over Sunday lunch at Louis Mayer's ranch, twit his father-in-law about the one that got away. Finally, if he hired the director and he failed . . .

Still not having seen *Young and Innocent,* Selznick urged Jock Whitney to withhold judgment on Hitchcock until the picture opened in Los Angeles, when Selznick himself could screen it and reevaluate the Englishman. The director "has certainly proven his great talent on mystery pictures of a unique and distinguished type," Selznick told

Whitney, "and I think that whatever deal we make we certainly should be able to use him for one picture a year of this kind." Whitney refused his partner nothing, including this simple wish for more time; after all, Selznick had at least backed away from a two-picture commitment. Meanwhile, as Selznick turned to more pressing business—the script of *Gone With the Wind* and the final cut of the more imminent *Adventures of Tom Sawyer*—Twentieth Century-Fox warmed to Hitchcock. In February 1938 Robert Kane, Fox's well-traveled managing director, offered Hitchcock $40,000 for thirteen weeks' work in midsummer 1938, guaranteeing him not only a handsome salary but a generous pro rata should the picture go beyond the allotted three months. Again, however, the company wanted Hitchcock to direct in Britain.

David and Irene Selznick saw *Young and Innocent* in late February 1938. Following the screening, Selznick praised Hitchcock as "the greatest master of this particular type of melodrama to be found either in America or in England today." Hitchcock saluted Selznick publicly. In the March 1938 *World Film News,* which Selznick's London representative Jenia Reissar forwarded to her boss, a reporter asked Hitchcock whether he intended to go to America. "The matter is still in the air," the director replied. "But if I do go to Hollywood, I'd only work for Selznick." Never had a relationship seemed so near consummation. Yet doubts about Hitchcock's ability to direct in America, bolstered by MGM's withdrawal and Fox's British-only proposal, still haunted Selznick. To reassure himself—and perhaps to seek a bargaining chip in negotiating Hitchcock's final salary figure—Selznick asked Jenia Reissar and William Burnside, his London talent advisor, to make discreet inquiries about Hitchcock's speed and efficiency.

Reissar, a Hitchcock partisan from the beginning, responded to Selznick in less than two days. The director shot *The Man Who Knew Too Much* in ten weeks, she said, "a very long time . . . because the unit went out to Switzerland." (Hitchcock's decision to replace a distinguished—but "hammy"—actor once shooting had begun may also have slightly extended the schedule.) The director finished principal photography on *The 39 Steps,* which also required location work but this time in England, in just under ten weeks. Edward Black, who produced *Young and Innocent,* reportedly threw a party for the cast and the director to celebrate Hitchcock's efficiency, yet bad weather had slowed even this production, which also finished in ten weeks. And like *Young and Innocent,* Reissar said, *The Lady Vanishes* is taking "a very long time, because of all sorts of difficulties, which, I am assured, have nothing to do with the director."

A skeptical David Selznick found Hitchcock's schedules, "in terms of our production habits, quite long." MGM's major releases averaged eight weeks, its smaller ones less than a month; *David Copperfield, Anna Karenina,* and *A Star Is Born*—all Selznick productions, with the last photographed in time-consuming Technicolor—had each been completed in fewer than ten weeks. Bill Burnside's tart report, more impressionistic than Reissar's and equally secondhand, may have further troubled Selznick. "Being the only one at G-B [Gaumont-British] who knew anything about pictures," Burnside wrote, Hitchcock "was allowed to be his own boss and, consequently, took his time doing everything he wanted. Also, he is a fat man and a little lazy." The substance of Burnside's note influenced Selznick throughout his association with Hitchcock; producer and director differed about many things, but none more than money and time. Even if Hitchcock never learned of the report per se, the rumors of his foot-dragging followed him to America, where he heard and attempted to silence them. Many directors wished to be known for their thoroughness and discernment, few for their deliberateness. In Hollywood, as MGM's enthusiasm for George Seitz implied, haste made careers.

In spring 1938, with dimming prospects of an American deal, Hitchcock asked Myron Selznick personally to represent him. Although the two men had met briefly in England in 1924, the reticent Hitchcock and the aggressive Selznick—whom Niven Busch remembered as a "tough little slant-hatted, ready-fisted Jewish boy from the East Side"—could not have had much to say to each other. Within five years, Myron had become a Hollywood agent; within ten years, driven by a vendetta against the studios, he had become a Hollywood agent nonpareil. Myron Selznick's name gave the English filmmaker instant prestige. Selznick represented such prominent stars as Carole Lombard, Fredric March, Errol Flynn, and William Powell, as well as directors Frank Capra, Gregory La Cava, George Cukor, Ernst Lubitsch, Leo McCarey, and William Wellman. Several of them worked for Selznick International (in which Myron had a financial interest), but never to their disadvantage: David "never paid a nickel less for anyone he got," recalled Marcella Rabwin, who worked for Myron, then for David. He might even have paid a nickel more. As Hitchcock may have reasoned, Myron would provide not only an "in," but a lucrative "in." Stirring the pot, the director again announced that he "really was keen on going with David Selznick."

Perhaps encouraged by the Selznick agency, Hitchcock spoke in spring 1938 of the "many offers" he had fielded—and rejected—while awaiting something other than protests of interest from David Selznick. If they existed, the "many offers" must have resembled Fox's. Hitchcock wrote to his press representative Al Margolies in New York that after *The Lady Vanishes,* "it looks as though I shall do a picture for Bob Kane [and Twentieth Century-Fox] here. . . . I have made no plans beyond a possible Gaumont picture early next year." The sigh seems almost palpable. As the king of British directors, Hitchcock presided over an increasingly impoverished realm. In 1937, London's *Daily Herald* had reported that film producers' "squandermania" had weakened relations between motion picture companies and the banks, drying up production loans throughout the industry; according to the *Daily Film Renter,* the British film bubble had burst. With the warning flags aloft, Hitchcock yearned to come to America but feared that no one would invite him. Another transatlantic crossing seemed in order.

The three Hitchcocks sailed again for the States on June 1. Although spring 1938 had brought another recession to America and a newsworthy "economy wave" to Hollywood, Myron Selznick assured his client that he would return to England with a signed contract, probably from David Selznick. In later years, Hitchcock said, he made his first trip to Los Angeles "to consummate the Selznick deal." But Myron must have scoffed at either the money or the terms offered by his brother, for he continued to press both Samuel Goldwyn and RKO to take another look at Hitchcock. Like Selznick, Goldwyn pursued quality. "He didn't always know how to get the best," said Olivia de Havilland, who later worked for him, "but he was *interested* in the best." Showing its mettle in 1939, RKO hired theatrical director Orson Welles and thereafter gambled on *Citizen Kane.* In 1938, however, neither Goldwyn nor RKO chose to compete for Hitchcock's services. Without too much exaggeration, David Selznick wrote to Frank Capra that Myron could "not get bids for [Hitchcock] at the time I signed him."

After stops in Manhattan and Palm Beach, the Hitchcocks went west to tour southern California and finally meet David Selznick. Each man knew the other by his work and, to some extent, his personality. Hitchcock anticipated a mogul, Selznick a clever Englishman; neither foiled expectations. To Hitchcock, Selznick and his world must have seemed immense. Selznick International's leased forty-acre lot, small by industry standards, contained twelve massive soundstages. "I made *The Lady Vanishes* in a studio ninety feet long," Hitchcock told a reporter, "and I was forced to build sets in perspective." Not in America. Though Selznick himself stood a head higher than his English visitor, his height mattered less than his enthusiasm and drive. Nature gave him his energy, Benzedrine his endurance. Wondering whether the experimental drug could harm him, he wrote his physician to report that "I am practically living on the stuff and would prefer that I do not explode for a couple of years." He carried the pills in his trousers pockets and passed them around to production assistant Lydia Schiller, editor Hal Kern, and composer Max Steiner. Some refused, others needed them to keep pace with their boss.

"We weren't used to people like that in England," British actress Ann Todd later said of the producer. "He was so big, a big personality." When he built Tara for *Gone With the Wind*, his Southern technical advisor urged him to reduce its grand scale. But Selznick, as Wilbur Kurtz wrote in his journal, took "the larger view." He even expanded his name to suit his persona. Following the example of his father-in-law, Louis Mayer, who invented the middle initial *B* for himself, Selznick added an *O* after "David." Like Louis B. Mayer, Jack L. Warner, and Darryl F. Zanuck, David O. Selznick became a name to be reckoned with. His high-voltage extroversion may have overwhelmed the more sedate Hitchcock, but his vision of the pictures that a willing producer and an able director could make together must have impressed the Englishman.

"David, I have no cock," the director may have said to Selznick, as he had to actor Barry Foster during their first meeting. Since the early 1930s, Hitchcock had attempted to shock people, particularly actresses, in order to throw them off their guard; paradoxically, he relaxed them and put them in his power. "I have no 'cock' " would have left Selznick astonished, then baffled, at which time Hitchcock would have said, "Oh, what I mean is you call me 'Hitch.' " Easily moved to laughter,

Selznick may have found Hitchcock's practical jokes and blue humor amusing. But the director's cinematic imagination truly captivated him. "He was fascinated by Hitchcock's ideas," Irene recalled, ideas articulated with wit, succinctness, and authority. During this period, color photography interested Hitchcock; given Selznick's experience with Technicolor, the men undoubtedly discussed the subject. "To my mind," Hitchcock had said to a British reporter, "color should be used not just to give pictorial effect, but as a means of expression." Some examples: "the red funnels of a steamer against a gray dawn; the blink of traffic lights through a pea-soup fog; a drop of blood on a daisy petal."

A surprising number of Hollywood directors—Mervyn LeRoy and William Wyler, for instance—communicated poorly. Hitchcock did not. Using his pudgy fingers to draw a quick sketch or to reinforce a point, he spoke with verve and precision. Moreover, he conceptualized in pictures. "The visuals" were hardly lingua franca among American studio executives, but the industry's most distinguished producer quickly understood the implication of Hitchcock's ideas for the movies that he and the director might make. Despite the risks of employing Hitchcock, Selznick recognized that he shared the director's passion for originality, quality, perhaps even experimentation. Finally, his instincts about Hitchcock's abundant talent vanquished doubts about his speed and adaptability. Delighting Hitchcock, the brothers Selznick agreed to come to terms.

Hitchcock's July 14, 1938, contract with Selznick was relatively brief. The year before, RKO had required sixty-plus pages to sign Howard Hawks to a two-year employment agreement; Selznick International and Hitchcock required only eighteen. The contract granted the company Hitchcock's nonexclusive services as director (and to a limited extent as producer) for one film, with four one-year, one-picture options. In return, Hitchcock would earn $50,000 for his first assignment ($2,500 per six-day week), and 10 percent more with each of the first three options exercised. (Myron would of course claim 10 percent of all income.) Prior to the beginning of the principal period, without remuneration, he would "assist and collaborate in the writing and preparation of the treatment, adaptation, script, dialogue and continuity." Although Hitchcock and Selznick had discussed possible maiden

31

In 1938 Hitchcock told a *New Yorker* reporter that the "increased pressure or more complicated methods in Hollywood" did not worry him—"as long as there's one mind in charge." The reporter was certain that Hitchcock meant his own.

films, the contract named none. Across town, the Feldman–Blum agency urged its clients to have at least budgets, if not film titles, specified by their employment agreements. Money, William Dover told director George Stevens in 1940, "can have a considerable influence upon the calibre of the picture you will be able to turn out in association with [a] studio." At Selznick International, however, David Selznick's exclusive slate of "A" films shielded Hitchcock from assignment to inferior projects.

Hitchcock's employment agreement lacked what agent Charles Feldman regarded in 1940 as "the shocking and objectionable features of general studio contracts." For example, Selznick permitted Hitchcock to veto loanout offers involving projects or companies abhorrent to him. As an unusual provision, he also consented to pay the $125 weekly salary of the director's assistant, Joan Harrison. Yet laid beside those of his American peers, with their fees, controls, guarantees, and contingent compensations, Hitchcock's contract paled. Under the terms of his 1937 RKO contract, for instance, Howard Hawks promised to direct up to three "Class 'A'" pictures each year for a $130,000 annual salary; the studio also promised him a bonus for speed, a percentage of the profits based on his films' gross receipts, the right to prepare a rough cut, and (under certain conditions) a producer's screen credit either at the top or bottom of the main titles. George Stevens's one-year, two-picture employment agreement with Columbia in 1940 gave him not only $200,000 but 15 percent of the profits, a figure comparable to Hawks's on Columbia's *Only Angels Have Wings* (1939).

Hitchcock and many other foreign directors approached Hollywood as suppliants. Without an American track record, an established immigrant director in the 1930s could not have expected (and in some instances would not have wanted) profit participation, something that Hitchcock fought for throughout his last Selznick years; neither could he have expected significant salary advances tied to options, nor the right to prepare a final cut of his work. (Selznick supervised postproduction at his studio, so unlike Hawks's and Stevens's contracts, Hitchcock's excluded editing from the list of services to be rendered.) Hitchcock could not even have expected—though he originally asked for and very much desired—a two-picture guarantee. No American company except Selznick International had offered him acceptable terms for even a single picture. Perhaps more than any other element of his contract, though, its limited, nonexclusive commitment disappointed Hitchcock. Theoretically, the contract permitted him to freelance for thirty-two weeks annually and thus expand his independence; yet in summer 1938, with Hollywood reticent to sign him and an "economy wave" still churning, Hitchcock feared *not* working for thirty-two weeks a year. Hitchcock had many anxieties—policemen, heights, confrontations—but the specter of financial insecurity perhaps disturbed him most of all. Unfortunately for the director, Selznick had the superior bargaining position.

One afternoon in that summer of 1938, while studio legal counsel Daniel O'Shea haggled with Myron Selznick over the fine points of the contract, a trolley from the Brown Derby restaurant rolled into David Selznick's office. The steaming pots, the cups and saucers, and the scones and crumpets arrived—but not the tea. Unperturbed, Hitchcock and David Selznick drank their hot water and amiably discussed *Rebecca* and *Titanic,* the two most likely Hitchcock assignments. For *Titanic,* Selznick half seriously proposed buying the *Leviathan,* an American merchant marine ship; Hitchcock could already envision a couple of scenes.

> I wanted to go to a card table, where four men were playing poker: go close to the whiskey and soda . . . the level is changing in the glass, tilting, you see? Same effect! Mind you, we've already told the audience that the ship has been struck. Then you go and say, "Here are the innocent people, they don't know what's going on." We might go down to the kitchen and I'd see a chef is putting the final touches to a beautiful cake with a pastry bag. . . . And the audience would say, "Don't bother! Don't bother! It's never going to be eaten! The ship's going down!"

Given Selznick's enthusiasm for Hitchcock's fertile ideas, their initial meetings undoubtedly left them exhilarated. Hitchcock's July 1938 contract may have disappointed him in certain respects, but as he, Alma, and Pat later boarded the *Normandie* for England, the director must have been optimistic about an American future in Selznick's hands.

Autumn came, then passed. On seeing the laudatory reviews of *The Lady Vanishes* in January 1939, Selznick concluded that "Hitchcock's free time will be grabbed up quick." Zanuck and probably others would soon see *The Lady* and might well reconsider their coolness to Hitchcock as a Hollywood-based director; Daniel O'Shea believed that Hitchcock's burgeoning reputation along with "the publicity attendant upon his [March 1939] arrival [in America] will bring him further offers that may be better than ours and which the [Myron] Selznick office will feel in duty bound to give to him." (Though Hitchcock later charged that the Selznick brothers colluded to his financial disadvantage, Myron apparently exaggerated the interest of other American firms in Hitchcock in order to force David to pay more for him.) Selznick thus decided to offer Hitchcock a modified contract: Under its terms, the Englishman would direct two pictures—instead of one—the first year, with options altered accordingly. Examining this revised contract some time later, Hitchcock's business advisor called it "replete with provisions unfavorable to Hitchcock and advantageous to Selznick"; the director himself would later come to regard it as a collar that rubbed and choked. In March 1939, however, with no pending offers from Zanuck or his peers, Hitchcock eagerly signed the amended contract.

In place of the cul-de-sac that England had become, Selznick had offered Hitchcock the Yellow Brick Road. "When he starts work for David Selznick early next year," *Newsweek* wrote in October 1938, "Hitchcock will not be regimented by Hollywood's communal method of moviemaking. As in England, he will dominate every phase of the film's story and production; the finished job will reflect no personality other than his own." No innocent, Hitchcock understood the difference between newsmagazine puff and Hollywood reality. The producer-director relationship, as Hitchcock knew, invariably mixed friction with harmony, frustration with compromise, and struggle with achievement. MGM had strewn the Yellow Brick Road to *Oz* with ten writers, four directors, and a prolonged shooting schedule; thereafter, the finished job bore no one's "personality." The film capital's modus operandi, if not David Selznick himself, might very well chew up Alfred Hitchcock. Yet more than perhaps any other executive in the American motion picture industry, Selznick also had the financial resources and the artistic flair to raise Hitchcock to international importance. For the ruddy-faced Englishman, pleased with his Selznick contract and happily anticipating his years in Hollywood, the horizon appeared bright if not clear.

3

ℛEBECCA

Among the hundreds of manuscripts, galley proofs, and published novels that poured into the East Coast offices of Selznick International every month, Kay Brown read only a few that she could enthusiastically recommend. Daphne du Maurier's *Rebecca* became one of them. *Rebecca* is "the most fascinating story I have read in ages," Brown wired Hollywood, a certain best-seller. In the novel, a plain and innocent young woman (the first-person narrator, whose name du Maurier never reveals) serves as paid companion to a crass American dowager visiting the Riviera. Gossip has it that the aristocratic Maxim de Winter has fled England to Monte Carlo in order to elude painful memories of his recently deceased, much-beloved wife, the fabulously beautiful Rebecca; yet almost inexplicably he proposes marriage to the unglamorous paid companion. Following a honeymoon in Venice, the newlyweds return to Manderley, de Winter's mansion. Here, the young bride confronts not only the memory of Rebecca—which seems to permeate the estate and to preoccupy and torment its owner—but also her mo-rose husband and the forbidding Mrs. Danvers, Rebecca's devoted housekeeper.

The second Mrs. de Winter feels ill at ease at Manderley. Her half-hearted attempts to assume her position in the house merely accent the differences between her and Manderley's former chatelaine, whose suite Danvers maintains as a shrine. A costume ball promises to cheer de Winter. Guided by the insidious Danvers, the new bride chooses a gown previously worn by her predecessor. When de Winter angers, she attributes his distress to his profound love of his first wife and momentarily considers Mrs. Danvers's suggestion that she throw herself from the second-story window into the stormy night below. Cries from outside divert her. A wind-tossed sea has produced the unexpected: the body of Rebecca, recovered from the boat in which she perished. De Winter finally confesses to his second wife that he in fact detested Rebecca, a wicked woman, and killed her, opening the sea cocks in her boat and sending her and the craft out to sink in the bay. Despite the attempt of Jack Favell, Rebecca's cousin and lover, to have de Winter convicted as Rebecca's murderer, a second inquest clears him. The distraught, avenging Mrs. Danvers burns down Manderley, yet its flames seem at last to release the de Winters from the ghost of the charming but deadly Rebecca.

Hitchcock, a voracious reader, skimmed the galley proofs of *Rebecca* while filming du Maurier's *Jamaica Inn* at Elstree Studios in spring 1938. Not yet under contract to Selznick, the director began negotiating for the screen rights, not only as an investment but as leverage in securing employment abroad: if the novel swept America, Hitchcock would control *Rebecca*'s future and possibly his own. For Selznick, who read a synopsis of the manuscript in late spring 1938, the story of the novel's awkward and shy heroine seemed ideal. Selznick's most impressive discoveries tended to be young women, including Ingrid Bergman, Vivien Leigh, and Joan Fontaine; furthermore, he had long been associated with the industry's premier "women's director," George Cukor. In certain respects a "women's producer," attuned to the sensibilities and psychology of the American female (at least as purveyed by the era's mass-circulation magazines), Selznick agreed with story editor Val Lewton that the second Mrs. de Winter "probably exemplifies the feeling that most young women have about themselves." On the commercial side, a couple's filmgoing decisions generally rested with the woman, and more than any other producer, Selznick considered himself capable of making the kind of film that would favorably influence a woman's choice.

Despite some concern about the title ("obviously a terrible one"), Selznick asked Kay Brown to begin negotiations for *Rebecca*. Sparked by towering sales predictions, the price of the novel's motion picture rights quickly escalated and eliminated undercapitalized bidders like Hitchcock. Nothing new there. "The Americans have left us very few stories to film," Hitchcock publicly complained as early as 1927, suggesting one reason for his pursuing work in Hollywood. The director, under contract to Selznick International by summer 1938, nonetheless was still interested in *Rebecca*. When Jenia Reissar suggested that his personal contacts with du Maurier might benefit his new employer, Hitchcock offered to help. Reissar believed that du Maurier, though "mercenary," might accept less from Hitchcock than from Selznick International; Kay Brown endorsed the strategy of Hitchcock as undercover agent and prodded Selznick to accede. Though preoccupied with the scripting of *Gone With the Wind,* which Brown had also prompted him to buy, Selznick paused long enough to authorize Hitchcock to pay up to $40,000 for *Rebecca.* Ultimately, Hitchcock deferred to a professional agent, Selznick tracked upward with the bidding, and du Maurier finally sold *Rebecca* to Selznick International for $50,000, a figure identical to that paid for Margaret Mitchell's Civil War epic just over two years before. Informed of the sale, Hitchcock was "vastly amazed at the price!"

Rebecca justified Kay Brown's opinion. It enjoyed wide exposure, not only as novel but also as story, radio drama, and (written by du Maurier herself) play. Shortly after its publication, the book was serialized in the London *Daily Express* and the *New York Daily Mirror,* which emblazoned the side panels of its delivery trucks with the word REBECCA. These syndicated digests—as Selznick knew—brought the story of *Rebecca* to a new readership; more important, they helped to keep the work's name before the public and created a vast potential audience for the film. Selznick, who owned the American radio rights to the novel, sold them for $1,000 to Orson Welles. The arrangement represented a bargain for the Mercury Theatre, but Selznick hoped to redouble his price in publicity. The media lionized the theatrical boy wonder, less than twenty-four years old and too young, if hardly too modest, to play de Winter. "Welles' generally unattractive physical appearance is not known to radio audiences," Selznick felt, so "he is probably the best bet for this broadcast outside of [Ronald] Colman." Welles hastily assembled ten or fifteen episodes from the book and aired them in late 1938. "A clever showman," Selznick observed, "he didn't waste time and effort creating anything new but simply gave them the original." That original proved a sturdy commodity in the marketplace.

In early September 1938, Selznick officially assigned Hitchcock to direct *Rebecca;* at the same time, he ordered a staff writer to draft a detailed outline of the novel. Should the studio encounter cash flow problems and wish to liquidate the property (always a real possibility for independents like Selznick), it could use the synopsis as a kind of prospectus. More to the point, Selznick intended to give the screenwriter a guide to use in faithfully adapting the novel. According to Selznick,

> the only sure and safe way of aiming at a successful transcription of the original into the motion-picture form is to try as far as possible to retain the original. . . . I don't mind letting my own creative instincts run wild either on an original, as in the case of *A Star Is Born,* or in the adaptation of an unsuccessful work, as in *Made for Each Other.* But my ego is not so great that it cannot be held in check on the adaptation of a successful work.

Selznick first offered the script assignment of *Rebecca* to du Maurier, the screenwriter most likely to protect the novel's character, but like Margaret Mitchell on *Gone With the Wind,* du Maurier declined. By transatlantic cable and letter, Selznick began conferring with Hitchcock on other possibilities. The first of their many differences soon became apparent.

Unlike Selznick, Hitchcock scorned original source material. "I believe that I owe much of the success I have been lucky enough to achieve to my 'ruthlessness' in adapting stories for the screen," the director said in 1936. In *Waltzes from Vienna,* where he ignored his own advice and clung to the musical that inspired the film, he misfired. In *The 39 Steps,* however, where he changed author John Buchan's setting, created a female interest, and added two suspenseful Music Hall sequences, he earned critical applause and aroused the curiosity of Hollywood. To rethink an existing property for the movies, Hitchcock scanned it (reading it might lead to a "mere photographic reproduction"), then extracted its narrative skeleton. Next came the period of invention, the days and weeks when he, his wife, Alma, his assistant, Joan Harrison, and occasionally another writer would attempt to fit his lively but often disparate visual pyrotechnics into a coherent story. Hitchcock loved this part of the filmmaking process best. The resulting treatment contained "a description of exactly what you saw. As though you had plugs in your ears," Hitchcock said. "Then I'd go to a playwright. I'd say, there's the film. Just a lot of steel girders, you see." Add dialogue, light, and shoot.

Hitchcock had been a silent or credited scenarist on most of his British sound films; ideally, the scripting of *Rebecca* would become an in-house project, a Hitchcock–Hitchcock–Harrison effort carried out with the director's accustomed "ruthlessness." But when Hitchcock delayed choosing a writer, his new employer began pushing him. Selznick first proposed Clemence Dane, whose *Bill of Divorcement* Selznick had made at RKO; "I would have you negotiate deal," Selznick cabled Hitchcock, "as you could probably get her cheaper than we could especially since it would be my thought to have her work with you in England on first draft and then come over to work on revisions with me." When Hitchcock rejected Dane, perhaps because she might miscarry his ideas across the Atlantic, Selznick proposed John Balderston *(The Prisoner of Zenda)* and Ben Hecht *(Nothing Sacred)*. Hitchcock remained unenthusiastic. Selznick then proposed Hugh Walpole, "perfectly charming to work with, very pliable and agreeable." Hitchcock sought iconoclasm, not complaisance. Again he stalled. The screenwriter should not endorse the original subject but supplement it, Hitchcock told Selznick by letter; "to use an analogy it must [be] like the idea of casting against type." Subtly asserting his case for a "more entertaining" adaptation of the novel, Hitchcock countered that Sidney Gilliat would be expert at "the writing of small parts [of] English characters to provide ingredient of humour." He had brought to *The Lady Vanishes* the qualities that Hitchcock wanted in *Rebecca,* wit and irony.

Not one to confront, Hitchcock preferred wars of attrition to wars of aggression; by indirection and persistence if not persuasion, he would

Hitchcock at work.

turn Selznick to his point of view. In London in November 1938, Hitchcock lunched with Kay Brown and Jock Whitney. They listened to his plans for *Rebecca,* particularly the changes in the second Mrs. de Winter's character, and came away excited. For $5,000, Hitchcock offered to prepare a treatment with elaborated dialogue sequences. "Please cable your reaction," Whitney asked Selznick, "personally think too good to be true." Once sealed, the bargain would accord Hitchcock a significant measure of control, for as the primary author of the treatment he would influence and perhaps even set the structure, action, and characterization of *Rebecca.* Selznick was wary.

Like expensive racehorses, thought Selznick, celebrated artists like Hitchcock could give spectacular performances but needed a trainer's professional grooming and watchful discipline. "I have never had much success with leaving a writer alone to do a script without almost daily collaboration with myself," the producer had written two years earlier. In 1938, he remained almost pathologically anxious about any major task completed without his supervision, including Hitchcock's adaptation of a $50,000 studio property. "Especially nervous changes second wife," Selznick wired Whitney, "since we have had overwhelming proof appeal of this character and further would challenge resentment if changed." Yet to become truly an "executive" rather than a "unit" producer, a course of action that Whitney and others had urged upon him, Selznick would have to loosen the reins. Perhaps feeling a subtle pressure from his business associate, Selznick reluctantly agreed to Hitchcock's proposal.

The novel was rife with challenges. For instance, first-person point of view, so important to the development of the second Mrs. de Winter's character, translated poorly to the screen. Orson Welles's hastily prepared yet successful adaptation of *Rebecca* used de Winter's wife as narrator, but radio actually benefited from a character-narrator; film had to use extensive voice-over or, as in *The Lady in the Lake* (1946), a camera that awkwardly stood in for the character-narrator, neither of which was very satisfactory. Selznick wanted to frame the narrative by opening and closing the film with the girl's voice-over commentary, but Hitchcock was doubtful. "Something might have to be substituted for the first person style of telling," he wrote Selznick, probably testing the waters for a less slavish adaptation. If only to attract a male star, they might find it necessary to expand the point of view. Hitchcock's idea was to make the girl "fairly bright, attractive and amusing" in the Monte Carlo scenes and bring her down on her arrival at Manderley. "As the book stands at present this contrast does not exist particularly; or, if it does, it is purely mental, and I feel unless we do something like this our early scenes in the house will not have the dramatic kicks that they should have, because visually we shall be unable to show any change in the girl."

Throughout the winter of 1938–39, Hitchcock worked on the *Rebecca* treatment with Alma, Joan Harrison, and British writer Michael Hogan, whom Selznick had implicitly approved. Among other problems, the director fretted about de Winter's explanation of Rebecca's murder. "Is it sufficient to put this over verbally through de Winter's own words," he wondered, "or must it be done pictorially, in order to make absolutely sure that we do not lose any sympathy for him?" Hitchcock recognized that an audience might need to see Rebecca in order to comprehend fully what a heinous woman she was, yet one of the novel's strongest points was its ability to make the reader *feel* rather than *see* Rebecca. When de Winter describes her to his second wife, Hitchcock said, his account is "practically a visual one. Flashback? . . . Ugh!" A two-page, single-spaced letter to Selznick in which Hitchcock shared his thoughts about the adaptation betrays his concern with the static quality of du Maurier's work, its limited settings, its monochromatic heroine, and its reliance on vague evocations of the past. When Hitchcock sought an option on the novel, he must certainly have been thinking of how he would have to dress it up, making it, as he told John Russell Taylor, more vivid and detailed, giving it more of an English flavor, less dreamlike and Gothic. In a September 1938 cable, Hitchcock had assured Selznick that he intended to "look after horrific atmosphere whatever writer we use," but if *Rebecca* veered toward the frisky tone of the British pictures, director and producer would clash.

With the unfinished treatment in hand, the director and his family left for America in early spring 1939, barely a month before the first twenty-week term of his contract began. While on the East Coast, Hitchcock addressed the History of Motion Pictures class at Columbia University. "If I were doing *Rebecca* in color," he told his audience, "the symbol of the dead woman's presence would be in a color. Obviously, it lends itself to exploitation. Why, just think, you might have a new color called 'Rebecca' sold in all the stores!" The students laughed, but Selznick would later make the naive joke seem prescient. In early April the Hitchcock entourage arrived in southern California. Greeted by the Myron Selznicks, the Hitchcocks drove to their penthouse apartment at the Wilshire Palms, near the Los Angeles Country Club and not far from Selznick International Studios. Joan Harrison lived downstairs and other neighbors included one of the Ritz Brothers and Franchot Tone, recently divorced from Joan Crawford. Behind the wheel of a little Austin, Hitchcock chauffeured Pat to her Catholic day school and himself to his handsome suite of offices (including bath and kitchen) in Culver City. Meanwhile, with Selznick still preoccupied by *Gone With the Wind,* Hitchcock worked diligently on the *Rebecca* treatment. The press covered his progress—and everything else about him—with steady interest.

To reporters as well as colleagues, Hitchcock strove to make himself interesting. Most Hollywood directors usually wore "sandals of Mexican derivation," the *World Film News* observed in 1938, "fancy slacks styled in the Broadway fashion, loud polo shirts . . . and sometimes either caps or sunglasses to protect their eyes from the klieg lights and the actions of the Thespians beneath." Hitchcock reinforced the eccentricity of his dark business suits with an amused if enigmatic expression; he would "tell you the dirtiest joke in the world," Marcella Rabwin recalled, "and never crack a smile." When he spoke to journalists, though, he proved immensely quotable, spicing his interviews with bons mots as original as the images in his films. On two topics—directing and eating—he became voluble. He had always been particular about food; according to his mother, he left one grammar school because he "objected to the cuisine." Newspapermen lapped up his aversions, preferences, and habits. Commissary chow disagreed with him, so he lunched at Perino's or the Victor Hugo. He never ordered eggs or shellfish, he loved steak and American ice cream, and he drank Château d'Yquem. Frequently after dinner, he dozed.

When Hitchcock, all 260 pounds of him, went on salary in April 1939, he and Selznick began conferring sporadically. During these sessions, the producer and the director must have first sensed the inevitable conflict to follow. Disliking surprises, Selznick reiterated his intention to preserve the structure and characterization of *Rebecca,* including all of "the little feminine things which are so recognizable and which make every woman say [of the heroine], 'I know just how she feels. . . . I know just what she's going through . . .' etc." Selznick approached a narrative intuitively; he leaned *toward* the human drama in fiction, whether Margaret Mitchell's or Daphne du Maurier's. An analytic filmmaker, Hitchcock privileged form over character, irony over romance. Throughout the spring Hitchcock listened to Selznick, read the memoranda, then went his own way. His forty-five page, double-spaced "storyline," dated June 3, changed relatively little of the novel, even if it rearranged certain scenes; yet it demonstrated the director's attempt—admittedly not always successful or subtle—to breathe cinematic life into du Maurier's often static, occasionally repetitive work.

The Hitchcock treatment opens briefly on a moving-camera shot of Manderley's "tangled and neglected wilderness," then quickly fades to "the sound of the scream of the boat train as it roars into the camera," a sound-image transition similar to those used in Hitchcock's *Blackmail* and *The 39 Steps*. (Two years later, Orson Welles's *Citizen Kane* would echo the fallen estate and the manner of photographing it, the shock sound cutaway, and notable other elements of *Rebecca*.) With great economy, Hitchcock used predominantly nonverbal scenes to introduce Mrs. Van Hopper, Maxim de Winter, and "Daphne," Selznick International's name for du Maurier's unnamed heroine. The director obviously wanted to *move Rebecca,* to convert the words of du Maurier's restrained fiction into lively images that incidentally expressed Hitchcock's love of travel and explicitly dramatized the picture-book world of the Van Hoppers and de Winters into which the heroine so uneasily fit. Act one, he insisted, "has to be charming, replete with quips and whimsey."

The treatment contains not only a number of Hitchcock signature scenes (a car racing along a precipice, some well-observed moments of English domestic life) but several of his "experiments." For the so-called confession scene in which de Winter tells "Daphne" of his hatred for Rebecca, Hitchcock first considered showing the discovery of Rebecca's body, but a local embalmer's explicit report about the effects of saltwater on a corpse dissuaded him. Instead, Hitchcock specified that while de Winter speaks, the camera moves "to a SEMI-CLOSE UP of him in retrospect as he goes through the various emotional experiences he describes." The lighting and background change constantly to reflect his relationship to the action and we even "get an impression of his physical movements as his voice narrative continues." Hitchcock intended the effect to differ from the "old fashioned 'flash back,'" and it does, for it dramatizes not the incident but a refraction of it in space and time. As scripted or even filmed, the scene might or might not have worked; it nonetheless represented Hitchcock's attempt to advance beyond a conventional mise-en-scène in a work that appeared somewhat resistant to cinematic treatment.

Selznick read the June 3 draft, marked his chief criticisms, and called in the stenographers for a lengthy session. The *Rebecca* treatment, he wrote to Hitchcock, left him "shocked beyond words." He spoke figuratively of course. In the almost three thousand words that followed, Selznick addressed the filmmaker's responsibility to a popular novel as well as Hitchcock's weaknesses as adapter. Beatrice, de Winter's sister, had been vulgarized, Mrs. Danvers detoxified, and Maxim de Winter left with "no charm, no mystery, and no romance." The changes in "Daphne" were especially harmful. "Every little thing that the girl does in the book, her reactions of running away from the guests, and the tiny things that indicate her nervousness and her self-consciousness and her gaucherie are all so brilliant in the book that every woman who has read it has adored the girl and has understood her psychology. . . . We have removed all the subtleties and substituted big broad strokes." Selznick served his new director well by forcing him to pay closer heed to character, for Hitchcock too often matched his cleverly reasoned visual logic with pallid characterization. He not only conceived pictures outwardly, from "big broad strokes," he also believed you first "decide what the characters are going to do. Then you provide them with enough characteristics to make it seem plausible that they should do it." This strategy compromised more than one of his films. Selznick sometimes let opulent but pedestrian visuals overwhelm his attention to subtle points of character, yet he attempted to render his characters' emotions fully and credibly. Selznick and Hitchcock made odd collaborators. The June 3 treatment represented the first skirmish in a long battle of contesting points of view.

"We bought 'REBECCA' and we intend to make 'REBECCA,'" Selznick dictated. Yet his ruminative June 12 memorandum repeatedly betrayed the hour and stressful circumstances of its composition. Principal photography on *Gone With the Wind,* a five-month drain on the small company's resources, was finally ending but providing no cause for relief. "Quite apart from the cost factor," Selznick observed, "everybody's nerves are getting on the ragged edge and God only knows what will happen if we don't get this damn thing finished." According to his wife, Selznick used increasing amounts of Benzedrine to maintain his "insane" hours on *Gone With the Wind*. He occasionally went without sleep, and occasionally was impossible to awaken. If *Gone With the Wind* had seemed to run out of control—Selznick may have thought—*Rebecca* would not. At the end of the memorandum to Hitchcock, he ordered a new treatment, "probably with a new writing set-up." That same week, du Maurier told Jenia Reissar that she was "weeping bitter tears over [Hitchcock's] 'Jamaica Inn'" and hoped for better from *Rebecca*. Selznick responded immediately. "I have thrown out the complete treatment on 'REBECCA,'" he wrote to du Maurier through Kay Brown; furthermore, he boasted, it is "my intention to do the book and not some botched-up semi-original such as was done with 'JAMAICA INN.'"

Hitchcock, Joan Harrison, and Scottish novelist-playwright Philip MacDonald (the author of three Twentieth Century-Fox "Mr. Moto" pictures) began work immediately on the new *Rebecca* treatment, and by the third week in June had completed an outline-script of over one hundred pages. In general, they followed the letter of the novel; they even added dialogue taken word for word from du Maurier's text. Eager to please Selznick but not yet resigned to producing a slavish *Rebecca*, Hitchcock attached a note to his revised treatment that seemed to challenge Selznick to accept it: This "will serve as a basis for discussion in order to decide what deviation may be permitted so as to remove some of the character weakness and slight static quality which I feel have emerged."

If Hitchcock thought that Selznick would regret having wholly embraced the du Maurier work, he erred. Once the treatment was set, Selznick intended to employ a dialogue writer who could readily finish the job: "We did not and do not now need a screenwriter," he told Kay Brown, "but simply someone to fill in that dialogue which we are not [yet] using from du Maurier." To cut *Rebecca* loose from its novelistic moorings, Hitchcock would first have to overcome his distaste for confrontation. An opportunity soon presented itself.

Toward the first day of summer, Hitchcock and his writers joined Selznick for an afternoon of business and pleasure on his boat. In the

1930s, John Huston recalled, "Sailing was the rage. Men who were mild-mannered and conservative behind their desks during the week put on yachting caps and brass-buttoned jackets and became Captain Blighs on their own quarterdecks each weekend." A nascent Mr. Christian, Hitchcock probably shed his accustomed dark suit but not his avoirdupois, 260-*plus* pounds fore and aft. On board, the foursome discussed *Rebecca*'s prospects, which for Selznick had brightened with the revised treatment. But transcribed into ten pages of single-spaced "minor notes," Selznick's response again signaled his intent to control the production, from treatment to direction to final cut. If Hitchcock wondered whether he should assert his independence, he had his answer between the lines. Of some added dialogue during de Winter's courtship of the heroine, Selznick observed: "I don't care for the girl's un-cued and unjustified disloyalty to her employer, as indicated by her gratuitous remarks about Mrs. Van Hopper to Maxim." An English director contemplating mutiny might well have taken the comment about labor and management personally.

As the writers revised the script, Selznick and Hitchcock discussed casting. A director at one of the five major studios generally secured actors from the pool of contract players; the notoriously frugal Warner Bros. would have forced Hitchcock to cast exclusively from its stock company, and later in his career MGM urged him to use contract actors Gregory Peck and Cyd Charisse as the leads in *North by Northwest.* Selznick International, which had only a few actors under contract, sometimes required its directors to look beyond the administration building's white colonnades. Hitchcock enjoyed searching for new faces, particularly at the theater, where he could audition performers without confronting them. In casting, Selznick generally supported his director.

For Mrs. Danvers, Kay Brown proposed someone new to film, Judith Anderson. The acclaimed stage actress demanded transportation from New York to Hollywood, a thousand dollars per week for the audition plus all other expenses, and a "written guarantee" that Hitchcock would direct the screen test, a tribute to Hitchcock's reputation if a slight to Selznick's. "Just who the hell does she think she is dealing with?" Selznick fumed to Daniel O'Shea. He nonetheless cast her. Throughout the summer of 1939, Hitchcock tested other, more malleable actors. His comments on the *Rebecca* auditions, while humorous, betray not only traces of condescension toward the performers, but a notable delight in pigeonholing them, objectifying them as he did so many characters in his films. Of Leo Genn and Anthony Ireland, reading for minor roles: "In a mild way they would fit into the parts mentioned, but actually they are quite unimportant actors." Of John Mills, established in England but just coming to America: "Very, very British and very, very short." Of Guy Middleton, the Harrow-educated English actor and Laurence Olivier's choice for the part of Favell: "A caddish David Niven. . . . Mentally light-weight."

Since reading an early treatment, Selznick had wanted Ronald Colman, whom the studio had under contract, for the leading role of de Winter; equally enthusiastic, Hitchcock liked the actor's flair for the poignant. But from the beginning, Colman's fear about the "murder angle" and also about the possibility of the picture's emerging as a "woman-starring vehicle" had made his acceptance of the part unlikely. In May 1939, Hitchcock visited Colman's home to plead the production's case, but finally the actor refused. Selznick asked Hitchcock to consider Melvyn Douglas, Walter Pidgeon (who Selznick thought was "coming along nicely"), Leslie Howard, and William Powell. Hitchcock found Howard "a little too scholastic for the romantic angle necessary" (a sly comment on Howard's casting in *Gone With the Wind*?) and thought William Powell's American accent "dangerous." At last, Selznick and Hitchcock settled on Laurence Olivier, who had returned to Hollywood in the late 1930s after an unhappy period in America several years before. Both Olivier and his lover Vivien Leigh preferred the stage to films: actors made money—not art—in Hollywood. According to one magazine writer at the time, Olivier had "a fund of disdain as large as the Italian treasury deficit." That manner could serve Maxim de Winter and *Rebecca* well.

Over *Rebecca*'s female lead, Hitchcock and Selznick clashed. The producer had found *Young and Innocent* "a very intriguing and a very exciting picture"; furthermore, he was convinced that Nova Pilbeam, its heroine, could convey the du Maurier narrator's "gauche behavior, awkward movements and general immaturity." With proper guidance, Selznick intimated to Jenia Reissar, Pilbeam could become a "great star for the world market."

Hitchcock balked. Pilbeam was "correct casting according [to the] book," the director conceded, but not to his conception of the script's

Maxim de Winter (Laurence Olivier) greets his brother-in-law, Giles Lacy (Nigel Bruce), dressed for the costume ball. In the screenplay—a Hitchcock touch—Lacy says that the weather does not favor a ball: "Very misty . . . very chilly, too."

heroine. Hitchcock obviously wished to influence *Rebecca* through the casting, if not the screenplay. Despite the objections to Pilbeam, however, Selznick pursued her, and without mentioning Selznick's name ("so as [to] keep [the] price down"), Jenia Reissar discovered that the actress was "very keen" on working in America. (Like Hitchcock, Pilbeam had suffered from the contraction of the British film industry; more to the point, Gaumont-British, her home studio in 1938, would neither cast her nor waive its restriction against her stage appearances.) Selznick's attempt to sign the young actress not only suggests his adamance about leaving intact du Maurier's book, heroine and all, but constitutes his implicit statement about the boundaries of Hitchcock's authority. By contract, Hitchcock had agreed to render his services "pursuant to Producer's directions, instructions and control." If Hitchcock could not veto casting selections, though, he could still twist arms. In October 1938 he had argued that Pilbeam was "too immature and difficult [to] handle in love scenes"; in November, that her range was too narrow. Meanwhile, as Selznick prepared a five-year contract for her, the lengthy term and binding exclusivity clauses of which troubled her agent, Hitchcock resorted to sarcasm. Referring to Colman's fear of *Rebecca* as a "woman-starring vehicle," Hitchcock wired Selznick: Why should Colman worry? With Pilbeam as de Winter's wife, the picture will be his.

To Hitchcock's relief, Selznick abandoned the notion of using Pilbeam. Olivier pressured them both to cast Vivien Leigh, whom Selznick International had under contract, but the director had other ideas. Since arriving in Hollywood, Hitchcock had urged Selznick to consider naming an *American* actress to play the heroine in order to stress her isolation at Manderley. The producer consented, the auditions began.

"Tested. Possibility," noted Hitchcock about Joan Fontaine's audition in midsummer 1939. She "has to show fair amount of nervousness in order to get any effect," he wrote. But he intended to test her again "to see how much we can underplay her without losing anything." Lucile Fairbanks, Douglas Fairbanks's niece and an alumna of Beverly Hills High, read in late June. She has "a sincere and naive hopefulness," Hitchcock told Selznick, but also "a husky voice reminiscent of Mae West in her youth (if any) and I don't really think we can take her seriously." On July 19, the director sent his producer a list of almost thirty women whom he had tested. Miriam Patty "should play the part of the cupid that is broken—she's so frail." Marjorie Reynolds, who had appeared in a number of programmers, was "absolutely not the type—too much gangster's moll." Though she had had some experience on stage and in film, Jean Muir was "too big and sugary." And Audrey Reynolds was "excellent for Rebecca who doesn't appear." Many of the actors with whom Hitchcock worked found him endearing, but his humor had a darker side, sometimes abusive and inescapably deliberate. In one of James Thurber's anemically drawn but telling cartoons, a fencer beheads his opponent. The caption: "Touché!" Hitchcock's épée was his wit, wielded with grace, speed, and a sometimes unexpected fatality.

As the casting process continued, the writers completed the first script of *Rebecca,* an amalgam dated July 29, 1939, which reflects both Selznick's and Hitchcock's ideas on du Maurier's story. The screenplay opens on a train en route to Monte Carlo, dramatizes the awkward meeting, brisk courtship, and civil marriage ceremony of de Winter and "I" (formerly "Daphne"), and settles into Manderley where it more or less follows the novel. Consistent with Hitchcock's earliest intention (the "second wife should be much less passive"), the heroine appears more assertive; in the "confession scene," having learned of her husband's act of murder, she exhibits a serene calm: "We must think up some way of explaining everything," she tells de Winter, as though Rebecca's death were merely an inconvenience. However, when Mrs. Danvers reverently shows "I" her predecessor's beautiful "things"— hairbrushes, negligee, and so forth—the young woman becomes paralyzed with despair. Hitchcock's best films privileged cinema's visual element over literature and the theater's verbal emphasis. The man who feared "things" also made them the centerpiece of his work, where glasses of wine, glasses of milk, dinner forks, cigarette lighters, and even hairbrushes frequently exert a latent yet menacing power over his characters. In *Rebecca,* they had exceptional resonance.

Selznick, overseeing the previews of *Intermezzo* and the cutting of *Gone With the Wind,* commented on the script in installments dictated over several days and transcribed in thirty-seven single-spaced pages. Then, less than two weeks before *Rebecca* went into production, he hired Robert E. Sherwood to trim and polish the screenplay and give its conclusion a fresh slant. For a flat $15,000 fee, the Harvard-educated dramatist became the production's seventh writer. During late August, Selznick met often with Hitchcock and Sherwood. Working with the producer always tested an artist's mettle. At late-hour conferences in his office or summerhouse, Selznick ran on adrenaline (and speed), Hitchcock and Sherwood on liquor. By three o'clock one morning, with Selznick still roaring, Hitchcock fell asleep and Sherwood, having drunk too much, tried to sail away in the model boat in Selznick's pool. When they all came to, the script's third act—particularly the manner of Rebecca's death—still awaited them.

In du Maurier's novel, Rebecca had gone to her physician because she suspected that she was pregnant by Favell, but further examination discovered terminal cancer. She kept the diagnosis secret and, to avoid suffering, provoked her husband into shooting her. The industry's censorship office had objected to de Winter's homicide and suggested that Rebecca trip and kill herself in falling. "The whole story of *Rebecca* is the story of a man who has murdered his wife," the producer wrote to Jock Whitney just after Labor Day, "and it now becomes the story of a man who buried a wife who was killed accidentally!" Although the censor prevailed, the three collaborators worked to vitalize the "confession scene" that unravels the story of Rebecca's death. Neither Sherwood nor Hitchcock felt that the actors portraying de Winter and his second wife could carry the sequence alone. Hitchcock rejected a flashback and Selznick wanted a *Rebecca* "without tricks," negating the director's earlier thoughts of superimposing a shifting background against a close-up of de Winter.

During his last days on the production, Sherwood devised an amended "confession scene" that Hitchcock liked and Selznick eventually approved. Shifting the sequence to Rebecca's boat house cottage, where the murder/accident occurred, Sherwood and Hitchcock used a subjective camera to etch in film the geography of the first wife's death, particularly the "things" associated with it. "She was lying on the divan—a large tray of cigarette stubs beside her," de Winter tells "I." "CAMERA PANS over to the divan, showing the tea table and a portion of the divan with a tray of cigarette stubs on it." Rebecca taunts her husband with her infidelity and the possibility of her having another man's child; he strikes her and she falls. "CAMERA MOVES over to take in the ship's tackle on the floor." Back in the present, the discovery of Rebecca's corpse jeopardizes de Winter's life with "I." "Suddenly the telephone rings, startling the two. CAMERA PANS to the phone, covered with dust, on the table. . . . CAMERA TILTS up to Maxim with the receiver to his ear." Despite the length of de Winter's monologue, a long take interrupted only once by a reaction shot of "I," the final shooting script sustains tension by counterpointing the agitato of de Winter's narrative and the legato of the camera's languorous movement.

The September 7 Final Shooting Script, the blueprint for *Rebecca,* resulted from the give and take of producer and director, neither willing to push the other too far. Selznick recognized that a mere re-creation would dull the picture. Though he preached fidelity, he endorsed those invented scenes that lent cinematic distinction to the narrative. Tenacious without becoming overbearing, he persuaded Hitchcock to distill the essence of du Maurier's novel, its most dramatic and best-remembered moments. Yet he also persuaded Hitchcock to explore the psychology of Maxim and his second wife, especially how love finally triumphs over masochism. British Hitchcock had been emotionally thin, *Rebecca* was robust. While seven writers might have defeated a lesser man and the script itself, Selznick held the project together and influenced its direction throughout the long spring and summer of 1939.

"This is a melodrama," noted one reviewer of the du Maurier book, "unashamed, glorying in its own quality." Although such "little British thrillers" as *Young and Innocent* and *The Lady Vanishes* also succumbed to theatricality, the presence of Selznick on *Rebecca* affected Hitchcock. "Things" still predominate, from the telephone in the cottage and the bones of a cold piece of chicken to Manderley itself. But unlike thirties Hitchcock, the *Rebecca* screenplay links the cool, stable surfaces of "things" to the perturbed characters' desires and fears. When de Winter screens the home movies from his second honeymoon (an invented scene), the two-dimensional figures mugging for the camera mock their now joyless counterparts; her wish unspoken, "I" longs to disappear into the character on screen, to become the "thing" before her, for it has the constancy that reality lacks. The shadow of Selznick had wrung the melodrama from Hitchcock.

During the evolution of the screenplay, Selznick never forced the issue of absolute control, for alienating Hitchcock made no sense. The critically acclaimed director was already the media's darling and potentially a major corporate asset. His name on Selznick International films could enhance the studio's reputation and swell its income; during dry periods, his name on loanout contracts could improve the small company's cash flow. Finally, despite the stinging memoranda and fatiguing conferences, Selznick liked Hitchcock. "You sent for me?" the director said when greeting someone. Only Selznick literally had.

The naturally circumspect Hitchcock was even more reluctant to press for a "Hitchcockian" *Rebecca* screenplay. With war clouds gathering abroad, Hollywood was contemplating retrenchment. International ticket sales generated roughly half of a film's revenue, and if war came, movie companies would probably trim their production schedules. "Film business here very sticky on account lost European market," Hitchcock cabled his brother in fall 1939, perhaps warning him not to count on any more money sent home. "Hope to be sublet to another company immediately following *Rebecca* otherwise will have twelve week layoff without pay . . . fear companies here will ask salary reduction near future even though one under contract." Although Selznick International had promised to pay the director for forty weeks annually, by force majeur the studio could cancel one or even both of his twenty-week terms. A too demanding Hitchcock might become known as "difficult" and thus perhaps unemployable in America. More than Selznick's memoranda, Hitchcock's financial insecurity shaped his deference to the producer throughout the writing of *Rebecca*. On his American debut, Hitchcock did not intend to win the round but lose the fight.

"Dear Jack," Hitchcock wrote to his London business advisor on September 1, 1939. "Please forgive silly question at this time but can you cable if furniture shipment at all possible because we are sitting on the floor." The floor belonged to Carole Lombard, whose home on St. Cloud Road the Hitchcocks had leased. Although the director missed not only his furniture but his growing collection of oils and certain delicacies like English strawberries and Dover sole, Los Angeles and Selznick International satisfied many of his needs. Habit conspired with the balmy climate to make him drowse occasionally (at private dinners, nightclubs, the theater), yet he remained fully awake to Hollywood's advantages, particularly its access to the media. Into autumn, Hitchcock continued to make excellent copy. *Life, Newsweek,* and *Collier's,* which usually reserved their feature pages for the stars, profiled the self-assured, eccentric director while he worked on his first American film. His corrosive comments about producers delighted journalists and their readers. "He smiled a little cynically when he discussed producers," Douglas Churchill reported in *The New York Times* in October, but impishly refused to be quoted. Said *Life:* "Judging from his past record it is only a question of time before he will give Louis B. Mayer the hot foot."

Selznick read the *Times* interview, noted Hitchcock's "snide remarks about producers," yet refrained from comment. Selznick could be charged with verbosity, perfectionism, and hard-nosed dealing, but not vindictiveness: secure in his own abilities, he not only vigorously promoted Hitchcock but allowed the director to vigorously promote himself. Hitchcock's courtship of the press opened another supply line (a free one at that) from the studio to moviegoers. Since content generally mattered less to Selznick International than linage, the studio recognized advantages in all of Hitchcock's pronouncements, even his earlier statement to *Newsweek* that his first film would "reflect no personality other than his own." This comment, a wish-fulfillment fantasy that the director would increasingly struggle to realize, gave to Hitchcock and the press a certain satisfaction and to Selznick International fodder for its public relations machine. No less than Clark Gable's love of sport or Joan Crawford's supposedly warm home life, Hitchcock's assertion of independence helped to define a persona that Selznick's publicity department and later Hitchcock himself could use in selling pictures. As long as Hitchcock played his act on the road and not in the executive offices of Culver City, no one strenuously objected; his contract, after all, negated his claims of authorship.

In late summer 1939, Hitchcock's whimsical opinions claimed little of Selznick's attention. The studio, inadequately organized to operate on an assembly line, had three pictures—*Intermezzo, Gone With the Wind,* and *Rebecca*—in various stages of production; the threat of war and a concurrent cessation of motion picture exports made each film momentous for the company's future. With less than two weeks remaining before principal photography began, however, Selznick had still not cast the second Mrs. de Winter. In late August, Jock Whitney told him that their company had "a very serious problem. I cannot assure the Pioneer stockholders or the Bank of America that all is well with

REBECCA until this most important part is cast"; in short, investors would not supply completion money for the film without a leading lady. "Such procedure has not been and is not good business," Whitney gently chastised his partner.

In later years, Hitchcock complained that Selznick had intended all along to cast Joan Fontaine, that his heralded search for the second Mrs. de Winter was a wearying promotional stunt for the film; but Selznick was genuinely undecided. Margaret Sullavan and Anne Baxter, both finalists for the role, seemed far more likely choices than Fontaine. After a handful of films in which she appeared to show little potential, RKO had eliminated Fontaine from its studio roster in 1938. Alma Hitchcock thought her manner intolerably "coy and simpering" and her voice "extremely irritating." Like Kay Brown, Jock Whitney also inveighed against her: "The last test of Joan Fontaine was so bad that I cannot see her playing the role otherwise than as a dithering idiot, or as her other version—a talking magazine cover." Even her fiancé, thirty-seven-year-old English actor Brian Aherne, described her as "young, pretty, gay, and utterly charming—and no actress, thank God." As Whitney noted, however, the decision was Selznick's, and as he had in Hitchcock, the producer sensed in Fontaine something that others had missed. When he finally offered her *Rebecca,* she deserted Aherne and sped from their Oregon honeymoon cabin to Culver City. The Pygmalion in Hitchcock nodded his approval.

Toward the end of August, Selznick changed the starting date of *Rebecca* from August 30 to September 5, then to September 8. Even before Hitchcock had exposed a foot of film, he had worked twenty-one weeks, all on salary. Selznick's attempt to serve as executive producer on *Gone With the Wind* and *Rebecca* had contributed significantly to the director's meager progress. Nonetheless, to a studio that had planned to get two pictures from Hitchcock in two twenty-week periods annually, the delay was costly. Despite the fact that they were not working, the contracted artists were being paid: Olivier $695 a day, Judith Anderson $291, Fontaine $166. An expeditious shooting schedule became essential. Hitchcock had first proposed a $947,000 budget with a forty-eight-day shooting schedule. Selznick ordered it lowered to $750,000 and forty-two days. "In view of the many speeches [Hitchcock] has made to me about how he pre-cuts a script so as to shoot only necessary angles [what the director called 'cutting-in-the-camera'], it is

Selznick and Hitchcock would finally cast the inexperienced Joan Fontaine as the heroine; she would perform with seasoned professionals Judith Anderson (*above*) and Laurence Olivier (*below*). Until she worked with Olivier, Fontaine had never realized that the screen actor must keep "doing the same thing over and over again, *exactly* the same way," repeating for the close-up what he did in the long shot. Olivier "did it to such perfection," Fontaine later recalled. In a breakfast scene, he "deliberately spilled some marmalade on his lap, or his chin, and it came exactly the same place" in every take.

a mystery to me as to how he could spend even 42 days." By the start of production, Selznick had established a thirty-six-day budget with expenses not to exceed $800,000. Calling for the completion of four script pages daily, the shooting schedule seemed almost reasonable. Victor Fleming had averaged three pages daily on the epical *Gone With the Wind*, Gregory Ratoff nearly four on *Intermezzo*. Yet the shooting schedule did not account for Hitchcock's unfamiliarity with American production methods and his customary ten-week British schedules, to say nothing of the still-unfinished screenplay. In agreeing to the thirty-six-day shooting period, the director built failure into his effort. The consequences would affect his career long after *Rebecca* had been released.

William Dieterle, a director who lived by horoscopes and numerology, might have sensed other negative vibrations. Several days before Hitchcock began shooting *Rebecca,* England declared war on Germany. Although the war would not come to America for over two years, the director and his predominantly British cast experienced its effects in September 1939. "We felt blighted right through," Olivier recalled, "careers, lives, hopes." Hitchcock frequently cabled London to inquire about his family, specifically his mother. An actress with ebbing self-confidence, Joan Fontaine brought different but no less disturbing anxieties to the production. Like the second Mrs. de Winter, she was a newlywed among strangers, all of them having come to *Rebecca* long before she. Between reading the script, enduring the hours of fittings and photographic tests, and trying to master the new role of bride at home as well as at the studio, she had set a challenge for herself worthy of the celebrated and poised Rebecca. As Selznick warned Hitchcock, she would need "an enormous amount of rehearsal." Yet the director's enthusiasm for the project remained steadfast. At the beginning of a picture, said production designer Robert Boyle, Hitchcock glowed.

As the first day of principal photography approached, Selznick and Hitchcock made final preparations. Nothing escaped Selznick's attention. Pursuing authenticity, he asked the art director to heed "the descriptions given in the novel in dressing the sets, the props, atmosphere, etc." He authorized construction of an enormous miniature—almost the size of the cavernous stage that held it—for close-ups of Manderley and a second, smaller miniature for long shots. Disappointed in some background footage made abroad ("it lacks mood"), he ordered retakes, if necessary with California standing in for Monte Carlo. The number of retakes made throughout the picture would stagger and finally tire Hitchcock, yet budget never stood between the producer and perfection. The actors concerned him no less. When the wardrobe department completed its work, the performers (not their stand-ins) modeled their costumes for Selznick. A photographic still could tell him how the actor looked once dressed, but not how he *moved.* His keen eye and long arm never failed to surprise. Just before shooting began, Judith Anderson recalled, "I was in Nevada getting a divorce, and I had word from Selznick, 'Don't pluck your eyebrows!' It was the least of my worries at that moment. [But] that's as far as he went with everything."

Hitchcock proved equally fastidious. Many pages of the screenplay's text already specified camera placement and editing selections that the director or his writers had devised and that, in some cases, Selznick had modified. But Hitchcock also filled his copy of a script with drawings, occasionally one for each shot; when complete, the director's heavily annotated screenplay resembled what one reporter called "a traveling artist's sketch pad." Hitchcock conceptualized each image by first positioning the characters' faces ("the first thing that one looks at"), then framing them in the screen's rectangle. Although he rarely discussed his characters' psychology with either actors or interviewers, he invariably caught a scene's emotional tone in his imagery. Part of the effect relied on scale, part on juxtaposition. As Hitchcock knew, long shots followed by close-ups—or vice versa—accentuated one another and lent vitality to a film; furthermore, cutting from a full shot to a small "thing" endowed an object with great power or menace. Finished with his sketches, Hitchcock had fully realized the film: "After all, once a chess player has worked out his moves, it's just a matter of physically moving the men."

On Friday, September 8, 1939, with Joan Harrison still revising the Monte Carlo sequences, Hitchcock began "moving the men." Ironically, considering Joan Fontaine's relative unfamiliarity with the part, the first scene scheduled involved the second Mrs. de Winter's getting lost in her new home. Hitchcock had planned his setup weeks before, but for half an hour he and director of photography George Barnes tuned the lighting. Having spent the 1930s shooting pictures on the

When Selznick altered the script, Hitchcock (with script girl Adele Cannon) had to reformulate the blocking and camera moves.

Warner Bros. assembly line, Barnes could work fast. As Selznick knew, the cinematographer could also work miracles. Barnes was known as "a Hollywood-woman cameraman," Hitchcock later observed, a specialist in glamor shots of leading ladies. Selznick wanted Joan Fontaine lit and photographed with enormous care, for he understood her role in the success of the picture. Hitchcock had founded his British films on action and things, not feminine beauty; he paid relatively little attention to stars. With pressure from Selznick, though, he learned to value photographic effects, particularly as they involved Fontaine. Soon his own demands for subtle, evocative light and shadow slowed him down.

Once the camera crew had set up, Hitchcock prepared Fontaine. While rehearsing, Frank Capra paced and Gregory Ratoff gesticulated and cursed; Hitchcock rarely left his canvas chair or raised his voice. Economy of movement became both condition and precept. "It is all the little nuances of expression that tell you what that character is feeling," Hitchcock said, "without reminding you that he is just an actor playing a part." A subtractive artist who exalted "things" and underplayed people, Hitchcock espoused "negative acting," an approach that he had developed in England and, to judge from the close-ups, had used to occasional advantage with Nova Pilbeam in *Young and Innocent.* "In other words," the director explained to Selznick, "you do not put a dramatic expression into a face, but you already have the face in a contrasting condition, say smiling, then to get a dramatic reaction you allow that smile to drain away from the face."

Preston Sturges and William Wyler rehearsed a scene extensively to find an interpretation they liked, while George Cukor, who stressed only the mechanical elements, forced his actors to save their emotions for the camera. Hitchcock belonged more to the Cukor camp. With experienced actors, Hitchcock provided little more than blocking; with younger performers whom he liked, however, he stipulated virtually everything, showing rather than telling them what to do. An expert forger, Hitchcock was also a fair mimic. With his actors rehearsed, Hitchcock said "Twirl 'em" and sat back to await the result. Several performers believed that he dozed while the camera turned. But on *Young and Innocent,* just as Derrick de Marney approached him after a shot, Hitchcock opened his eyes: "Too slow," he told the actor. "I had that scene marked for thirty seconds and it took you fifty seconds flat. We'll have to retake." Actors carried around loads of insecurity; Hitchcock, exuding enormous confidence, gave them a place to stow it. Like several young actresses before her, Joan Fontaine grew to love the director for his beneficent control over both a performance and a production.

Hitchcock provided both gestures and expression for Fontaine; as script supervisor Lydia Schiller observed, "She was practically a puppet." Yet early on, an impatient Olivier told Hitchcock, "This girl's terrible, old man, she'll have to be changed." Getting the desired effect from an inexperienced actress—especially at Selznick International— certainly consumed time. One Thursday afternoon in September, for example, the producer viewed a scene of the de Winters at dinner, with "I" typically ill at ease; for two hours Selznick halted work and scripted some new dialogue. Hitchcock shot Selznick's revision in ninety minutes, then devised his own, one in which strong images obviated the need for any dialogue whatsoever. The latter version, which appears in the completed film, opens with a close-up of a lace-bordered napkin, "R de W" embroidered handsomely upon it. As the second Mrs. de Winter lifts the napkin to place it in her lap, the camera pulls back until it is positioned well behind and above de Winter, seated opposite his wife. In the act of withdrawal, a movement duplicated elsewhere in the film, the camera contributes to the young bride's feelings of unworthiness and abandonment. Joan Fontaine, more self-conscious in this scene than in most others, could not sustain a performance through the shot; apparently in conversation with her screen husband, she moves her head lightly to and fro in a stilted parody of awkwardness. Because of the lost time and technical problems in getting the shot, multiple takes were not economically feasible; likewise, Hitchcock would have diffused the emphasis of the sustained, rearward movement had he cut away to de Winter, the dog Jasper, or even the young bride herself in a better acted close-up. At the end of this day, according to the production log, Fontaine felt "pretty tired."

During her first ten days on the picture, the young actress reported to the studio at 7:00 A.M. and often left after 8:00 P.M. The script revisions and intensive rehearsals—exacerbated by the coolness of her peers—so tired her that Selznick, at her request, willingly reduced her hours. "Even if you don't want to think about it from a standpoint of consideration of the player," Selznick told his production manager Ray

Klune, "in view of the bad times that we are faced with due to the War you must nevertheless consider it from a commercial standpoint, facing the possibility of a delay as a result of overwork." Thrown into disequilibrium by a first marriage and a first major role, a well-trained actress would have used her reserves to counter such obstacles as long hours and inhospitable colleagues; young and inexperienced, Joan Fontaine immediately drew on her capital and, at its rapid depletion, became vulnerable to fatigue and even self-destruction.

In addition to Selznick's tinkering and Fontaine's problems, Hitchcock's occasional tardiness as well as his method of discretely supervising actors and crew limited progress on *Rebecca.* By Saturday, September 16, his eighth day on the set, the director had completed just over eighteen minutes of usable film and twenty-one script pages, throwing the production three days behind schedule. Compared to his peers, Selznick concluded, Hitchcock was "the slowest director we have had." Selznick probably based his assertion in part on the record of *Intermezzo,* a film whose few physical challenges and relatively inexperienced leading actress made it superficially comparable to *Rebecca.* On short notice, Russian émigré director Gregory Ratoff had replaced William Wyler on *Intermezzo* and in his first ten days of shooting completed thirty-six minutes of usable film (compared to Hitchcock's twenty-two minutes) and thirty-three filmed script pages (compared to Hitchcock's twenty-six). On average, he also completed his first shot of the day thirty minutes earlier than Hitchcock. Since "cutting-in-the-camera" required shorter takes, Selznick reasoned, the British director should have gained time once he began filming each shot, but even averaging eighteen daily setups to Hitchcock's eleven, Ratoff moved faster than his colleague with no diminution of quality. Ratoff had been directing in Hollywood since 1935, Hitchcock for two weeks; nonetheless, while Hitchcock appeared to fiddle on *Rebecca,* Selznick began to burn.

The second complete week of principal photography began on Monday, September 18. Throughout the week and thereafter, Selznick visited the set, rarely staying long and just as rarely refraining from comment. The week before, he had urged Hitchcock to "speed the pace a little more, even, than you think is right . . . I would much rather err on the side of too fast a tempo than on the slow side"; he even suggested that Hitchcock ask editor Hal Kern to prod him along. Hitchcock's

Hitchcock rehearses Joan Fontaine, who sits at the long dining table at Manderley.

deliberateness and Fontaine's weakness in the exposed footage, seriously aggravated by worries about *Gone With the Wind,* made Selznick doubt *Rebecca*'s future. Cukor had been wrong for *Wind* (and fired); Hitchcock and Fontaine, whom the industry perceived as risks if not outright liabilities, might both be wrong for the du Maurier adaptation. Some weeks into production, Selznick asked his wife to view a rough assembly of the footage and decide whether to scrap the picture; looking at it, Selznick told her, he could not determine whether it was good or bad. Irene said that the problem lay not with the film but with the anxieties of the producer. As even Selznick admitted, the pressures of moviemaking had begun to weaken his constitution.

In early autumn 1939, Selznick decided to temporarily close the studio as soon as possible and take the vacation long promised to Irene. Meanwhile, however, fixed costs as well as interest expense on *Gone With the Wind* left Selznick International financially strapped. Other studios generated income by selling actors and directors; MGM had in fact exchanged Clark Gable's services for fifty percent of the profits from *Gone With the Wind.* Although no producer had been willing to compete for Hitchcock in 1938, the release of *The Lady Vanishes* (which had won the New York Film Critics Award) as well as the imprimatur of Selznick and *Rebecca* had given the director a certain cachet. With luck, Selznick's hefty English import might equal his weight in gold. During the second week of principal photography on *Rebecca,* Selznick the matchmaker sent Hitchcock to lunch with Walter Wanger, an independent producer of taste and political commitment; five days later, Wanger formally agreed to borrow the director for $5,000 a week upon the completion of *Rebecca.* Faced with possible suspension during Selznick International's retrenchment period, Hitchcock may have readily overlooked his employer's $2,250-a-week profit.

Hitchcock and Selznick, together six days a week, spent Sundays apart. Selznick would have liked to see Hitchcock socially, but Irene lacked her husband's instant affection for the Englishman, and generally excluded him from their weekends of tennis and movie screenings. Although a respected immigrant director like Hitchcock would have fit in, many of his colleagues would not. The industry's class system, Lydia Schiller recalled, "was not all that thick, but it was there." Producers sometimes mixed with writers, but never with lesser writers; stars occasionally mixed with featured players, but rarely with cameramen, language coaches, or script girls. Among the imponderables: income, an artist's studio affiliation, and even the box office returns of his latest picture. On entertaining, as on virtually everything, Selznick took "the larger view." Guest lists numbered thirty or so; after signing the leather-bound visitors' book (to document business parties for Internal Revenue), everyone had to greet David and, according to Joan Fontaine, kowtow to "the beautiful Irene." No affair worth throwing broke up before midnight. Hitchcock preferred intimate gatherings; "more than eight," he said, "is an insult to my friends." Select members of Hollywood's British colony as well as actors and his new secretary, Carol Stevens, enjoyed Hitchcock's wine and Alma's cuisine. When Hitchcock fell asleep after dinner, the evening ended.

Not long after Irene reassured her husband about *Rebecca,* Fontaine's performance ripened, Hitchcock's speed improved, and Selznick's prodding increased; with the producer's wind at his back, Hitchcock moved with an efficiency that had perhaps eluded him in England. The third week of principal photography, the director filmed twelve pages; the fourth, sixteen and a half; and the fifth, twenty-one. The number of usable film minutes also increased, from twelve minutes the third week to twenty the fourth. Although engrossed in the final cutting and imminent premiere of *Gone With the Wind,* Selznick kept a vigilant eye on *Rebecca,* primarily to insure that Hitchcock maintained speed without sacrificing quality. Despite the producer's intentions, though, Hitchcock resented all supervision. One morning during the third week of principal photography, Hitchcock began rehearsing the opening of the crucial scene in which Mrs. Danvers handles Rebecca's "things" as though they were religious relics. Having belittled and frightened the young bride, the housekeeper shows the second Mrs. de Winter her predecessor's room, then coyly invites her to remain and "listen to the sea." Selznick had prompted Hitchcock to include this dark moment from the novel in the screenplay. Moreover, he conveyed to Hitchcock some ideas on staging "I" 's entrance and expected the Englishman to follow them. As he blocked the scene contrary to Selznick's design, Hitchcock received a memorandum in which Selznick criticized him for not following directions.

Hitchcock felt ambushed. "You're supposed to be working with me, for me," he told Lydia Schiller, who had reported his deviation to her

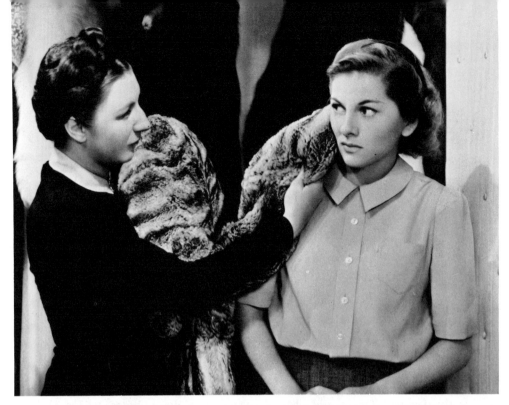

"Feel this," Mrs. Danvers tells the new mistress of Manderley as they stand in Rebecca's bedroom. "It was a Christmas present from Mr. de Winter. He was always giving her expensive gifts, the whole year round."

When the second Mrs. de Winter appears at the costume ball in a gown worn by her predecessor, her husband orders her to change. Distressed, she runs upstairs and follows Mrs. Danvers into Rebecca's bedroom. The housekeeper calls her to the window, then whispers, "Look down there. It's easy, isn't it? Why don't you? . . . Go on . . . Go on . . . Don't be afraid."

employer. "Do you think Mr. Selznick cares anything about you? The studio is going to close down soon and you'll be out of work. Had you helped me, we could have been loaned out together." The response suggests not only his fear of angering Selznick but his naiveté: every American studio maintained what Preston Sturges called a "News Gathering Service." Recalling the 1940s in Hollywood, director John Huston said that when filming began, "your work was monitored. . . . If they thought you were shooting an inordinate number of takes, there would be an inquiry. If a picture fell behind schedule, they would want to know exactly why. If anything untoward happened on the set, it was reported to the Front Office. You never knew who reported it, but no infraction was overlooked; the spy system was thorough." The daily log for the production (standard at all studios) also gave the front office such information as the time work began and ended; the number of setups, retakes, and completed script pages; the amount of picture negative exposed and the number of "film minutes" completed; and explanatory comments sufficient to provide a context for the daily figures.

By viewing the rushes (the day's exposed footage), scanning the log, and maintaining contact with his lieutenants on the set, Selznick closely monitored Hitchcock's progress on *Rebecca.* Unlike that of his peers, though, Selznick's interference often benefited a film. Against Hitchcock's wishes, for instance, Selznick had trimmed some dialogue in which Mrs. Danvers speaks of maintaining flowers in Rebecca's room; the line in question was, as Selznick argued, "silly" and the idea could more economically be conveyed by simply placing fresh flowers in the scene's opening shot. Selznick also decided that a picture of de Winter should sit upon Rebecca's dressing table, silently taunting "I"; he discussed the idea with Hitchcock and asked art director Lyle Wheeler to place "a handsomely framed photo of Maxim on dressing table, where 'I' will see and react. . . . It should be the only photograph in the room."

The middle and close of this key sequence with Danvers and the heroine had been subjected to numerous script changes and remained in flux the day before its filming. Not content to rely solely on the reports of underlings, Selznick came to the set in time for Hitchcock's rehearsal; the director reluctantly proceeded. He first led Anderson and Fontaine through the balance of the scene, demonstrating how Anderson should play it. He wanted Danvers to recall her moments alone with Rebecca. Assuming her role, Hitchcock showed Anderson how her eyes should reveal memories of dressing and undressing her mistress. "I knew I was in the presence of a master," Anderson concluded. "I had utter trust and faith in him." Though no one mentioned the underlying lesbianism of the Rebecca-Danvers relationship, Hitchcock sensed it. Esme Percy *(Murder!)* and Peter Lorre *(The Man Who Knew Too Much)* had appeared as fey, perhaps homosexual characters in earlier Hitchcock pictures; according to numerous observers, sexual aberrance intrigued the director. In *Rebecca,* the unnatural attachment of servant to mistress awaited only his "touch."

But the relationship between Mrs. Danvers and Rebecca, who called her companion "Danny," skirted the industry's censorship dictum against "sex perversion or any inference to it." Joseph I. Breen administered the Motion Picture Association Production Code's bluenosed guidelines with zest, fairness, and, when pressed, flexibility. After reading a synopsis of *Rebecca* long before production started, the Breen office hailed the novel as "a magnificent subject"; with a few minor changes, Breen said, its "moral values" would not jeopardize the sensibilities of American moviegoers. He had accepted with equanimity Favell and Rebecca's liaison as a necessary story point, and Selznick had reluctantly agreed to change the murder of Rebecca to an accidental death. But "Mrs. Danvers' description of Rebecca's physical attributes, her handling of the various garments, particularly the night gown," reddened his Irish Catholic cheeks. In the final cut, Breen told Selznick, "there must be no suggestion whatever of a perverted relationship between Mrs. Danvers and Rebecca. If any possible hint of this creeps into this scene, we will of course not be able to approve the picture."

Hitchcock moved by indirection. In England, he sat with the censor as he reviewed films. One British Board member wore glasses with a single opaque lens, and whenever an "offending piece of film approached, I said, 'Mr. Wilkinson—.' He turned his head toward me, and the objectionable scene went by on the screen without his seeing it." Breen had twenty-twenty and never looked away. Like Selznick, he also moved by confrontation. Breen had nibbled away at *Gone With the Wind*; he gave Melanie an easier labor, muted the cries of the wounded in the Plaza, and turned the Belle Watling brothel into a saloon. But Selznick protested the ruling against Rhett Butler's tag, "Frankly, my dear, I don't give a damn." Going over Breen's head in fall 1939,

Selznick decided to appeal to the Motion Picture Association Board. Meanwhile, reluctant to alienate Breen altogether, he offered more concessions than usual on *Rebecca*. An abortionist became a reputable physician, de Winter turned penitent, and Danvers loved "naturally." Asked by a reporter whether it would be necessary to kill him (meaning de Winter) at the end of *Rebecca,* Hitchcock replied: "You mean Breen? I don't think so."

As his producer watched, perhaps to assure conformity with the Production Code, Hitchcock blocked the body of the Anderson–Fontaine scene, then filmed it in an average of three takes per shot. Rather than minimize Selznick's additions, Hitchcock actually enhanced them. At the dressing table, he had "I" begin to touch one of Rebecca's hairbrushes, then recoil as though reprimanded by her husband's framed portrait. Hitchcock used the flowers even more tellingly. Danvers reverently holds out Rebecca's black nightgown and asks "I" whether she has ever seen anything "so delicate"; the young woman stands frame left, her face mottled by the spindly shadows of the cut flowers as though entrapped by all that Rebecca meant to those at Manderley. Cinematographer George Barnes lit the scene to evoke a fine mixture of wonder and Gothic horror; Hitchcock's staging, alternately widening and narrowing the spaces between the characters in the large, airy room, mirrored the attraction-repulsion theme that tortures the young heroine not only in the sequence but throughout the film. The concluding moments in the dressing room, however, were the most important. "I" attempts to leave, but the housekeeper, her pasty face ringed in a cool halo of light, stops her: "Don't you believe that the dead can see the living?" she asks. Hitchcock suddenly tightens the two-shot as the housekeeper speculates that Rebecca indeed watches her husband and his new wife. Although "I" shrinks from the malicious Danvers, her paranoiac taunt registers. In this shot, with its deliberately unflattering light (its source comes from below) and expressionistic shadows, the two actresses give controlled performances that just avoid the excesses of melodrama. But the climactic two-shot came hard. On it alone, Hitchcock worked for over an hour, photographing fifteen takes and printing only the fifth and tenth.

The production wore on. By the sixth week of principal photography, under its thirty-six-day shooting schedule, *Rebecca* was to have been

71

finished, yet all signs indicated that it would continue for at least another two or three weeks. The strain began to influence the actors, the director, and the producer. Hitchcock himself had cast Florence Bates as Mrs. Van Hopper. A lawyer by training, Bates had acted on camera only once before. "Well, Miss Bates," Hitchcock said over the public address system on her first day, the ears of a hundred cast and crew listening, "when did you start playing with yourself?" She may never have recovered from this blue practical joke. As much as Joan Fontaine, she slowed the pace on the set. A medium close-up of her sighting de Winter—"Why! It's Max de Winter"—required ten takes. In a more demanding shot, Hitchcock moved in from a three-shot of de Winter, Mrs. Van Hopper, and "I" to a close-up of the older woman just as de Winter announces his forthcoming marriage. Hitchcock obviously coached Florence Bates in "negative acting": she brightly asks de Winter the name of his fiancée, but when he responds, her smile "drains away from the face." The shot required twelve takes. Viewing the rushes in which she appeared, Selznick remarked, "I think there is no line which she could not improve upon."

The more experienced performers were capable of their own brand of "negative acting." With his mind on a love affair, George Sanders (the blackmailing Favell) showed up in complete "ignorance of his role." His first day on the *Rebecca* set, he received a good-luck telegram from the co-star of his just completed picture at Universal. "It would be absolutely wizard," she concluded her wire, "if you could come over here some time between four and six for a slight celebration." She signed her name simply "Love." Obviously Sanders's mind was in blue heaven, not Manderley; two days later, he still had not memorized his lines. On the other hand, C. Aubrey Smith, the seventy-six-year-old British actor who played the county constable, thought himself fully prepared; according to the production log, however, he had "learned wrong lines, had to memorize and rehearse correct ones."

Olivier also caused concern. As the film's de Winter, he painted the character in dark colors taken from a limited palette. When, near the end of shooting, Selznick asked Hitchcock to "try to get Olivier tender and sweet and perhaps with something approaching a smile" in the last scene, neither the producer nor the director could have been optimistic. Selznick worried about the intelligibility of Olivier's accent for an American audience, especially if the actor persisted in his habit of

In Monte Carlo, de Winter greets Mrs. Van Hopper (Florence Bates) and her timid paid companion.

Colonel Julyan (C. Aubrey Smith, second from right) reads a note from Rebecca that seems to challenge the interpretation of her death as suicide. De Winter, Frank Crawley (Reginald Denny), the second Mrs. de Winter, and Jack Favell (George Sanders) look on.

racing through his dialogue or "throwing away lines too much." He feared even more, however, that Olivier's smoldering silent reactions would retard the film's pace: "For God's sake, speed up Larry not merely in [his] close-ups, but in the rest of the picture on his reactions, which are apparently the way he plays on the stage where it could be satisfactory." Olivier, who began his screen career in 1931, alleges that his film apprenticeship lasted at least ten years, during which time his acting was "appallingly rough and ready, from sheer prejudice and ignorance." In spirit a man of the theater, he may have regarded *Rebecca* as an opportunity to experiment or, "happy with Hitchcock," merely a pleasant interlude demanding little exertion.

Olivier hardly worried Hitchcock. Joan Fontaine did. Unlike Archie Mayo, a director known for his long psychological discussions with actors, Hitchcock rarely chatted about motivation. (When actors asked about motivation, Hitchcock responded, "Your salary.") The English director offered physical rather than intellectual stimuli to his performers. His unorthodox methods could challenge the most adept actors. When filming alternating shots of two people in conversation, Hitchcock usually placed a stand-in opposite to feed the on-camera performer his or her lines. Accordingly, he shot Fontaine's close-ups with the script girl reading the absent Olivier's dialogue. An astonished Selznick ordered the practice stopped. On another occasion, the director resorted to violence.

> During the fifth take of a tearful scene from *Rebecca* [Hitchcock later recalled], Joan Fontaine told me she couldn't cry any more, that she was out of tears. I asked what it would take to make her resume crying. She said, "Well, maybe if you slapped me." I did, and she instantly started bawling.

"She was not a good enough actress to play in *Rebecca,*" Marcella Rabwin believed, "she really was not." Many of her fellow performers agreed. Shunned by the English community on the set, Fontaine felt isolated. "My grandmother was Lady de Havilland, the first lady of Guernsey," Fontaine told another cast member, hoping for acceptance of her English roots. "That's like being the first lady of Catalina," Hitchcock quipped. Despite the retort, the cockney director understood the alienation and diffidence that Fontaine (and the second Mrs. de Winter) felt. A self-confessed loner, the young Hitchcock had never dated; when he married Alma, he was a sexual naif. He rarely expressed his feelings, though, and directed his actors to contain theirs. A month into production, Selznick feared that a pair of monochromatic lead characters, the sullen Olivier and the reticent Fontaine, would deaden the picture: "I'd like to urge that you be a little more Yiddish Art Theater," an irascible Selznick wrote to Hitchcock, "a little less English Repertory Theater." Hitchcock ignored the note, Fontaine continued to underplay.

"I have been thinking about how difficult I must be to live with these days," Selznick wrote to Ray Klune; "the only excuse I can offer is that I am simply worn out, and I suppose my nerves are pretty well shot." Klune had earned the apology. As principal photography on *Rebecca* continued, the production manager's days stretched to fourteen hours, his weeks to seven days. Selznick matched him almost moment for moment. Anyone who worked (or lived) with Selznick fell victim to the unconventional, crisis-prone rhythm of his days. Well into the evening hours, with a secretary or production staff member in tow, he typically made last-minute script changes or other alterations. When they upset the next day's plans, Klune later recalled, Selznick would telephone at two in the morning and give the production manager six hours to overhaul the schedule, usually to the surprise of crew, actors, and director. During the days that followed such nights, Selznick would call meetings in his office, then fall asleep; his associates would quietly leave. Later, Selznick would awaken with a start, reconvene his conferees, and resume the meeting, fully attentive to the artistic and material elements of his productions. According to Hitchcock, working under a producer who rode such relentless herd over his staff inhibited rather than facilitated picturemaking.

But while Selznick's directives certainly ruffled Hitchcock, they benefited *Rebecca* and helped form the Englishman's reputation for efficiency. "Many people do their best when they work for me," Selznick believed. "I bully them, harangue them, coach them into doing better." Yet on numerous occasions, he neither bullied, harangued, nor coached. "I think today's rushes on the Confession Scene are wonderful," Selznick wrote Hitchcock midway through the period of principal photography, "and I am really hopped up about this sequence." Few producers more enthusiastically stroked their directors.

Few directors cared less. Hitchcock strove to create a family on his

The confession scene: "I've loved you, my darling—I shall always love you—but I've known all along that Rebecca would win in the end."

Rather than see the de Winters happy there, Mrs. Danvers destroys Manderley.

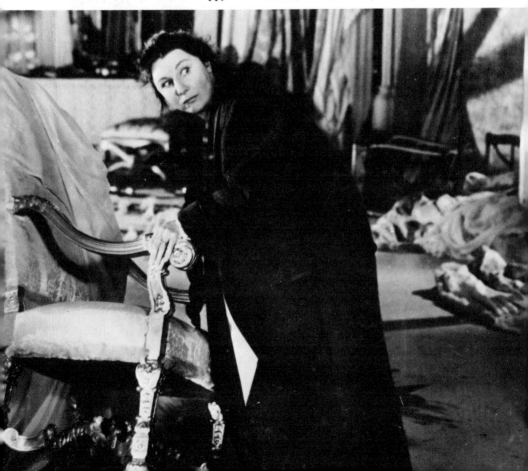

pictures, with himself as paterfamilias. The rites of passage included flowers and dinner invitations as well as cruel practical jokes and gossip. When Olivier privately criticized Fontaine, Hitchcock tattled to the actress; the "divide and conquer" strategy moved her into the Hitchcock circle. Selznick staffers often found themselves servants of two masters. Not long after the producer assigned Britisher Eric Stacey to *Rebecca* as a production supervisor, Hitchcock learned that Stacey reported to Selznick every evening. Hitchcock promptly shut him off: he ignored orders that Stacey brought from the front office and refused to answer his telephone calls after hours. Only when Selznick intervened did Hitchcock relent. The Lydia Schiller and Eric Stacey affairs had demonstrated to cast and crew alike that, as Fontaine observed, Hitchcock "wanted total loyalty, but only to him." Each Wednesday, however, Selznick International employees earned a vivid reminder that David Selznick—not Alfred Hitchcock—ran the studio. And until Hitchcock could sign the paychecks of his own company, he would bristle under the authority of his producer.

Like a machine taxed beyond its capacity, the *Rebecca* company threatened to burn out. Into the ninth week of principal photography, the film over three weeks behind schedule, Joan Fontaine contracted influenza. Between her hospitalization and a wildcat strike by IATSE, the stagehands' union, production ceased until Monday of the tenth week. During the last complete week of work, the company filmed primarily exterior shots, averaging two script pages and under two "film minutes" daily. The production ended as it had begun: slowly. The final scene photographed, a retake, was set in Rebecca's bedroom, engulfed in flames, the mad Danvers tearing at the curtains. The producer of "the larger view" and the director of "things" naturally argued about the film's close. At the end, with de Winter's stately mansion in flames, Selznick wanted Hitchcock to conclude on an image of smoke forming a gigantic *R* against the heavens; instead, Hitchcock wished to move from a long shot of the house into Rebecca's room, to her bed, to the *R* embroidered on her pillowcase. Although the director prevailed, Selznick found the rushes "a trifle slow in getting up to [Rebecca's] nightgown case"; he also wanted the "photographic effect" of "the flames rising as they devour the 'R,' to give us a natural curtain of flames as a background for our end title." To no one's surprise, the producer appeared on the set as Hitchcock began shooting retakes of this last sequence. Between some last-minute exterior shots and the problems of getting satisfactory footage in the bedroom, filming did not end until 4:30 A.M. On Monday, November 20, 1939, *Rebecca* had been in production 63 days (to *Intermezzo's* 35), had required 617 setups (to *Intermezzo's* 342), and had exposed 216,000 feet of film (to *Intermezzo's* 133,000). Numerous retakes and much dubbing still lay ahead, but the filming had ostensibly concluded.

In November 1939, *Rebecca* existed only in rough cut. Throughout principal photography, Hitchcock had screened the dailies to review the lighting, performance, texture, and pacing of the evolving film. Beyond "cutting-in-the-camera," however, he did not edit the film; that task belonged to Selznick, who believed "a picture could be ruined or made great in the editing." An inveterate tinkerer, Selznick enjoyed supervising final shot selection. The logistics of shooting a film involved hundreds of technicians, craftsmen, and artists; neither Selznick nor even Hitchcock, as an occasional dispute with cinematographers suggested, could control them absolutely. Editing, a solitary activity, involved only two or three persons and, furthermore, licensed an indecision that occasionally must have affected all moguls like Selznick. A journalist once conferred on David his father's "knack of making quick decisions"; yet production assistant Lydia Schiller recalled that "as long as a film was in his hands, he was never satisfied." Running an entire film endlessly through his fingers, Selznick could dictate not only the juxtaposition of shots, the pace and rhythm, but also the placement, volume, and cuing of the music. The next day, he could change it all. Whereas Hitchcock planned the editing in pre-production, directing his editor to cut by the numbers, Selznick experimented a great deal during post-production, which concluded only when chief editor Hal Kern said, "This is it; you cannot have that film anymore. Out it goes."

Selznick loved the freedom that miles and miles of footage offered him. By Thanksgiving 1939, nearly a quarter of a million feet of exposed film sat in the small clapboard editing room; much of it Selznick had requested in order to make *Rebecca* his *Rebecca*. When "I" and Mrs. Danvers met, for instance, Hitchcock filmed the sequence exclusively in close-ups; Selznick, on viewing the rushes, asked in addition for "a close two-shot of 'I' and Mrs. Danvers, or some other angle that will keep us from playing it in too many short cuts." *Rebecca,* like the

Selznick/Hal Kern *Gone With the Wind,* would have an even, almost stately pace; a concentration on emotions evoked from the performances; and a noticeable avoidance of "cuttiness." The opposite of a montage style, but one that Hitchcock would adopt by the end of the decade, Selznick's approach observed the rules of classic Hollywood cinema. The producer used a long shot–medium shot–close-up sequencing to highlight his investment in polished stories, major stars, and majestic exteriors and interiors. His long shots fused character and setting, the chief elements in his mise-en-scène; from *Gone With the Wind* to his 1957 *Farewell to Arms,* he seemed to weight the narrative and the pictorial (not necessarily synonymous with the cinematic) equally. His medium shots accommodated or privileged two or more actors engaged in dialogue; he moved further in—for two-person shots or, more rarely, one-person close-ups—to capture especially felicitous dialogue or to clarify a potentially obscured plot point. Following Hollywood's conventional shot–reverse shot protocol, he tended to cut not *against* the dialogue (as Hitchcock often did) but *on* it, satisfying the expectations of viewers accustomed to an on-screen harmony of speech and speaker. Words mattered to Selznick, who elevated the literary or verbal over the visual.

During the week before Christmas, 1939, Selznick worked full-time on cutting *Rebecca* and laying in Franz Waxman's hastily written score. Then, on Tuesday, December 26, he previewed a still very rough cut of the picture at the Huntington Park Theater. Although generally favorable, the response mandated further trimming as well as some additional rewriting and reshooting. With Hitchcock and Joan Harrison already at work on Walter Wanger's *Foreign Correspondent,* Selznick assumed post-production responsibility. He not only edited the retakes but also rerecorded much of the dialogue to correct technical problems and improve line readings. The velocity of Olivier's dialogue, to which Selznick had objected, was generally irremediable, perhaps a sign of the actor trying to control his performance: if his speech were slowed down, the image would lose synchronization with the sound. But the work of George Sanders, Florence Bates, and especially Joan Fontaine was extensively rerecorded.

Joan Fontaine dubbed *Rebecca*'s famous prologue ("Last night I dreamt I went to Manderley again . . .") as well as dozens of isolated lines. Later, the Academy of Motion Pictures recognized the film's achievement in almost every major category (eleven nominations in all) except one, sound recording. "We had so much dubbing after the picture was completed," Ray Klune said, that the sound was considered "far from perfect from a technical standpoint." With Hal Kern, Selznick carefully edited Joan Fontaine's portrayal of Mrs. de Winter. He often grafted improved line readings onto weak visuals, strengthening them; he also revised scenes to highlight Fontaine's best moments. When he had no suitable take of the actress from which to choose, he neutralized her performance on especially marginal readings by using (where possible) master shots or close-ups of other actors, as was done at the conclusion of the Lacy–de Winter luncheon scene. *Rebecca,* Selznick later maintained, succeeded only "after I got through completely recutting it, making wild lines [rerecording dialogue], etc." While the picture was not made in the editing and dubbing rooms, the increasingly favorable response of preview audiences, especially to Joan Fontaine's performance, indicates that it was remarkably enhanced there.

Anticipation built rapidly. In late January, belatedly showing interest in the editing, Hitchcock made specific suggestions about cutting the revised inquest scene, and Selznick implemented them. As February approached, the director and producer enjoyed a ripening bonhomie. "The picture looks perfectly swell," Selznick told Hitchcock and Joan Harrison, as he had on a number of occasions throughout the filming, "and I think we are all going to be very happy with it." Fully a week before the February 13 Santa Barbara preview, the director had announced the date and place to "everybody in Hollywood." Although Selznick himself had difficulty keeping such trade secrets, he changed the time and counseled his English protégé in discretion. Hitchcock's loose lips would deliberately sink a few ships over the years, but in this instance, he seemed merely overeager to watch his first American film projected for an American audience. Together, *Rebecca* and Hitchcock promised the studio great benefits; in fact, profitably loaned out to Walter Wanger, the director was already paying the studio a handsome dividend. In mid-February, Selznick decided to show his appreciation. "I know that Hitchcock would give his eyeteeth to spend a week with his writers in Palm Beach but can't afford it," Selznick wrote to Daniel O'Shea. "What would you think of our giving him this [working vacation] as a bonus?"

* * *

Two days after *Rebecca* played Santa Barbara, Selznick wrote to United Artists' Murray Silverstone, the distributor of Selznick International films: "It is with great pleasure that I am able to advise you we have seldom if ever had a more splendid audience reaction, and that judging by the enthusiasm of this preview audience we have what may prove to be the best and most successful picture we have made, with exception of 'Gone With the Wind.' " Selznick's telegram reads more as pep talk than report, for upon the sale of *Rebecca* rode not only such intangibles as Academy votes at Oscar time but company profits and an American future for Hitchcock.

Promoting the picture, Selznick authorized a movie edition of the novel as well as a "Rebecca Luxury Wardrobe," an idea that Hitchcock had inadvertently mocked a year before. The producer also revved up the studio publicity machine. "Extremely nervous, he paces his office as he talks," *Life* wrote of "Hollywood's Selznick" in December 1939, "but he talks well." The Atlanta premiere of *Gone With the Wind* (which occasioned the magazine's piece) and the subsequent openings around the country put both the Civil War epic and Selznick himself in the news for months. The linage naturally helped *Rebecca*. Hitchcock preceded Selznick in *Life* by several weeks; the November 1939 article that profiled the director also included photographs of him walking with his family, working on a script, and shooting *Rebecca,* whose budget he intimated was less than half that of most pictures. Several months later, a radio broadcast reinforced *Life*'s portrayal of Hitchcock as the compleat filmmaker. On *Your Hollywood Parade,* the host opened with an anecdote. Once, a man asked at a studio for the producer. He was sent to see Hitchcock. He asked for the screenwriter, again Hitchcock. For the art director, Hitchcock. For the director, Hitchcock. The radio host then introduced the cinematic superman "known to his friends as 'Hitch.' " The mild-mannered Englishman did not state that he worked for a great Hollywood studio, a deliberate oversight that would rapidly become a source of friction between producer and director.

The synopsis of du Maurier's *Rebecca* in newspapers, the Mercury Theatre radio adaptation, the merchandise tie-ins, and the selling of Hitchcock, Selznick, and the picture itself culminated in the selection of Manhattan's cavernous Radio City Music Hall as the site of the New

York premiere. *Rebecca* opened on Thursday, March 28, 1940. With the surprising exception of the trade press, which predicted that the pace and "English tone" might reduce the appeal to general audiences, critics hailed the film. *Theatre Arts* called *Rebecca* "a piece of suspenseful Hitchcock magic," and *Time* devoted two of six paragraphs to an analysis of the director's beautifully orchestrated "confession scene." Only Frank Nugent, writing in *The New York Times,* seemed to notice that while the American Hitchcock had become "less individualized," he had also developed his "widely-publicized 'touch' " into "a firm, enveloping grasp." The producer's guiding hand had contributed to that "firm, enveloping grasp."

Selznick International's *Rebecca* merited the praise of critics and moviegoers. As Nugent observed, however, the collaboration between Selznick and Hitchcock marked a change in the director's style. Hitchcock's British films lurched from one big moment to the next, the characters riding the roller coaster of plot; Selznick helped bring mood, seamless continuity, and psychological nuance to the director's work. The camera, which glides along the halls of Manderley, diminishes the second Mrs. de Winter in full shots, relentlessly envelops her in close-ups; meanwhile, Danvers appears or disappears ghostlike, eluding the enclosure of the frame. Under Hitchcock's direction, cinematographer George Barnes avoided the excesses of German chiaroscuro yet still evoked an artificial and oppressively stable world, utterly interior. Likewise, Selznick's editing smoothed out the narrative but retained—to great effect—Hitchcock's cutaways to the portraits along the stairway and the billowing window curtains, clattering teacups, latched doors. Throughout the picture, enhanced by Hitchcock's direction and Selznick's editing, Olivier, Anderson, and especially Fontaine skirted the edge of Gothic melodrama without ever losing their characters' humanity. The quintessence of the Hollywood studio system, *Rebecca* deserved to advance the careers of both its creators.

Along with the reviews and the plugs, good word-of-mouth sent urban moviegoers on both coasts scurrying to the theaters. The picture nearly sold out its opening days in New York, Montreal, and Boston. "Of course, you can always break a record at the Music Hall," Hitchcock later said with a snoot. "We had the best wet Tuesday in the history of the theater." Yet the director closely followed all box office reports. For Selznick, they proved disappointing. Although a studio

The Selznick touch: vast sets, rich appointments, and a shot wide enough to encompass them all.

like RKO would have considered the $700,000 profit on *Rebecca* grounds for celebration (only two of more than one hundred RKO releases between 1939 and 1941 earned over $700,000), Selznick wanted a blockbuster. Despite its popular and artistic success, *Rebecca* showed the producer a principal weakness of the independent: distribution.

Selznick nonetheless refused to abandon *Rebecca*. Although he gave it only "a fair chance" at the Oscar, he mounted another radio adaptation (with Ida Lupino and the elusive Ronald Colman as the de Winters, Judith Anderson as Mrs. Danvers) and reissued the picture. On Oscar night, the beneficiary of Selznick's talent for filmmaking and promotion, *Rebecca* captured the awards for Best Picture and Best Achievement in Black-and-White Cinematography. John Ford took home the statuette for Best Achievement in Directing *(The Grapes of Wrath),* an honor never accorded Hitchcock. Among the various factors influencing the academy's choice of director, one deserves particular notice. Members cast their 1940 Oscar ballots several months after the premiere of *Foreign Correspondent,* the Hitchcock successor to *Rebecca.* Although favorably reviewed and commercially successful, Hitchcock's second American picture marked a return to his British style, rough and melodramatic but hardly picture-of-the-year caliber. *Rebecca* may have suggested a burgeoning talent, *Foreign Correspondent* its contraction. Perhaps more than he imagined or wished, "Alfred the Great" needed the support of his producer. By having assigned *Rebecca* to Hitchcock, stretched its budget to nearly a million dollars, and forced the director to explore the psychological intensity of the narrative, Selznick had given Hitchcock an auspicious American debut. Few Hollywood moguls could have managed Hitchcock's transition to American filmmaking with as much distinction or visibility.

Years later, Hitchcock attempted to distance himself from the production. "Well, it's not a Hitchcock picture," the director said, explaining his dissatisfaction with *Rebecca.* "It's a novelette really." His possessiveness applied to people and pictures: unless he could control them, he dismissed them. Rather than cement the bond between producer and director, the Selznick connection with *Rebecca* made Hitchcock more eager than ever to declare his independence.

4

ʙETWEEN ENGAGEMENTs

The year 1940 marked a watershed in the careers of David Selznick and Alfred Hitchcock. For the first time in over a decade, a period of production activity lay behind Selznick rather than ahead of him. The dissolution of his company to secure a tax advantage should have brought something beyond financial rewards. Yet *Gone With the Wind* and *Rebecca* left Selznick emotionally and physically spent, almost too burned out to celebrate. Moreover, with two consecutive Oscars for Best Picture of the Year on his mantelpiece, he grimly contemplated the future. How could the producer of *Gone With the Wind* and *Rebecca*—not yet forty years old—top himself? Worse still, Benzedrine dressed him up with no place to go: the interaction of a chemical high and a spiritual low aggravated his disequilibrium. Feeling that he had crested, but driven to further achievement by dint of personality and a near addiction to stimulants, Selznick turned to making money rather than pictures. Hitchcock remained his commodity of choice.

Selznick and *Rebecca* had moved Hitchcock from the over-the-counter exchange to the Big Board (and from his small-scale Austin to a new Cadillac). RKO began labeling certain screen properties "of the Hitchcock variety," both a classification and a cachet. Rumor of his success with Joan Fontaine and his ability to direct *Rebecca,* a picture not "of the Hitchcock variety," attracted notice from actresses and even some producers, several of whom clamored to work with him. Back home in Sweden after completing *Intermezzo* for Selznick International, Ingrid Bergman cabled the studio to mail her a print of *Rebecca* so that she could see Hitchcock's work; Carole Lombard, whose house and agent the director shared, talked to him a few months later about collaborating on a film. The director of "little British thrillers" had crossed a threshold.

With *Foreign Correspondent,* Hitchcock hoped to advance his American career. When Selznick loaned him to Walter Wanger in late November 1939, both producers apparently contemplated a twelve-week schedule. Hitchcock consistently exaggerated his speed and may well have promised to develop the script in only three or four weeks, shoot it in eight or nine. A lax supervisor, Wanger gave the reins to Hitchcock and let the production take its course. Three months later, the screenplay remained unfinished and pre-production expenses had begun to soar. According to press releases, nearly six hundred craftsmen and technicians worked on *Foreign Correspondent,* many of them building the enormous sets. Hitchcock supervised construction of a three-story windmill, an Amsterdam city square, an airplane interior, and a mock-up of London's Waterloo Station. A replica of the *Clipper* ran $47,000, and the director's subtle lighting effects required a special relay system from the cameraman to the gaffer. By June 1940, costs approached a reported $1.5 million and would finally tower over those of *Rebecca.*

"As soon as I was working for someone I wasn't under contract to," Hitchcock later said, "the supervision was lessened." Selznick understood the consequences. Although Hitchcock's assignment to Wanger ultimately lasted thirty weeks and brought his employer a $54,000 gross profit, Selznick grew concerned about the picture's long schedule. United Artists had accused Wanger of inadequately controlling his operation and broken with him; through "improper supervision," Dan O'Shea told Selznick, Wanger had now made Hitchcock appear "an exceedingly slow director." Production manager Ray Klune confirmed the point: Hollywood had begun to gossip that the quality of *Foreign Correspondent* only barely justified its cost. As Selznick realized, unchecked extravagance would make Hitchcock difficult to handle and even more difficult to lend.

Hitchcock returned from Wanger with a fresh taste of independence. Discussions about securing an assignment beyond *Foreign Correspondent* invariably ended in rejection of Selznick properties not to his liking. While story editor Val Lewton found him "a peculiar person," resistant to headway, Hitchcock stalled for good reason. Export restrictions on British currency as well as the cost of setting up household in America had made him financially uneasy. Mindful of Selznick profits from the Wanger loanout, he desperately wanted to make an extracontractual picture, one that would pay him not his salary but his current market value. When he finally approached Selznick, the producer refused to suspend the contract: he would not "philanthropically donate [to Hitchcock] whatever profits there might be in [him] as a result of *Rebecca.*" Assuming his Buddha pose, Hitchcock rejected still more properties. Selznick considered threatening him with "lay off" (he would not use the word *suspension* lest its connotation "gain for Hitchcock sympathy to which he was not otherwise entitled"), then made amends with a $5,000 bonus from the Wanger deal. Though Hitchcock seemed pleased, he called such gestures contributions toward the "Fund for Starving Hitchcocks." The lord-to-vassal generosity must have rankled.

Despite friction, Selznick worked assiduously to find Hitchcock another loanout assignment. MGM wanted him for *Escape* and *A Woman's Face,* Universal for *Back Street,* Warner for *The Constant Nymph,* Twentieth Century-Fox for *How Green Was My Valley,* RKO for *Before the Fact,* and Columbia for anything at all. Selznick encouraged Warner's attention, Hitchcock encouraged RKO's. Warner's *The Constant Nymph,* a sentimental tale of a young girl infatuated with an older musician, seemed dubious Hitchcock material yet had tremendous commercial potential; moreover, by offering Hitchcock as well as Fontaine and Bergman to Warner Bros., Selznick hoped to snare a few of the Burbank company's male stars for possible future use.

To Hitchcock, eager for freedom from supervision, RKO seemed the better choice. A studio nearly bankrupt in the 1930s, RKO emerged from receivership in January 1940 and became a haven for independent filmmakers. To lure Orson Welles, RKO head George J. Schaefer had given the wunderkind free rein, including the final cut of his pictures. Schaefer took considerable abuse for his faith in Welles. When he announced a pay reduction for all RKO employees but kept *Citizen Kane* on the schedule, *The Hollywood Reporter* editorialized: "Mr. Schaefer evidently does not think an investment of $750,000 or more with an untried producer, writer, director, with a questionable story and a rumored cast of players who, for the most part, have never seen a camera, is a necessary cut in these critical times." Working at RKO— Hitchcock must have believed—would not only eliminate front-office interference but perhaps even allow him to lay groundwork for his own independent production company.

RKO producer Harry Edington lunched with Hitchcock in late spring 1940 and urged his superiors to close with Selznick. "If [it] takes liquor," he wired J. J. Nolan in June, "I will pay [the] bill." Among the properties that RKO considered for Hitchcock were *No for an Answer* as well as *Before the Fact.* Carole Lombard had agreed to star in the former, a screwball comedy eventually retitled *Mr. and Mrs. Smith,* but only on condition that RKO shoot it in thirty days. Could you direct a picture in five weeks? Edington probably asked Hitchcock. Eager to scotch rumors of his inefficiency, the British director would readily have assented. Throughout his life, Hitchcock claimed that he agreed to direct *Smith* as a favor to Lombard; more than likely, the looming threat of suspension and the promise of control influenced his decision.

Hitchcock was "very anxious" to work for RKO but learned that Selznick had stalled negotiations by driving a "terrifically tough bargain." The producer wanted "important assignments" for his director, ideally *The Constant Nymph* followed by *How Green Was My Valley.* Should neither Warner nor Fox meet his price, Selznick added, he might remake *The Lodger.* Faced with turning "a Hitchcock picture" into "a Selznick production," the director probably grew very, *very* anxious. He offered to review the preliminary budgets of *Mr. and Mrs. Smith* and *Before the Fact*—which all had now agreed would be his assignments—and show RKO how to remove sufficient fat to compensate for his heady salary. The stalemate persisted. An embittered Hitchcock told O'Shea that "he was seriously thinking of going back to

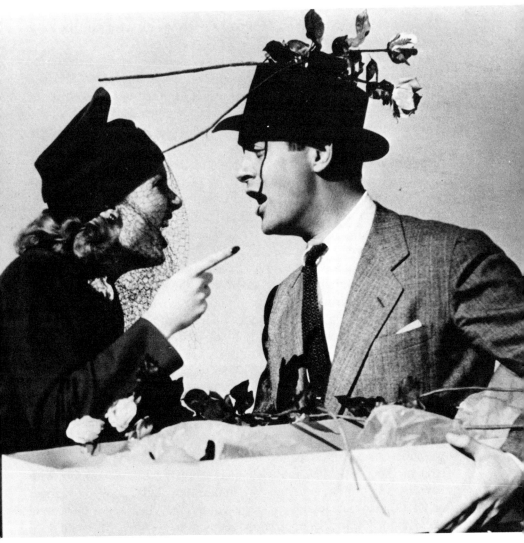

Carole Lombard and Robert Montgomery in *Mr. and Mrs. Smith*.

England to fight in the War." Unlike Olivier, the director said, he "was really serious about it."

When Warner and Fox lost interest in Hitchcock, perhaps deterred by reports of his pace on *Rebecca* and *Foreign Correspondent*, Selznick inched down his $100,000 asking price. RKO then agreed to hire the director at $5,000 a week, precisely what Wanger had paid Selznick nine months before. Under the contract that he had just renewed for another year, Hitchcock would earn $2,475 of that $5,000. Already the disparity chafed him. Yet Selznick had discussed extending his salary from forty to fifty-two weeks annually. The possibility of additional income, the expectation of minimal supervision at RKO, and the content of the second of his two RKO assignments lifted his spirits. So did an unexpected and lucrative offer from another medium.

Between *Foreign Correspondent* and the first RKO picture, Hitchcock made a "cameo" appearance on a broadcast of *The Lodger*. Radio producer Joe Graham soon proposed that the director host an anthology series; the format clearly adumbrated *Alfred Hitchcock Presents*, the 1950s television show that more than any of the director's pictures made "Alfred Hitchcock" a household word. Selznick waxed enthusiastic, for the offer demonstrated Hitchcock's burgeoning importance. "The more we can build up Hitch," Selznick told O'Shea, to whom he left a final decision on the matter, "the more valuable he becomes to us either for re-sale on individual pictures, or perhaps for sale of his entire contract, or for the value to the gross of pictures he does for us." O'Shea disagreed. "I understood it was always your theory to keep people economically dependent upon us in order to be better able to control them," O'Shea told Selznick, "and if we have trouble with Myron and Hitch now because we make a few dollars on [the Wanger or RKO] loan-out, imagine what it will be like when and if he is a big radio name." Many Selznick employees loathed O'Shea; Marcella Rabwin called him "an iceberg," Fontaine "a steel-hearted financial man." Yet Selznick heeded his advice. Hitchcock could drawl "Goood eeevening"—but not on radio.

The loss of one thousand easy dollars a week irritated Hitchcock, whose income hardly approached that of Mervyn LeRoy, Frank Capra, or others named in a July 1940 *Los Angeles Times* story that published the salaries of film luminaries. The director consoled himself with reviews of the just-released *Foreign Correspondent* and plans for his

RKO pictures. "Here are excitement, melodrama and thrill," noted *Motion Picture Daily* of the Wanger production, "susceptible of crackling exploitation by alert showmen everywhere"; *Film Daily* forecast "plenty of business wherever it plays." The New York critics praised *Foreign Correspondent* for its "romantic action, melodramatic hullabaloo, comical diversion, and illusion of momentous consequence" *(The New York Times)* as well as for its director's skilled "mingling of realism and fantasy" *(New York Sun)*. Only a few reviewers demurred. *The Hollywood Reporter* called the dialogue flat and the screenplay unoriginal; "by no means is it a Walter Wanger–Alfred Hitchcock super-super," wrote the *New York Daily Mirror,* "except possibly in cost." For Hitchcock, the prospects of a clear horizon at RKO removed the sting.

Hollywood professionals like Gregory La Cava and Howard Hawks directed sophisticated comedy as well as straight drama; on *Mr. and Mrs. Smith,* Hitchcock could demonstrate not only his speed but also his versatility. The script and cast fell into his lap, and for the first time in America, he dealt with two stars. Hitchcock both resented and needed stars, a double bind that accounted for his occasional callousness toward them. Jessie Matthews, whom he directed in *Waltzes from Vienna,* remembered him as "an imperious young man" who nearly badgered her into nervous collapse. He came to America with a reputation for harassing actors, shocking actresses, and working them both into sweats. According to Joan Fontaine, he also "had that habit of saying 'this silly old actor over there' or 'that idiot' or whatever it was, and probably did the same about me." Through memoranda and on-set visits, Selznick encouraged Hitchcock to esteem performance, especially star performance. Carole Lombard and Robert Montgomery gave the director an opportunity to consolidate his Selznick experience.

Tough-minded stars, Montgomery and Lombard evoked Hitchcock's professionalism and high spirits, both of which lent dispatch to the first weeks of principal photography. When a scene involving Montgomery and Gene Raymond fizzled, the director attacked the two men in order to dig a more committed performance out of them. Raymond grew fussed, yet the director's reported sadism kept the actors alert, the performances crisp, and the newspaper columns filled. The only disappointment: Hitchcock could not embarrass Lombard. Coming out of the projection room one day, he bumped into her. "Oh, you've looked at the rushes without me," she cried. "Everything's fine," Hitchcock assured her, commenting on the photography, the lighting, the performances. "I don't give a fuck about that. How did my new tits look?"

From Culver City, Selznick and O'Shea watched the director and from afar applauded his progress. "Hitchcock has been bearing down on the cost of *Mr. and Mrs. Smith,*" O'Shea told Selznick seven days into the picture, "in order to demonstrate to the world after *Rebecca* and *Foreign Correspondent* that he is not only a great director but a reasonably priced one." Neither producer Harry Edington (virtually a figurehead) nor RKO executives interfered with Hitchcock, who shot *Smith* in eight weeks, over schedule yet not terribly over budget. RKO seemed pleased with the result. A studio-commissioned Gallup poll taken in October 1940 forecast a predominantly female audience for the film, with the Hitchcock name a fillip to attract male audiences. A second poll quantified the power of that name. At RKO's request, Gallup asked a cross section of the population to identify four men and their films: Frank Capra, Alfred Hitchcock, John Ford, and Lewis Milestone. Hitchcock outscored Ford by four-to-one and Milestone by eight-to-one. The Hitchcock name added a tangible "cash *plus*" to *Smith,* Gallup said, and merited "conspicuous billing." Though Hitchcock must have smiled—he considered his peers his rivals—the difference between his value and his salary only served to highlight his promotion by David Selznick.

Mr. and Mrs. Smith had a happy ending: good reviews and modest box office success. While Hitchcock beamed, Selznick brooded. His contracts with actors and directors gave him little satisfaction, even if they permitted him to stay financially afloat. Moreover, Selznick knew that several artists under his management wished to bail out. Hitchcock clearly preferred RKO to Selznick. Hitchcock made pictures, RKO made space, neither bothered the other. Feeling at home after *Smith,* the Englishman hinted that RKO should enlarge his office and add a bathroom in order to make "a beautiful suite for some future director like myself." Selznick wanted Hitchcock treated well but not indulged, certainly not wooed. Yet RKO executive Dan Winkler had apparently suggested to Hitchcock that Selznick had "mistreated" and "exploited" him; "Alfred the Great" should be his own producer and director.

Hitchcock had nodded, then decided to ask Selznick for some of the loanout profits generated by Joan Fontaine, whom he had developed. "You'll never hide Hitchcock's light under a bushel," the amused O'Shea remarked to Selznick. Controlling Hitchcock would prove no laughing matter.

Hitchcock loved speeding. "We're going to have such a good time," he would say when his secretary chauffeured him to RKO, "Carol drives so fast!" By 1941, from the passenger seat of his Cadillac, he commanded "the larger view." *Rebecca* had broadened his style, *Foreign Correspondent* had transplanted his patented English thrillers to American soil, and *Mr. and Mrs. Smith* had demonstrated his ability to handle a routine studio assignment. Reviewers hailed his work. Journalists found him an eminently quotable subject for feature stories. Though screen credits for the Wanger and RKO pictures read "Alfred Hitchcock Courtesy of David O. Selznick" (per the Selznick contract), the director rarely mentioned his producer in interviews. He had packed the Hartman traveling case that Selznick had given him for Christmas, then taken off as the independent he longed to become. The more Selznick attempted to control him, the more he strove for autonomy. Fortunately for both Selznick and Hitchcock, RKO's *Before the Fact* diffused the tension.

Originally intended as a "B" picture, *Before the Fact* concerned a woman who allowed her playboy husband to murder her. Dramatist Samson Raphaelson wrote a first-draft screenplay, and the studio—given Hitchcock's participation—revised the budget figures upward. The director cast Cary Grant as the hero and pursued Joan Fontaine for the heroine. Without informing Selznick, another sign of his willfulness, Hitchcock sent Fontaine a copy of the novel. She responded in longhand, on her personal notepaper:

Dear Hitch,
Am returning 'Before the Fact' which I have read with avid interest and find my life completely changed: *I must do that picture.* Oh, please dear darling Hitch—I'm convinced it will be another 'Rebecca' and if anything, I find my enthusiasm even greater for Mrs. Aysgarth than for Mrs. de Winter. I am even willing to play the part for no salary, if necessary!

Selznick had refused to loan Fontaine to Wanger for *Foreign Correspondent,* banking on the appreciation of her worth after the release of *Rebecca.* Now that Fontaine had become a star, he offered her to RKO for $7,500 a week. RKO accepted, and Selznick pocketed over $4,000 a week in commission. Hitchcock and his protégée communicated well, especially when the conversation focused on their power as moneymakers for David O. Selznick.

Suddenly, the RKO honeymoon ended. After the sluggish box office performance of his company's 1940 releases, RKO president George Schaefer resolved to move from unit production back to central supervision, with all directors and producers reporting to his office; Hitchcock warily observed the changes and the consequences, including the defection of many of the independents who had come to RKO in the late 1930s. The new policies soon touched Hitchcock personally. The director had collaborated with cinematographer Harry Stradling on *Jamaica Inn, Mr. and Mrs. Smith,* and—until Selznick fired him—*Rebecca;* he had also secured him for *Before the Fact.* Just before shooting commenced, RKO reassigned the cinematographer to another picture. Selznick had occasionally shifted around personnel, including Stradling himself, but aesthetics, not economics, usually prompted the change; Schaefer moved Stradling to compensate for delays in starting *Before the Fact.* Already unnerved by the air of instability at RKO, Hitchcock protested. The director represented product flow and a certain prestige to RKO; at $5,000 a week, he also represented a bargain. Rather than alienate him, Schaefer returned Stradling to *Before the Fact.*

The Stradling affair, coupled with an incomplete script and an untested administrative policy, launched *Before the Fact* (eventually retitled *Suspicion*) into a choppy sea. Although principal photography began pleasantly enough on February 10, a coolness developed between the two stars and between Fontaine and Hitchcock; having put the actress through what she called his "finishing school," Hitchcock probably gave her less attention on *Suspicion* than he had on *Rebecca.* RKO executives had other concerns, especially the logistical problems that threatened to send the picture well over budget. After *Foreign Correspondent* and *Mr. and Mrs. Smith,* neither the equal of Selznick's *Rebecca,* Hitchcock returned to the burnished style of his only unqualified American success. His demands for glossy photographic effects and a spidery elegance consistently tested the cinematographer.

Selznick had removed Stradling from *Intermezzo* when the cameraman could not make Bergman "really look divine" and from *Rebecca* when the dailies proved "nothing to rave about." Stradling needed Hitchcock's patient guidance. Edington and Schaefer liked the footage but (with Selznick) abhorred the pace; the mounting interest on RKO's production loans as well as the absence of a satisfactory ending for *Suspicion* fueled their concern.

Ten weeks into principal photography, with at least two or three weeks of shooting to go, RKO considered scrapping the picture. But approaching Hitchcock seemed no less formidable than liquidating a costly investment. Some called Hitchcock shy, others distant. Whatever the case, he appeared unapproachable, autonomous. He never raised his voice and dressed in dark formal suits, suffocatingly inappropriate for the California sunshine. Asked what he would do if someone carelessly ruined a take, he replied: "I'd say 'cut,' look in the direction of the [crew member], and expect him not to be there." His imperious manner encouraged compliance and blunted argument. Although he insisted on his way less than reporters intimated, the seductive strength of his visual imagination more often than not prevailed. Both Hitchcock and Selznick had authority, but the cool assurance of Hitchcock could scald as surely as the hot bombast of Selznick.

Principal photography on *Suspicion* resumed, with RKO determined to speed up post-production to curb interest charges. Hitchcock blew up. "I have never in my 'puff' heard of an important picture being delivered 1 month after completion of its shooting," he wrote Edington. "Please, Harry, please, tell me this is only a joke so I may resume work on the picture with a feeling of reassurance that it is not going to be sabotaged; otherwise, how can I possibly dream of enthusiastically listening to RKO's suggestion that I make another picture here." When Hitchcock at last completed principal photography and briefly traveled east on vacation, producer Sol Lesser trimmed all hints of murder from *Suspicion*, reducing the running time to fifty-five minutes. Hitchcock again blew up. Schaefer ordered the original Hitchcock cut restored. The director made a last effort to change the title (from the "cheap and dull" *Suspicion* to *Johnnie*), then left the production and RKO.

Suspicion seemed to confirm Hitchcock, irrespective of the quality of his work, as a slow and expensive director. To counter the image and justify the loanout price, Selznick worked aggressively to promote the

"I put a light right inside the glass because I wanted it to be luminous," Hitchcock said of a key scene in *Suspicion*. "Cary Grant's walking up the stairs and everyone's attention had to be focused on that glass."

picture. With Hitchcock and Fontaine involved he would naturally prosper from its success; moreover, his goodwill might improve those contract artists' attitudes toward their employer. Swayed by Selznick, Universal agreed to waive a theatrical contract so that *Suspicion* could bow in at two Los Angeles theaters and make Fontaine's performance eligible for the Oscar (which she won). Selznick also persuaded the Hollywood Pantages Theatre to add $2,000 to its advertising budget for the film; while the splash might not woo audiences, it would direct industry attention toward Hitchcock. Despite the predictably negative comment about an ending necessary to meet censorship objections, *Suspicion* opened to good reviews and brought nearly half a million dollars in profit to RKO. The mellifluent photography and the unsettling tone of the major scenes between husband and wife added to the director's reputation for creating suspense. They also enhanced the value of Alfred Hitchcock to David Selznick.

By 1941, Hitchcock had become a thread in the fabric of American culture.

> THE GIRL: Is Capra nice, or don't you know him?
> SULLIVAN: Very nice.
> THE GIRL: Is Hitchcock as fat as they say he is?
> SULLIVAN: Fatter.
> THE GIRL: Do you think Orson Welles is crazy?
> SULLIVAN: In a very practical way.

These lines from the screenplay of Preston Sturges's *Sullivan's Travels* show Hitchcock moving in very fast company. Like Capra and Welles, Hitchcock knew what he wanted: the opportunity to make American studio films, preferably as his own producer or at least with minimum oversight. Unlike Capra and Welles, he had a long-term contract that blocked his independence.

Hitchcock also had a producer as unsure about his own future as he was about his principal contract director's. "I'm a wreck," David Selznick often remarked in the years after *Rebecca*. In summer 1940, the Selznicks and their two young sons moved to a picturesque farmhouse in Cornwall Bridge, Connecticut; here, David Selznick told himself and his wife, Irene, he could at last tackle the mountain of books that filmmaking had left him no time for. On weekends, Dorothy and Bill

Paley, the Averell Harrimans, Jock Whitney, and even brother Myron visited. From Monday to Friday, though, Selznick filled many of his idle hours not with reading but with melancholy reflection. Away from the industry, he dwelled on it. "He wasn't getting enough credit because people were envious," Irene heard him complain. " 'They're stealing my ideas. They're imitating my shots.' They would make his movie [*Gone With the Wind*] look hackneyed in no time." He needed another change of scene. Before their lease expired, the Selznicks left Connecticut and decamped for the Waldorf, where they rented an apartment.

Selznick pursued a gentleman's life. When Mrs. Cornelius Vanderbilt invited the distinguished producer of *Gone With the Wind* and *Rebecca* to her Fifth Avenue mansion in New York, the distinguished producer and his wife went. Hitchcock must have hooted at the meeting of aristocrat and parvenue. Despite the Beverly Hills lunches and the chauffeur rides to Culver City, the director remained an English burgher. He had "no pretentions, no other aspirations," Joan Fontaine recalled. "He was a devoted family man and liked a simple family life and his work." Such contentment was denied Selznick.

Returning to Los Angeles, he formed David O. Selznick Productions. Thereafter he auditioned Gregory Peck and Phyllis Walker (renamed Jennifer Jones), attempted to secure important parts for Ingrid Bergman, and mounted an ambitious three-week theatrical season in Santa Barbara. "I am taking on a tremendous amount of duties for the Chinese Relief," he wrote Irene in April 1941. "I cannot honestly say, though, that I am unhappy about it, and in fact I am rather enjoying accomplishing things which I am sure could not be put over by anyone else." He assumed a partnership in United Artists, joined Hillcrest Country Club, and traveled extensively. Abundant activity. Little focus. Many doubts.

Selznick predictably returned to thoughts of moviemaking. Not long after he exercised the second option on Hitchcock's contract, guaranteeing the Englishman $3,000 weekly (less 10 percent for Myron), he brought him back to Culver City with the intention of making a film for UA release. Story editor Val Lewton urged his boss to steer the director away from "the old-fashioned chase pictures which he turns out when left to his own devices," but while Selznick could have forced Hitchcock to choose a property from the studio hopper, he deferred to him on story selection. Hitchcock worked best when he enjoyed at least the illusion of control. Against Lewton's advice and his own better judgment, Selznick gave Hitchcock permission to develop an original narrative about sabotage.

Before starting the project, Hitchcock vacationed in Manhattan. There he met Sidney Bernstein—then head of the British Ministry of Information—and discussed not only the promotion of English propaganda films in America but other contributions that he might make to the war effort. The year before, Michael Balcon had told the press that a "plump" former associate had deserted England for the States "while we who are left behind short-handed are trying to harness the films to our great national effort." Hitchcock angrily responded that "the British government has only to call upon me for my services." Hitchcock may have pressed his friend Bernstein to search for a dramatic or documentary project that might serve the English cause and salve a troubled conscience.

After returning to Los Angeles, Hitchcock, along with Joan Harrison and Michael Hogan, developed a treatment for the Selznick picture. Their tale about a California munitions worker falsely charged with sabotage resembled *The 39 Steps;* the hero's search for the actual turncoat included a love interest, several humorous and suspenseful episodes, and the dynamiting of a new dam to be opened by the president of the United States. Whether Hitchcock dazzle could camouflage routine mechanics seemed questionable. Selznick read the story, noted the brittle plot devices, then called the stenographers up to Santa Barbara. He advised Hitchcock to "try to get something instead of [a] dam being blown up. This is not very new for a picture catastrophe." He also impelled him to address the weak human dimension, the characters' "heart and emotional relationships."

The brevity and tone of the memoranda suggested that Selznick lacked the concentration for sustained work and perhaps intended to sell both director and treatment to the highest bidder. Anticipating the Selznick windfall, Hitchcock attacked. He asked for a bonus before starting the writing and for the rights to the screenplay he produced; he also asked for a raise for Joan Harrison, who wished to leave her mentor and become a free-lance producer. Having allocated $10,000 of the RKO loanout profits to Hitchcock, Selznick tabled each request. Hitchcock had finally been listed among the filmmakers who dominated American payrolls, but many others—from William Wellman and

Henry King to John Cromwell and John Ford—still out-earned him. Make more pictures, Selznick reminded his contract director, and make more money. "We recognize your enormous standing today," the producer wrote to Hitchcock in an unsent memorandum, but we fear that "the mitigating factors of your cost and your slowness" have eroded it. No matter who produced it, the sabotage story had to reestablish the efficiency of "Alfred the Great."

To head the director away from his "old-fashioned chase pictures," Selznick assigned John Houseman to supervise the development of the screenplay and young Peter Viertel to write it. Neither choice benefited *Saboteur.* Houseman found Hitchcock a mesmerist, one who inspired not collaboration among equals but conspiracy between a master and his apprentice. Less fascinated than dominated by Hitchcock's mimicry and his enactment of moments from his British thrillers, Houseman gave the director nothing but breathing room. The callow Peter Viertel offered the Englishman even less of the discipline that his art needed when moving from idea to script. Hitchcock and his collaborators wrote at the multilevel home leased from Carole Lombard. A visiting magazine illustrator found them "rushing into different rooms with typewriters and manuscripts, taking over tables, chairs and lounges and at once starting to work feverishly, paying no attention to anybody but themselves." Hitchcock interrupted the sessions with huge goblets of Strawberries Romanoff, a concoction of ice cream, fruit, and liqueurs, then dozed off as the frenetic activity continued around him.

"I think it is ridiculous that a man who is getting his salary should not have to report for a full day's work at the place where he is employed," Selznick griped to O'Shea. Though he chose not to press the issue, the episodic Viertel–Hitchcock script hardly merited his trust. One Selznick reader called it synthetic and "loosely strung together," the work of "an inferior Hitchcock imitator." Never a Hitchcock fan, Val Lewton found it "the sort that every studio rejects after the most cursory reading." The director had conceived *Saboteur,* the director could sell it. Along with Houseman ("feeling rather like a pimp"), Hitchcock traveled from studio to studio, outlining the content of *Saboteur,* the settings, the principal characters and notable scenes. While he enjoyed spinning tales for new audiences, the roadwork humiliated him. "But there was one aspect of these visits that infuriated him," Houseman recalled, "the knowledge that David O. Selznick's asking price for the package, including Hitch's services as a director, represented a profit—to Selznick—of around three hundred percent!"

After Twentieth Century-Fox and RKO turned down *Saboteur,* independent producer Frank Lloyd bought it. Lloyd and Universal not only paid 30 percent more for Hitchcock than RKO had but also offered him 10 percent of the gross receipts provided he did not exceed the $750,000 budget. Though Selznick preferred bonuses to profit-sharing arrangements (which usually belonged to independent producers, not contract directors), he bent on this point. The prodigal Hitchcock would presumably not spend his own money as he spent others'.

One quiet December day, as Hitchcock worked on the West Coast and Selznick on the East, a nation at war blasted the course of history. Irene and David Selznick were visiting at Manhasset with the Paleys when the Japanese attacked Pearl Harbor. Selznick heard the news while in conference with psychiatrist Sol Ginsburg and writer Ben Hecht, probably discussing a story idea. Paley left immediately for the office, the Selznicks for home. As Irene recalled,

> David was going into the Army. He was going to be a soldier. A private. His reasons were complex, but they did include patriotism. His spirit was fine, his idea impractical—he was nearsighted, slewfooted, overweight, overage. He didn't need an enemy, he'd kill himself. "You'll put someone's eye out in your first salute and trip over your rifle."

But first things first. Almost immediately, Selznick wired Kay Brown to "drop everything" and register *Mein Kampf* with the producers' association Title Registration Bureau. "To point out importance of treatment I plan for subject, I am thinking about Hecht for script and Hitchcock for direction." A certain energy flows through the telegram as it would through the American economy and American spirit. Those who fought in the proud war served their country and themselves, but those who stayed at home, whether Rosie the Riveter or Selznick the Mogul, found new commitment and meaning in life.

Always reluctant to betray emotion, Hitchcock may have seemed the exception. On Sunday, December 7, he had gone to Universal to storyboard *Saboteur* with production designer Robert Boyle. The news of Pearl Harbor more seriously affected those in Hollywood than those in Manhasset. Selznick art director Lyle Wheeler recalled that "there was a lot of fear at that time that [the Japanese] might be planning an attack on California" and that hospitals and other areas would be evacuated. One of the few studio guards then on duty at Universal slipped on his air-raid warden's outfit (he was ready even if America was not) and scoured the lot for friends and aliens alike. Busting in on Hitchcock and Boyle, he flashed the news, then took off again. For a moment, neither man spoke. "Hm," said Hitchcock, "curious hat the fellow was wearing." He then resumed work.

Hitchcock roared through the making of *Saboteur.* He exceeded the budget by only $3,000 and completed both script and principal photography in less than fifteen weeks, faster than any of his four American pictures to date. His $15,000 profit share (treble the Selznick bonuses on his earlier loanouts) further sweetened the experience. Yet to his chagrin, reviewers criticized *Saboteur* just as Selznick had months before. Commenting on "a lack of versatility" in Hitchcock, *Variety* concluded that "it would be a greater tribute to a finer director if he didn't let the spectator see the wheels go 'round, didn't let him spot the tricks—and thus shatter the illusion, however momentarily." The director's friend Dilys Powell put the matter more succinctly in the London Sunday *Times:* "This is Hitchcock at his most Hitchcock, which doesn't necessarily mean at his best." Harsh notices sent the director into a deep funk, his secretary recalled. Two years and four pictures later, *Rebecca* threatened to become Hitchcock's *Gone With the Wind.*

Still, a long career in Hollywood seemed increasingly likely for Hitchcock. When Carole Lombard died, the director and his wife began house hunting, not to rent but to buy. Selznick lived in a large two-story home on Summit Drive, complete with tennis courts, tennis house, swimming pool, and two shifts of servants. "All I need," Hitchcock told a reporter, "is a snug little house with a good kitchen, and the devil with a swimming pool." The Hitchcocks chose a "well-hidden" story-and-a-half home at 10957 Bellagio Road, just beyond the fifteenth hole of the Bel Air Country Club golf course. Players soon found that balls rolling onto the Hitchcocks' lawn disappeared: the master of suspense tossed them to his dogs. Hitchcock cherished his privacy. Surrounded by trees, the house and its well-appointed kitchen afforded Hitchcock one of his greatest pleasures, cooking dinner with Alma on the maid's night out. Within months, the director also placed a down payment on a ranch in Scotts Valley near Santa Cruz. The weekend retreat provided even

Hitchcock cast Robert Cummings and Priscilla Lane in *Saboteur* when Universal cancelled the production to which they had previously been assigned.

greater seclusion than his Los Angeles home. By 1942, his West Coast roots stretched from southern to northern California.

Selznick, meanwhile, oscillated between New York and Los Angeles. "After being home for forty-eight hours," Selznick wrote Bill Paley from Hollywood in May 1942, "I told Irene that I was getting restless and wished we could plan a trip somewhere!" Depressed yet propelled by Benzedrine (up to six tablets a day), he turned from one pursuit to another. His "4-F" classification kept him off military active duty, and heading the China War Relief Committee, taxing and salutary as the job was, offered only minimal satisfaction. He wanted a post in Washington, one commensurate with his talent and stature in the industry. "I warned him to keep a low profile or they'd take a lesser man," Irene recalled. "The thing to do was to start small and build: his humility would take everyone by surprise; they would compete for him." But containment wasn't his. He would have a prominent position or none at all. The latter seemed inevitable as the months dragged on. Finally he gave up. "I have made a number of stabs and many trips to Washington," he wrote to a friend in late summer 1942, "but so far as I can see the government is convinced it can do very well without me."

Faced with Washington's apparent indifference, Selznick returned to motion picture activity to restore his self-esteem. He continued to entertain notions of producing a Hitchcock picture, but when Frank Lloyd's coproducer Jack Skirball sought Hitchcock for a second film, Selznick quickly negotiated a deal. The director's efficiency on *Saboteur,* which had just opened, no doubt prompted Skirball to agree to Selznick's steep terms: $150,000 for eighteen weeks, almost double what RKO had paid just over a year before. In addition to garnering the biggest return yet on a Hitchcock loanout, Selznick also enhanced Hitchcock's industry status by demanding that Skirball give the director one hundred percent of title; for the first time, the opening credits would place the Hitchcock name and the actors' names in equal-sized type. No filmgoer in Wichita would notice; none in Beverly Hills would fail to.

A Gordon McDonell short story entitled "Uncle Charlie" gave Hitchcock the idea for the Skirball picture. The narrative centered on a homicidal woman-hater who flees the police by moving in with his proper middle-class sister and her family. Although his niece (also his namesake) dotes on him, she comes to suspect and then to learn his dark secret. He dies accidentally while trying to kill her. The defects in *Saboteur,* more exaggerated on screen than they had been on paper, perhaps made Hitchcock more interested than usual in the screenplay of "Uncle Charlie." He especially wanted the writer to balance the elements of suspense against the mundane scenes of family life, the "comedy of small town manners." About the latter, the director had firm ideas.

> If possible I am extremely anxious to avoid the conventional small town American scene. By conventional I mean the stock figures which have been seen in so many films of this type. I would like them to be very modern; in fact, one could almost lay the story in the present day so that the social ambitions could concern themselves possibly with war work and such like. The only drawback to this is that it might date the film because things change so rapidly nowadays. But by modern I mean that the small town should be influenced by movies, radio, juke boxes, etc.; in other words, as it were, life in a small town lit by neon signs.

Using Santa Rosa, California, as their model, Hitchcock and Thornton Wilder collaborated on a script that Alma and *New Yorker* writer Sally Benson polished. By luck more than design, Hitchcock assembled an excellent cast for this second Universal picture, *Shadow of a Doubt.* Professional and personal antagonism between Selznick and Fontaine denied the director his first choice for the niece, Charlie Newton, whom he had called a "Fontaine type" in his earliest treatment. But he secured Teresa Wright and Joseph Cotten as the two Charlies and Macdonald Carey, Patricia Collinge, Henry Travers, and Hume Cronyn as supporting players. Casting himself as host, Hitchcock entertained most of them in Santa Rosa and San Francisco.

The glossy look of *Suspicion* and the smooth interiors of *Saboteur* gave way to an almost documentary approach in *Shadow of a Doubt.* On Stage 22 at Universal, art director Robert Boyle designed the Newtons' house for great flexibility, little cost, and maximum realism. A *New York Times* correspondent remarked on the set's "amazing adaptability to camera angles. As the camera moves into, out of, and through the house to record the action, windows come apart, the porch stands aside, the roof bends over, the kitchen walks away." The actors nonetheless felt at home. "No director was ever easier to work with," Joseph Cotten recalled. Teresa Wright echoed what so many actresses

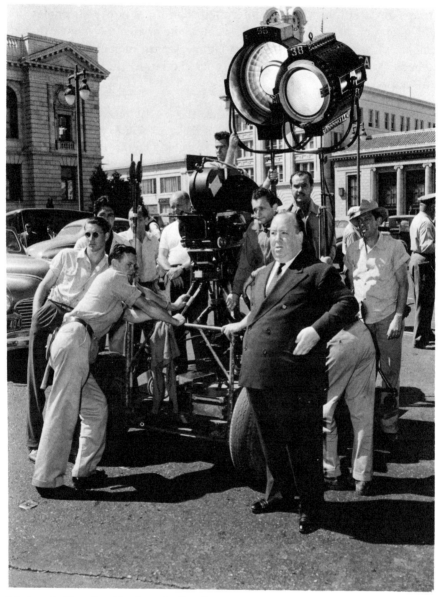

Hitchcock directing *Shadow of a Doubt*.

said of Hitchcock, that he gave them confidence. "During the shooting," Wright said, "he made us feel very relaxed. His direction never came across as instruction. We felt we could trust him, and he gave us guidance and a sense of freedom."

The slow evolution of the screenplay and the unhurried pace of principal photography stretched Hitchcock's time with Skirball from eighteen to twenty-six weeks. Yet *Shadow of a Doubt* demonstrated that Hitchcock could *produce:* his control over story, performance, cinematography, and post-production resulted in triumphant success. The trade ad in *The Daily Film Renter*—headlined "Hitchcock Back in Form!"—suggested the importance of the picture to the director. Aside from content, Selznick found the Hitchcock economies on the picture impressive; moreover, its $813,000 cost virtually guaranteed the Englishman a significant profit share. The Selznick contract notwithstanding, Hitchcock began to think of himself as an independent. When he joined radio host Bob Burns at the microphone in spring 1942, he mentioned neither Selznick nor Selznick Productions. The snub miffed Selznick but hardly affected matters of dollars and cents. Directors faced with prodding from the front office often replied, "Do you want it fast or good?" Selznick could change the *or* to *and,* offer Hitchcock to any studio in Hollywood, and hope to earn a windfall.

Passing by a shop window in Santa Rosa, California, where he filmed *Shadow of a Doubt,* Hitchcock chanced to see his reflection. The familiar profile sobered him. "I weighed just under three hundred pounds," Hitchcock recalled. "My ankles hung over my socks. My back ached." He vowed to diet. As his weight dropped, his price grew. Shortly before the release of *Shadow,* Selznick again loaned out the director, this time at nearly a thousand dollars a pound. Darryl F. Zanuck and Twentieth Century-Fox agreed to borrow not only Hitchcock, but almost everything Selznick had to lend: cameramen Stanley Cortez and George Barnes; contract actors Ingrid Bergman, Dorothy McGuire, Joan Fontaine, and Gene Kelly; contract director Robert Stevenson; and several major story properties, including *Claudia, Keys of the Kingdom,* and *Jane Eyre.* Industry rumor set the price at somewhere under $2 million; the Hitchcock slice alone guaranteed Selznick $300,000 for forty weeks. "The transfer of these assets does not signify Mr. Selznick's retirement," a Selznick official told *The New York Times;* yet those who followed the entertainment news must have been doubtful.

On his forty-third birthday, Hitchcock entertains the *Shadow of a Doubt* company. Seated at Hitchcock's right is his wife, Alma. To his left, Producer Jack Skirball and Director of Photography Joe Valentine. *Below*: Joseph Cotten (left) and Pat Hitchcock (second from right).

In late 1942, the loan of so many artists to Fox prompted not only Hollywood gossip but attempted raids on the Selznick stable. Around town as well as on the radio, Hitchcock played the free agent and thus encouraged outside offers. When Selznick heard that Sam Goldwyn had spoken to Hitchcock at Christmastime about a production deal, he ripped into his gin-rummy partner and occasional nemesis:

> You recently have sent direct for one of my people, Alfred Hitchcock, and talked with him without so much as either asking us, or even letting us know after the fact. . . . Hitch has a minimum of two years to go with me, and longer if it takes him more time to finish four pictures, two of which I have sold to Twentieth Century-Fox. And not alone did you try to seduce him, but you tried something which I have never experienced before with any company or individual—you sought to make him unhappy with my management of him. When you told Hitch that he shouldn't be wasting his talents on stories like *Shadow of a Doubt,* and that this wouldn't be the case if he were working for you, what you didn't know was that Hitchcock personally chose the story and created the script—and moreover that he is very happy about the picture, which I think he has every right to be.

The Goldwyn–Hitchcock interview occurred just after Selznick consummated the lucrative Fox deal. Since neither Selznick nor Fox intended to share the profits with the director, Hitchcock may have spoken with Goldwyn not only to test the waters for an independent production arrangement but to nettle his employer. In lighter moments, several artists under contract to Selznick jested that their association with the producer reversed the usual agreement: they earned 10 percent, their "agent" 90. The humor eluded Hitchcock but delighted Joseph Cotten; after the Fox sale, the actor twitted his English friend, "I see they're selling directors like cattle."

Myron Selznick may indirectly have prompted the Goldwyn-Hitchcock interview. Like many others by 1942, Hitchcock had begun to question Myron's power and ability. "Myron was drinking too much quite early on," said Niven Busch, who had been Myron's adolescent pal and later his client. "One writer at Warners said to me, 'You know, when Myron drops in and your option's coming up, it's a good idea to have a bottle of bourbon in the bottom drawer, because before he goes upstairs to see the brass, he'll want a slug.' So I kept one and he'd take a couple of fingers." Although Busch "never saw him smashed in the daytime," it became obvious shortly after the war that Myron the heavy drinker had become Myron the alcoholic. Consultation with doctors—not only for Myron but for himself and on behalf of his ailing mother—became a regular part of Selznick's week, as did the attempts to get Myron into a dry-out clinic. Three years younger and three inches taller than Myron, David quarreled with his brother yet always defended him. When Hitchcock determined to leave Myron for another agent in 1943, David intervened and Hitchcock stayed. Within a year, the problem of Myron Selznick would resolve itself.

Between *Shadow of a Doubt* and the commencement of the Fox period, Hitchcock's mind had time to dwell on the Selznicks' alleged collusion against him and the discrepancy between his skyrocketing value and fixed salary. Perhaps anticipating this, Selznick tried to keep him otherwise engaged. Hitchcock prepared an episode of *Forever and a Day,* RKO's 1943 paean to England, featuring Charles Laughton, C. Aubrey Smith, and seventy-six other name actors; he also conferred with Margaret McDonell about his wish to find a sea story. The idea of filming in cramped quarters fascinated him. While on *Shadow of a Doubt,* he had shown a magazine photo of a lifeboat to Robert Boyle. "It's a small space, like a closet, isn't it?" he asked the production designer. Hitchcock "had been intrigued with small spaces and photographing in them; now he'd found his location." Selznick would have encouraged the project. With the exception of rear-projection footage of the ocean, such a picture could be made in a studio and at little cost; the budget-conscious director of *Saboteur* and *Shadow of a Doubt* could thus consolidate his reputation for efficiency.

At Twentieth Century-Fox, where Hitchcock began work in November 1942, he again rummaged for a sea story. Lacking the spur of a financial interest, he read and discarded one property after another. He finally settled on an oceanic *Stagecoach* and began developing a treatment. Meanwhile, he received word from England that on January 4 his older brother William had done what he had so long threatened to do: commit suicide. William had cared for their mother until her death three months before, and the director (always generous to friends and family) had regularly sent money home. Still, Alfred and William had not been close. "When my brother comes up from Shamley Green to London," Hitchcock would say, "he always has to ride first-class because he's Alfred Hitchcock's brother. Why can't he ride third-class:

110

he's not paying for it." The deaths of Emma and William Hitchcock gave their expatriate son and brother even fewer ties to England.

Back at Fox, the sky darkened. John Steinbeck collaborated with Hitchcock on the treatment for *Lifeboat,* but the two regarded each other with suspicion. Hitchcock worried about the political baggage that the author of *The Grapes of Wrath* would bring on board, Steinbeck found the director "one of those incredible English middle class snobs who really and truly despise working people." By spring, almost twenty weeks into his scheduled term at Fox, Hitchcock had worked with MacKinlay Kantor and Jo Swerling yet still not finished the *Lifeboat* script. Casting proved equally frustrating. Zanuck's leading men had gone off to war, and his leading women—Alice Faye and Betty Grable—looked better in swimsuits than life jackets. Hitchcock settled on John Hodiak, William Bendix, Mary Anderson, Canada Lee, Walter Slezak, and Tallulah Bankhead. These lesser-known stars and the restricted setting (Hitchcock planned to shoot the picture without leaving the studio) strengthened the need for the vaunted Hitchcock "touch."

The long gestation of *Lifeboat* brought Zanuck close to canceling the production. Though Hitchcock may have perceived the threat as saber-rattling, he nonetheless promised to shoot the picture in eight or nine weeks. Accordingly, the studio refigured the budget so that the long months of pre-production could be offset by a brisk period of principal photography, one that would best even the speed of *Saboteur* and *Shadow of a Doubt.* Filming began. When Zanuck saw Hitchcock slowing down, he ordered him to trim the screenplay and accelerate the pace. On loan and unwilling to pay Zanuck the fealty he owed Selznick, Hitchcock bluntly answered the Zanuck memorandum with one of his own. "I have just received your note regarding the length of LIFEBOAT," Hitchcock wrote to Zanuck on August 20, 1943.

> I don't know who you employ to time your scripts, but whoever did it is misleading you horribly. I will even go so far as to say disgracefully. In all my experience in this business, I have never encountered such stupid information as has been given you by some menial who apparently has no knowledge of the time of a script or the playing of dialogue. ... Now let us get down to facts, and let us base our calculations on facts that come from persons of long experience and also the fact of actual shooting time.

111

The benevolence of RKO and Universal producers had perhaps made Hitchcock more sensitive than he should have been to Zanuck's concern; the director's reputation among critics and to some extent within the industry may also have let sarcasm creep into his response. Despite what seems a vulnerable defensiveness in the Hitchcock memorandum, Zanuck temporarily backpedaled.

The actors on *Lifeboat* enjoyed working with Hitchcock, yet his authority and independence had grown. "Once Tallulah tried to play a scene her way," Slezak recalled, "but Hitchcock said, 'No, no,' very quietly with that wonderful dead-fish face of his, and she suddenly turned to us and said plaintively, 'He won't listen to me.' And, of course, she did it his way." As the picture climbed toward the $2 million mark, grossly over budget, Zanuck found Hitchcock unresponsive. "On three different days," he lectured the director, "I have seen three separate shots of the German singing while he rows the boat. Would it not have been possible to have shot all three of these separate scenes at one time, when the camera was set up in this same position, and when the background was already rigged?" The question duplicated one asked by Selznick four years before during *Rebecca*. With little hope of expedition, Zanuck implored Hitchcock "to economize wherever possible," for the inordinate cost of the production had far surpassed its value to the studio.

Just before Thanksgiving 1943, one year after going to Fox with the promise of completing two pictures in forty weeks, Hitchcock finished *Lifeboat*. The aftermath left everyone feeling betrayed. Zanuck had paid $350,000 to a director for a picture whose gross receipts might not reach $1 million; furthermore, that same noted director had taken fifty-two weeks to do what a lesser known but no less competent director might well have done in twenty. The stockholders would not be amused. Steinbeck asked Fox to remove his name from the picture, and Dorothy Thompson (one of several hostile critics) gave *Lifeboat* "ten days to get out of town." Selznick believed that Zanuck had improperly supervised Hitchcock, jeopardizing the reputation that the Universal loanout had helped build. And even the director sulked. An artistic experiment, *Lifeboat* should have been enthusiastically sold; instead, Hitchcock said, Fox gave the film "a minimum of ad space" and let it die in the marketplace. Academy recognition for Best Achievement in

Henry Hull, Tallulah Bankhead, Hume Cronyn, Mary Anderson, William Bendix, and (facing away from camera) John Hodiak. Hitchcock was amused to learn that one of the young actresses in *Lifeboat* stuffed her brassiere with Kleenex. "An exaggerated bosom," he told reporters, "is a dull, elementary form of sex appeal."

Hitchcock on the "set" of *Lifeboat*, with MacKinlay Kantor.

Directing, Hitchcock's second Oscar nomination, offered slim consolation.

While a period of virtually independent production ended unhappily for Hitchcock, one resumed for Selznick. Overseeing the rerelease of Selznick International pictures and negotiating loanout agreements for his major contract artists, including Fontaine and Hitchcock, had hardly dented his creative energies. He attempted one creative project, then another, all helter-skelter. To Irene's chagrin, he planned to enlarge his house, add a bowling alley beneath the tennis court, put a bungalow-office on the property; these ideas expended, he decided to purchase land near Culver City and build an immense studio complex. But only motion pictures truly lent themselves to "the larger view." Finally he decided to produce one.

On *Since You Went Away,* Selznick himself outlined the treatment, wrote and rewrote the script, then sent it peremptorily to the set with instructions for director, cast, and crew. "He was more compulsive than ever about the tiniest detail," Irene recalled, perhaps because the picture starred Jennifer Jones, with whom he was falling in love. The level of supervision and the intensity of the memoranda suggest that the urge to produce and the desire for perfection had returned—with a vengeance. Meanwhile, the struggle with Zanuck and the dumping of *Lifeboat* had strengthened Hitchcock's resolve to enter independent production. Selznick represented the cloud on the horizon and, as Hitchcock learned, the producer had decided to make a picture with his acclaimed contract director. This second collaboration of David Selznick and Alfred Hitchcock, four years after *Rebecca,* would again bring together two men, each man more determined than ever to produce *his* film, *his* way.

5

$PELLBOUND

While Jennifer Jones and *Since You Went Away* brought Selznick back into the motion picture industry, his anxieties followed him. Realizing that his wide mood swings were affecting his judgment, he entered analysis with May Romm, one of Los Angeles's top psychiatrists. Selznick appeared to improve markedly during the early weeks of his treatment. His depression lifted, and he earnestly resumed film production. Psychoanalysis—or was it work?—alleviated the symptoms even if it did not give him a clean bill of mental health.

In fall 1943, as he became more deeply involved with *Since You Went Away,* he had less and less time for therapy. He canceled some appointments, slept through others, and occasionally showed up on Romm's doorstep at midnight, unannounced, for an impromptu conference. After less than a year, Irene later wrote, "he confided to me that he knew more than she did; *he* could analyze *her.*" What appears to be megalomania may simply have been a defense mechanism: Selznick would no more have allowed a psychiatrist the last word on his life than he would have allowed a director the final cut of his films. In addition, having spent thousands of hours in screenwriting conferences, examining the motives and behavior of characters in emotional turmoil, Selznick could claim some measure of analytic ability. Romm nonetheless gave him ideas, less about himself or his depression, perhaps, than about psychiatry as the subject of a potentially important film, one that would renew his association with his principal contract director.

Like his attitude toward psychoanalysis, though, Selznick's interest in making a movie about psychoanalysis ebbed and flowed. "I'd like to stress," he wrote to story editor Margaret McDonell in July 1943, "that I'm almost desperately anxious to do this psychological or psychiatric story with Hitch." On other occasions, he waxed unenthusiastic. "I don't think we should make this picture," he later decided. "In these times it is somewhat of a waste of Hitchcock." Selznick's depression accounts only partially for his indecision. To most producers, the subject of psychoanalysis seemed too far removed from the experience of the average moviegoer (and too vulnerable to censorship in America and England) to succeed commercially; as Selznick himself had once remarked, films should not be made "consciously to educate." Yet no subject could have been more topical. Toward the mid-1940s, the American popular press became a vigorous advocate of psychological counseling, especially for returning GIs. *Since You Went Away,* Selznick proudly told Karl Menninger, contained "a sequence that I personally conceived and wrote in the hope that it would have a value in making the American public aware of the work being done by psychiatrists to rebuild men who have been shaken by their war experiences." With the intellectual cachet of psychoanalysis, a picture with Hitchcock might further rebuild Selznick's own shattered reputation.

Since directing *Rebecca* for Selznick, Hitchcock had made six films away from his employer. He had originated or discovered the stories for two of the pictures *(Saboteur* and *Shadow of a Doubt)* and nurtured the scripts of the rest; he had closeted himself with writers at RKO and Universal, and even during production rarely saw a studio executive. He thus had the power—if not the salary—of the independent producer he yearned to become. Zanuck and *Lifeboat* had reminded him afresh of the authority that a mogul could exert over a director's work. Yet although he had tilted at Zanuck, he always deferred to Selznick. By contract, Selznick regulated loanouts, radio deals, and almost every

116

other aspect of the director's professional life. Hitchcock respected that control as much as he bridled under it.

Now Selznick had asked him to direct a "psychiatric story." While skeptical of psychoanalysis, Hitchcock had a coming appetite for perverse twists of character. The overwrought Danvers and the pathologically inferior second Mrs. de Winter of *Rebecca* blurred the line between the normal and the abnormal; the neurotic or psychopathic behavior of characters in *Suspicion, Shadow of a Doubt,* and *Lifeboat* also made many of them candidates for institutionalization. Yet Selznick contemplated a picture about psychotherapy, not psychopaths. For someone who regarded message movies as "impure cinema," the prospect of returning to Culver City must have been daunting. Still more discouraging, Selznick had become a man who knew too much: his confidence in himself as an expert on film *and* the subconscious promised close supervision of any "collaboration."

Selznick and Hitchcock never fought like cats and dogs; they preferred the subtler game of cat and mouse. Seeing the inevitability of a psychiatric project on his schedule, the director took the offensive. He had acquired the screen rights to a novel set in an insane asylum and offered it to Selznick as the basis of their film. Francis Beeding's *The House of Dr. Edwardes* (1927) might seem too unrefined for Selznick, perhaps even too raw for Hitchcock. High in the Alps, homicidal maniac Geoffrey Godstone locks up Dr. Murchison, the real head of Château Landry, and assumes management of this "house of rest for the mentally deficient." A new staff psychiatrist named Constance Sedgwick discovers Godstone's secret, but by herself cannot expose him and free Murchison. At the climax, Dr. Edwardes, a distinguished psychiatrist and the owner of the asylum, arrives and restores order; rounding out the narrative, Murchison weds Sedgwick. As a Selznick Productions reader said, it "is filled with diabolical maniacs running loose; black magic; weird ceremonies, rites and incantations; violence; attempted murders, etc." In short, hardly designed to impress Karl Menninger.*

*Unlike *Rebecca, Spellbound* diverged sharply from its literary roots. In the finished picture, John Ballantyne (Gregory Peck) presents himself as the new chief of Green Manors mental asylum. He soon admits to psychiatrist Constance Petersen (Ingrid Bergman) that he has killed the man whom he impersonates, Anthony Edwardes. Constance has fallen in love with Ballantyne and does not

Although he had some interest in the preternatural as well as the supernatural, Hitchcock probably intended to discard much of the claptrap of *The House of Dr. Edwardes* (as the film would be called until just before its premiere) and retain only selected action and characters. Divorced from the logic of plot, numerous incidents in Beeding's study of dementia gone amok lent themselves well to visualization, yet even these must have interested Hitchcock less than the central character. Psychopaths had not generally been the stuff of his British films; with *Shadow of a Doubt,* however, he had begun to explore the dark side of the mind. The fact that Hitchcock wished Joseph Cotten, the psychopathic Uncle Charlie, to play Godstone suggests a continuity in the director's design; with his smooth veneer and profound depravity, Godstone, had he survived the numerous script revisions, would have become the rough draft for Bruno Anthony *(Strangers on a Train)* and Norman Bates *(Psycho).* Seeing the potential for his characteristic "ruthless adaptation," Hitchcock urged Selznick to purchase the *Edwardes* film rights from him; in return, while abroad directing some propaganda shorts that Sidney Bernstein had finally contacted him about, Hitchcock promised to develop a first-draft treatment. At home, acting as editor and collaborator, Alma would supply the polish.

The $40,000 selling price and the prospect of a Hitchcock treatment written overseas should have prompted Selznick to reject the offer. After all, the farther the director stayed from his producer during the evolution of the treatment, the more he might control it. Surprisingly, though, Selznick acceded. Hitchcock had not earned a bonus on the

---

believe him a murderer. She determines to treat his amnesia through psychoanalysis. With the police pursuing them, Constance and Ballantyne flee to New York and then to the home of her mentor, Professor Alex Brulov (Michael Chekhov). Constance and Brulov analyze Ballantyne's dream, but Constance decides that only a trip to the ski slopes of Gabriel Valley, where he lost his memory, will heal him. There Ballantyne abandons the guilt complex that has made him assume responsibility for the accidental death of his brother and, by extension, the murder of his therapist, Dr. Edwardes. Constance returns to Green Manors to confront the real murderer, the aging man whom Edwardes would have replaced. Dr. Murchison (Leo G. Carroll) threatens to kill Constance, then turns his gun on himself. John Ballantyne and his lover are reunited.

Selznick-arranged Twentieth Century-Fox loanout, the producer apparently reasoned, so the $40,000 paid him for the screen rights represented double compensation; at least Hitchcock would not return to Selznick Productions (as he had after his loan to RKO several years before) crying poor. But Selznick distinguished between giving Hitchcock money and giving Hitchcock control over the *Edwardes* story. The ragged screenplays of *Saboteur* and *Lifeboat,* written under the supervision of the director acting de facto as his own producer, had undermined what little trust Selznick had in Hitchcock's narrative skills. If Hitchcock attempted to adapt *Edwardes,* Selznick feared, he would produce merely a farrago of "gags and bits of business and tricks," qualities at odds with the cinematic and personal goals that the producer hoped to realize.

The problem, as both men must have recognized, lay not only in their mutual touchiness but in their opposed aesthetics. From the beginning of their association, Hitchcock poorly concealed his desire for independence; accordingly, in the interests of good picturemaking, Selznick occasionally strove to give the director at least the illusion of freedom. Yet the two men held broadly different ideas about cinema and cinematic storytelling. To Selznick, plot meant "end"; to Hitchcock, "means." While foregrounding what Selznick called "gags and bits," Hitchcock often explored the terror within the commonplace, the horror within "things." Still, the "business and tricks" that Selznick disparaged worked best (as the director's pictures with screenwriters John Michael Hayes and Ernest Lehman later proved) when scenarists could blend them into a strong narrative. Seasoning then became substance. Selznick fully intended to force Hitchcock to confront the calculus of plot but naturally (given Hitchcock's disposition) preferred to work behind the scenes. After agreeing to the Hitchcock treatment, Selznick began looking for a screenwriter to tame the script if not the director himself.

Selznick's first choice was Ben Hecht. Capable of delivering finished work at remarkable speed, Hecht had penned his name across more paychecks than screenplays, for in addition to his credited work he had doctored for many major filmmakers, including both Selznick *(Gone With the Wind)* and Hitchcock *(Foreign Correspondent, Lifeboat).* Like Hitchcock, he had thinning hair, a coruscating wit, a mock disdain for actors, and—most important to Selznick—a reputation for quality.

119

Producer and writer had known each other for years, and Selznick had both affection and respect for him. If anyone could restrain Hitchcock's excesses, and thereby head off a producer-director confrontation, Hecht could. Tell Hecht, Selznick said to O'Shea, that for *Dr. Edwardes* we want "a well constructed emotional story on which to hang all of Hitch's wonderful gags; that they should not go off on tangents about gags; that Hitch has a tendency to fall in love with individual scenes and bits of business and to distort story line to accommodate these, so the effort should be to get a sound story. . . . I will count upon Ben to stick to story." The director, however, seduced authors as he did actors. He opened his conferences with snide comments about producers (he relished gossip), then proceeded to dazzle his writers with one cinematic *jeu d'esprit* after another. Without oversight from Selznick, Hecht might unwittingly fall for the "gags."

Hitchcock arrived in England at Christmas 1943. Two months before, the sober *Times* had formally announced, "Mr. Alfred Hitchcock's version of 'Rebecca' has been revived at the London Pavilion." While the so-called possessory credit would have delighted the returning hero, it would have dismayed the producer of *Gone With the Wind,* which (like *Rebecca*) had been billed "David O. Selznick's production." Selznick's filmmaking hiatus throughout the war years had made him sensitive to slights, which appeared to increase in direct proportion to the acclaim given his star director. By assigning Hitchcock the "psychiatric story" and, through Hecht, supervising the writing, Selznick intended to restore the apostrophe to *his* name above the title of a prominent picture. But Hecht would not begin until the director returned from England, by which time Hitchcock might regard at least the structure of *Dr. Edwardes* as a fait accompli.

The possibility also existed, Selznick realized, that while completing the Ministry of Information propaganda shorts for Sidney Bernstein, Hitchcock might plot more than the *Edwardes* treatment. Selznick knew Bernstein from a long Hollywood visit in the thirties. The Englishman dressed conservatively and spoke softly; government offices seemed more his proper milieu than the gilt movie palaces of his Granada Theatres chain. But Bernstein could surprise. From Orthodox Jew and entrepreneur, he had become an agnostic and a political progressive. Despite his commercial interests, he preferred "films" to "movies." Bernstein probably met Hitchcock at screenings of the Lon-

don Film Society, where they shared an enthusiasm for experimental cinema. They were not close friends: neither man easily traded privacy for intimacy. Bernstein nonetheless admired Hitchcock enormously for bringing the art of German expressionism and Soviet montage to the commercial cinema. Sam Goldwyn had sent for Hitchcock, Selznick probably reasoned; perhaps Bernstein also had.

In early January 1944, Alma lunched with *Shadow of a Doubt* producer Jack Skirball "to talk over some stories." Hitchcock clearly intended to leave Selznick, who could imagine the scenario. Bernstein and Hitchcock would form a British-American independent production company with Hitchcock as chief artistic director and—more significant—principal stockholder, a move that would weaken if not eliminate the director's dependence on Selznick. Though the wartime decimation of the English film industry would complicate shooting abroad, Bernstein and Hitchcock would have access to facilities and crews denied less important filmmakers. Hitchcock could then conduct his cinematic experiments away from the prying eyes of Hollywood and simultaneously enjoy the adulation of a largely sympathetic hometown press. Unlike his wife, the director had not filed for United States citizenship by December 1943; he also still banked abroad.

Complicating matters were the Ministry of Information propaganda films. To author these quasidocumentaries, *Bon Voyage* and *Aventure Malgache,* Bernstein hired forty-year-old Angus MacPhail. MacPhail and Hitchcock resembled Mutt and Jeff. The lanky Scot had been a title writer, scenarist, and member of the London Film Society; screenwriter Sidney Gilliat regarded him as a lovable eccentric with "no consistent faith in his own work." He "rewrote his own stuff wildly," Gilliat said, "and at all hours for sometimes no good reason." Apparently an alcoholic, MacPhail was incapable of sustained effort. Transatlantic correspondence between Hitchcock and Bernstein reveals both their concern and affection for MacPhail, and although hiring him for the Mo I films could not be construed as charity, Hitchcock did have a sentimental spot for many of the people whom he had worked with in the 1920s. The director thus suggested that once they completed the government pictures, MacPhail should author the *Edwardes* treatment. Had he been advised, Selznick would have balked. Unlike Hecht, MacPhail seemed a promising mark for Hitchcock's gags and bits; more to the point, while writing something possibly worse than the original novel,

MacPhail would free Hitchcock and Bernstein to plot financing of their joint independent production company.

By January 1944, MacPhail had begun work on what became a seventeen-page first-draft treatment of *Dr. Edwardes*. The quality and authorship of this outline have been questioned. "It rambled," Hitchcock told François Truffaut, and one Hitchcock biographer doubted its very existence. Selznick was convinced that Hitchcock intended to deceive him: "Any bets as to the resemblance of the adaptation which Hitchcock [brings back] obviously being written by Alma in Hollywood and not by Hitch in London?" The Hitchcock–MacPhail collaboration very much existed, however, and demonstrated that at this earliest stage in the film's development, MacPhail or Hitchcock or the two together established the structure and several of the major incidents for the film eventually called *Spellbound*.

In the first MacPhail–Hitchcock treatment, an amnesiac who identifies himself as "Dr. Edwardes" arrives to assume the headship of the Claremont Mental Home. The assistant director (Dr. Murchison) and the matron (Miss Curtis) are antagonistic; Murchison resents "Edwardes"'s appointment over himself, and Curtis is "a middle-aged woman, whose natural sweetness of character has been soured by her failure to achieve emotional happiness." As the plot unfolds, Murchison and Curtis try to discredit "Edwardes" and psychiatrist Constance Sedgwick, who eventually fall in love. Sedgwick realizes that "Edwardes" is an imposter and undertakes to cure him through psychoanalysis. At the climax on Devil's Leap, "Edwardes" rescues Constance from a mad patient and jars loose the memory that he has suppressed: the real Edwardes drove his car over a gorge; unable to accept his therapist's death or his role in it, "Edwardes" (really Eric Hunter, a United States Medical Officer) assumed the man's identity. The authorities clear him, and "as Constance and Hunter leave the court together, he pulls a lock of hair over his forehead, scowls, and gives the Nazi salute!"

Only Hitchcock could transform the pulling of the forelock into the thumbing of the nose. The levity notwithstanding, the writers had begun not only to distance themselves from the melodramatic shenanigans of Beeding's novel (particularly its homicidal maniac), but also to lay groundwork for an original psychoanalytic thriller. Although the love affair between Constance and "Edwardes" had been inadequately developed, the idea of a woman's using medicine in the service of romance was firmly in place. Linking the practice of psychiatry to a woman's nurturing instincts—a masterstroke—would make a scientific, thus foreign and cold, subject more palatable to motion picture audiences. As Selznick wished, the healing potential of psychiatry had become the work's theme; as he feared, though, MacPhail and Hitchcock had more fully realized the "gags and bits" than the narrative itself.

In their treatment, MacPhail and Hitchcock had had what they termed "a little not unkindly fun" with the inmates. One older patient, they wrote, believes herself "to be growing backwards and has now reached the age of ten"; another masquerades as Joan of Arc and following her conference with "Edwardes" takes a college pennant from her closet, "raises it proudly above her head, [and] exclaims 'Vive la France.'" An early adaptation of *Rebecca* had angered Selznick precisely because of its compromised tone; in one ostensibly comic moment, for instance, de Winter blew cigar smoke toward his future wife and caused her to throw up overboard. "If there is any humor left on the screen in seasickness," Selznick lectured Hitchcock, "let's for God's sake leave it to the two-reel comedies and not get our picture off on a low note by indulging in such scenes."

Perhaps anticipating Selznick's criticism of such bits of business as the Nazi salute and the daffy inmates, MacPhail and Hitchcock immediately began revising their first draft. Temporarily entitled *The Interloper, Dr. Edwardes* became increasingly serious. *Variety* reported that the director "worked with eminent English psychoanalysts before the adaptation was turned over to Ben Hecht," and the drafts of the treatment written in January and February 1944 exhibit some of their influence. Curtis, a melancholiac, loves Virginia, a nymphomaniac; their fellow sufferers include Mrs. Collett, being treated for schizophrenia; Anstey, for dementia praecox; and Trulow, for megalomania. Trulow would not be Hitchcock's last unflattering reference to his employer. But while he disliked Selznick's involvement and bristled under his authority, Hitchcock had begun to recognize that a "psychiatric story" combining his imagination with his producer's unerring taste, large budgets, and promotional skills might boost both their careers; after all, no film to date had brought the director more acclaim than *Rebecca.*

In revising the initial treatment, MacPhail and Hitchcock invented several of those plot turns that critics today call "Hitchcockian." Even Selznick delighted in those cinematic effects that served the story. The conclusion of the revised draft seems especially representative. Establishing that her patient's amnesia began somewhere on the ski slopes, Constance decides to return with him to Lake Placid and restage his slide down the hill. The unusual pictorial rhythms of skiers, zigzagging blacks on a field of white, had great photographic interest; the lovers' relentless, unstoppable downhill course also communicated the high risk of Constance's experiment. As she skis down before "Edwardes," nearing a precipice, he recalls how the real Edwardes—his psychiatrist and skiing partner—slipped into the canyon below before he could save him. In a moment of exquisite clarity, he saves Constance from a similar fate.

Falling, or the threat of falling, affects many of Hitchcock's characters, from the second Mrs. de Winter in *Rebecca* to the bickering couple in *Mr. and Mrs. Smith,* the treacherous Fry in *Saboteur,* and the innocent Charlie Newton in *Shadow of a Doubt.* The image of joined hands over a chasm—not an altar—concludes more than one of Hitchcock's romantic comedies. In Hitchcock's most accomplished films, the world is cold, indifferent, closed. "Sometimes I feel like a prisoner," "Edwardes" tells Constance in the revised drafts, "a prisoner struggling to get free." Perhaps Hitchcock, bound by long-term contract to bend his art to another's cinematic vision, created "Edwardes" out of his own anxieties and frustrations. Whatever his origin, "Edwardes" is another of Hitchcock's isolated heroes whose fear of falling points to the tenuousness of his position on earth.

A fall does not a screenplay make. Neither do personal anxieties and frustrations. For both drafts, Hitchcock had fished very close to shore.

> Constance says that a neurotic is like a man who shoves inconvenient letters and bills into the drawer of his desk and forgets all about them [the director wrote]. Then one fine day he is summoned for non-payment of his income tax. In the same way the neurotic shoves away his inconvenient memories and forgets all about them. But they have their revenge on him just as the neglected income tax does.

Police officers may not really have frightened Hitchcock, but tax men did. Shortly before he left for London, the director made a command performance at Internal Revenue to tally his income and pay all out-standing taxes. The meeting occurred in an office in downtown Los Angeles. "During the conference," Carol Stevens recalled, the director "never said a word—just sat straight in a chair with his hands crossed over his stomach in typical Hitchcock fashion." Because she main-tained his books, Stevens served as his mouthpiece. The "bureaucrats put the 'fear of God' into Hitch and were rude and showed no deference to his position." Had they remained on his mind in *The Interloper*?

Despite the elimination of the Nazi salute and the "not unkindly fun," *The Interloper* demonstrated Hitchcock's weakness in dramatic construction. He had gone off on tangents and stocked even the revised *Interloper* treatment with unworkable scenes. For instance, he had made Constance relate the narrative in flashback, a technique that not only retarded the pace but dissipated the audience's fears for her safety on the slopes of Lake Placid; he had also developed numerous belabored sequences centered on the inmates' production of Congreve's *The Way of the World*. In a cable sent to Alma in February 1944, he spoke confidently about the *Dr. Edwardes* treatment but added that he an-ticipated his wife's contributions to it. He certainly longed for home. The deprivation abroad had astonished him, the London air raids had frightened him. "I used to be alone in Claridge's Hotel," he said, "and the bombs would fall and the guns and I was alone and I didn't know what to do." He also "longed for Hollywood polish, Hollywood know-how," biographer John Russell Taylor believed. "He even longed, loath though he was to admit it, for the sounding-board of David O. Selz-nick." Even if Hitchcock did not long for Selznick, he needed him. To become a major motion picture, the "psychiatric story" would require the editorial expertise of Hitchcock's employer.

In March 1944, when Hitchcock returned to New York from Lon-don, he sent a copy of his third-draft *Dr. Edwardes* treatment to Holly-wood. Originally, Selznick would have ripped into the story and or-dered deletions, modifications, and additions; on March 23, however, his brother Myron died of complications from a liver disorder. Sibling rivalry aside, the brothers had been very close. "Myron is gone," the boys' mother would say in the months following his death. "I have nothing to live for." Between his own affection for Myron and the guilt engendered by his mother's lament, David sank into a deep depression in spring 1944.

126

Meanwhile, Hitchcock asked to remain in New York to confer with Ben Hecht and to research *Dr. Edwardes*. The proximity to notable medical advisors meant less than the distance from Selznick: although the two men planned to visit area mental hospitals and sanatoriums, their real interest lay in writing a script without the shadow of their producer falling across it. The more they talked, the more enthusiastic Hecht and Hitchcock became. Hecht had been in psychoanalysis and brought a special interest to the project; Hitchcock, who Hecht said "gave off plot turns like a Roman candle," usually brought out the best in writers with whom he felt congenial. Selznick normally wanted his writers on the premises, yet the death of Myron and the ensuing period of mourning had also left him unwilling to face a sullen Hitchcock. Since the presence of Hecht as both writer and watchdog seemed reassuring, he permitted his two salaried employees to remain a continent away.

Not long after he had buried Myron, Selznick began to question his liberality with Hitchcock. The director had begun to eat his way through script conferences at "21" and other posh restaurants. Without a wind at his back, Selznick feared, Hitchcock would malinger. "Fond as I am of Ben," Selznick also said some time later, "I wouldn't make him the trustee of my estate." Between them, Hitchcock and Hecht made $9,000 weekly, and thus merited at least some tactful overseeing. "Don't you think," Selznick asked Dan O'Shea, who was in New York as Hecht and Hitchcock worked, "you ought to give Hecht and Hitchcock a check-up every couple of days to see how they're coming, since they're working without supervision?" O'Shea's report only partially satisfied his boss.

Hitchcock conceptualized films outside-in; he built his scripts on neither character nor plot but setting and object. " 'What do they have in Switzerland?' " Hitchcock asked himself before beginning *The Man Who Knew Too Much*. "They have milk chocolate, they have the Alps, they have village dances, and they have lakes. All of these national ingredients were woven into the picture." *Foreign Correspondent* originated "with the idea of the windmill sequence and also the scene of the murderer escaping through the bobbing umbrellas. We were in Holland and so we used windmills and rain." (Like many directors, Hitchcock rarely set his films in Los Angeles. "How can you do anything about

127

Wilshire Boulevard?" asked Jean Renoir, one of Hitchcock's immigrant colleagues. "There's just no smell to it.") On *Dr. Edwardes,* despite the surveillance of O'Shea, Ben Hecht freed his collaborator to explore the windmills and rain of mental institutions.

Like *Blackmail,* which opens with a thumbnail documentary on police procedure, the first-draft script of *Dr. Edwards* (with the second *e* of "Edwardes" now eliminated) begins with a montage of the Green Manors Retreat. Touring the asylum but keeping his distance from the humanity of the patients, Hitchcock cuts quickly from one form of therapy to another—insulin and electroshock treatments, hot and icy water cures, the extensive use of drugs. Hitchcock depersonalizes the characters subjected to these experiments; he turns them into things, no more animate than "bobbing umbrellas." Mechanical things attracted Hitchcock, a draftsman turned director; he loved gadgets and even mail-ordered them, sight unseen, from radio advertisements. But mechanical things that controlled people especially captivated him. As a filmmaker who relied on suspense more than surprise, Hitchcock consistently elevated things over people.

When objects overwhelmed, Hecht restored the balance. Though he retained the jealous Murchison as well as the Constance–"Edwards" love story from the MacPhail–Hitchcock treatment, he not only humanized the characters (especially the psychoanalysts), but enlarged the setting. Hecht could also have some "not unkindly fun" with psychiatry. In his short story "The Adventures of Professor Emmett," a woman had "substituted Freud for Browning and was as versed in the horrors of love-making as her sisters had once been in its poetry." A therapist in another story, "Café Sinister," was "given to wandering the city after midnight and peering into its psychoses and, perhaps, looking for customers." On *Edwards,* Hecht directed his mockery toward the Green Manors staff rather than (as MacPhail and Hitchcock had done) the Green Manors patients. Throughout the first draft, he cut the sober discourse of the psychiatrists with humor, irony, and cynicism. One of the doctors finds Constance "withering away with science" and suggests a romantic diversion with "Edwards." "The mating of two psychoanalysts would be an event worth going miles to see," a colleague observes. "And study." Hecht gave "Edwards" still more nimble dialogue, ideally suited to the touch of Joseph Cotten, whom both collaborators imagined for the role. The light treatment of psychiatrists—

but not psychiatry—would help close the distance between the characters and the mass audience.

Along with Hecht, Hitchcock began taking the patients more seriously. The psychoanalysis of Mr. Trulow, the megalomaniac, runs through the script like a refrain. "I had that same dream again—about being pursued by the police and running up a long stairs. When I got to the top my father was standing there and I had to get rid of him—or he would tell the police where I was." Trulow also remembers his father, "when I was four years old—putting me in a closet because I'd been crying over something." Merely textbook Freud? Perhaps, yet the emphasis on a cruel father's betrayal of his son, especially a betrayal involving the police, again parallels the story of the elder Hitchcock's sending his son to the police station. The fear of authority figures and the depiction of a universe beyond the control of the individual appear repeatedly in the director's work. In many films, Hitchcock associates the moment of incarceration, usually photographed from above, with abject terror and helplessness. The Trulow dream complements the MacPhail–Hitchcock image of the "prisoner struggling to get free." In *Dr. Edwards,* Hitchcock would not allay the apprehensions of his personal and professional life, but he would obliquely bare them.

Constance falls in love with the amnesiac "Edwards," but an announcement about the mysterious disappearance of the real Edwards prompts the couple to flee Green Manors for Manhattan and points north. Hecht plotted the chase, Hitchcock visualized it. "We come in on a LONG SHOT looking down on the city of New York. THE CAMERA approaches the distant buildings. The city comes closer— THE CAMERA moves toward a large hotel. It moves toward one of the windows on the 30th floor. It passes in through the window toward a couch. J.B. ["Edwards"] lies on a couch. Constance is sitting in a chair, near his head." Practicing for the impressive opening of *Psycho,* in which the camera moves across the Phoenix skyline to peer into a hotel window, Hitchcock reduces the characters to specimens beneath a microscope. The camera becomes an instrument for framing, then enclosing and dominating them.

Routed from New York by unsympathetic Green Manors associates, "Edwards" and Constance train to the home of Alex Brulov, her mentor. After warmly greeting the "honeymooners," the German-accented therapist directs them to the guest bedroom. The dialogue there touches on lovemaking and therapy and the word *white* as a previously established clue to the amnesia of "Edwards." But Hitchcock generates the suspense through the lens. "Edwards" stands at the basin and draws out a straight razor. The whiteness of the shaving cream, associated with the whiteness of a suppressed childhood memory, makes him hallucinate; he cannot remove the lather from his face. He contemplates slashing his wrist, then enters the darkened bedroom. "The moon strikes the steel of the razor dangling from his hand. Holding the open razor at his side, he stands for a moment, looking around. Then he moves toward the bed." As he stares at the sleeping Constance, "the face on the pillow begins to turn white. It glistens as if it were made out of blinding white crystals. His eyes fill with terror and the arm that holds the razor twitches." The exaggerated, shifting tonalities (from darkness to bright light to moonlight) and the conversion of a pedestrian object into a threatening lethal (or sexually suggestive) weapon recur throughout Hitchcock's films; as much as the dream sequence that subsequently was planned, they dramatize the role of the unconscious in the characters' lives.

Once Constance assists "Edwards" in recalling the memory that he has suppressed (he imagined that he killed his younger brother as well as his psychiatrist, Dr. Edwards), she rapidly cures his amnesia; the last fade-out promises a real honeymoon. The marriage of Hitchcock and Hecht ended almost as happily. Although Hecht had liberally peppered the first draft with psychological dysfunctions—from jealousy to suicide, amnesia, and guilt complexes—Hitchcock had countered the talk with visual tours de force. Unlike some screenwriters, Hecht easily accommodated the Roman candles to the storyline: he made the bits of business and the chase seem organic. The May 1944 script also introduced authentic leading characters into the narrative. The Mac-Phail–Hitchcock "Edwards" equaled the sum of his afflictions; Hecht not only rounded "Edwards" and Constance but relieved the harshness typical of Hitchcock, the tendency to cartoon, to flatten the characters along the edges of the drama. Freudianism per se hardly engaged Hitchcock, but the pathology of interpersonal relationships fascinated him. The *Dr. Edwards* screenplay, attentive to the behavior of camera and characters, would permit the director to explore the human psyche from outside in and inside out.

Though the *Edwards* script had conspicuous weaknesses, the tension

Dr. Constance Petersen (Ingrid Bergman) with her amnesiac patient (Gregory Peck). Selznick wanted Bergman's wardrobe to "aid the characterization of a woman . . . who has deliberately disinterested herself in frivolity, kids herself that she is aloof from romantic interests, devotes herself entirely to science, and yet would have enough pride and fastidiousness and unaffected chic to look distinguished and smartly but severely groomed."

between two aesthetics had energized the story. Working with Mac-Phail, Hitchcock had "run for cover." He had resorted to the irony and stick figures of his "little British thrillers." Writers like Hecht drove Hitchcock from the bush; they forced him to confront narrative logic. When accomplished formula-writing collided with strong and original images, the chemistry could prove "Hitchcockian." One man would judge whether the collaborators had succeeded. With considerable enthusiasm for their work, Hitchcock and Hecht delivered the first-draft screenplay to their producer.

Overwhelmed by final cutting on *Since You Went Away*, Selznick asked his story editor to evaluate *Dr. Edwards*. Margaret McDonell enjoyed the objectivity denied Hecht and Hitchcock, but her opinion pleased neither the writers nor her producer: she found the screenplay "over-dialogued" and "too 'psychiatric' for the general public." Scanning her mid-May report, Selznick fretted. We may have "too much psychiatry" on our program, he told O'Shea; unless we are careful, it will become "a monopoly and be a trade-mark with our films." Unlike "Edwards" or Constance, Hitchcock personally mistrusted psychoanalysis. "They say psychiatrically if you can discover the origins of this or that, it releases everything," Hitchcock told Peter Bogdanovich. "I don't think it released me from a natural fear of the police." Yet the director understood that the *subject* of psychoanalysis, treated seriously, would rationalize some unusual experiments with narrative and photography, which of course delighted him.

Forced to defend the "psychiatric story," Hitchcock rushed to assure Margaret McDonell that he planned to create suspense by setting the action against a kind of "drawing-room tea party" background. Furthermore, he added, Joe Cotten as "Edwards" would lend excitement and mitigate the potential severity of a work about psychoanalysis. Selznick remained unconvinced. On the other hand, he argued, if filmgoers believed that "Edwards" had killed his analyst, they would perceive a greater physical danger to Constance in the third act. Weave this conventional murder-mystery angle into *Edwards*, Selznick told Hecht and Hitchcock, not only to heighten the tension but to balance the unconventional psychiatric elements of the narrative.

Hitchcock simmered. Although the murder mystery would increase the suspense, the suggestion marked the return of the director to junior partnership in the Selznick relationship. The equal of such independents as Capra or Ford, Hitchcock seemed at once outranked and intimidated by Selznick. Yet rather than confront him about *Edwards,* Hitchcock quietly retreated to his office. The more he meditated on Selznick and *Edwards,* the more his commodious lower lip drooped. Would the picture be an Alfred Hitchcock or a David Selznick production? With the answer altogether too clear, Hitchcock for the moment deferred to the inevitable. A week later, Selznick talked with Hecht, who "tells me that Hitch is still pouting about the murder mystery angle I inserted but is apparently working with Ben on straightening out the snags, albeit rather reluctantly."

Foot-dragging on the *Edwards* second-draft screenplay troubled Selznick. Without supervision, Hecht and Hitchcock might not address the structural problems in the script. Furthermore, their determination to lay the story against the background of contemporary psychiatric practice might not only make psychoanalysis "a trade-mark" with the studio, but open Selznick and company to criticism. "Ben and Hitch are both loaded with psychiatric misinformation," Selznick said, corroborating his wife's belief that he regarded himself an expert on such matters. "Ben knows a great deal about the subject—much more than Hitch—but he also has a lot of dope that is not accurate and that could be expected from an amateur." Fully expecting Hecht to "scream like a stuck pig about rewriting dialogue for technical reasons," Selznick named two technical advisors to the production: Eileen Johnston, a college graduate in psychology, and May Romm, Selznick's analyst and the technical advisor on *Since You Went Away.*

During the first ten days of June, Selznick, Hecht, and Hitchcock conferred amicably. All agreed to trim the opening montage and to plan a dream sequence with "less attention to interpretation of words, more to attitude, behavior, mood." They also decided to dramatize, through an unusually violent flashback, "Edwards"'s repressed childhood memory of having accidentally caused his brother's death. Most of the alterations plotted in these conferences gave the script a more visceral or sensuous dimension, aimed at making audiences perceive the film as entertainment rather than education. Within days, statistics confirmed the necessity of their course. Audience Research, Inc., which had tested interest in the "psychiatric story" in late spring, reported that "audience acceptance of the property is above average, although not by a great margin." For the second draft, Selznick urged the writers to push the romance and dramatic tension.

While Hecht revised the script, Selznick and Hitchcock began casting *Dr. Edwards.* Their selections were crucial. An absence of stars, coupled with a serious political statement, had mired *Lifeboat;* an absence of stars in a "psychiatric story" would write "didactic" across the lobby cards. Despite his resentment of stars, Hitchcock agreed with Selznick on their value: performers with box office appeal fueled the publicity machine. The greater the exploitation, the greater the enhancement of both producer's and director's careers. But the persistence of the war, which had claimed many male stars, reduced the filmmakers' choices for "Edwards." Those actors left behind in Hollywood either tended to work exclusively for their home studios or freelanced; the latter, because of the income tax structure, generally restricted themselves to two films a year. Earlier in the decade, Selznick had loaned or sold outright many of his contract performers but still controlled the services of a few. From this slim list, Hitchcock would have to draw his leading man.

Since Christmas, Hitchcock had envisioned Joseph Cotten for "Edwards." Cotten could project menace (as he had in *Shadow of a Doubt*) and romance (as he would with Jennifer Jones in *Love Letters*); his relaxed, instinctive approach to acting suited Hitchcock, who preferred to block the action and let the actor discover his motivation from the script or his fellow performers. A 1944 Gallup poll ranked the actor as "the great new romantic rage," yet the shortage of male stars forced Selznick to cast him in *I'll Be Seeing You,* the Dore Schary picture then in production for Selznick. Hitchcock regretted the loss. As the options shrank, Selznick turned to a contract actor unknown to the moviegoing public.

"He photographs like Abe Lincoln," Selznick wrote Kay Brown, who had proposed that her employer hire Gregory Peck in 1941. "If he has a great personality, I don't think it comes through." The paucity of male stars and the doggedness of Kay Brown finally made Selznick change his mind. He signed Peck in 1943, then sent him to Twentieth Century-Fox for *The Keys of the Kingdom,* his first major picture. As a missionary in *Keys,* Peck covered his dark good looks with vulnerability, partially calculated and partially the result of his naiveté before the camera. Since the advance word on *Keys* (ultimately released in December 1944) had been good, Selznick decided to cast Peck as "Edwards." The inexperienced Peck must have been excited by the chance to further his screen education. Yet although Hitchcock meticulously sculpted the performances of many youthful or untrained actresses, he could neglect actors. His superior pose and his preference for medium and close shots over the master shots that gave performers their bearings in a scene could strain relations between director and actor. And if Hitchcock did not like an actor, he could prove alternately sarcastic and distant. In choosing an insecure male performer for "Edwards," Selznick planted seeds of tension.

Hitchcock found his leading lady a far more congenial selection. "She had so much go, so much temperament, so much fire that she was a joy to watch," European liaison Jenia Reissar had reported to Selznick after meeting the young Ingrid Bergman in Stockholm in fall 1938. "It's a dangerous statement to make, but I believe if Scarlett O'Hara were Swedish, Bergman would be fine for her!" Bergman had come to America with one suitcase and a freshness about her that startled Hollywood. Irene Selznick recalled taking her to an Elsa Maxwell party at the Beachcomber where Joan Bennett audibly cracked, "We have enough trouble getting jobs as it is. Do they have to import kitchen maids?"

Bergman finished *Intermezzo,* her first American film, just as Hitchcock began *Rebecca.* If she credited the astonishing performance of Joan Fontaine to Hitchcock, as even Selznick and Fontaine herself had, she must have been eager to work with the director. For more than three years, the Selznick story department had grappled with "the Hitchcock–Bergman problem," the attempt to pair the Brit and the Swede in a picture. *Dr. Edwards* solved it.

In personality and artistic temperament, Bergman may have been the ideal Hitchcock performer. Both artists adored food yet often dieted. Both were social yet could be coldly professional. Both shunned the Hollywood class system yet remained Brahmins. And both disliked their binding contracts yet honored them. ("The terms are unbelievable," Bergman said of her renegotiated employment agreement with Selznick in 1942. "It is absolute prison.") Hitchcock and Bergman realized themselves through their work. His witty authority and her luminous sensuality blossomed on the set. If Hitchcock yearned for Bergman (as one of his biographers has suggested), the roots of his affection must have been as much intellectual as romantic. "Plunge an English actress into a bath of cold water and she still comes to the top trying to look aloof and dignified," the director told a London reporter. "Her whole concern is not how best to express her emotions but how best to bottle them up." American performers, on the other hand, too often wore their libidos on their sleeves. Or their chests. "Don't point those things at me," the punch line to an instructive Hitchcock joke went, "they might go off." In Bergman, the director found the actress who could at once express yet contain strong feelings. She provided the warmth that a "cool" director like Hitchcock needed.

Since most studios would have considered the box office prospects of a "psychiatric story" marginal, Hitchcock would probably have been urged to cast accordingly. At MGM, *Edwards* might have starred Van Johnson and Greer Garson. At Warner, Ronald Reagan and Alexis Smith. At Paramount, Alan Ladd and Dorothy Lamour. Hitchcock knew how casting worked at the majors. Universal had originally slated Priscilla Lane and Robert Cummings for *Mermaid in Distress,* to be produced in October 1941 by Vaughn Paul. When Paul squabbled with company executives about his contract, the *Mermaid* foundered. The studio then "imposed" Lane and Cummings on Hitchcock for *Saboteur.* Selznick regarded actors as neither cattle nor salvage, and he rarely cast by default. His selection of Peck and Bergman moved a questionable story into the mainstream. With Peck and Bergman as insurance against box office doldrums, Hitchcock had more room for experimentation. Selznick paid the premium, Hitchcock became the beneficiary.

In casting the secondary role of a Green Manors psychiatrist named Fleurot, Hitchcock used Selznick contract player Kim Hunter as stand-in for Bergman. The director mesmerized the auditioning actors.

> Hitch talked to each of the men at length, giving them a gorgeously articulate, detailed description of who they were, what their character wanted, what was going on in the scene, what the whole film was about. . . . It couldn't have been clearer, more beautifully outlined. Most of the actors, however, were so nervous they heard perhaps a quarter of what he was saying. Then at the end of each magnificent offering to the actor, he'd turn to me and ask, "Do you agree, Miss Hunter? Do you think

that's right?" I think he took an evil pleasure in seeing me blush scarlet and stammer some inanity in reply. He teased me unmercifully. But it didn't for one minute accomplish what I presume he also had in mind, to put the chaps who were testing at ease. At my expense, of course. It just made them more frightened.

Hitchcock responded to physiognomy and talent. He chose John Emery as Fleurot, Michael Chekhov as Brulov, and Leo G. Carroll as Dr. Murchison, the outgoing head of Green Manors. Emery's looks— mustache, slender figure, and loose limbs—had a certain dignity edged with bad intentions, an apt complement to the frigid Constance. Born in Petrograd, fifty-two-year-old Michael Chekhov had been trained at the Souvorine Dramatic School and subsequently acted and directed at the Second Moscow Art Theatre. Although he practiced what in America came to be called "the method," a studied approach to acting that Hitchcock abhorred, he proved an inspired selection as Brulov. He had the schmaltz to portray Constance's surrogate father and the strength to represent her mentor.

Casting Murchison involved a battle between Hitchcock and Selznick over characterization. When Selznick ordered Hecht to add a Murchison–"Edwards"–Constance love triangle, technical advisor May Romm supported the producer. "The argument that Murchison betrays a more than platonic interest in Constance, and that this is unlikely in a man in his late fifties, is not so. As you know, it is fairly common, and particularly in physicians." But Hecht and Hitchcock regarded the amorous complication as "a mistake." Several actors agreed. Fredric March "indignantly refused the role" of Murchison; Ralph Bellamy and Alan Napier tested, but Bellamy also turned down the part and Napier seemed unsuitable. Forced to sacrifice his "romantic red herring," Selznick permitted Hitchcock to cast his favorite character actor as Murchison. The cocker-spaniel jowls and earnest yet blank expression of Leo G. Carroll ideally suited the champion of "negative acting."

The artist who generated the most notoriety never appeared on screen. To design a dream sequence originated by Hitchcock and Hecht, Hitchcock urged Selznick to commission Salvador Dali. Selznick "probably thought I wanted [Dali's] collaboration for publicity purposes," Hitchcock later said. "The real reason was that I wanted to

Two Selznick contract artists:
Bergman and Hitchcock.

Freud with two accents: Swedish (Bergman) and Russian (Michael Chekhov). Selznick demande[d]
clarity. In mid-July 1944, he told his casting director that the *Spellbound* company had had [a]
costly delay on the set "as a result of having an actor with an accent when we didn't want anoth[er]
doctor with an accent. I don't understand why the part was re-cast without checking with me.[”]

convey the dreams with great visual sharpness and clarity, sharper than the film itself." Boldly self-conscious, Dali placed distinct "things" in aspatial or atemporal contexts, much as Hitchcock often placed his characters (and actors) among "things" in an alienating environment. Yet like Dali, Hitchcock also understood the dual value of art objects. In Hollywood, where the assets went home after five, Hitchcock regarded Dali as a capital investment likely to appreciate.

With approval from Selznick, Hitchcock and Dali met in summer 1944. As Dali thought the matter over, so did Selznick. The surrealist eventually asked $5,000 (a sum far in excess of the value of the dream sequence to the picture, Selznick felt), but the question involved more than salary. With a sense of his greatest years possibly behind him, Selznick no longer courted risk. He had gambled both on and off the lot during the years of Selznick International. He played high-stakes gin with Myron, Zanuck, and others; he bet on everything from Ping-Pong games and horse races to the popular standing of an actor or the gross receipts of a picture. When RKO released *Citizen Kane,* he bet Jock Whitney that "they'll have one hell of a time trying to break even." He won. By 1944, though, Myron had died and David had entered middle age; gambling inside the studio lost its edge. Selznick thus had personal and professional reasons for inviting pollsters to evaluate his production decisions on *Edwards.* What they told him hardly brought a Dali–Selznick contract.

George Gallup and Audience Research had discovered in June "a pronounced variation by size of community so far as [the *Dr. Edwards*] subject matter is concerned. 'THE HOUSE OF DR. EDWARDS' thus appears to be definitely a story for urban movie-goers." The data confirmed what Selznick already knew: the Selznick–Hitchcock film would play best in large cities. Yet although United Artists, Selznick's distributor, had neither the sales force nor the apparent interest to wring stacks of dimes and quarters from thousands of small-town exhibitors, such markets could not be written off. The question became: Would the stix nix the flamboyant Dali?

A celebrated fixture in American high culture, Dali's surrealism might communicate "inaccessibility" to those who, according to Audience Research, found the story of *Dr. Edwards* "too grim." Selznick's publicity department also demurred. Despite the fresh promotional angle that the artist's work would provide, a Selznick flack wondered whether "Dali's Phallic frescoes would be nice in juxtaposition with our Christmas tree, Miss Bergman. We would, of course, get kicks against the pricks from the Holy Men [probably a reference to the Legion of Decency or other pressure groups], who are undoubtedly convinced by now that Mr. Dali is a very unsavory character." Selznick continued to ponder the imponderables. Would Dali antagonize filmgoers? Create censorship problems? Shove "bits of business and tricks" into the crevices of the *Edwards* dream sequence? As Selznick vacillated, Hitchcock persevered.

Badgered and perhaps influenced by Hitchcock, Selznick opened negotiations with Dali. The artist dropped his price to $4,000 and, with the promise of a contract, headed for the drawing board. Far from blind to the "publicity purposes" of his Hollywood labors, Dali elaborated lavish production plans at least partially conceived to aggrandize himself. When Hitchcock endorsed them, art director "Calamity" James Basevi translated the Dali designs into cold cash. The $150,000 figure so shocked Selznick that he threatened to cancel the dream sequence altogether. Still sensitive to accusations of his profligacy and anxious to rescue the pending Dali contract, the director hastily painted himself into a fiscal corner by assuring his producer that with miniatures and rear projections he could effect the Dali drawings for only $20,000. At this minimal cost, Selznick could authorize the dream sequence but not obligate himself to use it. The producer gave his approval, Dali was signed, and *Dr. Edwards* had its "Phallic frescoes."

"Producers and what they do with scripts is like a chef making soup," a dialogue coach on *Gone With the Wind* observed. "The chef gets an idea from a soup he ate. He spends days making a stock that is just right. He tastes, adds seasonings, tastes again, adds again. Then he does more things to it until he has the finest soup in the universe. Whereupon, he calls in other chefs and they all stand around and pee in it!" After Hecht completed his speedy revision of *Dr. Edwards,* many—including Selznick—whipped out their blue pencils. Ingrid Bergman asked that the motivation for Constance's falling in love with "Edwards" be strengthened, especially since "she has been untouched by the other gents who are attracted to her." The English censors asked that the opening montage avoid the impression of a madhouse. Dore

James Basevi (left) would create the sets for the dream sequence that Salvador Dali (right) designed. Basevi had been an architect before going to Hollywood in the 1930s. After creating the storm in *The Hurricane*, the earthquake in *San Francisco*, and the plague of locusts in *The Good Earth*, he would find Dali's "phallic frescoes" relatively simple.

Schary, then employed by Selznick, asked that the love scenes strain less. May Romm asked for numerous technical corrections. And Joe Breen and the Production Code Administration had a short laundry list of troublesome areas.

Based on a first reading of the script, the Production Code Administration approved the basic story of *Dr. Edwards* yet recommended that Selznick consult with both the British Board of Censors (which presumably "refused to license pictures dealing with lunatic asylums, or with insane people") and the Federal Bureau of Investigation (one of the men pursuing "Edwards" was an agent) to insure that the completed film would not run afoul of its various supra-audiences. Selznick had no quarrel with these suggestions, for Hollywood always solicited open markets and Washington friendships. But for itself, the PCA also desired a little more superego, a little less id. "Please take care to avoid any characterization of Miss Carmichael [a patient] as a woman sexually obsessed, or anything bordering on nymphomania," Breen wrote to Selznick in June 1944; "such a flavor could not be approved under any circumstances." Breen also called for the deletion of a number of words—*tomcat, lecherous, libido,* and *frustrations*—as well as the wisecrack about "the *mating* of two psychoanalysts." Moreover, "Edwards" and Constance were to behave as patient and doctor, not husband and wife; their relationship should not bear the "flavor of sex." Ribaldry had its place but not in American film: "Please change the line 'Darling, what do you think goes on on a honeymoon—cannibalism?' "

Perhaps because he had tailored his earlier pictures to fit the more stringent requirements of the British censors (or because he disliked confrontation), Hitchcock quietly bowed to censorship changes. Not Selznick. "I have no fears of Mr. Breen," the producer told story editor Margaret McDonell, "and I am itching to get at his favoritisms and fight them out once and for all." The Motion Picture Association, if not its offspring, the Production Code Administration, may have discriminated against independents; especially after 1942, Breen resisted all films with even marginally controversial subjects. "He may act petty czar with others," Selznick fumed, "but he is not going to do it with me if I have to take the whole damn Code to court," an action that many producers contemplated yet out of self-protection never took. Within days, Selznick cooled off. Success lay in diplomacy, not brinkmanship. Selznick wisely appointed the reluctant Hitchcock his agent. Meet personally with Breen, Selznick asked Hitchcock, and convince him that *Dr. Edwards* is "no cheap titillating sex subject," but a serious attempt to educate the public about what *Fortune* magazine had called America's number-one postwar problem. Happily for Hitchcock, Breen delegated much of his work in summer 1944 to his less irascible and more liberal lieutenant, Geoffrey Shurlock. The changeover, McDonell told Selznick, "is a great relief to us all."

The withdrawal of Breen still left May Romm hovering over the soup. Romm and Hitchcock shared a wry sense of humor. Asked to supply some "psychiatric bits" for the opening montage, Romm suggested a manic patient at a writing desk "littered with pages of closely written script. . . . He writes furiously with incredible speed, and apparent indefatigability. NOTE: MANICS WRITE LETTERS BY THE HUNDREDS SOMETIMES WRITING THROUGH SEVERAL DAYS AND NIGHTS TIRELESSLY, UNTIL THEY FALL INTO A COMA OF EXHAUSTION." Could the inveterate memo writer David Selznick have been her model? (Only preview audiences could judge; before the final release, Selznick trimmed the introductory montage from the picture.) Though Romm meddled less than Hecht may have anticipated, Selznick endorsed virtually all her recommendations. "For God's sake," she told Hecht of a Brulov dialogue tag, "leave out the 'Aha!' " Selznick ordered the cliché cut. Constance and "Edwards" dancing in a dream, Romm told Selznick, "is a symbol of sexual intercourse. Is that what you wish?" Selznick ordered the scene cut. The deletion wounded Hitchcock more than the narrative. Had the director met with Romm, as Hecht and Bergman had, he might have scored more story points. Yet he apparently avoided her.

Perhaps Hitchcock feared that Romm's logic would impede his intuition. Perhaps he regarded psychoanalysis as just one more gimmick peripheral to the real work of telling a story on film. Or perhaps, a very private person, he did not wish to reveal even so much as his professional life to a professional analyst. Romm nonetheless significantly improved the script. She supplied both logical motivation for each character and nontechnical but accurate names for emotional disorders; she provided truth and facts about psychoanalysis. Not everyone within the psychiatric community would hail the script, yet thanks to Romm few would condemn it. Though Selznick shared credit with Romm for the authenticity of *Edwards,* the director who resented some of her decisions again became the real beneficiary.

Hecht completed *Dr. Edwards* by August 1944. The varied collaboration had produced a shooting script at once serious and commercial. The major plot points would remain unchanged in the finished picture, from the romance between Constance and the amnesiac "Edwards" to the flight from Green Manors, the assistance of Brulov in interpreting the dream, and the climax. Director and producer deserved joint credit for the exciting final moments of *Edwards.* Hitchcock and MacPhail had originated the suspenseful downhill run that threatened Constance but unblocked "Edwards," while Selznick had pushed Hecht to devise the confrontation between Constance and Murchison, the head of Green Manors. The fact that Constance used science and psychology to expose Murchison as Edwards's killer, when common sense had already led audiences to accuse him, perhaps diminished the worth of psychoanalysis, but made for powerful cinema.

Selznick liked *Edwards.* The tony setting, the affair between doctor and patient, and the standoff between Constance and Murchison provided strong screen values, as did the polished dialogue and strongly drawn characters. "I can't think of any other writer alive who could have done this particular job with anything like the quality we have secured," the producer said of Hecht. Hitchcock also liked *Edwards.* The provocative visual imagery, particularly the associative links between white and the hero's "guilt complex," would demonstrate a sophistication in Hitchcock that audiences had not seen since *Rebecca* and *Shadow of a Doubt.* As the director prepared to enter production, he tucked under his arm one of the best—and most "Hitchcockian"— screenplays of his career.

"What makes Hitchcock so important," Selznick had remarked in 1937, "is that he is a producer as well as a director actually." The years between 1937 and 1944 had demonstrated even to Selznick that Hitchcock could capably produce films in America. Like Selznick, Hitchcock could negotiate with the Production Code Administration, formulate budgets and shooting schedules, supervise departments, and cut film. Despite his mixed track record, critically and commercially, he brought both fiscal conservatism and artistic largesse to the Universal pictures.

Selznick knew that Hitchcock wished to exert greater control over the final product; he had granted Hecht and Hitchcock their New York sojourn in part because he recognized the director's need for freedom. Yet although Selznick wanted to distance himself from the production process, he found total withdrawal impossible. Even after hiring Dore Schary exclusively as a producer, Selznick often retraced Schary's steps on *I'll Be Seeing You.*

Selznick could hardly expect Hitchcock to renew an employment agreement that would limit his control as a filmmaker. But the tiff over the "murder mystery angle" and the shocking Dali figures reminded Selznick anew of what happened when he left Hitchcock alone. Selznick effected a compromise: he delegated certain responsibilities as producer to Hitchcock, then shadowed him. Confusion bloomed in late spring. Margaret McDonell raised the question of an *Edwards* technical advisor with Selznick in May, yet wondered, "Am I correct in communicating with you on these matters rather than Mr. Hitchcock?" A month later, when Romm had been hired as technical advisor, McDonell did not know whether to send the psychiatrist's comments on the script "to you . . . or Alfred Hitchcock, or jointly." When McDonell began forwarding the reports to Selznick, she and her employer clipped some directorial wings. The opportunity for an amicable Romm–Hitchcock relationship may have ended here.

Observed Hitchcock: "One day that great producer David Selznick said to me about that great producer [Irving] Thalberg, 'He's wonderful with a finished picture.' He should have said, 'What's he like with it before it's being shot?'" With Selznick never far away, Hitchcock began his meticulous planning. He conferred with art director James Basevi, editor William Ziegler, and cinematographer George Barnes, all of whom would collaborate on the storyboards, the small, rough drawings of each composition in the film. Some of his colleagues have said that Hitchcock drew everything prior to the beginning of principal photography (a practice not unknown in Hollywood), while others recall that he hastily sketched a setup just prior to shooting it. On *Edwards,* numerous screen directions had been included in the script, so in certain cases—for instance, the celebrated razor sequence at Brulov's—the screenplay fully detailed the placement of camera, performers, and even lights. Hitchcock relished the management of verbal and visual pre-production details.

While artists and craftsmen built the sets, Hitchcock supervised the wardrobe design, for the things that draped a character interested him. Selznick often asked actresses to model their outfits for him in his office; Hitchcock occasionally took them shopping. At a place like Green Manors, the studio researcher told Hitchcock, the patients would dress comfortably, in anything from lounging clothes to suits for women and from sweaters to sports jackets for men. Illustrated brochures from the Hartford Retreat as well as the Hitchcock and Hecht visits to several such institutions in the East supported the point. For the dream sequence, however, the director planned to break away from the monotony of straight fashion. Ingrid Bergman, more specifically, was to slip out of the severe business suits she had worn throughout the film and into a blond wig, a white saronglike evening gown, and a gold choker that resembled a well-tended dog's collar. Playing couturier to Joan Fontaine and Ingrid Bergman satisfied the Pygmalion in Hitchcock; because Selznick heralded the commercial and aesthetic rewards of glamor, the director could here indulge himself and please his employer.

Edwards at last seemed ready for the camera. Much had changed in the five years since pre-production setbacks on *Rebecca.* A long war was nearly over, and the studios and the public seemed ready to confront something besides death at the battleground and life on the homefront. The six-month gestation of the *Edwards* screenplay had resulted in what reviewer Bosley Crowther later called "some notably fine writing and construction"; the film had been cast quickly and reasonably well. Except for the usual tension between producer and director, the path to production had been smooth.

When Hitchcock proposed a budget for *Edwards,* however, he shattered the pre-production calm. To Hitchcock, the fifty-seven-day shooting schedule and $1.25 million estimated cost seemed fair, especially given the tendency of the producer to tinker with the script throughout the period of principal photography. To Selznick, though, the figures seemed dangerously inflated. Selznick promoted his films by invoking his record of distinguished motion pictures, several of which had enjoyed successful rerelease. But investors ranked fiscal responsibility over prestige. Although studios rarely defaulted on loans during and immediately after the war, the failure to set judicious budgets and subsequently to monitor costs damaged a producer's relationship with

Much of the footage shot for the dream sequence fell to the cutting room floor, including moments when Bergman appeared in costume.

his most discriminating audience, the bank. As Hitchcock prepared the *Edwards* figures, Selznick was completing *Since You Went Away,* whose $1.5 million original budget had doubled. The producer needed the economy of *Shadow of a Doubt;* the director gave him the prodigality of *Lifeboat.*

Was Hitchcock manipulating him? The quick revision downward of the dream sequence budget had confirmed the great slack in an earlier estimate. Increasingly in the 1940s, Selznick believed that production personnel as well as attorneys, physicians, and others outside the studio exploited him. Although he took issue with many of them, his presumed wealth as the producer of *Gone With the Wind,* along with his managerial style, left him vulnerable to gouging. The runaway finances of Selznick Productions began with Selznick himself; on *Since You Went Away,* his characteristic involvement with the production had swelled both shooting schedule and expenses. But he insisted that *Edwards* constituted a small production. Short script, competent cast, simple physical action and sets. Hitchcock could make it reasonably, or not at all: "I would much rather face the music now and abandon the Hitchcock picture if it is going to cost too much or if we are so poorly organized that we can't get an accurate estimate that can be depended on." Canceling *Edwards* with over $150,000 spent on the screenplay and considerably more committed to sets and actors would have been injudicious, but *threatening* to cancel the picture—as Zanuck had done with *Lifeboat*—might sober a capricious Hitchcock.

Was Selznick manipulating him? the director wondered. Although Selznick and Hitchcock agreed upon the necessity of economical film production, a tapered shooting schedule pinched the Englishman's ample frame. Directing pictures required the ability to provide instruction for a score of artists and technicians prior to each run of the camera; directing them well required the time to provide instruction imaginatively. No "One-Take Woody" (the nickname given Metro's speedshooting director W. S. Van Dyke), Hitchcock moved deliberately, achieving remarkable lighting and photographic effects. His calm assurance inspired confidence and bred a certain efficiency. A conservative estimate of fifty-seven days, he perhaps thought, might even move the company ahead of schedule, thus enhancing efficiency. But Selznick controlled the purse, which in turn controlled the clock. After a period of negotiation, Hitchcock shaved his figures. Principal photography could at last begin.

On July 10, with Ingrid Bergman celebrating her seventh wedding anniversary to dentist-turned-physician Petter Lindstrom, Hitchcock began shooting *Edwards,* largely in sequence. The director arrived promptly at nine, took his first shot within the hour, and eight setups later had completed almost three minutes of usable film; he barely found time to rib Bergman. The first scene featured the Swedish actress and Rhonda Fleming, whom Selznick had borrowed from Fox and cast as a nymphomaniacal patient. Between takes, the still photographer snapped shots of Fleming provocatively stretched and preened upon a couch. The young Selznick had quit Metro because of a dispute with producer Hunt Stromberg over *White Shadows in the South Seas:* "David thought it an idyllic story," Irene recalled; "Hunt said he wanted lots of tits." Seventeen years later, the Production Code notwithstanding, Selznick yielded to the public clamor for full-figured pinups. The director who could not "stand those women who wear their sex around their neck like baubles" had other uses for Fleming. When the male attendant delivers Virginia to her analyst, Constance Petersen, she scratches him. The bleeding lines down his hand subtly foreshadow the grooved white figure that haunts "Edwards." The juices flowing, Hitchcock quit work at 6:30—almost a quarter day ahead of schedule.

Edwards never fell behind. Though Selznick gave his life's blood to a picture, Marcella Rabwin felt that "he also took the life's blood out of everybody who had anything to do with it." But Hitchcock "was the most thoughtful person. He was charming, he was nice, and he closed the set on time." By the end of the first week, *Edwards* had advanced two days ahead of schedule; by the end of the second, three days ahead. Hitchcock averaged seven setups and just over three minutes of completed film daily. Unlike some of his colleagues who did not speak "cinema," Hitchcock knew the function and technical name of lights and lenses; in only minutes, he could telegraph directions to a crew. He used a similar shorthand—strong on externals, weak on rationale—with his actors. "The next shot, Norman," he reportedly told Norman Lloyd, who portrayed an inmate named Garmes, "will be a close-up of you in a sweat. Please start sweating now." Cameras came equipped

149

The nymphomaniac patient Mary Carmichael (Rhonda Fleming) has just scratched Harry (Donald Curtis) when she enters Dr. Petersen's office.

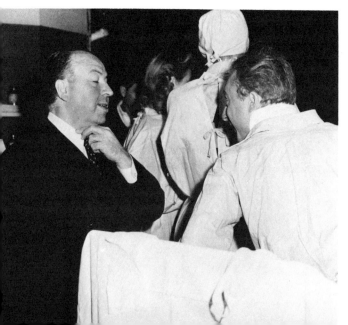

Hitchcock directing Norman Lloyd: "Please start sweating now."

with twenty-one-millimeter lenses, performers with beads of perspiration. Did one thing differ substantially from the other?

" 'You just behave as you normally would,' " Hitchcock told some puzzled extras assembled to shoot the introductory montage; he then walked away, Frank Nugent reported, "leaving them staring suspiciously at one another." Though actresses commanded more of his attention than actors, Hitchcock could be maddeningly terse with both. From the language of *action*—"walk to here" or "take her hand there"—Hitchcock expected the performer to assume the aspect of *being*. The director apparently felt that intellectual analysis of motivation stifled the subconscious and diluted the emotion. According to Norman Lloyd, Hitchcock used the actor as "a figure in a story, so if he told you to look to the right or look to the left, this was part of how he was telling a story. 'Don't worry about your performance so much, just do it, and you'll be fine.' " Bergman had doubts. Early on, Hitchcock blocked a scene around a desk. Bergman questioned the movement, Hitchcock evaded. "But why do I . . ." Bergman persisted. Hitchcock "just waited until she saw it [his] way," Lloyd recalled, "and that's the way it was done." Later when Bergman told Hitchcock that she felt uncomfortable with a line of dialogue, he provided succinct advice: "Fake it." The sardonic humor of his work ethic—"it's only a moo-vie"—amused Bergman and ended all discussion.

Gregory Peck seemed less persuaded. Theatrical and screen acting, as Peck would learn, differed considerably. Onstage, the actor disappears into the character; on film, the character disappears into the persona of the star: whereas Othello transcends Burbage, Garrick, and Olivier, "James Stewart" outlasts his every part. Drawing upon *Adam Had Four Sons, Dr. Jekyll and Mr. Hyde,* and *Casablanca,* Bergman could "fake" Constance Petersen. But *The Keys of the Kingdom* opened no doors for Peck. His work with the Stanislavsky system and the Group Theatre in New York had emphasized movement from internals to externals. When Hitchcock switched the order, Peck felt stripped, for he lacked the screen persona that would free the director to concentrate on externals. Since he could not merge the "Edwards" role with a nonexistent "Peck" persona, he could only "act" rather than "be" the romantic amnesiac.

"I felt I needed a good deal of direction," Peck later said, but when he asked for assistance, Hitchcock offered only his theory of "negative acting." "My dear boy," the Englishman replied in answer to a question about motivation, "I couldn't care less what you're thinking. Just let your face drain of all expression." A director more sympathetic to male actors and the shaping of cinematic masks (say Howard Hawks) might have helped Peck mediate between his inexperience and the demands of the part. Hitchcock declined. Although he and Peck exchanged pleasantries on and off the set, the former Berkeley athlete sensed the lack of support from his director. Selznick might have improved matters by leaning on Hitchcock to meet Peck halfway, but the producer attended more to the actor's appearance (particularly the shade of his beard) than his performance. Meanwhile, as Peck considered the suppressed anger and deep passion of "Edwards," yet reflected on the parentheses imposed on his interpretation, his confidence slowly ebbed.

Hitchcock shot *Edwards* faster than *Rebecca* and almost as fast as *Saboteur* and *Shadow of a Doubt.* He rarely rehearsed a sequence through or filmed the equivalent master scene, the shot that allows actors to perform the action from beginning to end; when he used long takes, the actors adjusted to the moving camera rather than vice versa. The pace suited Bergman, slow of study but once rehearsed, eager to go. The normally relaxed Peck felt rushed. Hitchcock "liked his actors and movements to be as much under his control as the camera movement or the props or the scenery," Peck said, but "my soul-searching and my lack of ready technique" tested his patience. Treated like things, actors broke down. A pull-back dolly shot of Constance and "Edwards" walking toward the train that would take them to Brulov's house required sixteen takes, as did a moment later in the film when "Edwards" awakens on Brulov's couch following his drug-induced sleep. These shots, which ultimately consumed less than two minutes of screen time, required almost three hours to photograph. Matching live action to rear screen necessitated some of the repeated takes on the train platform, but Peck caused others. Truffaut later called the actor "shallow," with "a lack of expression in his eyes." Less "drainage" in the direction might have deepened the performance.

Selznick passed the early weeks of *Edwards* contemplating the mixed reviews of *Since You Went Away.* Although *Time* hailed its "taste, shrewdness, superiority, [and] life," others found it glossy, sentimental, and overlong. Selznick dismissed the criticism, yet soon realized that the prestige and grosses of *Gone With the Wind* would easily tower over

those of *Since You Went Away.* The personal disappointment almost outweighed the professional, for Selznick had put himself fully into the picture: its props even included a bronzed baby shoe from his home and a published poem written to mark Danny Selznick's birth. These sentimental touches aside, Irene and David Selznick had loosened the bonds of matrimony. She grew tired of playing "my husband's keeper"; he became romantically involved with Jennifer Jones. Selznick might have hoped that *Since You Went Away* would mark a joint triumph for the actress and the man who discovered her, perhaps increase her esteem for him. But their first collaboration fell short of success. While Hitchcock shot *Edwards,* Selznick reluctantly decided to trim the "overlong" *Since You Went Away* for general release.

Preoccupied with *Since You Went Away* and out of Hollywood much of the summer, Selznick left *Edwards* to Hitchcock; when he visited the set, Ingrid Bergman recalled, the director simply stopped the camera, announced "a mechanical fault," and shut down production. "I think Hitchcock was the only director who was independent of Selznick," Bergman said; "he wouldn't stand for the notes." Although the producer still intimidated his director, Hitchcock drew strength from the contract negotiations that had begun in summer 1944. Selznick and Hitchcock still needed each other, but Selznick *wanted* Hitchcock more than Hitchcock wanted Selznick. Previously that year, the director had even conferred over lunch with Alex Ardrey and other Bankers Trust vice-presidents in New York about his future in independent production, and Selznick had heard rumors "of a deal pending in England . . . to take effect after the war." The balance of power thus favored Hitchcock.

Free of direct supervision (Selznick monitored the rushes), Hitchcock shot accomplished footage with notable economy; after all, should he not re-sign with Selznick, the director wanted to position himself attractively in the Hollywood marketplace. *Edwards* had engaged him from the beginning, yet planning and shooting the nonverbal scenes energized him. From Saturday, August 5, to Tuesday, August 8, Hitchcock photographed one of his most famous sequences, "Edwards" and the razor. This montage defined "Hitchcockian." Breen and the Production Code Administration, fixated on the "sex suggestiveness" of Constance and "Edwards" sharing the Brulov guest room, had left the razor sequence largely undisturbed. Today, its redolent sexuality seems almost too obvious. The brush in the shaving cream and the open straight razor carried at the waist suggest Freudian symbols of female and male genitalia; the porcelain bathroom fixtures and the moonlight falling across the sleeping Constance add sensual grace notes. In sequences like these, Hitchcock exhibited not only enormous control but freshness and imagination.

A second production unit, working under instructions from Hitchcock, photographed shots of the bathroom chair, basin, commode, and tub; the director himself filmed the inserts involving Peck, including a close-up of his mixing the lather in the shaving cup. Next came the heart of the scene. "Edwards" looks menacingly at the sleeping Constance, then walks downstairs. When he nears the bottom step, he stops so that his hand and the open razor are in close-up (three takes, each of which demanded that the actor subordinate his movement precisely to the placement of the camera). Cut. Brulov rises from his desk to get "Edwards" a glass of milk. The camera pans from right to left, following Brulov into the kitchen but stopping so that the razor again appears in close-up in the left foreground (five takes). Cut. "Edwards" accepts the milk as Brulov returns to his desk (three takes). "Edwards" drinks. Lining up the "trick shot" close-up through the raised glass required over an hour, rehearsing it forty-five minutes, and shooting it one and one-quarter hours. Although the shot lasts only a few seconds on screen, the irony justified the multiple takes. "Edwards" and the razor seem the assailants, Brulov the victim. Only after "Edwards" drinks the milk, containing a sedative, does Hitchcock reveal that he has switched the roles of assailant and victim. The Englishman controlled more than actors and props. He controlled audiences.

Time later criticized Peck's "dazed somnambulism"; Hitchcock's preference for "things," however, denied the actor, any actor, a sense of context. Portraying a stunned, then drugged, man, Peck found himself playing against inserts of gleaming bathroom fixtures (as would Janet Leigh in *Psycho*) or holding a prop steady for the camera (as dozens of actors in television commercials would do). On technically complicated shots, the director's control increases, the performer's diminishes: in the razor/milk sequence, the lighting, the second production unit's close-ups, and the camera movement tended further to objectify the performer, yet another irony in a film about a man attempting to recover his lost humanity. The Brulov sequence thus belonged not to the "puppets," as Hitchcock called his actors, but to the puppeteer. Peck grew increasingly unhappy with his work in *Edwards,* and although he hesitated to blame Hitchcock (the "business and tricks" were marvelously evocative), he looked forward to the period of post-production and the opportunity to improve at least pieces of his performance through retakes and overdubbing.

At the end of four weeks of filming, the production was six days ahead of schedule. "I have seldom seen so smooth-running a crew, or as obviously efficient a company as the 'Dr. Edwardes' unit," Selznick told his production manager. With *Since You Went Away* complete and *Edwards* on course, Selznick considered his options. "David, in the days he loved movie making, was a brilliant plotter," Ben Hecht wrote in his autobiography, but Selznick now seemed to prize "tough trading" over pictures. After Myron's death in March 1944, Irene observed, "his deals grew more outrageous, I couldn't grasp what it was all about." To the detriment of a marriage he cared increasingly little about, he often transacted business in tense half-hour telephone conversations at the dinner table. Although the hard-nosed negotiations for contract renewals and new stars irritated Irene and even such close friends as Ingrid Bergman, they gave Hitchcock still more freedom on *Edwards.*

The director's momentum never flagged. When Hitchcock discovered a way to eliminate scenes in a police station and Constance's room, the production gained an entire day. By the seventh week, in late August, the company was filming the Lake Placid scenes, some of which used skiing doubles for Constance and "Edwards." (Neither Bergman nor Peck could ski; in the studio, they gamely jumped onto a pile of mattresses from a makeshift twenty-five-foot-high gypsum-and-cornflakes slope.) Technical problems with the ski lifts as well as "continual airplane motor interference" temporarily halted work but did not jeopardize the company's unhampered efficiency. Hitchcock retained his wit throughout. To discourage visitors, he communicated in his arcane cockney rhyming slang, where "relax" was "actual chopper" ("real axe") and a wife was a "storm" (from "storm-and-strife"). Finally, sailing into the end of his eight-week schedule, Hitchcock confronted the surrealist dream sequence.

Interpreters of the Dali sequence included Drs. Petersen and Brulov as well as Drs. Breen, Romm, and Hitchcock; their collaborative analysis nearly turned the "Edwards" dream into nightmare. Doublecast as a "kissing bug," Rhonda Fleming played a scantily dressed woman who flits about pecking men's cheeks. Breen eyed her suspiciously. She must be "more covered," he told Selznick; "there must be more rags around her midriff, considerably more rags to cover the inside of the left thigh, and . . . to cover the breasts properly." Hitchcock draped her, then turned to Romm. The sexual symbolism overlooked by the Production Code Administration bothered the psychoanalyst. Several inexplicable objects, including a sack of coal suspended from the ceiling of a ballroom, vaguely connoted genitalia, but a gigantic pair of pliers could only be phallic. They "might prevent whatever possible endorsement we might otherwise get from a psychiatric society," Romm warned Selznick. Just two weeks before, Karl Menninger had offered his friendly cooperation to the producer, but rumors reached the American Psychoanalytic Society headquartered in Detroit that "the psychoanalysts in this picture are represented as maladjusted persons, that an actual treatment situation is depicted incorrectly and that there are other effects which place psychoanalysis in an unfavorable light."

Hitchcock scoffed at public opinion and special interests. The National Creamery Buttermakers' Association had condemned *Foreign Correspondent* for showing people drinking milk and suggesting "that milk drinking is an object of ridicule." Hitchcock responded by associating milk with Mickey Finns in both *Suspicion* and *Edwards.* Psychiatrists carried no more weight than dairy farmers, Hitchcock believed, and he wanted no professionals turning the art of the dream sequence into a mere case study. But Selznick respected public opinion and pressure groups, especially the prominent men who influenced both. Money and privilege impressed him; he loved people who were important. Joan Fontaine said that he courted the Long Island social set and their notice. Though Romm could not confer status upon him, she could protect him from offending those who might. Hitchcock fought to retain some of the Dali imagery; the audience would follow the action, not the objects, he told Selznick. But fearing the wrath of the psychiatric community, Selznick yanked the gigantic phallic pliers.

Between the myriad cooks standing about the soup and the work of a second-unit director presumably supervised by Hitchcock, the dream sequence and its empty ballroom, speechless characters, stylized props, and raked angles barely jelled. Producer and director blamed each other. Selznick criticized "the photography, setups, lighting, et cetera,

Two scenes from the *Spellbound* dream sequence. It was designed by Dali to Hitchcockian specifications ("long shadows, infinity of distance, and converging lines of perspective"), but the finished sequence would please neither Selznick, nor Hitchcock, nor Dali.

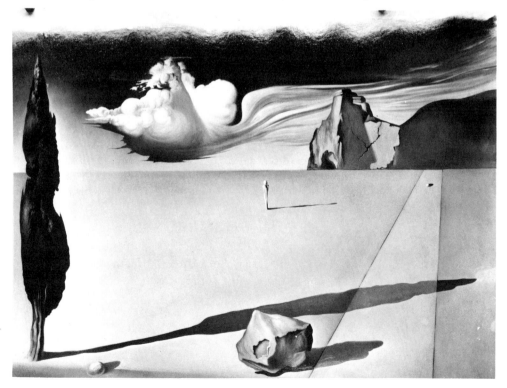

all of which are completely lacking in imagination and all of which are about what you would expect from Monogram," a studio on Hollywood's poverty row. Hitchcock maintained that Selznick's refusal to allow the sequence to be photographed outside deprived it of the "sharpness" of De Chirico, "the long shadows, the infinity of distance, and the converging lines of perspective." Yet responsibility for the deficiencies belonged chiefly to Hitchcock; after all, shooting *Nights of Cabiria* and *I Vitelloni* on Italian soundstages, Federico Fellini would manage to catch the essence of De Chirico. Hitchcock apparently wanted the Dali name more than he wanted the Dali images, for he often played against them. Constance and Brulov not only explicate the dream, assigning each object and action a meaning, but also pepper their explanation with humor. By diluting Dali with wit and popular psychology, Hitchcock raised the entertainment value of the film but compromised the dream sequence. "There's the constant pressure," he told a reporter. "You know: people asking, 'Do you want to reach only the audiences at the Little Carnegie or to have your pictures play the Music Hall?' So you compromise." The schism between the literal and the metaphoric—not the interference of Selznick—would become even more of a problem during post-production.

On the Saturday before Labor Day, seven and one-half days ahead of schedule, Hitchcock completed principal photography on *The House of Dr. Edwards*. Gregory Peck was still "very anxious to make loops and wild lines," Selznick learned, but the performances of Bergman and Michael Chekhov more than satisfied the producer. On the censorship front, Breen had only minor criticisms, and May Romm "found no technical inaccuracies, and approved the body of the film with whole hearted enthusiasm." The Motion Picture Division of the Office of War Information reviewed Darryl Zanuck's screen biography of Woodrow Wilson *(Wilson)* and Selznick's *Edwards* on the same day; both received high marks for their positive contributions to public opinion. *Edwards,* the OWI told Margaret McDonell, was especially important "because of the increasing significance of psychiatric treatment, particularly in relation to the problems of returning servicemen the world over." The social if not the entertainment value of the film had thus already enhanced the careers of producer and director. More important, Hitchcock had demonstrated to Selznick and (crucial after *Lifeboat*) to Hollywood a quantifiable efficiency. The length of the *Rebecca* and *Edwards* screenplays differed by less than a page, but there the similarity ended. Hitchcock used 617 setups on *Rebecca,* 382 on *Edwards,* as much a dramatic example of the economy of his preplanned "cutting-in-the-camera" as evidence of his movement toward longer shots. *Rebecca* was in production 63 days, *Edwards* 48; *Rebecca's* first cut ran 145 minutes, *Edwards's* 125. The quality of his work aside, these figures alone suggested Hitchcock's value to a studio and to David Selznick.

Although most directors in the American studio era routinely walked from the soundstage to their next film, independents like Stevens, Capra, and Hawks supervised the editing, the scoring, the design of the titles, and similar matters of post-production. Lacking their clout, Hitchcock and his peers controlled the final cut only through their producers' generosity or indifference. Selznick might relinquish the reins by invitation but not by default. Especially after the mixed reception of *Since You Went Away,* he wished *The House of Dr. Edwards* to succeed and relied on his own skill and aesthetic distance from the film to supply the necessary polish. Hitchcock had directed *Edwards,* Selznick would henceforth produce it. Yet Hitchcock protected his work far better than many of his more profligate colleagues. Directors who shot "around the clock," photographing a scene from every possible angle, left their producers numberless options; Hitchcock's "cutting-in-the-camera," unimpeded by Selznick on *Edwards,* gave his producer few opportunities to remake a film in post-production. Selznick could hijack *Edwards,* but except for the long dream sequence he could not materially change it.

Once *Edwards* moved into the House of Mr. Selznick, conflicts immediately arose. Despite Hitchcock's affection for it, Selznick considered *The House of Dr. Edwards* an unwieldy title. Testing *Edwards* against *The Couch* (posed as titles for two separate films), Audience Research discovered that filmgoers preferred the former by nearly 50 percent. Selznick wavered. A dispirited Hitchcock suggested *Hidden Impulse,* studio secretary Ruth Rickman offered *Spellbound.* Only a quarter of those moviegoers sampled in August responded favorably to *Hidden Impulse;* the rest liked *Edwards* and *Spellbound* equally well. " 'Edwards' persists in all these studies," Hitchcock argued, but Selznick remained incredulous. Demographics decided the issue. Men

160

preferred *Edwards* to *Spellbound* by a 15 percent margin, women preferred *Spellbound* to *Edwards* by 13 percent. Since women "bring men to the theatres much more than men bring women," Selznick reasoned, the title must appeal to women. Besides, Hitchcock's name would guarantee the film its "masculine appeal." Changing *Edwards* to *Spellbound* vexed Hitchcock, yet boosted the marquee value of the picture.

In preparation for the previews, retakes and looping (rerecording of dialogue) began in September; Hitchcock directed the former, Selznick the latter. The Englishman's loss of post-production control, along with the usual Selznick demand for endless retakes, translated into a loss of enthusiasm. In one important early scene, "Edwards" and Constance picnicked near Green Manors. The original footage lacked scenic beauty, a key (like music) to the developing romance between the couple. When Hitchcock reshot the sequence—Selznick believed—he worsened it: "The location was such that when Miss Bergman looks off and talks about how lovely the place is we haven't the remotest notion of what she is talking about nor any idea as to why she thinks it is so lovely when clearly it is just a lot of barren California hills." Selznick cut around the pictorial weakness to achieve what he called more "mogo on the gogo." Still more acute problems emerged during the looping sessions that changed or improved line readings. Although Selznick had virtually taught Hollywood how to rerecord dialogue, MGM and Goldwyn had long since surpassed him. Selznick labored with Peck over many individual aural retakes, but inaccurate synchronization and improper sound engineering made the work unusable. His speech remained the speech as Hitchcock had directed it on the set.

If Hitchcock dozed through retakes of a principal love scene (the picnic), he roused himself for murder. At the climax of *Spellbound*, Constance returns to Green Manors to confront Murchison. Practicing psychology on a psychiatrist, she tells Murchison that his killing Edwards was the act of an insane man, whereas killing her would be "cold, deliberate murder." Hitchcock quickened the sequence with his dynamic shot composition. Murchison holds Constance at gunpoint, the revolver in extreme close-up in the foreground, Constance in the background. Again, the "thing" dominates the people. The Hitchcock strategy: "Constance rises, walks R., gun, mounted on free head follows her, CAMERA panning with Constance to door, keeping gun in f.g. CON-

STANCE exit o.s.R, closing door behind her. CAMERA stays on gun as it turns slowly R-L and fires into CAMERA." Audiences had been blasted before: in the postlude of the 1903 *Great Train Robbery,* a cowboy fired his gun directly at the lens. In *Spellbound,* Hitchcock punished not only Murchison and the audience, but the actors. On September 22, Ingrid Bergman and Leo G. Carroll spent the morning retaking this complicated shot. It required combining photography on the set and hand coloring of four frames of film (to yield a sixth-of-a-second explosion of red on screen) with two offstage stunt and rear-projection shots; it also demanded that the actors subordinate themselves in movement and scale to an object. Victimized by technical problems, the sequence required thirty takes to complete.

On September 27, 1944, Selznick and Hitchcock nervously previewed *Spellbound.* The print was riddled with splices; the music not yet composed, much less laid in; the dream sequence in disarray, lengthy and too literal; and the film itself too long by at least ten, even fifteen minutes. Jaded southern California preview audiences could opt for the jugular, often from the fade-in of the studio logo. But like the MGM lion and the Paramount summit, the colonnaded administration building that stood for David O. Selznick Productions often sparked a buzz of happy anticipation. The picture let down few moviegoers. Although reaction to Bergman and (slightly less so) Peck was enthusiastic, respondents lauded Michael Chekhov as Brulov: "He stole the picture." Those who demanded only entertainment were pleased: "Bit off all my fingernails," one moviegoer wrote. Four others praised the film for its "timely subject, worthwhile because of importance psychology will play after war."

But not everything pleased everybody. The introductory montage, with its realistic footage of hot and icy water cures and insulin treatments, provoked comment. The sequence reflected as much a review of contemporary psychiatric practices as a Hitchcockian interest in "things" and how they worked. Hitchcock had yielded to the documentary impulse in *Blackmail* and would again in *The Wrong Man* (1956); he once contemplated abandoning fiction for a straightforward motion picture about food, from distribution to preparation.

The end of the film would show the sewers, and the garbage being dumped out into the ocean. So there's a cycle, beginning with the gleam-

162

ing fresh vegetables and ending with the mess that's poured into the sewers. Thematically, the cycle would show what people do to good things.

The Green Manors montage would show what things did to people. After thumbing through preview cards that criticized the sequence, though, Selznick decided to cut all of it. Unlike the skeptical Hitchcock, he respected public opinion. He may also have sensed that the documentary footage lengthened an already slow exposition. "It takes too long to get into the meat of the picture," production executive George Schaefer later advised Selznick; "the establishing of characters and motivation is much too long." The montage vanished, a brief explanatory foreword appeared. Though Hitchcock mourned the loss, Selznick improved the picture: electroshock treatments belonged more to such exposés as *The Snake Pit* than to *Spellbound*.

After falling on the opening, the Selznick machete advanced through the film. The producer retook individual shots to improve narrative clarity, dubbed individual lines to insure greater intelligibility, and trimmed the beginnings of shots to enhance the pacing. He retook the close-up of the attendant's scratched hand and strengthened the association of vertical lines with "Edwards"'s amnesia. "Brulov hard to hear," one moviegoer noted, "because of moustache." In responding, Selznick and editor Hal Kern turned this benevolent father figure from supporting to secondary character. Both Bergman and Chekhov spoke with accents, Chekhov's the stronger; Chekhov's speech often needed the close-up for the impact of his personable dialogue to register. Some three- and two-shots of Brulov, "Edwards," and Constance thus became close-ups of Brulov. As he congratulated the couple on their marriage, for example, he wished them "babies and not phobias." Selznick's switch from a three-shot to a close-up of Brulov gave the word *phobias* greater audibility and "visibility"; as a result, the line played better. Credit for Chekhov's Oscar nomination belonged at least partially to Selznick.

The aroma of film cement may have been a stimulant for Selznick. One evening he stayed up "until all hours with [director William] Dieterle and [producer Hal] Wallis recutting a good deal of [*Love Letters*]," a fact that he reported with exuberance, not irritation. Hal Kern, who cut *Gone With the Wind* as well as *Rebecca* and *Spellbound*, grew accustomed to having Selznick beside him throughout the period of post-production. Together, they ran scene after scene, trimming and supplementing here, interchanging and deleting there. According to Lydia Schiller, Selznick controlled the projector—not simply the projectionist—from the projection room and thus could stop the film on a single frame in order to mark the precise location of a cut. Hitchcock was also a formidable editor. But his method annoyed Selznick. "As somebody said," Selznick wrote in a memorandum to Hitchcock, dictated but not sent, " 'Hitchcock shoots like [Woody] Van Dyke—except that he gets one third as much film,' which means that you cut your film with your camera the way Van Dyke does but that he gets three times as much cut film per day."

Artistic differences between Selznick and Hitchcock naturally surfaced during post-production. The unsettling complexity of a Hitchcock picture grew from what Selznick called the director's "goddamn jigsaw cutting." On *Spellbound,* Hitchcock filmed the ski run climax in six setups. The last featured "Edwards" in profiled close-up. Wedged between a head-on close-up of Constance and a head-on two-shot of "Edwards" and Constance, the outré close-up would have violated the Hollywood rule of "invisible editing," the smooth movement from one shot or angle to another. Hitchcock intended subversion. He wanted the climactic shots to play against each other without harmonizing effect. But editor Selznick placed this odd piece in the Hitchcock puzzle immediately after a head-on shot of "Edwards" and thus minimized, even negated, its power to disrupt the established point of view and make us *feel* the hero's agitation. With the destabilizing effect neutralized, the action-montage sequence became conventional.

Between the evening of the preview and the day of his mid-autumn departure for London, Hitchcock spent only one day at the studio. After October 15, the film—and its ever-complicated dream analysis scenes—belonged to Selznick. William Cameron Menzies, the stalwart visual consultant on *Gone With the Wind,* worked briefly on the Dali sequence, but neither he nor studio art director James Basevi could effect anything superior to Hitchcock's original, much less the luminousness that Hitchcock had desired. The director had shot enough film to create a fifteen-minute sequence. He had animated things as correlatives to an agitated mind, as unassembled pieces to an elusive puzzle. From a seven of clubs to the proprietor of a casino, whose stocking-covered, mannequinlike face was more thing than human, the familiar but surrealistically rendered objects lent a sense of dislocation to the dream and the dreamer. "It was beautiful," Ingrid Bergman recalled. "We worked on it so much. That statue . . . my death mask was made and then this whole body of a statue. Then the body flew away, revealing the real woman underneath."

But the dream sequence would not "play." Although Selznick earnestly cabled and telephoned the absentee director for suggestions, Hitchcock provided little assistance beyond warning his producer against "the so often done montage *à la* Vorkapich." The frenetic, "cutty" style of the Slavic émigré was so long out of vogue in "A" pictures that Selznick may have regarded the advice as demeaning. Hemmed in by commitments to Dali, the producer began trimming the footage and trying to make the best of George Barnes's "strictly effect photography." The Selznick version privileged words over objects. A man approached a ledge, "Edwards" says in voice-over, recounting his dream. "Then he went over, slowly, with his feet in the air." The man falls, in long shot. "And then I saw the proprietor again, the man in the mask. He was hiding behind a tall chimney and he had a small wheel in his hand. I saw him drop the wheel on the roof." The heavy narration demotes the images to illustrations. Hitchcock's subjective shooting revealed *what* a character saw, his subjective editing demonstrated *how* he saw it. The Selznick version that trimmed more than ten minutes from the Hitchcock original realized neither what nor how. The distant Hitchcock proposed another glib solution: "Score entire seq."

Hitchcock had few original ideas about music. "Romantic music" here, a "love theme" there, he noted in some comments left for composer Miklós Rózsa. Hitchcock and Selznick nevertheless agreed that Rózsa should provide a "new sound" for the paranoia at the center of the film. Rózsa suggested scoring the razor/milk and other key sequences for orchestra and theremin, a forerunner of today's electronic instruments. Its high-pitched sounds were produced by a player's running his hands over two tuning rods; the closer the hands to the instrument, the more intense the vibrato and the volume of sound. "Hitchcock and Selznick hadn't heard of the theremin and weren't quite sure whether you ate it or took it for headaches," Rózsa said, "but they agreed to try it out." The promotional possibilities especially appealed to Selznick. Rózsa's *Jungle Book* score had sold fourteen thousand copies on 78 rpm; with luck, a *Spellbound* album might engage the imagination and unbutton the pocketbooks of filmgoers. Working with a rough cut of the film, Rózsa began scoring the film, liberally using the theremin.

Hitchcock "left the editing [of *Spellbound*] to me," Selznick later wrote. Guided by the Pasadena preview audience, which had probably seen something approaching a rough cut, Selznick eliminated about fourteen minutes from *Spellbound*. According to one biographer, Hitchcock found Selznick's action "galling." Still, much of the reduction undoubtedly came from tighter transitions between scenes, not (except for the documentary montage) wholesale deletions. And although the producer enhanced Michael Chekhov's performance and substantially altered the dream sequence, he sought the director's advice and approval. *Spellbound* remained vigorously "Hitchcockian." When the director requested not only possessory credit but also the appearance of his name above the title, Selznick obliged. The credits would read " 'Alfred Hitchcock's *Spellbound,* ' using 'Hitchcock' half the size of the title," the producer said, "solely and simply because I think he is entitled to it." The Hitchcock grievances persisted. The response to a second advance screening makes their source appear even more obscure.

With the Rózsa score complete, Selznick previewed *Spellbound* on February 16, 1945. Nearly 90 percent of those who returned the questionnaires called the film "outstanding" or "excellent." Although Bergman received an overwhelming share of the stars' praise, Peck's approval rating almost doubled. "Could take place of Van Johnson," one moviegoer scribbled. (Since the first preview, Fox had released *The Keys of the Kingdom,* which undoubtedly enhanced Peck's appeal in *Spellbound.*) Echoing an earlier respondent, someone said of Michael Chekhov, "He stole the show." Rhonda Fleming was "hot stuff," the picture itself "something for [the] mind to chew on," and the credit all the director's: wrote one Huntington Park patron, "Give Hitchcock his due." Ten persons objected to the "slow, boring" foreword, so the producer ordered it trimmed. One respondent found the background music "too loud"; Selznick ordered a new mix. Otherwise, *Spellbound* was ready for release. On February 22, even Joe Breen stamped his final approval upon it.

During the tottering Schaefer regime, RKO had accidentally released *Mr. and Mrs. Smith* on news stock rather than fine grain. Perhaps fearing a repetition of this embarrassment, Selznick gave exacting instructions to the lab "because I would consider it the height of folly to spend a fortune getting the best possible photography and lighting effects and often spending money on retakes that do not benefit us commercially to the extent of a dollar but are remade solely to maintain our reputation and my own standards of quality, and have all of this go to waste simply because New York or someone else out there doesn't understand our attitude on these questions." Unlike some of his peers, Selznick understood printing. Before he ordered new prints for *Rebecca*'s rerelease, he made extensive notes for the lab. "At door of cottage, Fontaine with dog: Shot of her in raincoat at door of cottage is too bright. All the mystery is lost. Panning up shot ought to be way down. Her subsequent CU should be printed down to match, in overcast quality." *Spellbound* had cost $1,696,377; happily for Hitchcock, Selznick intended to lose none of its production values in the lab.

What happened to *Spellbound* in the editing room ultimately concerned Hitchcock far less than what happened to it in the marketplace. Like all contract directors and even many independents, Hitchcock exercised no control over distribution and exhibition of his pictures. When Zanuck abandoned *Lifeboat,* Hitchcock could only grumble. Selznick and United Artists, an uncomfortable partnership, could not hope to match the distribution network, theater chains, and ample promotional departments of the majors, but neither could they afford the luxury of dumping the occasional picture with questionable box office prospects. The "psychiatric story," dramatizing the triumph of "modern science" over "the emotional problems of the sane," would require and receive careful selling. And however much Hitchcock resented the power and interference of Selznick, he trusted his showmanship. Given the producer's relentless drive, the cheering audience for *Spellbound* might even include bankers willing to finance an English director with a yen for independence.

Capturing an audience worried Selznick. According to pollster George Gallup, the general public had little idea of the content or even the existence of *Spellbound* only weeks before its scheduled release. With interest mounting on his production loans, another producer might have tossed the picture into theaters and hoped that Hitchcock and Bergman would counter the absence of "penetration" and gloomy predictions of "disaster." Selznick decided to postpone release until summer. As the release date approached, Selznick reviewed his promotional package. Print ads in *Vogue, Mademoiselle,* and other fashion magazines would feature Rhonda Fleming garbed in snake chain, pendant, and earrings standing next to a phallic statue; for the less sophisticated, a plane would skywrite "Spellbound" over Los Angeles. Bergman's 1944 Academy Award for *Gaslight* would strengthen her popular appeal, and at previews of *Spellbound* "the dames" were already " 'ohing' and 'ahing' and gurgling" over Peck. Almost as important as his stars, Hitchcock curled no bobbysox yet generated a buzz among filmgoers. Neither producer nor director disputed this point, which had already prolonged contract negotiations between them. While sharing "the name above the title" discomforted Selznick, he would not sacrifice the welfare of the picture to ego. "Critics and public already refer to him as Hitchcock with no Alfred," a Selznick publicity man had noted; "suggest we do same as we did Lubitsch as Hitchcock even bigger bo [box office]." Selznick complied. The ability of the Hitchcock name to attract male filmgoers increased the director's importance to a producer confronting "disaster": we must "exert extra pressure on all potential audiences," Selznick told his promotion department; "therefore, I think it behooves us to go after a man."

"May I say here," Don King, Selznick's director of advertising told his boss in early 1945, "that Mr. Hitchcock has been wonderfully helpful and cooperative and that all of us in the department are duly grateful for his attitude." A mixed blessing, Selznick thought. Like all producers, Selznick wished to manage the news flowing from his studio, especially to insure that reporters perceived his company not as a way station for independents but as an authentic studio. Once Hitchcock opened his office to the press, though, Selznick could not always shut it. The director's caustic wit, facetious anecdotes, and thumbnail lessons in cinema played well with reporters, and while a forthcoming picture usually occasioned their visits, the Englishman could deftly turn a conversation from his actors (his "cattle") or his patron (Selznick) to himself. Feature stories on *Spellbound* (a David O. Selznick production) somehow became feature stories on Hitchcock (distinctly *not* a David O. Selznick production). Ignoring Selznick delighted the impish Hitchcock, and eased his transition to independence. Since production loans partially hinged on stars, the director enhanced his appeal to the financial community by packaging himself as a celebrity capable not only of making but of selling his own films. Gregory Peck aimed for the cover of *Photoplay,* Hitchcock for the notice of Bankers Trust.

When long-running pictures kept many scheduled releases out of theaters in summer 1945, Selznick postponed the *Spellbound* opening until November 1. At a special Halloween-night screening, a black-tie fund-raiser for Victory Bonds, the producer threw a premiere apparently intended, at least in part, to convince Hitchcock to extend his Selznick contract. The instructions, which demonstrated an attentiveness to optimum viewing conditions unknown today, covered lighting ("kill all house lights that it is possible to kill," usherettes should not "flash their lights any more than is essential"), music (the length of entrance and exit music, each to be coordinated with the dimming and raising of the lights), and short subjects (nothing comic, "medical or scientific," or in color—*Spellbound* was in black and white). In addition to the usual security precautions, Selznick also requested that police be stationed around the theater, "to avoid a repetition of what we once had—the ruining of the picture at a special showing by children and fans pounding at the side exit doors during the performance. . . . We must be doubly careful because of coping with Hallowe'en." Jean Arthur, Joan Crawford, Norma Shearer, Alexander Korda, and Fiorello La Guardia enjoyed Selznick's remarkable hospitality; together with other members of the full house, they pledged $1,314,500 for the Victory Bond drive and spread the word around Hollywood that the second Hitchcock and Selznick collaboration would be a winner.

The reviews followed. For better or worse, many credited *Spellbound* to the director. *Newsweek* found it "a typical Alfred Hitchcock exercise in crime and astonishment and, as such, a superior and suspenseful melodrama." In *The Nation,* James Agee dissented: the film was "worth seeing, but hardly more." Though Agee also wrote for *Time,* that magazine's second-stringer covered *Spellbound* and likewise found it "good entertainment" but lacking "Hitchcock's usual sustained suspense. There is always the suspicion that there's a doctor in the house." (*Time*'s Al Wright saw *Spellbound* "cold," without an audience, Selznick discovered; the producer ordered his publicity department henceforth to monitor press screenings more closely.) Most reviewers hailed the picture, but several hoisted warning flags. *Spellbound*'s "scientific theories are, for the masses, somewhat high falutin'," one English reviewer believed. Summarized another, it "may be over the heads of some popular house audiences." *Variety* cautioned exhibitors not to "let the scientific words fool you. While an adult picture all right, beautifully played and photographed, it's still for the women patrons, containing all the suspense and characterization made to order for them." The question remained: Could the dames be convinced?

By Christmas 1945, Selznick had separated from his wife, Irene, yet bought her a diamond necklace; the anticipated profits on *Spellbound* would not make his gift seem extravagant. United Artists had estimated a $5.5 million domestic gross on the film. By February, however, that figure appeared in jeopardy. The problem, as with *Rebecca*, was the sale of *Spellbound* to small-town markets. The newspaper and movie poster advertising for *Spellbound* had favored images over words: names (stars, director, and title) and a commanding illustration (Bergman embracing Peck, who holds an open straight razor in his hand). According to Audience Research, which sampled the public, the graphics were "too sophisticated" for towns under fifty thousand in population. To achieve "greater penetration," Gallup suggested, tell more of the story. Selznick rejected the pollster's argument. The problem lay not with the poster's evocative simplicity: "I do not see why [a] typical campaign should result in anything more than typical or average business." Rather, the projected indifferent showing in small towns would result from United Artists' lackadaisical sales effort after the picture completed its big-city first run.

In less sophisticated markets, however, Selznick hedged his bets. The reviewer for the *Daily Oklahoman* had called *Spellbound* "heavy psychological going," and a still from the film featured in the Sunday entertainment section was captioned: "It is another Alfred Hitchcock thriller with a lot of psychoanalytic stuff." As though he anticipated the response, Selznick approved advertising copy that, as George Gallup had recommended, told the story: "WOMEN will be strangely moved, fascinated . . . men will be intimately intrigued, thrilled . . . by this bold woman who risks everything in one reckless experiment to unlock the fearful secret in the heart of a man . . . a man suspected of murder!" *Spellbound* demonstrated its staying power by remaining in Oklahoma City for two weeks, replaced on March 7, 1946, by *Getting Gertie's*

Dr. Petersen supports her amnesiac patient. After *Spellbound*, Bergman would tire of the parts that Selznick wanted her to play, women "so good all the time it makes you ill."

Garter. Both the advertising and the publicity heralded the name of Alfred Hitchcock.

In 1946, the Academy of Motion Pictures nominated *Spellbound* for six Oscars, including Best Picture, Best Achievement in Directing, Best Performance by an Actor in a Supporting Role (Michael Chekhov), Best Achievement in Black-and-White Cinematography, Best Achievement in Special Effects, and Best Music Score. Except for the Selznick-produced *Rebecca,* no Hitchcock picture had received as many nominations. Or as much acclaim abroad. On May 19, the day of the British premiere of *Spellbound,* London's Tivoli Theatre turned away a reported six thousand people. "Even a driving rain failed to disperse the crowds," Selznick's London representative cabled his employer. A month later, playing in two theaters, *Spellbound* had broken every house record, "including records for a single day, week, month, holiday and Sundays." Victory Week, celebrating the first anniversary of the end of World War II, had caused "virtually a rebirth of show business in the historic Strand," and *Spellbound* was among the beneficiaries. Hitchcock attended the Paris opening of *Spellbound* in May, then returned to London to be feted as the director of one of the season's indisputable hits.

To celebrate the completion of *Spellbound,* Dali gave Hitchcock a drawing inscribed to him as *"Le chevalier de la mort";* Selznick gave him his weekly salary. Even with little exposure in American small-town markets, *Spellbound* returned worldwide receipts of over $6 million to its distributor, enough for Selznick to buy a dozen diamond necklaces. Hitchcock realized less than pocket change. The inequity rankled, the wormwood spread. Yet *Spellbound* and Selznick unquestionably furthered Hitchcock's career. Selznick had initiated the "psychiatric story," assigned Ben Hecht to the script to insure its integrity and polish, and cast Bergman and Peck, for whom he accurately predicted stardom. While his style owed much to the classic Hollywood school, his demand for excellence and glamor played superbly against the director's journey into paranoia and fear. *Rebecca* and *Spellbound* may have discouraged the experiments that Hitchcock so loved (and would soon carry to an unfortunate extreme), but they reached an enormous international audience; they may have been glossier than certain pictures he directed in between, but they—and the Selznick publicity department—gave him the kind of attention within industry circles that paved the road to independence.

Along with *Rebecca* and *Shadow of a Doubt,* but no other pictures between 1939 and 1945, *Spellbound* and Selznick moved Hitchcock a commanding distance away from the fairy-tale melodramas of his British period and toward the profound psychological realism of his 1950s masterpieces. In tempering science with slickness, didacticism with entertainment, and Dali with wit, Hitchcock reacted to the direct and indirect shadow of his producer. Gracefully acknowledging the debt proved impossible for Hitchcock. When Constance and "Edwards" kissed for the first time in *Spellbound,* the director superimposed doors opening into infinity; he said that they represented the psychiatric symbol for two people falling in love. Yet just as Selznick began opening doors for Hitchcock, courting him with a share of the profits as well as other blandishments on condition that he sign another contract, the director assiduously worked toward freedom. Strangely, the tension would soon produce their best collaboration.

6

NOTORIOUS

California summers found Alma and Pat and assorted Hitchcock dogs among the redwoods near Santa Cruz. "We can see the whole of Monterey Bay from our house," the director told Hedda Hopper. Throughout the forties a host of journeymen tramped about making improvements. Though the original property included chicken houses (Hitchcock hated eggs), the new landowner added a professional greenhouse for his wife and a wine cellar for himself. Alma loved gardening, a solitary hobby. "The more I see of people," she once told her husband, "the more I like my dogs." But Hitchcock loved entertaining.

"If Hitch invited you to Santa Cruz and you said no," one screenwriter recalled, "he was very hurt." Usually accompanied by guests, Hitchcock sped north on Friday afternoons to his remote Spanish-style villa. The interior, a blend of Chinese Modern and Early American, may have startled some visitors, while the paintings may have impressed others. Not one for ostentation—except an occasional cinematic flourish—Hitchcock kept much of his growing art collection at the ranch, where the Klees and Sickerts enriched his psyche, not his Hollywood social status. Even on weekends, Hitchcock continued to direct. He passed around the imported tobacco, mixed the experimental cocktails, and placed the Hitchcock "touch" on the gourmet meals. According to Carol Stevens, Alma "adored Hitch, was extremely proud of him and defended him no matter what." Less gregarious than her husband, though, she may have welcomed the calm of Monday mornings.

In Hollywood, between pictures, Hitchcock indulged himself. He shopped for paintings, smoked expensive cigars, and lunched almost daily at Romanoff's. A small steak, potatoes, perhaps asparagus, Stevens recalled; "wouldn't dream of eating a tomato." The restaurant always seated Hitchcock at Table One, where he could see and be seen. In July 1944 alone, his monthly bill ran $257, the equivalent of over $1,500 today.

Meanwhile, Selznick pressed Hitchcock to choose his next film. Thinking about an independent production arrangement abroad, not to mention his next meal, the director seemed vague, but story editor Margaret McDonell sensed finally that he wished to follow *Spellbound* with a picture about a calculating rather than a diseased mind. Hitchcock would "very much like to do a story about confidence tricks on a grand scale in which Ingrid could play the woman who is carefully trained and coached in a gigantic confidence trick which might involve her marrying some man. He is fascinated with the elaborateness with which these things are planned and rehearsed and I gather that his idea would be to have the major part of the picture with the planning and training and the denouement more or less as the tag." A "woman who is carefully trained and coached." A woman not herself. A thing. Hitchcock "trained and coached" many of the actresses with whom he worked; he taught them technique ("negative acting") and philosophy ("it's only a moo-vie"). He seemed naturally drawn to the story of a woman made over, a woman as sex object.

"These things" and how they worked deeply engaged Hitchcock. His interest in process and organization displayed itself in his hobby (reading and memorizing railway schedules), his picturemaking (elaborating a sequence on storyboards prior to its photography), and his interviews (where he eagerly explained his camera and editing procedures). His pictures themselves were "gigantic confidence tricks." By carefully designing a project long before the performers entered the soundstage, Hitchcock achieved machinelike efficiency on the set; the resultant films at once thrilled and manipulated the audience. To some critics, his completed works were sleek dynamos, the product of an American industrialist posing as a British artist. To more severe critics, they were time bombs, full of sound and fury on detonation but signifying nothing. No matter. The more Hitchcock considered a "confidence trick" story, the more he liked it.

Short on confidence, long on tricks, Selznick had not yet decided whether to produce the next Hitchcock film, especially since loaning out Bergman and Hitchcock might generate a handsome return. Such "tough trading," however, would certainly jeopardize an already precarious relationship with his distributor. In 1941, Selznick had become a partner in United Artists. Although the company expected the producer of *Gone With the Wind* to supply pictures, he supplied only excuses. Between *Rebecca* in 1940 and *Since You Went Away* in 1944, Selznick contributed nothing to United Artists. Moreover, using monies advanced by the distributor, he acquired three properties *(The Keys of the Kingdom, Claudia,* and *Jane Eyre),* sold them to Twentieth Century-Fox, and turned an impressive profit. UA founder Charlie Chaplin became apoplectic: rather than lift the company from its doldrums, Selznick had betrayed it. Selznick tried to appease Chaplin, for the producer not only enjoyed low distribution fees but apparently entertained notions of buying out UA. With discretion, Selznick ordered Hitchcock to pitch his "confidence trick" idea to RKO.

During his three-month visit to London in early 1944, Hitchcock spoke with Sidney Bernstein, however tentatively, about founding a British-American independent production company. Bernstein later sounded out United Artists about an affiliation, but as the months passed and the war endured, nothing materialized. The uncertainty of English or American financing soon enhanced the attractiveness of a proffered Selznick contract and the studio hopping that accompanied it. The employment agreement then in negotiation committed Hitchcock to five pictures over five years, his total compensation $150,000 per picture; for each Selznick release that he completed, he was likewise permitted to direct an additional outside film. The high salary would grant Hitchcock at least a portion of any Selznick windfall on loanouts. Hitchcock implicitly approved the contract yet delayed signing it: the prospect of another long-term agreement sobered him. Yet loanouts paid two dividends. While they allowed Selznick to profiteer, they also gave Hitchcock a measure of freedom; furthermore, a tour of duty at RKO would allow him to cement his already good relationship with a studio again friendly to independents. The director lunched with an RKO executive in fall 1944 and outlined the story of "a woman sold for political purposes into sexual enslavement." Having sold himself into financial enslavement for artistic purposes, Hitchcock spellbound his audience of one: William Dozier declared himself interested.

Shortly after Margaret McDonell found a suitable property to base the "confidence trick" picture on (John Traintor Foote's "The Song of the Dragon," from a 1921 *Saturday Evening Post* story), Hitchcock and Selznick conferred about a screenwriter.* Though both quickly agreed on Ben Hecht, Selznick warned Hitchcock that availability and fee would determine the final selection. Meanwhile, his contract still unsigned, the director left for England. A disappointed Hitchcock apparently found that independent financing still eluded him and Sidney Bernstein, for he not only decided to return to the States earlier than previously expected but cabled Selznick about his eagerness to find a screenwriter for the "Dragon." "In any case," Hitchcock wrote, "better cut short activities here so as to be on hand if any change takes place regarding subject ['The Song of the Dragon']. Will telephone you on arrival NY. Alma will advise you approximate time." Once again, the director needed his producer. Given what Hitchcock called the "old-fashioned" quality of the "Dragon," he also needed Hecht.

---

*The "confidence trick" picture evolved into *Notorious*. In the RKO release, American government agent T. R. Devlin (Cary Grant) recruits Alicia Huberman (Ingrid Bergman) to infiltrate a Nazi cell in Rio. Though she falls for Devlin, he seems uncertain of his feelings and wary of her reputation as a playgirl. "This is a very strange love affair," she tells him, because "you don't love me." Alicia meanwhile pursues her assignment to seduce Alex Sebastian (Claude Rains), the head of the secret German war machine in Brazil. When Sebastian proposes marriage, Devlin allows Alicia to accept. The Nazis openly welcome the new Mrs. Sebastian, but Alicia's spidery mother-in-law seems jealous and suspicious. Alicia soon learns that her husband has hidden something valuable in the cellar. During a tense search, she and Devlin find uranium in some wine bottles, yet their discovery leads to her exposure. Slowly the Sebastians begin to poison Alicia. At last expressing his love, Devlin rescues her from the Sebastian home and leaves Alex and his mother behind to face their vengeful Nazi associates.

The director *and* producer of *Notorious*.

The demand for Hecht jumped his salary. As *Spellbound* proved, though, Hecht could harness the director's flights of fancy and produce dialogue at once romantic and urbane. Moreover, he wrote fast. Selznick hoped to have a completed script for the "Dragon" by February 1, in six weeks' time. With principal photography concluded by April (for himself or RKO), the producer could then schedule two other 1945 pictures for Ingrid Bergman, his most popular contract star, and maximize her earning potential to the company. "We have everything to gain and nothing to lose" from this plan, Selznick believed. Yet Hitchcock marked his projects andante, not allegro. Although he might waltz through the period of principal photography, he enjoyed the luxury of false starts, blind alleys, and woolgathering while preparing a script. Rushing just to brighten a Selznick balance sheet hardly suited him. Hecht thus became the courted screenwriter: Selznick needed his speed, Hitchcock his skill in construction. Shortly after Thanksgiving 1944, following a brief period of negotiation, Selznick convinced Hecht to beard the "Dragon" for $5,000 weekly (two-thirds what Hitchcock had been offered in his still-unsigned Selznick employment agreement) with a fifteen-week guarantee.

As they had on *Spellbound,* Hitchcock and Hecht were to complete the "Dragon" treatment in New York, then confer with Selznick in California; afterward, Hecht would return to New York to complete a final draft. Selznick's trust in his two employees had grown since *Spellbound,* when a reluctant Dan O'Shea had been asked to watch the men: the producer allowed Hitchcock and Hecht to develop the "Dragon" unsupervised. Still strange bedfellows, Hecht and Hitchcock differed in their politics but not their mock contempt for performers. "There are no idiots or villains in Hollywood," Hecht once wrote of actors. "There are only egos that have snapped their moorings." The New York Jew and the rotund Englishman proved exemplary collaborators. During December and early January in Manhattan, Hecht and Hitchcock met several days a week from nine in the morning until six at night. Hecht either paced or lay on the floor; Hitchcock "would sit primly on a straight-back chair, his hands clasped across his midriff, his round button eyes gleaming." Hecht dealt in narrative structure and development, Hitchcock in visual pyrotechnics. During the days between conferences, Hecht would type out the story-to-date, then return to Hitchcock for reconsiderations, alterations, revisions. By January 9, less than three weeks after they had begun, they had produced a fifty-page first-draft treatment. The pace pleased Selznick.

Notorious, as Hecht and Hitchcock called their tale from its inception, opened in Brazil. The setting would entertain audiences and gratify the distributor; with so many European markets closed to Hollywood, the studios counted on Latin America for much of their foreign income. "The Germans are very busy organizing for the next war," American intelligence officer Walt Boone tells his civilian recruit Alicia Wyman, "building political and propaganda machines in the U.S." A German fifth column in the States—including Alicia's treasonous father—moves its dollars to the neo-Nazis through Alex Sebastian. By marrying Sebastian and remaining in Rio, Boone says, "You've got a chance to shoot down tomorrow's Luftwaffe." Alicia, a "loose" woman, consents. Sebastian's mother first suspects an amorous liaison between Alicia and Boone, then perceives the real danger to her son. Adding arsenic to Alicia's milk, the Sebastians slowly poison her. Boone notices her failing health, yet only when she begins passing false information does he understand that the Nazis have penetrated her cover. Like any romantic hero, Boone wants to rescue the woman-in-danger. But Alicia is "a soldier on a mission—a soldier in a battle. And she'll have to fight it out alone," his supervisor tells him. "That's part of the game." Boone violates the rules. He sweeps Alicia out of Sebastian's house and leaves the exposed German patriot to face his menacing colleagues. Armed with a presidential citation for her work, Alicia returns to America and the home of Boone's parents to await Walt's return from the war.

What did they have in Brazil? A casino, a beach, nothing too special. While the treatment set the structure of *Notorious,* Hitchcock's signature scenes were neither elaborate nor particularly compelling. In one, Boone meets Alicia on a beach. There a fellow agent who had been spying on Sebastian lies buried in the sand, apparently asleep, actually dead. Hitchcock had devised better "business and tricks" than this, which would not survive the final draft. What was wrong? What had changed? Perhaps striving to earn his fifteen-week guarantee in record time, Hecht had poured water on the director's legendary Roman candles. Perhaps disillusioned by the lack of progress in securing financial support from abroad, Hitchcock had been uninspired. The answer was not quite so simple.

What did they have in Manhattan? Hitchcock in transition. Forced by Hecht and Selznick to address characterization, Hitchcock opened himself to people, not things. The sound and fury of *The 39 Steps, The Lady Vanishes, Foreign Correspondent,* and *Saboteur*—those dynamically edited action sequences—signified nothing compared to the emergent psychological intensity of *Notorious.* Even in first draft, as it explored the emotional realities of male and female relationships, the narrative proved subtle and complex. Sebastian and Boone, for instance, do not see Alicia; they *imagine* her. Sebastian creates a madonna, Boone a whore, no "stranger to insincere love making." Like the amnesia of "Edwards," these false perceptions insulate the men from passion and risk. Most of all, the relationship of Sebastian and his domineering mother boldly introduced a new Hitchcock.

"A witty and slightly eccentric fellow," Alex Sebastian "utters sly jokes, and his manner and words are drenched with an actorish and listless cynicism." Although the description fits Hitchcock, the character also presents the first of the director's "mama's boys." Hitchcock drew two types: the high-strung eager-to-please (Norman Bates in *Psycho*) and the effete charmer (Bruno Anthony in *Strangers on a Train*); Sebastian originates the latter category. When his mother begins chipping away at his faith in Alicia, at his gullibility where women are concerned, Alex affects complacency but experiences a debilitating hurt. The first-draft treatment does not make Madame Sebastian into the spider woman that she would later become; still, her overprotectiveness fosters his dependence and leads indirectly to the final confrontation with his Nazi associates. And as mother and son have lived, bound inextricably to each other, so must they die. Even in this rudimentary treatment, the moral implications of male-female relationships enriched what might otherwise have been a routine Latin American thriller. Their extraordinary first draft complete, Hitchcock and Hecht returned west in mid-January 1945.

What did they have in Hollywood? Selznick in transition. Still married to Irene, Selznick continued his affair with Jennifer Jones. Her youth and beauty touched Selznick as it touched so many filmgoers. Under another mentor, she might have remained the girl-next-door, a role she played in both *The Song of Bernadette* and *Since You Went Away.* Selznick had other plans: their next picture, he said, would be *Duel in the Sun.* Audience Research sampled moviegoers to determine their interest in the "sexy story of a wild, passionate girl" and found 57 percent receptive. Unless the Production Code Administration blocked his efforts, Selznick would give the public what it wanted. The author of *Duel* (both novel and screenplay) had known Selznick from their boyhood days. In the 1930s, Niven Busch recalled, Selznick had had a rough attractiveness, an engaging snorting laugh, and a sense of humor; he turned "heavy and bloated" in the 1940s, his jokes more cruel, at others' expense. Hitchcock apparently sensed the difference, perhaps even stalled on signing his contract for that reason. Yet Selznick remained an extraordinary editor. He read the *Notorious* first draft, criticized the occasionally precipitous story turns or mediocre treatment of certain plot points, and scribbled double question marks and triple exclamation marks in the margins.

Selznick also realized that Hecht and Hitchcock had drafted a potential box office hit. "Please keep [*Notorious*] strictly under cover even from sales heads," the producer advised his East Coast representative, for "I am sure the picture will emerge as something really outstanding." Selznick underestimated the value of neither artist. During January 1945, negotiating with the screenwriter for yet another Bergman script, Selznick urged O'Shea "not to do anything that would give Hecht an excuse to take one of the other offers that I know for a fact he is receiving." Courting Hitchcock, Selznick displayed an uncharacteristic largesse. When the director returned with Hecht to Manhattan to develop the treatment (continuing to work without supervision, that in itself a privilege), he would be "free to take Mrs. Hitchcock and/or his daughter to New York with him," at studio expense. The Hitchcocks packed their suitcases full but reserved room for Selznick's critique. One unusually terse suggestion influenced writer and director more than any other: noting the omnipresence of Hecht in the treatment, Selznick cried, "More Hitch."

Written in New York, Hecht and Hitchcock's second-draft treatment had both "more Hitch" and more hitches. It opened with Alicia Sebastian singing in a Colón bar, her celebrity resting on her "loose" reputation, not her voice. The narrative proper then unfolds in flashback. In a long first act, while falling in love with Wallace Fancher, a flyer assigned to the State Department's code desk in Brazil, Alicia gradually uncovers her father's role in a German conspiracy to prepare

The Hitchcocks on the town in Manhattan.

for a post-war Nazi resurgence. Confused and disturbed, she becomes an FBI recruit and, without telling Fancher the reason, marries Nazi Alex Sebastian. Soon after moving with her to his aerie near Petroupolis, Sebastian realizes that Alicia is a spy and begins slowly to poison her. At the climax, Wallie happens on the Sebastians at an outdoor restaurant in the mountains, provokes Alex into a fight, and both topple against a railing and plunge to their deaths. Back in Colón, Alicia looks at her presidential citation: "Most of those who got this aren't in a position to enjoy reading it," Alicia says to Prescott, the South American FBI liaison. "In my case, some of me is still alive—and I'm luckier than those others who helped—much luckier." As Prescott leaves, she rises to sing.

The somber second-draft treatment featured a number of Hitchcock trademarks. Responding to a Selznick criticism about the absence of Latin American atmosphere, Hecht and Hitchcock incorporated the city's famous statue of Christ into the narrative. This Rio landmark mounted atop a 2,300-foot peak offered a splendid panorama of the city, the bay, and the ocean. Typically, though, Hitchcock played "against" the monument. Beneath this masterwork, where only "a skimpy railing guards against a 500-foot plunge," an Alicia torn between love and duty contemplates suicide. Hitchcock often stood his characters near the edge and forced them to cling tenuously to life. As early as *Blackmail,* when a man falls through the roof of the British Museum to his death, Hitchcock had shown that monuments to humanity were particularly indifferent to humanity, a theme epitomized by the Statue of Liberty finale of *Saboteur.* Maxim de Winter *(Rebecca)* nearly falls into the sea and "Edwards" *(Spellbound)* into a snowy abyss; after struggling beside a "flimsy" railing that "would hardly protect anybody from plunging 1,000 [feet] to their death were they to stagger against it," Fancher and Sebastian do stagger and do die. The earlier Selznick pictures differed from *Notorious* by more than degree. Although the sea and the snow evoked "the past," the railing held neither people nor metaphors. The story had the Hitchcockian fall but needed an echo.

Hitchcock immediately began the revisions. The February 1945 third draft eliminates the Colón frame-tale and the climactic plunge. Like the picture, the story opens with the sentencing of the traitor Huberman, dissolves to the party where the drunken Alicia Huberman (formerly

184

Alicia Homer) meets T. R. Devlin (formerly Wallie Fancher), then moves to their first love scene in a speeding car. The second and third acts occur in Rio, where Nazi botanist Alex Sebastian raises hothouse orchids. Hecht and Hitchcock strengthened Sebastian, adding a translucent Oedipal subtext to the treatment, but they also developed the relationship between Alicia and Devlin. The lovers' passion and desire battle their fear and mistrust; once Alicia begins her assignment, the acrimony has hardened. Thereafter Sebastian dominates the action, Devlin withdraws. Selznick recognized the danger: no leading male star would want to portray a character who *did* so little. Hitchcock threw some balls into the air—two stabbing victims, one gushing blood over a kitchen stove, another falling from his opera box—but once they tumbled down, the Devlin problem remained. And though the hero's attempt to rescue Alicia showed his courage, his death at the hands of the Nazis finally suggested his weakness.

This third-draft treatment had a peculiar tone. More than *Spellbound,* an overt "psychiatric story," the narrative veered toward the grotesque and the depraved. A Sebastian associate, bizarre even by wartime Hollywood standards, became a "George Grosz German, fat necked, flat faced, bulging bodied, small nosed, watery eyed." Government agents stationed in Brazil regarded Alicia as the ideal spy to trap such nefarious creatures: "a real lady" outside, "inside—dry rot." At the track in Rio, where Alicia returns the pressure of Sebastian's knee as they watch his horse run, her abasement is complete. Devlin watches Sebastian take his future wife to the winner's circle; he "sees Alicia's arm go around the sweating, gleaming neck of the race horse—and sees the foam from the animal's panting mouth drip on to her shoulder as the photographers take their pictures."

Hecht and Hitchcock sent their hybrid third draft—part screenplay, part expository narrative—from New York to California in mid-February 1945. This time, Selznick required not "more Hitch" but "more *original* Hitch." The kitchen and opera house corpses too closely resembled those of British Hitchcock. Must *Notorious* raid *The 39 Steps* for its effects? Besides the death of Devlin, the characterization of Alicia bothered Selznick. Hitchcock had asked Hecht to model her speech after Tallulah Bankhead's—deadpan, brash, and sexy. "Better take your coat," Devlin tells Alicia before taking her for a ride; "it's chilly."

185

Selznick brought two stars together for *Notorious*. Still under long-term contract to the producer, Ingrid Bergman could demand only her salary, but Grant bargained for "all customary conditions" of his free-lance employment agreement, as well as a percentage of the gross receipts.

She responds: "You'll do." Selznick found Alicia "vastly overdrawn," and while in sympathy with her talking "in Tallulah fashion," he believed "that Tallulah would be shot before she would say anything like these lines, too many of which are horribly coarse without being witty, and many of which contain jokes and words that date back to the Hecht and MacArthur of 'Front Page.' " The draft may have told Selznick that Hitchcock could hardly serve as his own script editor, much less producer.

By winter 1945, with the war near its end and international sensibilities frayed, Selznick recognized that any film dealing with espionage abroad would require official clearances prior to its release. Assistant Secretary of State Archibald MacLeish promised to cooperate on government approvals, even to meet with Hecht and Hitchcock in the capital. The Selznick employees could easily train down from Manhattan. Several years before, however, producer Pandro Berman had flown to an important Washington conference with Hitchcock and found that the director spoke a sardonic English almost offensive to bureaucrats. Unless Selznick demonstrated his willingness to share producer duties with Hitchcock, though, the director would probably not renew his contract. Selznick compromised. He would send Hitchcock to Washington with "a company representative who can advise us accurately and in detail exactly what has to be done and who can get the approvals in writing and not come back without them."

While Selznick continued to chase after a renewed Hitchcock contract, Irene Selznick told her husband in early 1945 that she wanted a divorce. "My revolt had been sudden and without provocation," she recalled. "No threat, not even a warning." The couple agreed not to announce her decision to the public or to friends, and outwardly life went on. A breakup with Hitchcock seemed equally likely and equally disruptive. Negotiations for a new contract had stalled. Hitchcock wanted $6,000 a week—with an unlimited number of weeks per picture—and a title credit equal to that of his stars. A 10 percent share of the profits would ice the cake. Selznick could add: Hitchcock had worked on *Rebecca* and *Spellbound* for thirty or more contractual weeks, *Lifeboat* for almost a year. With the tap dripping $6,000 a week indefinitely, Hitchcock would malinger and drive up costs. Selznick counteroffered $7,500 a week, twenty weeks maximum per picture. Billing "not less than 75% as large as star name." No profit share.

David and Irene Selznick. "He would have liked me to be the best-dressed woman in town," Irene wrote about her husband; "he wanted me to knock them dead. I said, why? Sartorial elegance had never been my goal. Every party, every gift, every movie must be the best [he said]."

To Hitchcock, each contractual point represented a building block in achieving both financial and artistic independence. One demand ("Article Twelve") required the studio to pay "all expenses for a two week trip to New York after each picture for publicity purposes," including first-class transportation with Pullman compartment. Such junkets gave Hitchcock a working vacation and an opportunity to cultivate important broadcast and print journalists in the East. Selznick understood that these trips accomplished their goal, the promotion of a Hitchcock picture. According to his daughter, who accompanied him on these tours, Hitchcock could go into Baltimore or Philadelphia, conduct numerous radio interviews throughout the day, yet offer each broadcaster a totally different angle. The chatter could offset negative or indifferent reviews (or word-of-mouth), raise the visibility of the film in question, and thus benefit Selznick Productions. It also fattened the image of Alfred Hitchcock as independent producer. The more Selznick thought of Article Twelve, the more he resented it. Since the cockney director had aristocratic taste in lodging and restaurants, Selznick believed that any new contract should specify "a limit to the expenses." After Hitchcock filed travel expenses from his 1944 trip abroad, Selznick became even more convinced that Hitchcock intended to make the studio his exchequer. In memoranda, Selznick began to refer to this contract demand as "the 'humiliation clause.' "

As relatively unimportant as it was, Article Twelve filled out an agenda: whomever he signed with, Hitchcock wanted considerable fiscal benefits and artistic controls. The money mattered in unexpected ways, for Hitchcock lived simply. He bought the Santa Cruz villa and the two-bedroom, two-bath Bel Air home to please himself, not Hollywood. Irene Selznick had employed one cook for David alone; the Hitchcocks had only a housekeeper. Though he added a custom-designed kitchen and a wine cellar to his southern California home, Hitchcock drove the same Cadillac for years. He could spend money, for expensive oils, Baccarat crystal, the handbags he loved to present as gifts. And he could be very generous. He loaded down his secretary with books and wine whenever she chauffeured him to book and liquor stores, and he cheerfully maintained an apartment for Alma's cockney mother and sister, who moved to Los Angeles in the early forties. ("Suddenly you get married," Hitchcock would say, "and you find yourself being nice to people you wouldn't even speak to on the street.")

Hitchcock rarely carried money: he signed for everything. Despite burgeoning wealth, though, financial insecurity whistled through the cracks. The fiscal benefits might help seal them.

Money also translated into power. Hitchcock would never find complete freedom in Hollywood. He might leave David Selznick, but other collaborators would naturally influence his work, from bankers and distributors to screenwriters, production designers, cameramen, and censors. He nonetheless wanted artistic control for both professional and personal reasons. America and Selznick had altered Hitchcock. The longer takes, the diffused lighting, and the attention to close-ups in *Rebecca* and *Spellbound* were matched by an enriched psychology of character. The "gags and bits" that Selznick red-penciled sometimes brought not only thrills, but pathos and pain. The more complex the theme, Hitchcock believed, the more necessary his hand alone on the wheel, for a supervising producer could compromise the vision. Personal reasons also shaped the push for control. "If Hitch liked you," one writer recalled, "he wanted you to work for him forever." He was "extremely possessive of people who worked for him," Carol Stevens added, "especially the crew." As long as the director and others on a picture were employed by the producer, Hitchcock could not command absolute loyalty.

Other clauses made apparent the goal of complete artistic control. Hitchcock wanted a provision that gave him "approval of story, script and cast, such approval not to be unreasonably withheld" as well as a screen credit that read " 'an Alfred Hitchcock Production.' " In addition, he asked that Selznick eliminate force majeure options, exercise no restraints over the director's activities beyond an individual studio picture, and in a loanout agreement grant the director the right of final approval of story and cast. In effect, had Selznick agreed to Hitchcock's terms, the director would de facto have become an independent producer, with the conspicuous advantage of a weekly salary as safety net. Such an arrangement, Selznick believed, was "completely untenable."

"This whole contract is bad enough as it is," Selznick wrote in a February 1945 memorandum to O'Shea, "without agreeing to something that to the best of my knowledge has never been agreed to with any other contract in Hollywood, even with a star of the first rank." Force majeure options would remain. Other Hitchcock demands were equally abhorrent to Selznick. If the earlier contract had been "replete with provisions unfavorable to Hitchcock and advantageous to Selznick," though, perhaps the contract under discussion simply balanced old accounts. Perhaps more than he could admit, Selznick understood that Hollywood was changing, that the future belonged to the independent director-producer. Final negotiations would center on one issue: who ran David O. Selznick Productions. In her column, Hedda Hopper had already advised Ingrid Bergman to negotiate a contract similar to Hitchcock's, its purported terms a matter of public knowledge because of the director's boasting. Selznick feared with good reason that the contract with Hitchcock might threaten the welfare of his entire operation.

His inflated demands notwithstanding, Hitchcock was not worth his weight in gold. Still, he offered Selznick both product and prestige. The courtship continued. For *Notorious,* Selznick offered the reluctant contract artist his choice of blue-ribbon cinematographers Arthur Edeson *(Casablanca)* or Lee Garmes (parts of *Gone With the Wind*). While Hitchcock devised the script in New York, Selznick appeared eager to impress upon him that the studio had strived diligently in his behalf ("we may have worked on the [cinematographer] situation so thoroughly and successfully that we may have an embarrassment of riches") and to remind him of his boss's cordiality in all matters artistic ("I should appreciate hearing from you by wire as to which man you would prefer"). Selznick also deferred to Hitchcock on casting. The producer wanted Clifton Webb for Sebastian, Hitchcock objected; the producer began looking for others who had "played straight leads and not heavies," including such men as George Sanders (Favell in *Rebecca*) and Metropolitan Opera bass Ezio Pinza. Preoccupied with *Duel in the Sun,* Selznick gave Hitchcock what the director most wanted: time to complete the *Notorious* script without supervision.

In their ninety-five-page final treatment–script, Hecht and Hitchcock again sent the camera prowling. From the courtroom opening, the story dissolves to the Huberman home, under FBI surveillance. First the agent "peers into the window," then "we go through the window to the bungalow's bedroom. Alicia Huberman is having breakfast in bed." Like other anticipatory moments in Hitchcock films, this shot leads the viewer to expect one incident (despite the hour, a bedroom scene), then provides another. Subtly the director shifts the guilt from Alicia, innocently dining, to first the government agent patrolling the house and

191

then the viewer whose prurience also stands nakedly revealed. Devlin recruits Alicia, they journey to Rio, and the intrigue begins. Responding to Selznick criticism, Hecht and Hitchcock stabbed one less victim (the agent gushing blood over a kitchen stove disappeared) and further shaded the characters of Alex Sebastian and his mother. They also wove Devlin more prominently into the plot by bringing him to a dinner party at the Sebastians', where he rescues Alicia amidst gunfire. The tag finds the couple before a judge, exchanging vows.

The final treatment bore several Hitchcock traces, from a romantic scene with Alicia and Devlin making love while discussing their chicken dinner to the discovery of a corpse on a massage table in a Rio beauty salon. But the addition of the MacGuffin distinguished the draft. Hitchcock defined the MacGuffin—a term coined by Angus Mac-Phail—as "the pretext for the plot," the device or gimmick that occasions the action.

> It might be a Scottish name, taken from a story about two men in a train. One man says, "What's that package up there in the baggage rack?" And the other answers, "Oh, that's a MacGuffin." The first one asks, "What's a MacGuffin?" "Well," the other man says, "it's an apparatus for trapping lions in the Scottish Highlands." The first man says, "But there are no lions in the Scottish Highlands," and the other one answers, "Well then, that's no MacGuffin!" So you see that a MacGuffin is actually nothing at all.

The MacGuffin for *Notorious* became "chemicals and mechanisms" for building a "new German weapon," the plans for which resided in the memory of one of Sebastian's associates. The plot device seemed sufficiently vague, sufficiently topical.

Hitchcock and Hecht returned to Los Angeles in March 1945. The producer assigned the Englishman to another director's vacant offices, but Hitchcock refused to occupy them unless they were overhauled. Thinking of the still-unsigned contract, Selznick allocated $2,000 to redecorate the suite. Hecht presented other challenges. "Plotted all day, lunched with [William B.] Ziff and two million dead jews [the number believed to have been exterminated by the Nazis], working on radio show tonight," Hecht wired his wife Rose (at Selznick's expense). "Have hired bellboy to humor and drive me." In early April, Selznick requested an accounting on Hecht and found it "getting a little thick": the writer had been on salary for *Notorious* for over three months and collected in excess of $60,000. Should Selznick package the film for sale, high pre-production costs would erode some profit. More important, Hecht's vendetta against Germany and his Jewish activism spilled over into *Notorious,* particularly in the crude portrayal of the Sebastians and their George Grosz associates. In early spring 1945, Ethel Barrymore read the treatment-script and through an intermediary informed Selznick that she "did not like the part of Madame Sebastian and is not at all interested, even in discussing possible development with Hecht."

Despite problems on *Duel in the Sun,* riddled by poor weather on location and organized labor troubles in Culver City, Selznick humored Hitchcock if not Hecht, for overall the script looked promising. He hired ace cinematographer Gregg Toland to shoot the South American rear-projection footage and began to consider Technicolor for the entire picture. For Hitchcock, these deluxe fringe benefits partially compensated for the less appealing elements of a Selznick production, including the inevitable script conferences. Hitchcock later recalled the drill. After dining together at Romanoff's, Hitchcock and Hecht would drive to Selznick's home at 11:00 P.M., the appointed time; for four hours, the producer would pace, discourse, and digress, then at three in the morning finally turn to the project at hand. Interestingly, Hitchcock's method of operation, if not his hours, resembled his producer's. Hitchcock began story conferences by discussing everything except the story. The tea trolley would call at tenish, then the luncheon trays. Sometimes only after the empty plates and wineglasses had been removed, and the gossip of Hollywood exhausted, would Hitchcock settle down to work.

At his conferences with Hecht and Hitchcock, Selznick provided only minor suggestions. He ordered Madame Sebastian toned down and Devlin built up; he also encouraged the collaborators to develop their proposed new MacGuffin. Armed with the Selznick critique, the writers worked throughout April on the film's dialogue treatment. Although Madame Sebastian remained waspish and the Germans as odious as before, Hecht and Hitchcock clarified the Nazis' machinations. "Our original intention had been to bring into the story government officials and police agents and to show groups of German refugees training in secret camps in South America with the aim of setting up an enemy army," Hitchcock recalled. "But we couldn't figure out what they were

193

going to do with the army once it was organized." The new Mac-Guffin—"simpler, but concrete and visual"—became an atomic bomb, "a little shell as big as your fist that could destroy a city." The Mac-Guffin sparked the writers. Tossing out the opera house scene where Sebastian first realizes that Alicia is a spy, Hecht and Hitchcock devised a suspenseful episode that chillingly involved Alicia. Late one night, having learned that Sebastian keeps in his basement a mysterious substance pertinent to his group's scientific research, Alicia explores the wine cellar alone. She accidentally breaks a bottle and spills its contents—"sand"—to the floor. American intelligence identifies the substance as uranium. In April 1945, a month before the military began work on deployment of the atomic bomb, two months before certain of Churchill's advisors knew of it, and three months before the Alamogordo test that demonstrated its efficacy, Hecht and Hitchcock brought uranium and atomic warfare to *Notorious.*

Hitchcock leaked the news to Thornton Delahanty, who alluded to the director's "secret researches" in an April 1945 *Herald Tribune* feature story. Yet the unfamiliar term "atomic bomb" caught the studio off-guard. A stenographer transcribed "automatic bomb," production assistant Barbara Keon called it an "automic bomb." Hitchcock had heard of secret projects in New Mexico and "was also aware that the Germans were conducting experiments with heavy water in Norway. So these clues," he said, "brought me to the uranium MacGuffin." By early summer, the director had asked the research department to determine whether Brazil had sufficient "deposits of minerals from which Uranium can be obtained." Still later, Hecht and Hitchcock visited California physicist Robert Millikan in order to confirm the scientific element of their plot line. Millikan paled at their query and discouraged them. Yet the Nobel Prize winner also told them that "such a bomb need be no larger than an egg to do the dirty work of a dozen blockbusters." Amused by this topical MacGuffin, Hecht began calling his son "the little atomic bomb."

Hitchcock later accused Selznick of believing it "absurd to use the idea of an atom bomb as the basis for our story." Yet Selznick not only called the decision to use uranium and the bomb "a tremendous thing," he even urged Hecht and Hitchcock to devise a culminating scene in which the Germans reveal the power of their discovery: they use "a bomb that could be held in the palm of one's hand" to blow up an entire mountain. An earlier draft had contained an allusion to such an experiment; Selznick now wished to use the trick department to realize it. Exploding the bomb "makes the whole thing real," he told Hecht and Hitchcock, "and will give the picture size and spectacle."

The French originated the *auteur* myth, but moviemakers like Hitchcock nurtured it through stories that championed directorial genius. The roots of Hitchcock's apparent pride of authorship were deep. As the relationship with Selznick began to unravel, with the director seeking an independence that might still link him to his producer (if only as distributor of independently made pictures), his resentment of the years of financial and artistic servitude quickened. The plump expense account reports from London, the cat-and-mouse contract negotiations, even the demand for a refurbished suite of offices connoted a Hitchcock bent on flexing his muscle and manipulating Selznick. Selective memory helped. In the late 1930s, Selznick had rescued Hitchcock from drowning in the tempestuous waters of British film production; by the 1960s, when the director began seducing not only the press but French cinéastes and American scholars, Selznick had become the ogre pushing Hitchcock and his brilliant MacGuffins under for the third time.

Although securing the necessary approvals for a film script involving an FBI man and an "automatic bomb" could prove dicey, Selznick fought for both. Margaret McDonell knew that the bureau could be circumspect about its activities and methods, so suggested that her boss appeal to "J. Edgar Hoover's personal liking for publicity. I know that Warners have made use of this and in our case I think it would be a very good plan if a script of 'Notorious' went to him personally, possibly from you personally, above all if a line were written in somewhere in which a character refers to something like 'the long arm of J. Edgar Hoover.' " Jock Whitney's intercession with NAACP executive secretary Walter White had helped keep the Negro organization away from *Gone With the Wind*. Selznick adopted a similar strategy for *Notorious,* which—at least initially—worked. While the atomic bomb was a "ticklish subject for [a] picture," Hoover aide Lou Nichols told Selznick that because the Germans and not the Americans were the bomb's inventors, the notion seemed acceptable.

Revising, polishing, and inventing, Hecht and Hitchcock worked on the *Notorious* script in an atmosphere of both domestic and national uncertainty. On April 12, 1945, Franklin Roosevelt died. Although the Hitchcocks (especially Alma, who had applied for American citizenship) may have mourned FDR, Ben Hecht did not. The president who had refused to charge the Germans with mass murder "was being wept over, and all his great fine deeds acclaimed. In my mind," Hecht wrote in his autobiography, "his chief monument remained—the dead Jews of Europe." Matters nearer home concerned Selznick. Leaving his writers alone, he attempted to manage the labor disputes victimizing *Duel in the Sun* and to tend his foundering marriage. He promised his wife to dine at home and to spend more time with his young sons; his attempts failed. The big party and the $60,000 diamond bracelet that he gave Irene for their fifteenth anniversary on April 29 healed no wounds. "I put [psychiatrist May] Romm through some turbulent months," Irene recalled. "She tried to stem the tide by stepping me up to five times a week, often in double session." David found his therapy in *Duel* and in Jennifer. As if they weren't enough, the 156-page May 9, "temporary screenplay" of *Notorious* gave him plenty to do.

Hecht and Hitchcock had retained the opening scenes between Devlin and Alicia, then moved the action to Rio, where the romance struggles to bloom. They intercut scenes developing the love-hate relationship—more pointed than ever—with scenes showing Devlin in conference with the American and Brazilian authorities. When Devlin brings Alicia her assignment, he wants her to refuse, she wants him to refuse for her. However cloudy the logic, the impasse throws her to the Sebastians. The Hecht pen still dripped venom. The writer gave Alex a world-globe prop straight out of *The Great Dictator* and had Madame Sebastian abuse Alicia. After the tongue-lashing, Alicia says, "Really, Madame Sebastian, you are a bit insufferable." Alex nonetheless introduces Alicia to his Nazi associates, the seduction proceeds, the couple wed. Her love for the ever-absent Devlin, combined with the Sebastians' calculated poisoning, lend Alicia and the final act an emotional charge rare in Hitchcock. Again Devlin goes to the ailing Alicia, but in this draft she dies in his arms.

Selznick advanced on the script like an avenging field marshal. He left in the wake of his dictation numerous dead issues, from the specific ("I urge avoiding references to Nazis who are going to be pretty dead ducks nine months from now") to the general (Madame Sebastian behaves "like an idiot"; "Devlin just doesn't make sense to anybody but

Ben Hecht"). He railed at exposition "dragged in by the ears," the abrasive characterization of Alicia, and the static action. The various FBI-office scenes—"radio technique, and not very good radio technique at that"—hauled the narrative from point to point with the efficiency and finesse of a locomotive. Moment after moment of "people sitting down and exchanging dialogue" could ruin the film, Selznick lectured Hitchcock, especially when the dialogue was not only prodigious but bad. Too many sequences lacked direction. "It's just a lot of dialogue," the producer said of one scene; "it has no construction—no beginning, no middle, no end."

The steely dialogue of Hecht seemed rusted. At a Brazilian sidewalk café, Alicia and Devlin pass time awaiting a call from the FBI. Devlin orders a drink, the notorious Alicia refuses one. Laughing, he calls her abstinence "a phase." She urges him to relax his defenses, to "give that copper's brain of yours a rest." Later at her apartment, they are still waiting. "Don't we have fun together?" Alicia deadpans. "Terrific," says Devlin. Hitchcock apparently found such dialogue serviceable, but the more verbal Selznick cringed. He accurately termed "insufferable" the retort that Alicia offered Madame Sebastian, "a line that no actress in the world could read to come off properly." Fearing that his scenarist had gone "out of season" or gotten "bored and stale on the subject," Selznick considered replacing him for the rewrite. "I really couldn't even play hearts again with a man who in this day and age uses such a line as 'That's what you think.'" For Hitchcock, the images and not the dialogue conveyed cinematic truth. While the romance of Devlin and Alicia languished, the director foregrounded such "things" as a decanter of arsenic-laced red wine for Alicia, coming "nearer and nearer the CAMERA until the tray fills the screen." Between the "business and tricks" and the savaging of the Germans, Selznick believed, Hitchcock and Hecht had lost the trail of the narrative. How else could the producer account for Alicia's dying at the end, a plot point "incompatible with a story of this kind"?

Selznick would not permit the Hecht typewriter to become a blunt instrument. He offered numerous suggestions—from smoothing out the exposition to deepening the romantic feelings that Devlin has for Alicia—and used sarcasm, cajolery, and outrage to enforce them. Shielding Hecht (who was simultaneously writing an anti-Roosevelt drama), the contrary Hitchcock defended the *Notorious* script. Certainly the

197

tone and substance of the Selznick critique must have rubbed raw. It reflected the Selznick of *Duel in the Sun* and *Notorious,* more pompous, more querulous, more arrogantly self-important than the Selznick of *Rebecca* or even *Spellbound.* In 1939, *Gone With the Wind* publicity director Howard Dietz had so wearied of the Selznick ego that he erected a sign over his desk: "Please don't be FAMOUS around here." The Selznick of the late thirties could laugh at the epigram; the Selznick of the mid-forties might have torn it down.

The critique embodied the professional differences that lay beside the personal ones. Selznick defined cinema in terms of the past, applying to it the rules of another medium (the novel) and another century (the nineteenth); like Orson Welles, Hitchcock thought of it as a ribbon of dreams. The producer remained bound to the logical and the verbal; the director embraced the inexplicable and the visual. "I'm trying to figure out what these people would do if they were simple, rational human beings," Selznick confessed at the end of his notes. Hitchcock might have been tempted to tell his boss, "It's only a moo-vie." But the director's films are only a movie in the same sense that our nightmares are only a dream: they are in their irrational way quite real. And in an irrational world, irrational actions have their own irrational acceptability. Selznick complained that Hitchcock's characters were "puppets in a melodrama." Would Selznick or Hitchcock pull the strings?

Hitchcock had already become puppeteer, or at least apprentice puppeteer. Although he would participate only casually in revision of the screenplay, he would continue to draw his paycheck each Wednesday. Selznick had put the director on salary four months before, per the terms of a five-picture contract still in negotiation, but with *Notorious,* "the most expensive script in the history of my career," the producer now confronted a financial black hole. Production delays on *Duel in the Sun* made an idle Hitchcock even more onerous. "Just because Hitchcock uses up a big fat chair in Dan's [O'Shea] office and distracts him from other work is no excuse for paying him almost a thousand dollars per day," Selznick groused. Perhaps the director should be reassigned to a different project or simply "laid off."

Selznick might assign the director to *Some Must Watch,* then being scripted and presumably an apt work for a director associated with voyeurism. Used to seeing a project through, however, the director would complain about the unfinished business of *Notorious*. The other alternative, suspending Hitchcock, was less desirable but certainly not without precedent. When jurisdictional labor disputes had closed down *Duel in the Sun* earlier in the year, Selznick had taken director King Vidor off salary. But "the risk of losing Hitchcock in the future" finally outweighed the "disgrace for our management that the highest amount ever paid in the history of the picture business to a director should be paid by us on this subject." Afraid to alienate Hitchcock, whose long-term commitment to Selznick remained indefinite, the producer neither reassigned nor suspended the director. Hitchcock—the producer sighed—"has the Indian sign on us."

As a third alternative, Selznick could peddle the project around Hollywood. Along with Hitchcock, the tentative casting of Ingrid Bergman and Cary Grant—appearing together for the first time—would give a *Notorious* package great appeal. The big names would mitigate what Selznick perceived as problems in the screenplay, and the sale would not only relieve the company of a financial burden but pour needed cash into *Duel in the Sun*. Earlier in his relationship with Hitchcock, Selznick would have preferred Brazilian sex and intrigue over "lust in the dust." The participation of Jennifer Jones, however, strengthened his commitment to *Duel*. And with his marriage and career in transition, he may have lacked the psychic energy needed to sustain multiple productions. *Notorious* may have seemed suddenly expendable.

Selznick's offer of the Hitchcock project—script, director, and stars—to Hal Wallis typified his approach, yet demonstrated just how little *Notorious* mattered to him at this point. Although Wallis and his associate Joe Hazen were major producers, Selznick believed that their pictures reflected Wallis's assembly-line mentality. In January 1945, while editing *Love Letters* with Wallis, Selznick found his colleague impatient, "but boy, I certainly see how he turned out pictures in quantity. I could turn out about a hundred a year the way he makes them." When Selznick mentioned to Hitchcock the potential sale to Wallis, the director must have smiled inside: a producer unwilling to overhaul a picture in the editing room gave the director considerable power. Ingrid Bergman likewise had no objections. Though the producer hardly sought their resistance to a loanout, he resented their indifference to the contribution that a Selznick as opposed to a Wallis could make to a picture. Their response, Selznick told O'Shea, struck "a blow to my ego."

Whether Wallis would buy remained doubtful. The MacGuffin may have posed a significant threat to the sale; Hazen later told Hitchcock that he and Wallis regarded the bomb as "a goddamn foolish thing to base a movie on." After reading the screenplay, the prospective buyers also worried about receiving the necessary approvals for such sensitive topics as espionage and atomic warfare. The project was "far from clean" with the FBI, Selznick conceded, and neither the Office of War Information (OWI) nor the Production Code Administration (PCA) had yet approved the story. Unless a workable script could be produced, the project could not be sold. Swimming through the alphabet soup of regulatory agencies required dexterity; each office guarded its terrain, and the approval of one hardly insured that of the others. Negotiations with governmental bodies again fell not to Hitchcock but to Margaret McDonell.

While the local OWI office provided only a moderately bumpy path for *Notorious,* Joe Breen scattered nails in the road. Breen read the May 9 temporary screenplay and called it "definitely unacceptable under the provisions of the Production Code." Alicia in particular offended. Virtually a prostitute, she appeared to Breen as "a grossly immoral woman, whose immorality is accepted 'in stride' . . . and who, eventually, is portrayed as dying a glorious heroine." The writers, Breen concluded, had not met the code's requirement of "compensating moral values," whereby the immoral acknowledge and pay sufficiently for their immorality. *Notorious* posed problems, Breen had solutions. If Alicia lived it up (as a "gold-digger," not "a kept woman of loose morals") yet retained her virtue, the script could be approved. "I think most of [Breen's] criticism from the sex angle is nonsense and is clearly not consistent with the Lauren Bacall character and what he passed in it in 'To Have and To Have Not,' " Selznick complained. PCA approval of two James M. Cain works, *The Postman Always Rings Twice* and *Double Indemnity,* further encouraged producers to test Breen. Refusing to "be left with milk and water," Selznick prepared for "a good fight."

The sale of *Notorious* and the approval of Joe Breen hinged on an adept shooting script. Although he feared that Hecht would not "get

200

down to business" on the revision, Selznick knew that even "out of season" Hecht excelled many of his colleagues. The enthusiastic reactions of Ingrid Bergman and Cary Grant to the May 9 screenplay and the Hitchcock defense of Hecht persuaded Selznick to leave the writer on *Notorious*. With Hitchcock pressing him to hurry—the director wanted to leave for England—Hecht did not disappoint.

The result of the producer's stimulus and the writer's and director's invention, the June 11 "temporary screenplay" built the Alicia–Devlin romance, relieved the static quality of the expository scenes, and increased Devlin's participation in the third act. At the producer's insistence, Hecht finally trimmed Madame's claws. Rather than attack Alicia on their first meeting, Madame Sebastian envelops her in a razor-sharp aristocratic charm. Sebastian then introduces his cronies to Alicia. Photographed one by one from Alicia's point of view, in close-up, the big heads resemble animated wanted posters. Scale alone conveys danger. As Alicia struggles to associate names with faces, the Nazis come close enough to sniff out her identity as an American agent. Yet unlike her countrymen, they peer warmly into her eyes and see only her beauty, not her checkered past or agenda of betrayal. Notorious to Devlin and her friends, chaste to her enemies, Alicia abandons herself with equal resignation to Sebastian's affection and, later, his arsenical poisoning. "David sent me the synopsis of *Valley of Decision,*" a frustrated Ingrid Bergman remarked several weeks before she read the Hecht–Hitchcock screenplay. "My, what a woman's part. It is just what [Selznick] would like me to do . . . a courageous, strong, sincere, GOOD BORE!" Alicia and *Notorious* promised a brisk change of pace.

Selznick supplied the impetus, Hecht the dialogue, Hitchcock the visualization. Writer and director added the key-to-the-cellar sequence and the tense final departure of Alicia and Devlin from the Sebastian home. What became one of the most famous "Hitchcockian" scenes had begun with an order from Selznick some weeks before. Regarding the earlier draft that sent Alicia into the cellar alone to discover the uranium, Selznick noted: "We certainly missed Devlin seriously through this section of the story. The whole love story falls apart with him out of the picture for this length of time." Hecht and Hitchcock responded by having Alicia lift the cellar key from Sebastian's ring and slip it to Devlin; after the two of them discover the uranium, Sebastian discovers them. Suddenly Devlin kisses Alicia, then tells Sebastian that

In early drafts of the script, Alicia had searched the cellar alone; Selznick urged Hecht and Hitchcock to add Devlin to the scene. Here Alex Sebastian (Claude Rains) discovers the couple in an embrace.

they came downstairs to make love. Alicia pales: Has Devlin lied to both her and Sebastian? One reel later, his climactic rescue answers the question.

When Devlin goes to the dying Alicia, a prisoner in her bedroom, he tenderly helps her from her bed to the landing. Madame Sebastian appears, then Alex. The quartet slowly descend the stair. Sebastian here cedes Alicia to Devlin, who assumes the trust in her that her husband once had and lost. Below them stand the Nazis, puzzled. If Sebastian betrays Alicia, he betrays himself; if the Germans become suspicious, they may kill them all. The scene on the stairs gathers tension less from simple plot mechanics than from its complex characterization, the metaphysical thrill of Sebastian's fear, Alicia's redemption, and Devlin's leap of faith. Had Selznick not consistently objected to endings that found either Devlin or Alicia dead, Hecht and Hitchcock might never have devised this suspenseful climax on the stairs.

Still not altogether pleased with some of the dialogue ("Bergman shouldn't say 'You three-toed sloth!' " the producer had earlier complained, "or 'Holy Jehosophat!' "), Selznick nonetheless rushed the shooting script to the regulatory agencies. Their approvals would allow him to package *Notorious*. Though previously amenable, J. Edgar Hoover now objected to the portrayal of an FBI presence in Brazil and the relatively blunt sexual subtext. *Notorious,* he informed Selznick, might "subject the FBI and you to some criticism on the grounds of morality." Why not make the Bergman character an impersonator of the real Alicia Huberman? Since the ersatz Alicia would presumably not be an American citizen, the real Alicia would emerge from the scheme with her patriotism—and her virginity—intact. The OWI also decided to play screenwriter. The liaison officer protested the vagueness of Sebastian's political and economic plans and the implication that his death eliminated all danger to the West. "This," the OWI agent reiterated, "is the kind of over-simplified attitude which would make overseas audiences question our political maturity and our understanding of the true nature of Fascism." Selznick questioned "what authority these people have"; Hitchcock insisted that *Notorious* was "simply the story of a man in love with a girl who, in the course of her official duties, had to go to bed with another man and even had to marry him. That's the story." After questioning and insisting, though, Selznick and Hitchcock would comply: Hitchcock quickly made Devlin an agent of the

Stage actress Leopoldine Konstantin made her only screen appearance in *Notorious*. Here Madame Sebastian watches with her son as Devlin and Alicia make their escape.

Brazilian government and turned the scarlet Alicia pale pink. The director then left for England and Sidney Bernstein.

Summer 1945 brought many changes for Hitchcock, Selznick, and the world. The end of the war with Germany signaled a period of adjustment and a subtle shift of alliances, both around the globe and in Hollywood. Relationships between Alma and Alfred Hitchcock, between David and Irene Selznick, and between Hitchcock and Selznick were changing. Having been her husband's helpmeet on the sets and in the cutting rooms of most of his British and earlier American films, Alma Hitchcock participated neither officially nor unofficially in the development of *Notorious*. The couple still entertained at small dinner parties, biographer Donald Spoto wrote, but Hitchcock reportedly became "pouting, moody, and glumly attentive to the small, active woman who was his creative counselor and his motherly muse." Along with anxiety about realizing his independence, concern about his size may have fed his malaise. The hundred pounds lost several years before had begun to creep back on; although he maintained three wardrobes for his three body sizes, he preferred leaving the Tweedledum suits in mothballs. For various reasons, including age, the forty-five-year-old Hitchcock seemed to slow down. From 1939 to 1942, he directed six films; from 1943 through 1946, he would direct three. The incentive for speed and renewal lay in formation of a Bernstein–Hitchcock independent production company. Much rode on that trip to England.

The threat of losing Hitchcock depressed an already gloomy Selznick. Though superficially placid, his domestic relations were deteriorating, yet according to Irene he could not bring himself to leave home. "He would have liked to find commitment for himself as well as for me," his wife believed. "He simply couldn't." Her patience gone and the Jennifer Jones affair an embarrassment, Irene decided on separation. Meanwhile, $1 million over budget and seventy-five days behind schedule, *Duel in the Sun* finally resumed principal photography on June 25, 1945. Selznick and director King Vidor clashed almost immediately, and the animosity grew throughout the long shooting schedule. The romance between the producer and his leading lady only partially relieved headaches caused by the Hitchcock mission abroad, the pending divorce, and the morass of *Duel*. Selznick felt himself losing ground. The two-punch of *Notorious* and *Duel* could restore his preeminence in Hollywood, but the Western had acquired a monstrous fiscal appetite. Selznick now *had* to sell *Notorious*—and fast. Unless a firm starting date for principal photography could be set, Cary Grant would fall out of the package.

When Hal Wallis abandoned *Notorious* and its topical MacGuffin, RKO offered to purchase the package for an $800,000 cash consideration and 50 percent of the net profits. Selznick realized almost $500,000 from the sale, Hitchcock nothing. For the first time since coming to America, though, Hitchcock would both direct and produce. *Really* produce. Hitchcock had worked at RKO in 1940 and 1941, only two of the studio's many years of turmoil. With George J. Schaefer turning out almost as many executives as pictures, Hitchcock even then had reasonably little supervision. In 1945, he could expect still less. Such director-producers as Leo McCarey, Frank Capra, William Wyler, and George Stevens had already located their production companies at RKO, an apparently hospitable environment for independents. RKO furnished studio space, office facilities, and distribution; largely unsupervised, the director-producers furnished product. The RKO purchase delighted Hitchcock. Supervising everything from the polishing of the script to the negotiation of myriad post-production details, the director could demonstrate to the industry at large his skill as an executive.

The purchase delighted RKO. "We had no stars of our own," RKO production executive William Dozier recalled, "so we had to take what we could get, treat them well, make them feel at home, give them a lot of cooperation." Besides "product," the *Notorious* sale would give RKO an opportunity to woo the Englishman as a future independent producer-director. Hitchcock had of course come with strings attached, but the RKO final contract attempted to cut several of them. An amendment to the original agreement brought the scissors into the open. Clause Thirty-three, added in early August 1945, denied the lending producer "any voice in the production, or the supervision of production, of the PHOTOPLAY." This late entry seems a courtship gift from studio to director. Hitchcock himself may even have selected it. With Selznick guaranteed 50 percent of the profits, however, RKO could not hope to silence its silent partner. Soon after having purchased the *Notorious* package, the studio had the benefit of Selznick's advice.

RKO assumed responsibility for *Notorious* in mid-July; within

206

weeks, its latest acquisition turned white-hot. On August 6 and on August 9, the United States dropped atomic bombs on Hiroshima and Nagasaki. Few realized even then just what an atomic bomb was. To the general public, this "superbomb" concentrated an enormous amount of TNT in a very small package. Contemplation of radioactivity, megatons, and megadeaths belonged to the future, not to a present buoyed by the reality of a Japanese surrender. Interest had been awakened in nuclear energy, of course, and *Notorious* stood to profit by it—but only if Hitchcock's picture beat the others to the theaters. Two days after Hiroshima, Selznick predicted that half a dozen pictures would probably reach the box office before *Notorious.* "Not only will we miss the opportunity to get the additional gross by being out first, but if we are out last with such a subject, we are going to suffer greatly." Selznick urged RKO to ease out Cary Grant (who was unavailable until October), hire Joseph Cotten, and rush *Notorious* into production.

RKO demurred. Hitchcock was abroad, the script needed a final polish, and the romantic pairing of Grant and Bergman promised a box office bang comparable to an atomic blast. The studio left the start date set for early October and assigned the dialogue revisions to Clifford Odets. Best known for his proletariat dramas *Awake and Sing* and *Waiting for Lefty,* Odets had just written and directed RKO's *None But the Lonely Heart,* a resolutely depressing story of a cockney (Grant) and his cancer-stricken mother (Ethel Barrymore). Selznick must have questioned the choice of Odets. The fictional world of the playwright was dismal, its characters downtrodden. Alicia needed redeeming, Devlin humanizing, and the dialogue leavening, all tasks for which Odets seemed uncomfortably suited. To William Dozier, however, Odets "seemed a pretty good candidate" for the *Notorious* revision. Selznick was immersed in *Duel* and Hitchcock theatergoing in New York, yet both men monitored Odets through Barbara Keon, a Selznick production assistant who had been tossed into the *Notorious* package and sent to RKO. In late September, Keon laid a copy of Odets's 136-page rewrite on Selznick's desk.

Odets tried to bring an atmosphere to the story that previously had been absent. Extending the characters' emotional range, he heightened the passion of Devlin and Alicia and the aristocratic ennui of Alex Sebastian. He also added a soupçon of high culture to soften Alicia: she quotes French poetry from memory and sings Schubert. "That ocean doesn't stop," she says to Devlin on her balcony. They kiss. "Far off the pounding surf. FADE OUT." Odets had used Hollywood shorthand to send Alicia and Devlin to bed together. Reunited after the Sebastian affair, Alicia and Devlin dance. " '. . . Ce soir M'a plongé L'amour,' " she whispers in his ear, and "they whirl away."

"Merde," Hecht later said upon reading Odets's work. (Scribbled in the margin beside a purple patch of dialogue, the writer's actual comment read: "This is really loose crap!") But with Hecht unwilling to lift his pen until RKO opened its checkbook, an Odets second draft became inevitable. The time required would further erode the impact of an atomic MacGuffin. Selznick made his displeasure known, indirectly. The "characters have lost dimensions," the producer told Hitchcock, who had just returned from New York and, unlike Selznick, could communicate with RKO. Alicia, "a cross between Bankhead and Bacall," became hard, then soft, for no reason. In addition, the "audience won't understand Alicia's French." Devlin still lacked charm; moreover, his sleeping with Alicia "may cheapen her in the eyes of the audience." Selznick lectured Hitchcock about the "bald exposition" and the characters who "don't talk like real people." He urged the director to have Odets rework the climax, which in both writers' screenplays had "not enough emotion nor drama nor wallop." Hitchcock promised to make the rough places plane, then slipped his leash and fled to RKO for late-September script conferences with Odets.

Hitchcock had only half his mind on *Notorious,* for his summer trip to England had revived hopes for an independent production company. Daydreams alternated with nightmares. Bernstein had asked Hitchcock to edit some footage of Nazi atrocities, a proposed seven-reel film to "help rouse the personal consciences of the Germans who have allowed these cruelties to multiply within their midst." The documentary evidenced a Hitchcock aesthetic-in-progress. According to film editor Peter Tanner,

> Hitch was very careful to try to get material which could not possibly be seen to be faked in any way, and one of the big shots I recall was when we had priests from various denominations who went to one of the camps. They had a Catholic priest. They had a Jewish rabbi. They had a German Lutheran and they had a Protestant clergyman from England. And it was all shot in one shot so that you saw them coming along, going through the camp, and you saw from their point of view all that was

208

going on. And it never cut. It was all in one shot. And this I *know* was one of Hitchcock's ideas, and it was very effective. There was *no way* for somebody seeing it that it could have been faked.

In *Notorious* and *The Paradine Case,* Hitchcock would experiment further with the extended take, a cinematic strategy that he would push to the limits in two later pictures.

The director spent his days manipulating footage of concentration camp horrors, his nights complaining to Bernstein about Selznick and his interference. Since Bernstein ran a chain of theaters, he had the wherewithal to finance their nascent partnership, but he agreed to become Hitchcock's partner and executive producer, not his benefactor. Their future would rest on external funding. Hitchcock approached *Notorious* cheered by the increasing firmness of his artistic plans and slightly depressed by their fiscal indefiniteness. Selznick meanwhile pursued Hitchcock with a contract and RKO with suggestions. Ignoring the infamous Clause Thirty-three, Selznick pushed RKO to cast Claude Rains as Alex Sebastian. Rains offers "an opportunity to build the gross of NOTORIOUS enormously," Selznick told his company secretary; do not "lose a day in trying to get the Rains deal nailed down." Such interference helped the picture but irked its English director. Until a Bernstein deal became impossible, Hitchcock would avoid the Selznick dotted line.

The elusive Hitchcock and the "terrible siege" of *Duel in the Sun* challenged Selznick by day, his domestic crisis by night. However flawed, the marriage to Louis B. Mayer's daughter Irene, Hollywood royalty, at least represented continuity, his ties to a past when all things were not only attainable but attained. *Duel* might vindicate him as a producer, yet its uncertain future and even the affair with Jennifer Jones provided nothing like the mooring that Irene had once given him. *Gone With the Wind,* the important pictures with Hitchcock, the development of stars like Vivien Leigh, Joan Fontaine, and Ingrid Bergman— all promised immortality and all were behind him. The separation from Irene would close the door with ominous finality. In the days before Irene telephoned the gossip columnists to announce the news, David resisted packing, moving, or telling his children. "He'd thought we would talk it over again," Irene remembered. "He wanted one more day." But no retakes were possible. Gratifying her readers with an account of the split, Louella Parsons mourned that neither Selznick's "fame, his money, nor his enviable position in the business world have been enough to make him happy." Myths of the rich and miserable have long been an American stimulant, but Parsons and Irene herself may have underestimated Selznick's affection for Jennifer Jones. She and *Duel in the Sun* demanded his attention. *Notorious,* by contract, prohibited it. In August, Selznick became involved with both productions.

Without Selznick to drive him, Hitchcock apparently gave Odets a free hand on *Notorious.* The dramatist proved all thumbs. "We all of us have to stop sometimes and seriously sum up, asking ourselves who and what we are," Devlin tells Alicia, trying to persuade her to work for the government. "I won't stand here in moral judgment. But the past is a heap of dead leaves, and what I'm trying to do now is confirm in you your possibilities . . . you can really have some sort of decent future. (A humorous addition) With hot and cold running water." The convoluted syntax, the uneasily mixed tone, and the impoverished figures of speech hint at Odets's lack of affinity for the FBI agent. His thoughts elsewhere, Hitchcock busily investigated the nature of Brazilian uranium. Odets meanwhile signed his October draft "A. B. Clifford" (perhaps an indication of his own dissatisfaction), collected a final $5,000 payment, and left *Notorious.* The revisions did nothing to alter Selznick's opinion that the script was "very poor, particularly from the emotional standpoint." The producer urged RKO to contact Ben Hecht.

When Hecht agreed to tackle another rewrite, Hitchcock made a number of suggestions, from the racetrack sequence ("stay with Sebastian and his mother for a short scene subtly [not on the nose] getting over the mother's jealousy") to Odets's revised climax, much of which (including a wild Schubert serenade) the director apparently liked. Hitchcock asked Hecht to end Devlin's climactic scene with Alicia and the Sebastians in a speeding automobile. "It should be an odd sort of quartette," Hecht said, his typing a match for his spelling, "something like in Rigelleto. . . . I811 write it one night this week when the afflatus strengthens." Though Hecht could not top the stairway finale that Selznick had earlier prompted him to write and to which he ultimately returned, he made the changes as requested. With principal photography imminent, speed became essential. "Dear Hitchy," Hecht began that crudely typed letter, his last screenplay draft virtually complete.

210

"If there are . . . cuts, filler scenes or rewrites that are needed let me know. Being a good boy, my nights are always open."

My dear Ben, Hitchcock responded, write some lines that will demonstrate Sebastian's concern about his age and appearance. Alex should not be "pompous or bombastic or silly in his vanity, merely a little naive and tiresome"; he should continually seek Alicia's reassurance. "This 'Do I look tired?' gag," Barbara Keon wrote to Hecht, "is the thing Hitch wants to keep running through the picture—Sebastian, the egoist! Always 'Do I look well tonight?' 'I had a good night's sleep'—'How do I look tonight?' etc., etc." Hitchcock biographer Donald Spoto argues that the director, stirred by sexual feelings he neither understood nor desired, identified with both the Cary Grant and Claude Rains characters. Certainly the stronger parallel lies with the Rains character: Devlin is but an agent (a player), Sebastian is an architect (a director). His are also the doubts of an aging man, not unlike Hitchcock, who at this time experienced a bout of mild hypochondria. "Business is such a bore," Alex tells Alicia. "But the worst thing about it is that it makes you act old, think old, look old." Not long after his forty-sixth birthday in August 1945, with his independence still hanging fire, Hitchcock may have reflected on the divergence of his vanished youth and his artistic future.

When Hecht completed a shooting script acceptable to Hitchcock, RKO, and their never-silent partner David Selznick, principal photography began. RKO had a new president in Peter Rathvon and a fresh set of challenges, including labor problems and rising costs. But along with *It's a Wonderful Life, The Best Years of Our Lives,* and *The Spiral Staircase* (based on *Some Must Watch* and directed by Robert Siodmak), *Notorious* promised a better-than-average year for production. The cast included Bergman, Grant, Rains, and in her only American screen performance Leopoldine Konstantin as Madame Sebastian. All were superb professionals whom Hitchcock respected.

The RKO staff insulated Hitchcock against interference and made the shooting of *Notorious* a "clear horizon." Oddly, the Selznick in Hitchcock gave the picture the glossiness of *Rebecca* and *Spellbound,* a quality absent in *Shadow of a Doubt* and *Lifeboat* but appropriate to the exotic Brazilian milieu and the physical beauty of the performers. Consummate stars like Bergman and Grant again found Hitchcock an

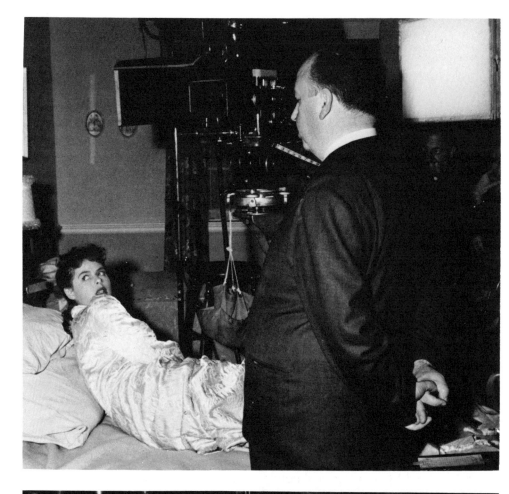

ideal director. Sardonic but precise, formal but accommodating, devious but talented.

> He wanted an actor to bring something to the part, and he would not do any direction until he saw a rehearsal first, and he saw what the actor would bring to it [Pat Hitchcock recalled]. Then he very quietly would talk to the actor, you know, and say, 'Now I think it might be . . . why don't you try such and such a thing,' and of course you did and it worked beautifully. But there were no bombastic ravings or anything like that on the set. The sets were very quiet and very happy and very normal.

Though privately Hitchcock may have resented the power of Cary Grant, especially his 10 percent share of the gross receipts, the director and his "puppets" disagreed only rarely. When they did, Hitchcock prevailed.

During the filming of one sequence, Alicia and Devlin walked from the terrace to the telephone, nuzzling and kissing in close-up. "We feel very *awkward* in this position," Bergman complained to Hitchcock. "Don't worry," he replied, "it'll look all right on screen." The idea of retaining the continuity of a romantic moment had occurred to Hitchcock in France.

> I was on the train going from Boulogne to Paris and we were moving slowly through the small town of Etaples. It was on a Sunday afternoon. As we were passing a large, red brick factory, I saw a young couple against the wall. The boy was urinating against the wall and the girl never let go of his arm. She'd look down at what he was doing, then look at the scenery around them, then back again at the boy. I felt this was true love at work.

Hitchcock often told far bluer stories to his actresses prior to a take. Depending on her temperament, the performer would either relax or stiffen. Bergman generally took the ruddy-faced Hitchcock in stride. She laughed at his teasing, indulged his curious habits, and turned away his practical jokes and tricks. She may have resisted the terrace-to-telephone scene, though. RKO executive William Dozier saw Bergman and Hitchcock "go at it with hammer and tongs" for half an hour one morning. "Very well, Hitch. We'll do it your way," the actress finally said. "It's not my way, Ingrid. It's the right way." Hitchcock "knew what he wanted to see on the screen," one of his actresses said, and "the most important thing to him was what was going to be up on that

Hitchcock and two stars who contributed to his "clear horizon." The director would work once more with Bergman (*Under Capricorn*) and twice more with Grant (*To Catch a Thief* and *North By Northwest*).

screen." The actor accommodated himself to the camera, not vice versa.

Working with Claude Rains must have especially pleased Hitchcock. The height of the actor immediately posed the kind of technical challenge that Hitchcock embraced. Though Bergman and Rains played lovers, she towered over him. The effect in mid-range two-shots seemed almost comic. The director stood Rains on a box for static close shots, but a moving long shot posed problems. When Alicia and Sebastian approached together from a distance, Hitchcock said, "we couldn't have any boxes out there on the floor, so what I did was to have a plank of wood gradually rising as he walked toward the camera." Rains belonged to the no-nonsense school of cinema. The performer called moviemaking factory work; like Hitchcock, he regarded screen acting as a mechanical skill. At rehearsals, he counted. Lifting a cup to the mouth required five beats. Drinking required two. Restoring the cup four. When the camera turned, Rains marked time silently but nonetheless marked time. One . . . two . . . three . . . He puzzled and amused colleagues yet at least gave Hitchcock an alternative answer to the perennial question of behavior. If actors could not locate their motivation in their salaries, perhaps they could look to their numbers.

While *Notorious* progressed, the long-delayed New York premiere of *Spellbound* and post-production chores on *Duel in the Sun* preoccupied Selznick. Barbara Keon nevertheless kept him informed. Meanwhile, producer Hitchcock gave director Hitchcock the freedom to stop mid-production for extensive retakes, a practice that Selznick had forbidden on *Rebecca*. Although RKO again declined to muzzle Hitchcock, Selznick had no such inhibitions. Thinking of his 50 percent interest in *Notorious,* Selznick urged the director to postpone retakes until the end of the schedule when he would have a better notion of what really needed retaking. Hitchcock nodded, then ignored the advice. A resentful Selznick appealed to a higher court: unless RKO forced Hitchcock to abandon the retakes, Selznick would "pull Bergman if necessary" and make her inaccessible to *Notorious* immediately after the period of principal photography. Long distance, the game of cat-and-mouse continued.

Unpleasantness over retakes aside, principal photography moved seamlessly along. In late January 1946, it ended. "Working as I do," said Hitchcock of his "cutting-in-the-camera," "you're sure that no one in the studio is going to take over and ruin your film." Yet generally at this point, Hitchcock submitted his rough cut to the producer and held his breath. Selznick came "from the school of film-makers who like to have lots of footage to play around with in the cutting room," Hitchcock said. (An understatement: *Duel in the Sun* originally ran twenty-six hours.) With enough footage, Selznick could remake a picture.

Hitchcock probably expected Selznick to shadow the RKO cutting room. But although restraint came uneasily to the producer, he had compelling reasons for his uncharacteristic "containment." In part, editorial work on *Duel in the Sun* occupied his waking hours. Selznick and Hal Kern had trimmed *Duel*'s twenty-six hours to a rough-cut four by February, yet the preponderantly negative response cards from an Oakland preview drove the producer back to the soundstage for two months and $500,000 worth of supplementary scenes and retakes. In part, as Selznick may have recognized, absenting himself from involvement with the RKO production—per the difficult-to-enforce Clause Thirty-three—might further his courtship of Hitchcock, an artist with an expiring contract and a free spirit.

As the producer of *Notorious,* Hitchcock enjoyed the final control that he had lacked on *Rebecca* and *Spellbound:* he firmly placed his stamp on the arrangement of the images, what Selznick called the "goddamn jigsaw cutting." The rhythm of the close-ups, the concentration on objects, and the depiction—largely through editing—of a world of constricted vision are typically Hitchcock. Frame by frame, shot by rapidly shifting shot, *Notorious* not only broke with the Selznick ethos but fully anticipated the director's masterpieces of the 1950s, all works that created unnerving cinematic environments through montage.

Despite differences in style, Hitchcock and Selznick followed a similar modus operandi in the editing room. On *Notorious,* editor Theron Warth (later an RKO producer) used the continuity sketches and the transcriptions of Hitchcock's detailed "cutting notes" to construct each scene. Once the footage had been assembled, Warth screened it for Hitchcock in the projection room. A stenographer seated beside the director recorded his comments for later reference. Having "cut-in-the-camera," Hitchcock sought few major changes; he required neither significant added scenes nor retakes. Yet he called for numerous alterations of camera angle and distance, cutting speed, and the sequence and duration of close-ups, particularly of objects.

Slight adjustments often paid large dividends. In one scene, the Sebastians know that Alicia is a spy; their colleague Anderson does not. When the professor talks too specifically of his work, Alex changes the subject: "Would you care for some more brandy, Otto?" The innocent bumbler next reaches for the poisoned cup; the agitated Sebastians warn him that he has mistaken Alicia's coffee for his own. Hitchcock supplies some of the tension through composition. One setup paints a mordant cinematic still life, with the poisoned cup in the right foreground, Alicia in the middle ground, slumped in a large wing chair with "blinders" on each side. Theron Warth rough-cut the body of the scene in alternating two-shots of Alex/Madame Sebastian and Alicia/Dr. Anderson. Revising, Hitchcock intercut close-ups of Alicia immediately after each Anderson gaffe. Forced into the chain of images, these flashes disrupt the dull progress of alternating two-shots. They not only block our access to the Sebastians (what are they thinking? what are they doing?), but tighten the frame around Alicia when she most needs breathing room. By separating Alicia from the group, Hitchcock also wed style (isolation) to content (isolation). The jigsaw eventually created an evocative psychological pattern.

Hitchcock did not always cut against the Hollywood norm; if he had, his deviations from it would have lacked the ability to affect the audience. He could, when he wished, impose a rigorous form of "invisible editing" on his work. When Alicia awakens from her drunken debauch in Miami, she sees Devlin standing over her with a hangover cure. "You copper!" she says. "Cut to: Devlin," Hitchcock noted, "ONLY IF she looks up when Devlin says 'Finish it.' IF she hasn't looked up, don't cut to him." Selznick might have cut the sequence identically. Yet the sheer variety, the arrangement, and the tempo of Hitchcock's shots finally distinguished him from his producer. Discontent simply to track his characters' emotions through a long shot–medium shot–close-up protocol, he juxtaposed images to create emotions both within the frame and without the film. Shot by shot, then sequence by sequence, Hitchcock's "proper rhythm" led his audience to rely on only one certainty, the director's mastery over the narrative. His critics often focused their praise on his signature shots, those moments that seem most "Hitchcockian": the Albert Hall climax of *The Man Who Knew Too Much,* the vaudeville finale of *The 39 Steps,* the assassination scene of *Foreign Correspondent,* the Statue of Liberty chase of *Saboteur,* and the better-known set pieces of his later pictures. But their positioning within their respective films—their relationship to the cutting of sequences around them—makes them great filmmaking. Key moments in *Rebecca* and *Spellbound* bear Hitchcock's distinct mark; cut by table saw rather than jigsaw, though, they lost some of their effect. Postproduction control at RKO gave Hitchcock the power to make the first American picture he could call his own.

By early April 1946, Hitchcock had finished *Notorious,* and RKO began preparations for the picture's release. Production Code Administration approval headed the agenda. "As you know," RKO executive William Gordon told the director, "the PCA have run and re-run NOTORIOUS, at which times some very heated discussion and argument ensued." Censorship changes rarely worried Hitchcock on the Selznick pictures: the final cut belonged to a producer who would contest the slightest changes. For *Notorious,* Hitchcock had photographed protection footage but hoped the Breen office would not require its use. After Hitchcock departed for England and an appointment with Sidney Bernstein, the studio made some minor concessions to the PCA, yet what remained would shock critics and moviegoers. Alicia and Devlin's passionate, uninterrupted embrace on arrival in Rio (the director's observance of the letter, if not the spirit, of a PCA taboo against "lustful and prolonged kissing") and Devlin's intimacy at the dying Alicia's bedside (his head on her pillow, at her face) exemplify a kind of sexuality rare in Hollywood cinema of the 1940s. Perhaps Breen had nodded for once.

In London, meanwhile, Bernstein announced formation of Transatlantic Pictures to the public and, presumably, to David Selznick. The *Daily Film Renter* reported in early April 1946 that Bernstein and Hitchcock would produce films in England and America and that their first release would be *Under Capricorn,* starring Ingrid Bergman. Besides the artistic advantages, Hitchcock could reap a financial bonanza, for the government taxed corporations far more favorably than it taxed individuals. But declaring independence and achieving independence remained separate matters. Until Transatlantic could convince one of the major Hollywood companies to distribute its product, no bank would lend Bernstein and Hitchcock money to shoot *Under Capricorn.*

For the publicity still, the photographer sat Bergman in an ordinary chair. In the film, an enormous wingback chair encloses Alicia as she realizes that her coffee has been poisoned.

Devlin comes to rescue the poisoned Alicia.

The uncertainty of financing meant that Hitchcock could not yet end the association with David Selznick.

When Selznick learned of Transatlantic (oddly enough, from Ingrid Bergman at a Sunday evening dinner party), he intensified his efforts to sign the director to a nonexclusive contract. The Hitchcock journey abroad coincided with the British premiere of *Spellbound.* Persuaded by Selznick, two London exhibitors agreed to play the film concurrently in first run, a coup that promised to enhance the distributor's early profits and the director's status in his homeland. Hitchcock should "know what we accomplished on SPELLBOUND which couldn't have been accomplished by anyone else," Selznick wrote to O'Shea; it would have "a tremendous psychological effect on . . . Hitchcock's attitude toward us and even to the new deal with him." Selznick finally chose not to play this card: he feared that Hitchcock's bragging might harm relations between Selznick's nascent distribution company and London theatermen. Yet having seen *Notorious* and recognized its potential for box office success, he made the Hitchcock renewal an imperative.

On several occasions after the war, Selznick remarked that Hitchcock had made two outstanding pictures in America, *Rebecca* and *Spellbound.* Although both prominently bore Selznick's name, RKO's *Notorious* would not. The omission troubled him. He had conceived the picture and shepherded the screenplay through numerous drafts; considering his justifiable pride of accomplishment (and the uncertain future of *Duel in the Sun*), he wanted the following RKO screen credit: "Services of Alfred Hitchcock and Ingrid Bergman, and scenario, by arrangement with David O. Selznick." The reference to a "scenario" would let the industry and its critics know that Selznick functioned as more than an agent on *Notorious.* Unfortunately, it would also broadcast his involvement with RKO product. Charlie Chaplin had publicly excoriated Selznick for failing to honor his United Artists commitment; if Chaplin saw his partner's name on an RKO picture, he might sue for breach of contract. Selznick deferred to the advice of his attorneys.

Released in August 1946, *Notorious* enjoyed both critical and popular success. "Hitchcock at his subtle best," wrote *Newsweek,* which found the rescue of Alicia "an exercise in suspense by a past master in the business." *The New Yorker* called the film "a happy example of

220

what Alfred Hitchcock can do when he is really bearing down." Some reviewers deprecated the routine plot, and especially Devlin's character. *Commonweal*'s Philip Hartung called Cary Grant "cool and calm and almost dull"; writing in *The Canadian Forum,* D. Mosdell noted that Grant had "very little to do but fold his arms and look ominous." But to James Agee, who knew an American agent similar to T. R. Devlin, Grant's "cultivated, clipped, puzzled-idealist brutality" seemed well-observed. According to Bosley Crowther, who had praised *Spellbound* highly, "Hitchcock has directed in brilliant style a romantic melodrama which is just about as thrilling as they come—velvet smooth in dramatic action, sharp and sure in its characters and heavily charged with the intensity of warm emotional appeal." Ten days later, Crowther devoted his Sunday *New York Times* column to the film, focusing on Hitchcock's mastery of romance: "One little sequence of ardent courtship in the first part of this film," he wrote, "is about as emotionally combustible as any we've seen on a screen." The public agreed. RKO tentatively planned to send Hitchcock to New York to publicize the film, but three days after Crowther's initial notice appeared, the studio canceled the junket. "In view of fact NOTORIOUS breaking all records [at Radio City] Music Hall," RKO's president wired O'Shea, "seems unnecessary have Hitchcock make trip."

Hitchcock closely followed the box office performance of his pictures. *Spellbound,* he bragged to Truffaut, "cost us about a million and a half dollars to make, and it brought in seven million to the producer"; *No-torious* (as he called the "confidence trick" story) "cost two million dollars to make and grossed eight million dollars for the producers." The figures were rounded (*Notorious* in fact cost $2.3 million and grossed $7.1 million) and the references to "the producers" tinged with rancor. As early as 1942, Jack Skirball had given the director a share of the profits—in addition to compensation—on *Saboteur* and *Shadow of a Doubt.* Although Selznick had not objected (he himself had given and would give Hitchcock a number of bonuses), he permitted Skirball to amend Hitchcock's loanout contract only on condition "that your giving of this bonus [a percentage of the gross] to Mr. Hitchcock, his acceptance of it and our acquiescence, can in no wise affect, or have any bearing on, or in any manner or sense be amendatory to, our contract of employment with Mr. Hitchcock." By Hollywood standards, Skirball's percentage arrangement and Selznick's bonuses had been modest.

221

On *Notorious,* RKO and Selznick earned about $1 million each; Hitchcock earned his salary.

Although Hitchcock lived to make pictures, not money, financial insecurity dogged him. He once bought a "piddling amount" of oil stock, his secretary recalled, yet so closely monitored the investment that "he drove us crazy." Hitchcock demanded an almost weekly accounting of his net worth—savings, insurance policies, bonds, and cash. With her vacation clothes packed and her train waiting, Carol Stevens often found herself preparing a last-minute current balance sheet for "Hitch." By July 1946, Selznick finally recognized that his erstwhile contract director might respond to a profit-sharing arrangement, one that had advantages for both parties. A percentage deal could conceivably "cost us considerably less for Hitchcock's services as against a chance to make considerably more . . . because of [Hitchcock's] increasing habit of taking a year per picture." In return for a share of the profits, the director might also be persuaded to accept a lower weekly salary, reducing Selznick's commitment of front-end money. Moreover, as an investor in a film, Hitchcock would surely work to minimize cost overruns. All hinged upon bringing the Hitchcock signature to the bottom line.

On a visit to England in early spring, Hitchcock modestly told a journalist, "They say in Hollywood Selznick respects me." Selznick indeed pursued Hitchcock for at least one nonexclusive picture annually. He bombarded the director with projects—*The Lost Weekend, The Spiral Staircase, The Turn of the Screw, The Devil's Disciple*—and hoped that one would command his interest. Hitchcock hemmed and hawed. "It's the same old story," Selznick complained to his corporation's secretary early in the Hitchcock chase. "Months and months of negotiations, endless conversations, yackety-yackety, and no deals; and if we do get anywhere near a deal, we spend enough time defining it and drawing contracts that the horse is stolen." The "farcical negotiations with Hitchcock" continued for months. Selznick realized that his company had become known for the "mysterious and almost notorious length of time it takes us to close negotiations on the preparation of contracts."

Dodging Selznick throughout the summer, Hitchcock watched his weight cross the two-hundred-pound mark. "I'm not a heavy eater," he protested, "unless you mean I'm heavy and I eat." The more he gained, the more evasive he grew. Although the Tanner Tour of Hollywood now cruised by the Hitchcock home, the guide could only guess at the nature of the personality within. Is America your permanent home? a reporter asked Hitchcock in 1946. Pretty much. Will you become a citizen? " 'Raised-eyebrow department,' he said with a twinkle." Again the future seemed to depend on transatlantic overtures.

7

THE PARADINE CASE

In 1946, while *Notorious* was still in post-production, Hitchcock took off for New York to confer with Sidney Bernstein about a future without Selznick. Cary Grant and Ingrid Bergman had tentatively pledged their services to Transatlantic, and they accompanied Hitchcock east. Several other performers, writers, and directors had talked to Bernstein or Hitchcock about an affiliation. In England, Frank Launder and Sidney Gilliat, the coauthors of *The Lady Vanishes,* had met with Bernstein about directing some pictures for Transatlantic. But when they learned that Bernstein would make the final business decisions, they withdrew. Fond of Hitchcock, they may have perceived Bernstein as an interfering producer like Selznick. No impression could have been more mistaken.

Hitchcock fought influenza the entire seven days in Manhattan, and instead of training home decided to fly Howard Hughes's *Constellation.* After numerous delays, Hitchcock and Hughes's friend Cary Grant finally took off, with Hughes himself in the cockpit. As Hitchcock recalled,

> we thought we were as good as home, but then [Hughes] began to make stops. In Chicago, I believe, for a change of clothes. Then in St. Louis to go to a nightclub. The problem was, as difficult as it was to get commercial passage from New York to Los Angeles, it was all but impossible from anywhere else. So there we were, dropping in on some cabaret in Denver, or a restaurant in Nevada. It took almost two days to fly from New York to Los Angeles.

On the ground in Hollywood stood David Selznick, contract and assignment in hand. According to the terms of the proffered nonexclusive agreement, Hitchcock would direct one Selznick film a year for $100,000; a percentage share of the gross receipts could raise his income by another $300,000. Once he had satisfied his annual commitment, he could then make an outside picture for his own company. He seriously considered the offer: Transatlantic remained unfinanced, and a Selznick contract would provide security. But as Selznick pressed, Hitchcock stalled.

Meanwhile, the two men began work on the last film under their existing contract. Since his tenure at MGM, Selznick had been trying to film Robert Hichens's *The Paradine Case* (1933). Based on a scandal that rocked the legal circles of London, the ponderous five-hundred-page novel centers on a beautiful but enigmatic Danish woman (Ingrid Paradine) accused of poisoning her blind husband, the ruthless war hero, Colonel Paradine. Malcolm Keane, a middle-aged lawyer known for his grandstanding before juries, believes her innocent; though happily married, he also falls in love with her. When Keane confirms a liaison between Mrs. Paradine and her husband's manservant, he grows jealous but determines to blame the valet for the murder. She meanwhile uses Keane's affection to further her defense. Finally the case comes before the unctuous Judge Horfield. After perjured testimony wins Ingrid Paradine an acquittal, Keane finds his career in shambles and returns to his wife, Gay.

" 'The Paradine Case' is built on scenario lines," a reviewer for the *New Statesman* wrote. "The style is luscious; the husky voice of Greta [Garbo] alone might make it acceptable." Though other critics had

The Weather:
It's the Fog in the morning and the Smog at night
—Edith Gwynn

WORLD NEWS

EXTRA

15th Day of Old Bailey, 1947

POISON: CLUE IN PARADINE CASE!

As the Paradine Case spotlight centered yesterday on Stage 11 at the Selznick Studio, Director Alfred Hitchcock sternly clamped down on outside investigation. Attorney Gregory Peck, still wearing his barrister's wig for "The Paradine Case," and his colleague Charles Coburn are shown as Hitchcock barred them from dressing rooms of Valli, Ann Todd and Joan Tetzel.

Wine Glass Spurs New Police Probe

BULLETIN

Search for the slayer of Richard Paradine quickened this afternoon on Stage 10 at the Selznick Lot in Culver City. A spokesman in the Hitchcock office who refused to be quoted said a break was expected before morning. A wine glass was rushed to police headquarters for laboratory tests and fingerprints. The wine glass was thought to be the first important break in the mysterious killing. Hitchcock, when reached by telephone by a News reporter, was very crisp and said "No comment. See the picture when it comes out."

The Medical Examiner early today established that "a deadly poison," probably taken with his nightly burgundy, killed Col. Richard Paradine, distinguished Army career officer whose body was found under mysterious circumstances last week in his continental style West End residence.

(Continued on page 3)

CASE HAS CLASS

With yesterday's poison discovery the death of Col. William Paradine (above) may force court appearances for socialites Joan Tetzel, left, and Ann Todd, daughter and wife respectively of prominent attorneys Charles Coburn and Gregory Peck.

found the novel old-fashioned in 1933, Selznick purchased the rights from Metro and decided to make the picture in 1946. The reasons seem obvious. Both *Rebecca* and *The Paradine Case* centered on an otherwise strong man dominated by a malevolent woman and ultimately redeemed by his selfless wife. A "woman's producer," Selznick understood the emotional power of smoldering love. The involvement of Hitchcock may seem puzzling. Today, many regard *Notorious* and *The Paradine Case* as the zenith and nadir of Hitchcock in the 1940s. Dissociating himself from the picture, the director later intimated that he accepted the assignment to work off his Selznick contract. But his producer never forced anything on him. Especially in 1945, trying to sign Hitchcock to a nonexclusive employment agreement, Selznick offered him a choice of properties. Hitchcock freely selected *The Paradine Case.*

The youthful Hitchcock had wished to become a barrister. "What I wanted most of all," he told a reporter, "was the opportunity to be a ham in court." Though Hichens had written an exciting trial sequence, the mature Hitchcock found other attractions in *The Paradine Case.* The director wore the clothes, followed the sports, and read the newspapers of his homeland. *Spellbound* had been based on an English novel, *Rebecca* and *Suspicion* had been set near London. Preparation for *Paradine* would naturally include a trip abroad to research the script and view prospective locations. The director longed to work overseas, not simply away from Selznick but close to his Transatlantic partner. "For me, Sidney, what counts is who you work with every day," Hitchcock told Bernstein; though they met sporadically, the men conferred by telephone every Sunday morning. Selznick and *Paradine* would foot the bill for their next face-to-face meeting.

If *The Paradine Case* itself interested Hitchcock, the character of Ingrid Paradine must have intrigued him even more. She embodied the dark side of his feminine ideal, the kind of woman whom he fully realized in another flawed work, *Marnie.* While *Blackmail* had opened with the apprehension of a suspect, *The Paradine Case* would begin with the arrest of what Hitchcock called "a soignée society woman." The gabardine aura of the plainclothesmen and the humiliation of Mrs. Paradine in her high-class milieu appealed to the director; from such odd juxtapositions he built both domestic comedy and ironic drama. The climax in Old Bailey, another of the Hitchcock monuments, would embody a vivid contrast, the director said, "supremely dispassionate conversation about the most passionate things." Hitchcock undoubtedly read *The Paradine Case* as a cautionary tale about the need for control and the wages of "letting go." Because "containment was his," its obverse roused him.

Efforts to adapt *The Paradine Case* at MGM came to nothing in 1933, 1936, and 1940. Joe Breen told Louis Mayer that a leading lady who is both adulteress and murderess, who is acquitted as the result of perjured testimony, and who escapes justice by committing suicide—yet who emerges on balance as a sympathetic character—was highly problematic; a judge who "revels in his power to inflict the death penalty and who enjoys seeing people suffer, is also highly questionable from the standpoint of general industry policy." A decade after the novel's publication, Salka Viertel and two other MGM screenwriters had satisfied most of the PCA's criticisms, but their screenplay draft apparently strayed from Hitchens's original. "If there are faults in construction," Selznick continued to believe, "it is better to keep them than to try to change them around, because no one can certainly pick out the chemicals which contribute to the making of a classic. And there is always the danger that, by tampering, you may destroy the essential chemical." In the laboratory of the soundstage, Hitchcock performed his own experiments—originals, not replications. *Rebecca* had emerged the Selznick–du Maurier *Rebecca;* would *The Paradine Case* become the Hitchcock or the Selznick–Hichens *Paradine Case*?

Hitchcock, Alma, and Barbara Keon, a Selznick stalwart assigned to the *Paradine* project, retired to the Hitchcock home to develop a treatment. Each Wednesday, Selznick paid the director more than double his initial $2,500 weekly salary, yet the evolving Bernstein–Hitchcock arrangement, along with the elusiveness of the director during contract renegotiations, piqued Selznick. The *Hollywood Reporter* said (apparently erroneously) that Hitchcock was writing a book, and Alexander Korda told Selznick that Grant and Bergman had something cooking with the director. Meanwhile, Hitchcock was supervising post-production on *Notorious.* "I am sure we are really getting finagled on the Hitchcock matter," Selznick told O'Shea, whom he asked to monitor the Bellagio Road "country club." Fearful of queering a deal with Hitchcock, though, Selznick kept his distance. He told the writers specifically what he wanted—a *Paradine Case* dialogue treatment for budget purposes—and generally left them alone to produce it. The trio completed its assignment in April 1946.

In his 195-page first draft, Hitchcock closely followed the novel, suggesting more haste of completion than lack of involvement. Yet the work evidenced his participation and influence. When Gay Keane compares Ingrid Paradine to a Strindberg woman, she also sketches a type of Hitchcock heroine who emerged during the Selznick period.

> They're usually beautiful, calm and self-possessed—but so much behind the face.
> (she thinks for a moment then continues)
> Almost mysterious—maybe a touch of deep hysteria. There's something merciless in them—terribly merciless. And they're brainy with a horrible sort of perching braininess. And they keep at it—yes, they keep at it.

The intelligence, the obsession, the relentlessness characterize the leading women in more than one Hitchcock film, from the unseen Rebecca to Madeleine in *Vertigo*. Hitchcock said that he knew women like this; they had an easy sexuality yet protested when someone around them cursed. As usual, the director approached *The Paradine Case* with more zest than he later cared to admit.

In the treatment, Hitchcock told Selznick, he tried to capture "the flavor of the 'back-stage' of the law." What do they have there? he asked. The Inner Temple with its Dickensian backgrounds, the "Pump Court, little bay-windowed wig-makers shops, and other characteristic backgrounds." The British "things" that charmed Hitchcock alienated many Americans to whom *Paradine* would have to appeal. "We all like 'dear Old England,' " a small-town exhibitor complained to RKO on the release of *Suspicion,* but "why, oh, why do you spoil a good plot and good artists by making it so very English that a big share of our patrons object to it & don't come to see it?" Three years later, that question escaped Selznick and Hitchcock. The consequences affected Selznick Productions, then Transatlantic Pictures.

Having nailed down his free trip to England, Hitchcock addressed other matters. He told Selznick that Sir Simon Flaquer (Keane's associate) and his bright daughter Judy (Gay's friend) lent themselves to comic treatment and could relieve Hichens's sobriety. The "grim-faced, humorless" Keane, reminiscent of "the old silent movie heroes like

Conway Tearle or Clive Brook," also needed "some extra dimensions, especially a sense of humor, so that we get some change of color when he goes into his purple moods about Mrs. Paradine." Gay, "fairly dull" yet "a very vital person structurally," also needed development; Hitchcock could remedy her reticence with "a sufficient number of 'mental' closeups" but hoped to achieve something in the writing that would lift her from her reserve. Selznick must have read the "Notes" attached to the treatment with a jaundiced eye. In addition to the old battle over wit compromising serious drama, the architecture seemed raw. "The picture starts off being the story of Mrs. Paradine," some magazine editors later told Selznick, "then it becomes the story of [Malcolm] Keane, then the story of Gay Keane, and once around again Willie before the tale is finally concluded." Hitchcock and company had failed to blend the two obvious love triangles of Keane–Paradine–Latour (the valet) and Keane–Paradine–Keane. A minor conflict between Horfield and Gay Keane as well as the subplot of Horfield and his callous treatment of his wife, Lady Sophy, also remained unintegrated. Hitchcock needed a scenarist, and Hecht was unavailable.

The Paradine Case may have begun to fall apart with the hiring of the screenwriter. In spring 1946, Hitchcock convinced Selznick not only to hire James Bridie but to permit him to complete an unsupervised first draft. Though previously acquainted with the Scottish physician-turned-playwright, Hitchcock remained blind to his weaknesses. The director needed someone with a strong grasp of dramaturgy, which Selznick had formerly provided. Yet Bridie cared little about structure. Asked about illogical twists or slack motivation, the Scot would respond, "What does it matter?" These revelations lay ahead. Earlier in his association with Hitchcock, Selznick would have vetoed Bridie. But the producer had surrendered much of his control over the director. Neither actors, company executives, nor Selznick himself readily denied Hitchcock anything. More than the formal business suits he wore, his manner discouraged give-and-take. His moody withdrawal when crossed and his evasiveness when pursued (especially with contracts) lent him the control that Selznick had lost in their relationship. Having usually managed Hitchcock with kid gloves, Selznick found his hands now tied behind his back.

* * *

In early May 1946, Hitchcock and Bridie spent a day together in New York, Hitchcock en route to Britain and Bridie having just come from there. While they met, Selznick moved forward on set designs and casting. Still haunted by the specter of *Gone With the Wind,* Selznick determined to make *The Paradine Case* a picture worthy of his reputation and his now tarnished motto, "In the Tradition of Quality." The budget and the commitment would not only enhance Selznick Productions but convince possible defectors like Hitchcock to maintain their allegiance. Casting offered the first evidence of Selznick's intention. Given the potentially narrow commercial prospects for *The Paradine Case,* another studio might have tried to offset the English setting and high seriousness by casting a major box office attraction in the lead. For Malcolm Keane, however, Selznick wanted Laurence Olivier; the Shakespearean actor could depict the obsessive within the character and lend the film prestige. When Olivier proved unavailable, Selznick thought of Maurice Evans. With a hairpiece and a "crack cameraman," Evans would test well, Selznick believed. "He is no romantic dream prince but [I] think this is all to the good for the picture since the woman does not go for him but for [the valet Latour] and actually I think the picture would be off balance if he had either any more or any less romantic appeal than he has."

Perhaps anxious to impress potential Transatlantic backers with his savvy, Hitchcock campaigned for either of two Selznick contract players, Joseph Cotten or Gregory Peck. The *Spellbound* reviews and gross receipts convinced Hitchcock that whatever the limitations of Peck, the actor enjoyed an enormous following. Moviegoers thought almost nothing of Olivier or Evans, but they informed the Gallup poll that only Bing Crosby and Alan Ladd outranked Peck in their esteem. *The Paradine Case* would be hard to sell, Hitchcock probably realized; irrespective of the content, though, Peck could draw audiences into the theaters. Selznick and Peck himself hesitated. Would his youth and his American accent militate against a convincing performance as an experienced, dazzling British trial lawyer? Hitchcock persuaded Peck to test for Keane. Peck warmed to the lawyer, Selznick again hesitated. The role imperfectly fit the actor, the producer intimated to O'Shea; if the picture failed, Peck's career might dip with it. Selznick proposed Alan Marshall (who hated the part) and James Mason; Hitchcock touted Cotten and Peck. Finally, the sales department joined forces with Hitchcock and Peck against Selznick. *The Paradine Case* had its Anthony (formerly Malcolm) Keane.

Casting the enigmatic Mrs. Paradine challenged the endurance of both Hitchcock and Selznick. After Greta Garbo rejected the part, Selznick offered it to Ingrid Bergman. The Selznick–Bergman relationship had become as knotty and sensitive as the Selznick–Hitchcock relationship. The Swedish actress had called David "my father" and "my second husband," terms of endearment that he had encouraged through his paternalism. But the honeymoon had ended. According to Petter Lindstrom, his wife, Ingrid,

> disliked Selznick for several reasons. He kept her out of work when she wanted to work. He wanted to prolong her contract against her will. He refused to let her appear on radio. When he sold her services to other studios, he never gave her an increase in salary, though even despite the wartime labor law, he could have found a way to give her more money. She had firmly decided never to make another contract with him.

Hitchcock could have recited the same litany. About to break with Selznick, Bergman refused Ingrid Paradine. More disappointed than angered by the attitude of his Scandinavian import, Selznick next considered Hedy Lamarr, a weak third choice. But Hollywood had somehow homogenized the mystery and sex appeal that the young actress had brought to *Ecstasy,* the motion picture that had made her a star. The options shrank. Rather than film *The Paradine Case* with a "compromise cast," though, the producer who had no stars decided to make one.

Selznick turned to Europe for a new face, one that would brighten *The Paradine Case* and affirm his power as a mogul. When the vigilant Jenia Reissar suggested a young but celebrated Italian performer named Alida Valli, Selznick ordered a screen test. The March 1946 footage confirmed her talent as well as her starchy figure and lame English. The producer nonetheless reasoned that her association with him would not only attract other Italian artists whom he wished to sign, but perhaps favorably influence Italian distributors whose work on his behalf could help thaw frozen currency. Although the prolonged negotiations threatened to collapse when Valli heard that Bergman had left Selznick, few Europeans could resist the lure of Hollywood, especially when a deal included Hitchcock and Peck. By fall 1946, Valli had agreed to play Maddalena (formerly Ingrid) Paradine.

For the pivotal roles of Latour and Gay Keane, Selznick cast actors largely unknown in the States, Louis Jourdan and Ann Todd. Hitchcock objected to the former, endorsed the latter. Producer and director reached an uneasy agreement on the remaining roles. After Claude Rains turned down the licentious Horfield (not "quite my dish"), Hitchcock cast Charles Laughton, really the better choice since the director wished to temper the judge's sadism with humor. The regal Ethel Barrymore agreed to portray Horfield's abused wife. Hitchcock picked the supporting cast from among his English actor-acquaintances: Isobel Elsom, John Williams, Phyllis Morris, and the faithful Leo G. Carroll. (Many of these performers cost Selznick dearly. With the various delays that slowed production, the actors remained on salary much longer than originally planned; no one dared ask Hitchcock to terminate them.) Years later, Hitchcock grumbled about the casting. According to Carol Stevens, though, Hitchcock returned from *Notorious* as Selznick Productions' "key asset"; since he behaved accordingly, he never would have been deliberately crossed by his producer. And surely he recognized the potential of a cast that balanced handsome young actors from two continents with the seasoned talents of Laughton and Barrymore as well as the box office appeal of Gregory Peck. Selznick taught Hitchcock to appreciate the power of stars, their purpose and their special light. In *The Paradine Case*, the director had a galaxy.

While James Bridie struggled alone with a dialogue script and Selznick negotiated the various actors' contracts, Hitchcock tramped around Europe. In Nice and Paris, where the war-delayed French premiere of *Spellbound* occurred, he searched for an alternate Mrs. Paradine, an actress-in-reserve in case Valli fell through. In London, besides conferences with Sidney Bernstein on their Transatlantic pictures, he explored possible backdrops for *Paradine*. Selznick production manager Fred Ahern and Hitchcock spent nine days looking at railway stations, restaurants, Holloway Prison, the Bow Street police station, and Old Bailey. On May 15, they flew to Cumberland where they selected the railway stations, houses, roads, inns, and gardens used to represent the Paradine country estate; a second unit would later film these and other sites as "dear Old England" backgrounds.

Italian actress Alida Valli (shown here with Gregory Peck) opened doors for Selznick. "I haven't yet met anyone who hasn't told me he would like to work for you," Jenia Reissar wrote to Selznick from Italy, "though most people wince at a seven-year contract."

Anthony Keane (Peck) pleads for Mrs. Paradine in Old Bailey.

In letters home, their content pipelined to Selznick, Ahern sketched a rosy picture of Hitchcock. Selznick could read between lines: Hitchcock devoted his days to *The Paradine Case,* his nights to Transatlantic. Perhaps so, but *Paradine* hardly suffered. In London, Hitchcock and Ahern asked a prominent judicial wig and robe maker to add *Paradine* to his case load. Hitchcock also attended a session at Old Bailey, sketchbook in hand. He intended to rebuild the most famous of English criminal courtrooms and, like Selznick, insisted on accuracy; he even persuaded the Keeper to permit a camera crew to film the vacant court. Talking with reporters later, Hitchcock emphasized the preparation that he would bring to the picture. "As I watched the judge," the director said, "I even knew what lens I would use to photograph him." Hitchcock projected imperturbability, utter confidence, supreme knowledge. Against this sardonic mountain of assurance, the balky performer and the interfering producer (more and more frequently, the interfering producer) found themselves disarmed. Bankers, Hitchcock hoped, would also get the message: the owners of Transatlantic Pictures would spend money efficiently.

The bridge between drawing board and soundstage still eluded Transatlantic. Although Frank Capra reportedly financed his independent production company with only his reputation and earning power as collateral, Bernstein and Hitchcock would have to offer lenders something more substantive: a distribution contract with an established Hollywood company. The distributor was the silent partner of most independent producer-directors. He guaranteed bankers that the finished picture would receive adequate promotion and exhibition; he also pledged his assets as security against default. From abroad, Bernstein explored Transatlantic options. The slow pace must have worried Hitchcock, not only because of his financial insecurity but because of his relationship with Selznick. Despite producer-director meetings about major decisions, Selznick remained the employer, Hitchcock the employee. Hitchcock might know which lens he would use, but Selznick could demand retakes. And unless Bernstein soon arranged distribution contracts and production loans for Transatlantic, the director might be forced to sign another contract with Selznick.

In England, Hitchcock worked through the day and sometimes into the night on *Paradine*. Costs began to rise when the second unit experienced the vagaries of the British climate. Fred Ahern scheduled five days to shoot the Cumberland exteriors, but finally required five weeks. Added to rain and clouds, Ahern said, were the inferiority of equipment and personnel. The implications—if not the expense—should have concerned Hitchcock, for Bernstein wanted to split the Transatlantic production schedule between England and America.

Back in Los Angeles in June, Hitchcock conferred with production designer Mac Johnson on the interiors for *The Paradine Case*. Pressed, the director could tick off three ways—the $1,000, $5,000, and $10,000 ways—to build a set; the Universal pictures and their percentage compensation had demonstrated his cost-consciousness. Unsupervised or unmotivated, he aimed for the sky. The money-no-object environment of *Foreign Correspondent* became the model for *The Paradine Case*. The trouble began with ceilings.

Selznick International had always matted in its on-screen ceilings through special effects, but on *Paradine* Hitchcock asked that they be constructed. A strong production manager like Ray Klune, who bitterly departed following *Duel in the Sun*, might have challenged Hitchcock; many key people associated with Selznick over the decade, however, now worked elsewhere. Hitchcock outranked those who remained and intimidated the rest. Selznick had not transmitted a money-no-object message to the set of *The Paradine Case*. Still, the reports from England, the frayed lines of command within his small company, and his own reticence to cross Hitchcock cast a mood of laissez-faire over the lot. When department heads and bookkeepers nodded, Hitchcock naturally ran. By the time Selznick discovered that every member of his staff had acquiesced to Hitchcock, the $15,000 ceilings—hardly visible when filmed—were already in place. The bill for *Paradine* scene design finally exceeded that of *Gone With the Wind*. Selznick may have wondered whether he could afford Hitchcock.

Throughout summer 1946, Hitchcock worked long-distance with James Bridie on the script. Anxiety again affected Hitchcock. Hypochondria ran in his family, the director maintained, and doctors found no significant medical cause for his malaise. Biographer John Russell Taylor suggests that Hitchcock suffered from a form of male menopause, a mid-life crisis triggered by a change either hormonal or mental; Donald Spoto locates its source in a "dissatisfaction with the Selznick empire, which was diminishing in effectiveness and prestige and efficiency." However supportable these reasons (though Hitchcock himself contributed to the diminished efficiency), another also seems viable. Hitchcock stood poised between the known of contract work and the unknown of independent production. Selznick had given him the luxury of prominent writers, overstuffed budgets, major stars, and indulgent crews, all of the resources to make important motion pictures with none of the attendant financial risk. While *The Paradine Case* did not worry Hitchcock, the *end* of *The Paradine Case* would mark the end of filmmaking as Hitchcock had known it. And for a man who feared many things, especially financial uncertainty, the removal of the safety net may have been daunting.

Selznick had fixed a late-autumn starting date for principal photography on *The Paradine Case,* but much script work remained. After a brief working vacation in New York, where he met Fred Ahern returning from two frustrating months of second-unit filming in London, Hitchcock retired to his home in Santa Cruz to confront unanswered questions about the script, particularly its opening and its climax. Although he liked the idea of beginning with Mrs. Paradine's arrest, he felt that the audience should see the Paradine murder, perhaps in a prologue as "silent pantomime." As written, the drama promised a more refined narrative; as amended, a more visceral, evocative one. The climax offered Hitchcock and his transatlantic collaborator another dilemma. If the prosecution broke down Mrs. Paradine on the witness stand, Keane would vanish from the ending and weaken the drama. Selznick and *Notorious* had reminded Hitchcock of the importance of moving the leading man all the way through the script. We must "get our character conflict pyramiding as a climax to our story as a whole. Otherwise," Hitchcock told Bridie, "there's a grave danger of the whole thing dissipating into an anti-climax."

The long-distance work with Bridie posed more problems for Selznick than Hitchcock. As Selznick came to realize, Hitchcock used the transatlantic delays to formulate Transatlantic plans; the director had in fact invited Bridie to adapt *Under Capricorn.* Selznick must have resented Hitchcock conducting Transatlantic business on Selznick time, but he said nothing. By October, Bridie had forwarded to Hollywood his last contributions to *The Paradine Case.* A preoccupied Hitchcock sat on the script until Selznick prodded him. Like *Lifeboat,* *The Paradine Case* was overlong, partly the result of Bridie's attempt to solve story problems yet retain those elements in which the director had special interest. Selznick told Hitchcock to trim the script, specifically to eliminate a trial scene written solely to prove Keane's histrionic ability and some other scenes depicting the pomp of Old Bailey, of greater interest to British than American audiences. He also asked Hitchcock to address censorship concerns, for the studio could not send Joe Breen a script that contained the elements to which he had previously objected.

The dawdling necessitated a postponement of the starting date and a hasty revision by a willing Ben Hecht. Working at his Oceanside home with the Hitchcocks, Hecht wrote with his characteristic dispatch yet left Selznick much to do. "I am on the verge of collapse and not thinking clearly, and am having under these conditions to try to patch up and rewrite the Hitchcock script," Selznick wired O'Shea on the day before Hecht left the production. He fully anticipated putting the picture into production "willy-nilly"—increasingly a problem at Selznick Productions—and achieving the necessary quality through expensive retakes, all this with a budget already in excess of $3 million. The feelings of Hitchcock aside, *The Paradine Case* more than ever needed producer David Selznick. Benzedrine by day and barbiturates by night fueled Selznick. The combination made him, at best, difficult to work with, not only because of his nocturnal hours but because of his erratic performance. In years past, during periods of pre-production, he had focused on the goal at hand, the picture; now his center had become the self. Ego had increased his command over the script and principal photography of *Duel in the Sun*. A strange blend of arrogance and insecurity would prompt him to continue rewriting *The Paradine Case* well into production.

With principal photography set to begin on Thursday, December 19, Hitchcock invited Ann Todd to join him and Alma in Santa Cruz for a last long weekend before stepping onto the treadmill of production. Away from Los Angeles, Hitchcock worried about the return of Selznick to the throttle, yet found time for a stern practical joke. He and Alma met Ann Todd at the Mark Hopkins bar, where they immediately turned to bicker with one another over something. When a tall cowboy with studs running up and down his white suit made a pass at Todd, she turned to Hitchcock for support. The droll Hitchcock cast her as an unknown actress whom he intended to audition: "Well, Miss Todd," he said in a loud voice, "let me see your legs." To no avail, Alma shushed her husband. "Well," he told Todd and her by now sympathetic Texas friend, "you're coming to Santa Cruz with us. We'll talk it over during the weekend."

Back in Hollywood, Selznick demanded a star buildup for his new imports. Valli (as he would bill her) began trimming inches from her figure, and Jourdan had his teeth capped, his heels elevated, and his hair fashionably barbered. Selznick wanted both Valli and Ann Todd smartly dressed in *The Paradine Case*. Hitchcock cautioned Selznick that English audiences would laugh at Mrs. Paradine if she wore clothes obviously beyond the means of even a wealthy English woman in postwar London; the producer snapped that he would not drape Valli in suits that a moviegoer could find "in Dubuque and in Dallas." Hitchcock conceded the point, partially because he shunned confrontation. When Selznick chose an enormous brocade dressing gown for Ann Todd, which she deemed grossly inappropriate, the director suggested that she take up her dissatisfaction with the producer.

> I marched into Selznick's office [Todd later recalled]. "Mr. Selznick, 1 don't think I want to wear this dressing gown, a husband and wife in their bedroom alone. I wouldn't be wearing a brocade." "Yeah, you would." "Well, I don't like it and you brought me all these thousands of miles from England and told me, 'We're very real with our films.' " So he said, "People in Arizona have got to know you're rich."

Hitchcock could not have strongly objected: the chic wardrobe complemented his smooth camera movements and longer takes, two elements of Hollywood glamor photography influenced by David Selznick.

Just before Christmas 1946, his storyboard sketches complete, Hitchcock began shooting *The Paradine Case* with his characteristic glow. Lee Garmes would photograph the picture in continuity, a signal advantage to Jourdan and Valli, both of whom would be learning the script as well as the Hollywood modus operandi. Early in the schedule, Hitchcock shot one of the sequences that had drawn him to the picture, the arrest of Mrs. Paradine. The director had adequate counsel. A technical advisor from the police read the script and warned Hitchcock to keep his detectives "coldly polite, terse, firm, to the point, not too warmly disposed towards a person's social rank, but mannerly all the time"; Hitchcock obliged by playing the officers almost straight (as he rarely did in his pictures), with just a scintilla of humor. Selznick oversaw the distaff. Though the producer sometimes regarded young actresses as chattel, he arrayed them as goddesses. On *Intermezzo* a decade before, he had told Ingrid Bergman that he wanted her "arrival in the American film world to be like a shock that would just hit people between the eyes"; accordingly, the retakes of her entrance continued through her last day in Hollywood. Selznick must have told Hitchcock to photograph Valli with equal care: unless the director gave her allure from her first appearance on screen, audiences might not accept her as Peck's seducer, much less as a star. To introduce Valli, Hitchcock moved the camera through the foyer and into the study where Mrs. Paradine receives the police; once they arrive, the camera circles around her in a fluid motion that looks back to a few isolated but important shots in *Notorious* and ahead to the Transatlantic pictures. The long gown that Mrs. Paradine wears, her smart hairstyle, her composure— all find their apotheosis in the sweeping camera movements that typify what Hitchcock learned from Selznick.

Yet the early footage revealed something ominous. Hitchcock consistently emphasized the need for performers to contain rather than demonstrate expression. While Selznick hovered over Valli, supervising her makeup and costume, the director urged her to "do nothing well." Novelist Robert Hichens had created a puzzling character in Mrs. Paradine. By including so little psychological detail about her, he obscured the reasons for the murder of her husband and left even careful readers wondering whether she were woman or chimera. The *Times Literary Supplement* had called her featureless, "the female puppet in a thriller." Hitchcock had preserved the thin characterization and, along with the refinement of makeup and costume, pushed Valli toward dryness of performance. His doctrine of "negative acting" worked only too well: Valli posed rather than performed. Her stasis and the cool visuals promised a claustrophobic experience for moviegoers.

The visual strategy of the opening sequence in *Paradine,* particularly that interplay of moving camera and fixed subject, became even more predominant in the remainder of the picture. "I chose medium shots to establish the scene," Hitchcock said, "and struck hard for dramatic impact by concentrating at close range on the key figures." Since Hitchcock did not edit his Selznick pictures, he had limited control over just how the producer would cut together his images; as much as possible, however, he shot the picture to mandate the "jigsaw cutting" that would disorient and thus "thrill" the audience. Part of his technique, exemplified by the downhill skiing sequence of *Spellbound,* involved cutting into close-ups that did not match adjacent shots. For *The Paradine Case,* Hitchcock composed a number of close-ups head-on rather than fully or three-quarter profiled; since the eyes looked slightly above rather than into the lens, the composition did not break through the cinema's "fourth wall" yet adequately stirred viewers accustomed to a smooth flow from image to image. An alarmed Selznick caught these shots amid the first rushes. However suitable for highly dramatic moments, the shots were "ugly as to composition" and "most unattractive of the individuals, as well as being jarring to mood and smoothness," Selznick informed Hitchcock and his cinematographer. Precisely the point. Only reluctantly would Hitchcock stop shooting them.

On other pictures in other years, Selznick brought a certain humanity to character development that happily threw Hitchcock's more dispassionate style into relief. On *The Paradine Case,* which he extensively rewrote, Selznick occasionally demonstrated his good ear for an original piece of dialogue, either borrowing freely from Hichens or writing his own. "Men are such horrible beasts," a friend tells Gay Keane. "I hope—no, I don't hope they hang her. I don't like breaking pretty things." Much of the remaining dialogue that Selznick authored and hastily sent to the floor lacked spontaneity. Because of the immediacy of cinema, its photographic realism and apparent proximity of actor and audience, motion picture dialogue cannot sustain much inflation; it must be pithy but without self-consciousness. Jo Swerling, with whom Hitchcock worked on *Lifeboat,* could bend language from another medium, the stage in his case; Selznick lacked that talent. Too novelistic, his dialogue turned as arid as Hitchcock's images. Their previous pictures had succeeded in part because of the tensions between their narrative and visual styles. *The Paradine Case* would fail because of an unexpected consonance.

Some dissonance remained. By January 1947, with costs mounting, Selznick told O'Shea that Hitchcock had "slowed down unaccountably" and grown "out of hand." But when the producer finally spoke to the director about the inefficiency, Hitchcock charged that Selznick had gone into production with photographic and recording equipment

On the loading dock at RKO-Pathé. Standing: Hitchcock, Louis Jourdan, Selznick, Charles Laughton, Charles Coburn, Gregory Peck. Seated: Joan Tetzel, Ann Todd, Ethel Barrymore.

"twenty years behind the times." On the second day of filming, a camera had to be replaced because of scratches on the lens; in succeeding days, problems with a boom and another lens caused delays. Since *Spellbound,* Selznick and his operation had become vulnerable to attack. Larger studios making a number of pictures simultaneously could spread the inevitable waste over a number of production budgets and thus dissipate the effect. Selznick could not. But the real problem lay in personnel, not matériel. Over the five years of Selznick International, Selznick had formed a cadre of people experienced in high-quality independent production, a rarity around Hollywood. When administrative positions became vacant, he could promote from within. Seven years later, with so many former employees free-lancing, those days seemed very far away. His meddling in every department of the company resulted in the usual counterproductive double bind: Selznick begged his staff to show initiative, then oversaw—and criticized—their every move. No longer an inexperienced director of "little British thrillers," Hitchcock bridled under the supervision.

The relationship between Selznick and Hitchcock demanded restraint from both men, especially since both wished to preserve the fragile status quo. Having launched a distribution company to handle *Duel in the Sun,* Selznick would soon need other pictures from other independents to help absorb overhead; whether as contract director for Selznick Productions or independent producer distributing through the Selznick Releasing Organization, Hitchcock represented a potential asset. Meanwhile, doubts about Transatlantic encouraged Hitchcock to continue toying over a new long-term nonexclusive contract with Selznick. George Cukor knew Hitchcock only slightly but well enough to call him "so perverse! He'd never tell you what he really thinks, never, never!" That "perversity" irritated Selznick. In his cathartic memoranda, the voluble producer told his unfortunate targets what he really thought—and more. Hitchcock dodged frontal attacks with the grace of an athlete. Few others could have kept Selznick negotiating a new contract for almost two years.

Displaced tensions surfaced elsewhere. Gregory Peck later recalled that the differences between Selznick and Hitchcock made the Englishman seem "really bored with [*The Paradine Case*], and often we would look over to his chair after a take and he would be—or pretended to be—asleep." Though the hot lights and the occasionally heavy lunches may have prompted a catnap, the mixture of stars, character actors, and discoveries whom Selznick had cast would not permit Hitchcock to nod long through the period of principal photography. He may have dozed to conserve energy, or he may have pretended to doze to win control. Either way, Hitchcock projected confidence. And if through his behavior this notable director implied that the performances were at least not unsatisfactory, could any actor dispute him?

The snoozing Hitchcock must nonetheless have roused or confirmed suspicions of inadequacy within his leading man. Though Ann Todd found Peck very relaxed, the part felt as unnatural to him as the Ede and Ravenscroft juridical wig. Too young for Keane, Peck tried various mustaches for aging, then grayed his temples. He studied audio transcriptions of an Anthony Eden speech to blend his voice with that of his English co-stars, but could not maintain a convincing accent. Hitchcock offered only one suggestion: "Negative acting." The result produced stolidity rather than inexpression. Uncharacteristically mute, Selznick left Peck and Hitchcock to share blame for the weak performance. Actors like Cary Grant and Joseph Cotten needed little from Hitchcock, which suited him. When men like Peck sought more than their blocking, the director could turn sarcastic, even sullen or mute. During filming on *The Birds,* a reporter asked Rod Taylor what the picture was about. "Hell, I don't know," he said. Hitchcock "never told us."

The Hitchcock perversity affected women differently. Although he could scorn actresses, including frosty English girls, he courted Ann Todd and Alida Valli. "Now remember," he told Todd, taking her aside at the beginning of principal photography, "you're playing the wife in this, and I want you to be the most exciting personality on that screen." His precise direction, stated in few words, pinpointed an emotion with extraordinary clarity. Keenly involved and attentive, he watched Todd through most takes. "You'd feel his alertness throughout his body," Todd recalled. Afterward he would compliment her. "Hitch was very human; he would say, 'That was wonderful,' which very few directors could do. He could lift you up." And occasionally weigh you down. Once, while Todd sat on a stage bed, mentally preparing for a difficult bedroom scene with Peck, the director ran from the back of the stage and jumped on her. "Relax, girl, relax," he said. Despite his professed scorn for actors, many stars loved working under Hitchcock. And as performers replaced producers as centers of power in Hollywood, his reputation as a magnet for actors would have increased his value to Selznick.

"Negative acting is what I want most," Hitchcock said in 1947, "the ability to express words by doing nothing. That is the hardest thing on screen—to do nothing well—and that is what I demand." For younger actors like Alida Valli, Hitchcock used his authority to exact his demand. But persuading experienced actors to "do nothing" required more tact and tenacity than Hitchcock possessed. The sluggish progress of *The Paradine Case* resulted in large part from problems with actors —none more so than Charles Laughton.

"A Laughton picture is one long battle from start to finish—Laughton versus Laughton," Hitchcock said. "He frets and strains and argues continuously with himself. And he is never satisfied." Though the struggle actually pitched Laughton against Hitchcock, the two liked each other. Laughton had his own perversities. A loosely guarded secret in Hollywood, his sexual ambivalence may have contributed to his acid charm and provided Hitchcock, off the record, with some of his most pointed but amusing gibes. The role of Horfield—sadist, lecher, public official—seemed ideal for Laughton. But neither containment nor negative acting was his. Less than four weeks into principal photography, with the English actor obliterating the punctuation from his speeches and thus making them unintelligible, it became apparent to Selznick and even Hitchcock that the Laughton scenes would require extensive retakes.

Laughton's performance worsened over time. Rather than mine the subtle wit from Horfield, he stalked big laughs. An apelike gait and exaggerated facial expressions and gestures further enlarged his already outsize performance. In one scene, playing Ann Todd's seducer, he roughly took her hand and squeezed so hard that she winced; five takes produced the same result. "Charlie, do remember this time, it's too much, it's getting hammy," Hitchcock urged. Laughton "yessed, yessed" the director, then changed nothing. Hitchcock altered the setup to get the shot. Screening the dailies, Selznick worried not only that the shift in key from the Laughton performance to that of the other actors would disrupt the picture but that the British Board of Censors, always sensitive to the presentation of judges, would view his mugging as

"That's a charming ruby," the lecherous Lord Horfield (Laughton) says to Gay Keane (Todd).
"Did your husband earn all that whacking away at juries?"

offensive to English jurisprudence and call for major cuts in overseas prints. Selznick warned Hitchcock to sit on Laughton, yet the director could neither reason with nor intimidate the actor. The Horfield juices flowed. Toward the end of principal photography, Laughton told Hitchcock that he wanted to make a dress for his wife out of his bright red wool judge's robe. "Nonsense," the director replied, only partly in jest, "you want to wear it yourself around home and make life hideous for people."

As production moved toward the midpoint, Selznick freighted *The Paradine Case* with his nervous involvement, again conveyed not always through Hitchcock, but often directly to the cast or crew. Some of the memoranda that appeared in staff mailboxes or on dressing room mirrors were complimentary and encouraging. The producer called the dailies of Jourdan's first scene "superb. My enthusiasm for you and my confidence in you have grown even more," he wrote to the Frenchman, "although previously I didn't think this was possible." But other memoranda, notable for the mood shifts of their author, addressed Hitchcockian "things" rather than character and story. "For God's sake, stand up," Selznick ordered Todd, "you've got a bust, haven't you?" After viewing another set of dailies, he told Peck not to return to the set until the makeup man straightened the actor's eyebrows. A more attentive producer would have constructively criticized the performance. The tone of the "notes" would darken as the period of principal photography neared its end, both because of difficulties with *The Paradine Case* and because a number of other matters demanded attention, few of them promising a pat resolution.

Portrait of Jennie, the story of a painter and his beautiful but phantom young lover, had hastily gone into production on location in Manhattan, where Selznick hoped to capture the New York milieu convincingly. Not yet fully recovered from her own or Selznick's pending divorce, Jennifer Jones starred in the picture with Joseph Cotten, but despite the potent box office of the cast, the picture threatened (in Selznick's words) to become "one of the most awful experiences any studio ever had." Selznick predicted cost overruns when cast and crew traveled three thousand miles away from his control. They indeed occurred. Linked to problems in financing his distribution company, finding parts for his young contract stars, and fighting the lingering censorship battles over *Duel in the Sun,* as well as his own fatigue, the

247

Jennie crisis made Selznick a poor choice to bring grace and line to the *Paradine* script. Nightly, however, he scanned the rushes and then revised the screenplay.

The Selznick rewrite inevitably slowed production. Hitchcock would "see those blue pages in the morning and he would just retreat to his bungalow," Gregory Peck recalled; "in all fairness to Hitch, the dialogue was invariably worse not better." As the actors memorized their new lines, Hitchcock revised his prearranged setups to accommodate the changes. Meanwhile, a studio car sped the rewrite, four and five script pages daily, to Joe Breen; only after the censorship office approved the alterations could Hitchcock begin. "So very often we didn't shoot anything until eleven o'clock or twelve o'clock or even until after lunch," Peck said. Hitchcock naturally resented the violation of his sense of order. Moreover, the tension between producer and director caused an undesirable imbalance between director and actors, director and crew. "A very poor method of work," Hitchcock believed.

When Ben Hecht joked about the midnight dictation of new pages, Hitchcock saw that the gag reached Selznick. Constant rewriting is "not a new job for me," the injured producer told Hecht, "nor a new method, that either the studio or Hitch is contending with, and the sympathy and criticism of those involved is accordingly completely without justification." Selznick was right. And wrong. The balance of power between Selznick and Hitchcock seemed more precarious than ever. Director of photography Lee Garmes felt himself caught between Selznick's increasing involvement in bringing glamor to the picture and Hitchcock's demand for a harsh tonality. Although in earlier years Selznick let the director guide the cinematographer, the producer himself had written pointedly to Garmes about elements of the footage that needed correction. He paid fastidious attention to his nascent stars. Striving for a chiaroscuro effect, Hitchcock ordered Jourdan photographed in shadow (Latour being a shadowy figure); Selznick ran the rushes and ordered the Frenchman brought into the light, especially so that filmgoers could see his best feature, his eyes. Garmes tried to strike a middle path but succeeded only in bringing both Selznick and Hitchcock down on him. In a memorandum to the director about the flat photography, Selznick wrote:

David Selznick with Jennifer Jones, 1946.

There is no shading or attempt to photograph Jourdan interestingly as there was the first few days, and if we're not careful this will be true of Valli. In filling in light for the eyes, [Garmes] failed at this objective and lost what he had before. I can't figure out for the life of me why he can't give us what he had originally, and why he can't give us eyes that are not black sockets that give us nothing.

The problem may have been that Selznick perceived Garmes as Hitchcock's man, while Hitchcock perceived him as Selznick's man. Selznick had unwittingly played the Hitchcock game of divide and conquer. The director already maintained a certain distance from the lesser members of his crew, but toward the end of *The Paradine Case,* he even gave his photographic instructions to Garmes through the intermediary of an assistant director.

One day, looking ahead to the fluidity of his Transatlantic pictures, Hitchcock prepared an elaborate tracking shot of Peck and Todd. While grips frantically pulled away furniture to make a path, the probing camera followed the actors through a long and arduous take. Todd called the shot "frightening," but Selznick had the last word: "Theatrical." Appearing on the set, he ordered the sequence filmed conventionally. Hitchcock unwillingly obliged. At least three scenes between Valli and Peck occurred in a spare five-by-six conference room at Holloway Prison. A minimalist, Hitchcock often put actors in confined places to make them (and the audience) sweat. The stark scenes in this virtually unfurnished room—the antithesis of the mahogany-and-marble home of Maddalena Paradine—adumbrate the documentary style of *The Wrong Man.* Valli and Peck worked on the set for nine days, producing footage remarkable for its severity. Selznick meanwhile badgered Hitchcock to leave the gangster-in-a-cell style to other, lesser studios:

We can't go on photographing the walls and the windows, making passport photos, without any modeling to the face, any lighting designed to give the woman interest and beauty and mystery, no study of her best angles and how to light and photograph them (in today's stuff we actually shot down into her mouth, which wouldn't be attractive if she had the most beautiful teeth in the world, much less what she has), any composition or modern camera angles on her to excite the audience and thereby understand Keane's fascination.

250

The memorandum pinched. Hitchcock would like to have explored the tension arising from a glamorous star portraying a debased woman, but Selznick demanded that Valli be cinematically idealized. Until Transatlantic began production, the director would have to forgo such experiments.

Largely because Selznick ended his memoranda with a conciliatory phrase, Hitchcock tolerated the written interference. Visits to the soundstage were another matter. "What am I to do?" the director said as he approached the end of principal photography. "I can't take it any more—[Selznick] comes down every day, he rewrites the scene, I can't shoot it, it's so bad." Ann Todd recalled that even as the actors worked, they could tell when Selznick walked on the set. "It used to throw Hitchcock very much indeed." Despite an occasional practical joke, Hitchcock ran a cool set. Cukor kept things lively; Sturges employed a piano player to tinkle between takes. Unlike his convivial peers, Hitchcock manufactured authority out of reserve. The construction supervisor said that the infamous ceilings had been built because of "Mr. Hitchcock's insistence of an acquiescence with Mr. Hitchcock's wishes"; Fred Ahern, who found the director great company in London and New York, nonetheless believed that anyone who crossed Hitchcock on the set "would be worthless in their [future] association" with him. The intimidating presence of Selznick compromised the intimidating presence of Hitchcock. Naturally the director discouraged his producer's appearance on the soundstage. The need to maintain that delicate status quo kept tempers cool.

As late as February 1947, when *The Paradine Case* entered its last month of principal photography, Hitchcock and Selznick continued negotiations for Transatlantic Pictures to share its director with Selznick Productions. Even with *Under Capricorn* announced, Selznick hoped to snare Hitchcock for part of each year; he also hoped that the Selznick Releasing Organization might distribute Transatlantic product. Had Hitchcock been thoroughly disenchanted with Selznick or had he had solid and remunerative offers elsewhere, the talks would never have occurred. This "yackety-yackety" produced an impasse on both sides. Hitchcock offered to make two pictures annually, one for Selznick, the other for Transatlantic. Since 1942, however, the director had generally worked a year on a single picture. So Selznick agreed to meet the Hitchcock financial terms, including a 10 percent profit share, only if the director promised to discontinue his salary twenty-six weeks into a film. Hitchcock liked the money, nearly $6,000 weekly, but not the qualifier. With Selznick as producer, the writing and even the production period could extend well into the half year reserved for the Transatlantic picture. "This is of course impossible because they might have me working for a year or if necessary two years," Hitchcock told his accountant. The director did not close the door, he pushed it to. Selznick would soon tap again.

Hitchcock vigorously entered the last weeks of principal photography, driven not only by his interest in the production but by his eagerness to speed away to *Under Capricorn*. With Selznick discreetly pushing him, he decided to shoot the long trial sequence of *The Paradine Case* in an experimental manner that foreshadowed the three-camera style of television. During cross-examination scenes, Hitchcock would bring as many as four cameras to the mock-up Old Bailey, each focused on one of the principals: Judge Horfield, Keane, the prosecutor (Leo G. Carroll), and the witnesses (Jourdan or Valli). Once he positioned the cameras, Hitchcock would shoot each sequence through and presumably save the time normally lost in preparing new setups. The long examination of Latour ran almost twenty script pages; at Hitchcock's earlier speed, even allowing for the minimum setups required in a courtroom, the sequence would have consumed at least a week. With careful planning—Hitchcock told Selznick—he could complete the sequence in a single day. "Certainly I hope we will make this our goal," the producer said, "because if we don't thoroughly organize such a plan, we are going to waste a fortune in Old Bailey on top of the inordinate amount of money already spent on the film."

The presence of four cameras and four booms in the well of the courtroom necessitated a legion of grips and operators. Not only did the congestion block the performers' vision of one another, forcing them to play to things rather than people, but the heat and confusion broke their concentration. Any technical achievement, irrespective of success or of popularity with his actors, interested the director. Hitchcock could lose himself in experimentation, in lenses, angles, and (when he had faith in his cinematographer) lighting effects. "We know that Hitchcock is having a wonderful time in Old Bailey," Selznick told O'Shea, "and will stay there forever if we don't do something about it." Yet the ratio of one day to twenty pages narrowed as the amount of

As the days on the Old Bailey set evolved into weeks, Selznick compared Hitchcock to Erich von Stroheim, a director noted for his extravagance. The London *Times* would later commend *The Paradine Case* "for the care it brings to the business of conveying the feel and atmosphere of an English murder trial."

footage swelled. Feeling the picture slipping beyond his grasp, Laughton took action. He began to slow down the reading of his lines, especially those most likely to feature him on screen; he also pulled smirks and clucks from his arsenal and thereby demanded attention. Leo G. Carroll also began to slow, and within the week Jourdan and Peck had entered the game. Hitchcock perhaps encouraged his actors to work against the melodrama, but "negative speaking" could bring the entire production down on the studio's head. Selznick rolled the dailies and sounded the alarm.

> We must not forget that Keane is characterized as an emotionalist, that Latour is a Latin, that the defense attorney is violently jealous of the witness, and madly in love with the defendant. I don't think that any of these points could be said to be true of the way today's rushes were played.

The attention to character came too late; more to the point, the dialogue that Selznick authored sometimes contributed to the leadenness. Finally, on March 13, ninety-two days after it had begun (setting a record for a Hitchcock picture), principal photography on *The Paradine Case* ended.

Thanks to the Old Bailey sequence that finally saved money, *The Paradine Case* closed $100,000 under budget. Immediately terminating Hitchcock's salary would further economize. Principal photography and the director's compensation often ended concurrently, even when the director cut his own pictures. Selznick stopped the Wednesday paychecks for Hitchcock but urged O'Shea to have a "candid talk" with the Englishman: "I do not want him to have any issue about being taken off so unceremoniously."

Although an arrangement between Selznick Productions and Transatlantic still appeared possible, Bernstein had offered Transatlantic product to two distributors, RKO and Warner Bros. In return for the vast promotional resources of the distributor, Bernstein promised special financial incentives and the almost predictable fixed return of a Hitchcock picture. With Transatlantic apparently nearing a deal with one of the majors, Selznick must have believed that Hitchcock would not sign another Selznick Productions employment agreement without enormous concessions. Selznick would not knowingly alienate the director, for the Selznick Releasing Organization might eventually become his associate. But neither would he pay him $1,000 a day to perform a task that the producer himself intended to supervise. His thoughts elsewhere, Hitchcock neither protested nor pouted.

Losing Hitchcock would close an era for Selznick. By 1947, his roster of defections included East Coast representative Kay Brown, production assistant Barbara Keon, story editor Val Lewton, art director Lyle Wheeler, and production manager Raymond Klune. *Portrait of Jennie* would add two more casualties. Cinematographer Joseph August died of heart failure on the set, and Selznick fought with and fired his long-time editor, Hal Kern. Contracts with Rory Calhoun, Guy Madison, Rhonda Fleming, and the mature Shirley Temple replaced expiring contracts with such stars as Ingrid Bergman, Vivien Leigh, and Joan Fontaine. Major stars and major directors no longer belonged to producers but to themselves. "Oh, it's wonderful to feel free," Fontaine said when she formed her own company in 1947; "there are a lot of advantages to being a producer of one's own picture." Selznick turned pensive. "When I think of what we were," he reflected, "I commence to regain some perspective and some objectivity." Recreating the past had failed, charting the future became difficult. Though Jennifer Jones remained with Selznick, the imminent Hitchcock departure undoubtedly affected him.

In 1947, Selznick drove himself relentlessly but to less purpose than in years past. His simmering quarrel with Charlie Chaplin and Mary Pickford erupted into a $3 million suit against United Artists and required countless meetings between Selznick and O'Shea, and between O'Shea and the attorneys, before Selznick finally abandoned his case. Maintaining a distributorship (the Selznick Releasing Organization) on a shoestring budget demanded more energy. Though the business of filmmaking dominated his attention, Selznick attempted to influence the creative element as well. In January 1947, despite orders from his physician, he left his sickbed to minister to an ailing *Paradine Case* script; he later worked on the picture for three days without sleep. Benzedrine provided the extra hours. Nearly fifty years old, Selznick lacked the youthful resilience that once chased the aftereffects of the drug from his system. Just before filming of *Paradine* ended, he vacationed in Florida, then visited his estranged wife, Irene, and his sons,

Jeffrey and Daniel, at the Pierre in New York. He continued to play the tireless executive. According to playwright Arthur Laurents, Selznick would "go into the bathroom and lock himself in and sleep on the floor rather than let anybody know that the legend wasn't true." He contracted food poisoning in Manhattan and, probably because of his depleted physical condition, returned home no better than he had left it.

By working on *The Paradine Case,* Hitchcock apparently conquered his imaginary invalidism. Sidney Bernstein's visit to Los Angeles during the last weeks of shooting as well as the repeal of the excess profits tax in 1946—not unrelated events in Hitchcock's future—brightened his increasingly clear horizon. Internal Revenue had recently cracked down on "collapsible" production companies, those independents who made one picture, dissolved the corporation, and reaped large dividends and small taxes. But neither Bernstein nor Hitchcock conceived Transatlantic as fly-by-night. They envisioned a partnership as durable as their friendship. Bernstein may have known his witty countryman more intimately than most others knew him. The magician-director happily exposed his technical tricks, how he managed the plane crash in *Foreign Correspondent* or the halation of the milk in *Suspicion,* but revealed little else. "You never knew quite what Hitch was thinking," Frank Launder said, "because he always played his cards close to his chest." Even when negotiation of a contract between the director and Selznick appeared hopeless, the producer would not discount the chance of an agreement. Hitchcock acknowledged many of his fears, exhibited others. Financial insecurity—what John Houseman called "Hitchcock's lifelong and highly neurotic preoccupation with money"—had brought him to the bottom line of a Selznick contract once before, and the soft ground beneath Transatlantic might once again. Who could tell what Hitchcock now thought, what he would do?

Meanwhile, as *The Paradine Case* lay uncut, Hitchcock and Bernstein conferred about their Transatlantic future. Besides screen adaptations of the novel *Under Capricorn* and the drama *Rope's End,* they contemplated a Shakespearean release: "Sidney Bernstein presents Cary Grant as Alfred Hitchcock's *Hamlet,* a modern thriller by William Shakespeare." Some might have snorted, yet the political and cultural credentials of Sidney Bernstein demanded respect. Stringing along the producer of *Rebecca* and *Nothing Sacred,* Hitchcock men-

Alfred Hitchcock with Sidney Bernstein.

tioned *Hamlet* to Selznick, who found prestige and even showmanship in the project. The Olivier *Henry V* had demonstrated the limited but very strong box office appeal of the Bard; desperate for product, the Selznick Releasing Organization could use the shillings that a Cary Grant *Hamlet* would generate. Finally, however, a plagiarism suit brought by the author of a twentieth-century *Hamlet* not only chilled the plans but involved Hitchcock and Bernstein with lawyers for over three years.

For Hitchcock, the costs demonstrated the price of independence. "My dear Joe," he wrote to his New York attorney after receiving a dun, "I am saving hard in order to pay your fee in a few weeks." Transatlantic inched forward. As the partners sorted out the clauses of possible distribution deals, a 1947 Bernstein-sponsored poll confirmed what Selznick himself might have guessed: English filmgoers called Alfred Hitchcock their favorite film director.

During the second week of April 1947, Hitchcock roughly edited *The Paradine Case*. Still enamored of the footage shot in his four-camera courtroom, he presented Selznick with an almost three-hour movie, then left. The end of his weekly paychecks no doubt lessened his interest. Since the content obviously could not support the length, the producer immediately searched for expendable footage. He called up the Old Bailey sequence and found it both long and—as he had predicted—"excessively cutty," a criticism sounded earlier on *Rebecca* and *Spellbound*. With opposing lawyers Peck and Carroll held at their seats by the conventions of English court procedure, Hitchcock had deployed montage to counterbalance the weight of the single setting and tedious questioning. Yet *Paradine* was not *Saboteur*. The montage style seemed jagged, at odds with the cool manner of Valli and the sobriety of Old Bailey. For Selznick, the subject of the picture was not passion and murder but glamor and allure. A noisy narrative style would clash with Mrs. Paradine, who looked no less soignée at the trial—having lived for weeks in jail—than she had upon her arrest. Selznick returned to the invisible one-shot, one-speech approach that had sustained him in *Rebecca*, as well as in his own best pictures.

By summer, Selznick had edited nearly an hour out of *Paradine*. Several languorous tracking shots notable for their aestheticism fell before the scissors, for the producer detested the "torturous and unnatural camera movement" of the picture. Although he feared that the cutting room held "a lot of stuff which [Hitchcock] may have shot ridiculously and unnecessarily," Selznick nonetheless ordered the retakes for which he had become famous. Hitchcock agreed to shoot the additional footage—at his $1,000 a day salary. The period had its share of anxieties. Since "Hitch's sloppiness about story points" necessarily concerned Selznick, the producer assigned Lydia Schiller to check the finished print for severed links in the narrative chain, moments when cutting to gain time resulted in loss of coherence. Selznick also supervised the dubbing, including the bedroom confrontation between Keane and his wife, the one Peck called "my worst scene." A couple of lackluster previews did nothing to alleviate Selznick's worries—if anything, they demonstrated the importance of making the picture as good as superior craftsmanship could make it. To that end, he shopped around for a composer who could give *Paradine* the warmth that Hitchcock had perhaps sapped with his cold lighting and occasionally labored tracking shots.

Selznick considered hiring Bernard Herrmann to score *Paradine,* but when sound engineer James Stewart warned him about Herrmann's "musical independence," the deal soured. Selznick was enough of a prima donna, especially given the problems with *Portrait of Jennie* and the Selznick Releasing Organization. The *Paradine* assignment fell to Franz Waxman, the composer of Hitchcock's *Suspicion,* Selznick's *The Young in Heart,* and Selznick–Hitchcock's *Rebecca;* among the beautiful themes he produced for the picture was a sinewy nocturne for Maddalena Paradine. The insecure Selznick fretted over one last question: Should *The Paradine Case* finally be called *The Paradine Case?* The producer considered *Fascination, Bewitched, Under Oath,* and *The Lawyer's Secret,* all of which George Gallup said out-tested *The Paradine Case.* Even the whimsical title *A Streetcar Called Mrs. Paradine,* named for a play that wife-turned-producer Irene Selznick then had in rehearsal, seemed a more propitious choice. Indecision racked Selznick. Barely a day before the premiere, he returned to his original title. The art department quickly and crudely lettered *The Paradine Case* onto the credits, and within hours audiences got their first glimpse of the finished picture.

In 1938, when Hitchcock and Selznick joined forces, the director envied the reputation of his American producer. But when Hitchcock and Selznick neared the end of their association, they had reversed positions. Selznick could appreciate why Hitchcock wanted his independence: Selznick had broken with MGM in 1935 to shape his own future, in his own way. And Selznick could also understand—even if he could not quite accept—the seating of Hitchcock at the head of the bargaining table. Producers who intended to survive in a changing industry would have to cede points to directors-cum-entrepreneurs. Yet personal and professional events seemed to conspire against Selznick in 1947.

His marriage remained a sensitive point. Though David loved Jennifer Jones, neither he nor Irene had filed for divorce. Irene "had a floating, prowling way of moving," playwright Enid Bagnold recalled. "Turning, seeming about to speak: not speaking. She seemed a thinking-machine, making intermittent contact, brimful of resolves." In August 1947, she forced David to discuss matters of custody and the division of property. The moment caught Selznick in a particularly depressed state. Taking a leaf from Howard Hughes and *The Outlaw,* he had promoted *Duel in the Sun* ostentatiously. The critical failure and the contumely of certain elements within the industry preyed on him; *The Paradine Case* would be unlikely to alter the climate. More concerned about posterity than he would have been during the years of Selznick International, when his selection of properties all but obviated worry, Selznick brooded over the smudge on his name and considered a public relations blitz to remove it.

> In view of what happened with the picture [*Duel*] and in view of the consequent great loss and prestige with the trade and press and public, I think the campaign on me is needed very badly, if only from the standpoint of my own morale and my own thinking—for even if I am wrong in exaggerating the extent of the loss to my position, there is the matter of my family to think of, and it is also a fact that if I think the damage has been done, it must affect my state of mind and of my work, and therefore must be met exactly the same as though I were not exaggerating the damage—and mind you, I don't think I am exaggerating.

The divorce continued a pattern of loss for Selznick: easy to understand, difficult to accept. His liberal settlement on Irene suggests that even in the twilight of the relationship he sought her approval. Spending Thanksgiving 1947 in Manhattan with his sons, he observed her debut as an East Coast impresario. The success of *A Streetcar Named Desire,* whose premiere and opening-night party at "21" Selznick attended, must have touched a nerve. Irene had aligned herself with the kind of raw young talent—Elia Kazan, Marlon Brando, Tennessee Williams—that her husband had once nurtured at MGM, RKO, and of course Selznick International. By December, back in Los Angeles, Selznick had seen many of the *Streetcar* reviews and telegrammed his wife, "It is a joy to know that all my predictions of your success are commencing to come true, and in a big way. I am sure you are well on the road to recognition as the theater's best and most distinguished producer." The genuineness of the sentiment conveyed his admiration, the reference to "all my predictions" salved his ego, and the formality communicated his envy.

Hitchcock enjoyed a peace of mind denied his producer. In summer 1947, after the British government imposed a 75 percent confiscatory tax on American motion picture earnings, Bernstein and Hitchcock must have fielded numerous queries from potential distributors. As a predominantly British-run venture, Transatlantic may have seemed the loophole through which American companies could carry away profits from their richest foreign market. Still, despite their hunger for product, distributors could prove tough negotiators: They wanted maximum percentages and controls, and independents like Bernstein and Hitchcock naturally sought minimal fees and interference. Even after an agreement had been reached, the parties might spend months ironing out details. Meanwhile, plans firmed for *Under Capricorn* and *Rope's End.* Though Hitchcock could at last smell freedom, neither he nor Bernstein regarded a complete break with Selznick as advisable. The excesses of *Duel* showed just why. While the picture offended the critics, the advertising campaign drove millions to the box office. Selznick and the Selznick Releasing Organization offered Hitchcock and Transatlantic a skilled personal commitment to the promotion of Transatlantic pictures. SRO remained an outside candidate for Transatlantic distributor.

Selznick would aggressively promote *The Paradine Case.* The big campaign would not only help the picture but demonstrate to independents like Hitchcock that SRO could sell lurid spectaculars as well as more refined screen entertainment. The chance of turning a profit seemed questionable: the distended production schedule and the interest on the long-due production loans pushed costs beyond $4 million. Yet an undercapitalized promotional campaign would doom the picture. With his reputation again on the line and a Hitchcock contract hanging however remotely in the balance, Selznick threw money at *Paradine.* The publicity budget finally exceeded that of any other Selznick release.

In addition to plans for sending Hitchcock on the road ("he is superb with the press and is great copy," Selznick told his East Coast distribution head), the producer "shot the works" for a gala double-theater premiere on New Year's Eve, at the last possible time to qualify for Oscar nominations. The industry-dominated audience in Los Angeles, undoubtedly in the mood for more bubbly entertainment, greeted *Paradine* with polite applause. The mixed reviews followed. Always sympathetic to Hitchcock, *The New York Times* found *The Paradine Case* "a slick piece of static entertainment"; *Commonweal* disliked Laughton's "hammed-up" performance and Selznick's "verbose script" but promised readers an interesting story. "It is now time to forgive David O. Selznick for 'Duel in the Sun,' " *Newsweek* announced. "Once again, with 'The Paradine Case,' he has produced a fine movie." Other reviewers granted no absolution. Howard Barnes thought the picture had "too much production." Acknowledging the polish and intelligence of the style, *Time* damned the lifelessness of *Paradine.* John McCarten of *The New Yorker* went for the jugular: "One picture may be worth a thousand words," he began, "but you'll never prove it by David O. Selznick." Hitchcock emerged with only a scratch. "It is with great reluctance that I am compelled to announce that 'The Paradine Case' was directed by Alfred Hitchcock," McCarten ended his notice. "The Selznick script must have caught him nodding."

Selznick regarded the critics dubiously. Over the years, he complained to his friend Harry Luce about the rapping that *Time* reviewers often gave his pictures, but the *New Yorker* piece—blaming Selznick and pardoning Hitchcock—stung. Selznick banned the magazine staff from preview screenings, then took a second swing in a letter to *New Yorker* editor Harold Ross:

> I happened to witness Mr. McCarten's performance and that of his associate, Lillian Ross, in the projection room [the Selznick publicity man told Harold Ross]. They came in late, uninvited, and apparently

262

fortified against any contingency. Miss Ross' juvenile giggling and loud comments to McCarten disturbed those of the invited audience who were near them. [McCarten has] a chronic distaste for motion pictures and perhaps that is the reason he so often attends previews insulated.

The negative reviews fed Selznick's own dissatisfaction with *Paradine*. Prior to the general release, Selznick commissioned George Gallup to measure viewer interest moment by moment at a special screening. The resulting Audience Research graph demonstrated that while Jourdan excited moviegoers, Valli did not. Ironically, Hitchcock had fought Selznick on the only cast member in the picture who drove interest above the "neutral" line. Though Selznick could not beef up the Jourdan part, he could trim Valli. Still more of the Old Bailey sequence fell to the cutting room floor. The producer frantically considered every other element that could affect audience response, including a title change.

"I have goosed around this film a dozen different ways," Selznick wrote in early 1948, "and get a lot of values out of it that aren't in the original film." He spent $400,000 promoting the recut *Paradine Case,* well over 100 percent more than the budget for more notable (and salable) pictures. Eager to square himself with the industry and with Hitchcock, he advertised widely in the trade press and worked steadfastly to have Hitchcock nominated for the Best Achievement in Directing Oscar. Olivia de Havilland had finally won a Best Performance award in 1946, Joan Crawford the year before, both more for work they had done in years past than specifically for their nominated films; a consolation Oscar, Selznick reasoned, might go to Hitchcock "with far more justice. It might be brought out, which would be beneficial in reminding everyone that Hitch directed REBECCA, that REBECCA won the best picture award but not the directorial award." The Academy chose to nominate not Hitchcock but Ethel Barrymore. Selznick ruefully eyed the honor: "How ironic that Barrymore should have won a nomination on a performance which I have cut to ribbons."

The balance sheet on *The Paradine Case* contained a grim message. As a 1947 Gallup poll had demonstrated, the older the consumer, the less likely he attended the movies. Persons from twelve to thirty bought over 60 percent of the tickets; persons over forty-six, who constituted an "untapped market," bought only 15 percent. A producer who selected "adult" subject matter could hope to profit only by trimming costs or creating a motion picture appropriate for the youth market. Neither course appealed to David Selznick, whose staid *Paradine Case* probably attracted mostly the over-thirty audience. Only reluctantly did Selznick concede defeat. "We should devise a new advertising campaign on the sex angles omitting the mystery and court room angles," he suggested in time for the picture's second run in summer 1948. By the following January, however, when *The Paradine Case* opened in London, Selznick had finally lost interest.

Some years later, a Spanish reporter asked Gregory Peck which of his pictures he would like to burn. *The Paradine Case,* he replied. Hitchcock also tried to disown the film. He encouraged cinephiles to divide his American career into the Selznick and post-Selznick eras, with *Paradine* demonstrable proof of the malignant Selznick influence. In the years immediately ahead, the years without Selznick, Hitchcock would face a more powerful opponent than his producer: the force of aestheticism. Though the style of the Transatlantic pictures would differ minimally from that of *Paradine,* the obsession with craft—lenses and cranes, dolly shots and break-apart scenery, Technicolor temperatures and hydraulically manipulated flats—would leave no room for the Selznick "touch," the ability the producer once had to balance a distant technique with conventional Hollywood story and pictorial values. The experiments in the Bernstein pictures would trumpet the independence of Alfred Hitchcock. Yet they would also threaten to ruin him.

8

TRANSATLANTIC POSTLUDE

In early August 1939, Selznick and Hitchcock had gone off to see the wizard, MGM's wonderful *The Wizard of Oz*. They had breezed by the Trocadero to congratulate director Victor Fleming, then continued on to a fashionable Los Angeles night spot for dinner and drinks. "We talked—stories!! *Rebecca* and *Titanic* and Benedict Arnold were my gaiety. He's not a bad guy, shorn of affectations, although not exactly a man to go camping with," the producer had remarked. But Selznick practiced engagement, Hitchcock evasion. Over time, suspicion and resentment, along with the stresses of production and the collision of temperaments, had iced the bonhomie, the respect, the awe. Their only bond became their contract.

A break seemed inevitable for personal reasons alone. Within and without studio grounds, Selznick and Hitchcock wanted absolute control. When Selznick entertained at a restaurant, Joan Fontaine recalled that he told everyone what to have, then went into the kitchen to tell the chef how to prepare it. At Santa Cruz, Hitchcock also plied visitors

with food and drink. "Usually the weekend was more than one's diges-
tion and capacity could stand," Hume Cronyn said. Hitchcock "took
a marvelous, malicious delight in seeing his guests fall apart with all
those vintage wines and liquor he'd force." Both producer and director
were power brokers. Selznick had worked to have Petter Lindstrom
(Bergman's husband) admitted to the University of Rochester Medical
School, tamed the controversy surrounding Alida Valli's immigration
to America, and stage-managed the wedding of contract player Kim
Hunter. "Since my father wasn't alive," Hunter remembered, "Mother
gave me away, but I think [Selznick] would have preferred it if I'd asked
him to do it." Hitchcock also regarded himself as the master, the center
of attention. One afternoon at RKO, before accompanying the director
back to his trailer-office on the stage, Carol Stevens chatted with several
studio employees. Later Hitchcock told her, "You think everyone likes
you—well, Cary Grant hates you!" Stevens reeled, then privately questioned Grant about the remark. "Good heavens," he replied, "*you*
ought to know how possessive Hitch is." Both Hitchcock and Selznick
were generous though dominating men. Both commanded authority.
Both clashed.

Following the war, Selznick demanded more—more control, more
money for more loanouts, more involvement in more elements of picturemaking. On *Paradine* he wrote the script, on *Duel* he directed some
of the sequences. He produced not wisely but too well. Hitchcock grew
equally self-absorbed. "The subject doesn't count," the director later
said. "You get your satisfaction through your style of treatment. I'm
not interested in content." Spoiled by the Hollywood publicity machine
no less than the bounty of the studios, he regaled journalists with tales
of the development and execution of his experiments. The linage that
corrupted more than one Hollywood starlet may have convinced Hitchcock that the public shared his passion for "things," that his name
above the title would indemnify him against box office failure.

By 1948, Selznick and Hitchcock had begun to lose touch with their
audience. Television offered moviegoers wrestling and Milton Berle,
while the European cinema gave them social problems and neorealism.
The middle ground between slapdash entertainment and intellectual
challenge still belonged to Hollywood. But Hitchcock could certainly
not command the middle ground with *Rope's End, Under Capricorn,*
or *I Confess,* all properties optioned by Transatlantic. Patrick Hamil-

Hitchcock would periodically have an optician bring a large selection of frames to the studio and insist that secretary-business manager Carol Stevens choose four or five pair. "And if I came on the set without my glasses on, it irritated the devil out of Hitch. He had a fetish about glasses."

ton's *Rope's End* dramatized the Leopold–Loeb murder case. Although the 1929 play exploited elements of the grotesque that Hitchcock had toyed with in *Shadow of a Doubt* and *Spellbound,* it seemed stagey and dated. *Under Capricorn,* Helen Simpson's 1937 novel about nineteenth-century Australia, seemed even more problematic. Hitchcock lacked affinity for costume pictures, and the "highly-coloured, improbable" narrative (Simpson's own description) called for a director fluent in comedy of manners, someone like George Cukor or even Max Ophuls. When early on Hitchcock and Sidney Bernstein chose the turn-of-the-century drama *I Confess,* Kay Brown remarked to one of her colleagues: "Please don't tell Hitch, as it's none of my business, but I thought the story frighteningly bad, and I hope he makes enormous changes before he does it as a picture." These were not screen properties that challenged the Hollywood studio system, properties so radical in content that only an independent could produce them; rather, they were weak properties that the major companies, using their better judgment, had passed over.

For good reason, the break with Selznick occurred gradually. Though Bankers Trust had pledged a $5 million production loan to Transatlantic, Bernstein and Hitchcock still lacked American distribution. Their small company floundered. Plans ballooned, then deflated. Bernstein announced construction of a six-stage studio in England, half the size of Selznick International, but nothing materialized. Personnel came, personnel went. Bernstein hired a former colleague to run the Transatlantic story department (a room tucked away in the Granada Theatres empire), but she lasted only a few months; production manager Victor Peers combined his duties with hers. Yet Hitchcock remained optimistic. In 1944, when Bernstein had cabled his acquaintance David Selznick about a share in United Artists, the producer had responded, "Forgive my saying so probably need you less than you need me." The intervening years had made Selznick the beggar.

The 1940s profoundly altered the movies' labor force. The capital gains tax and the complete unionization of craftsmen and technicians prompted countless artists to turn free-lance. Once as common as pigeons along Wilshire Boulevard, seven-year contracts became rarae aves. In 1945, fewer than one quarter of the working members of the Screen Actors Guild and the Screen Directors Guild were under contract to one of the major companies. Though Selznick had remained afloat in the early forties by loaning out talent under long-term contract, he could not depend on such profits in the late forties. Like other producers, he would have to serve independent filmmakers rather than employ them. He thus came to regard the Selznick Releasing Organization as necessary for survival in the new Hollywood. Anxious to supply SRO with pictures to distribute, the producer courted his former contract employee. The odds were against him.

Apparently trying to fence out Selznick, Bernstein and Hitchcock pursued RKO as a hospitable American home for their new company: RKO not only encouraged independents but imposed reasonable overhead charges. Three years before, the director had tested the waters. He told RKO president Peter Rathvon that when the Selznick contract expired, he would make four pictures annually, two for RKO and two for himself. Even had Hitchcock gone into overdrive and met the agreement, the salary from picture four would have belonged almost exclusively to Internal Revenue. Yet the reason for his hyperbole seems obvious. Hitchcock knew that his efficient Universal pictures had not effaced the production figures on *Rebecca* and *Foreign Correspondent,* much less on RKO's *Mr. and Mrs. Smith* and *Suspicion.* Speed mattered. Soon after Peter Rathvon pointed out "what a slow worker Hitchcock has been in the past," RKO executives quietly slipped away from the bargaining table. The success of *Notorious,* as well as Transatlantic salesmanship, brought them back.

Hitchcock offered RKO two notable incentives. The director would film his first two productions—*Rope's End* and *Under Capricorn*—in long takes. Rolling the camera for five, six, even ten minutes at a time, Hitchcock could halve the usual ten- or twelve-week schedule required for principal photography. Selznick had worked with Hitchcock on "the whole idea of the month's rehearsal and the week's shooting" several years before. While he resented the director earning Transatlantic interest from capital not his own, he must have admired how shrewdly Hitchcock had read and begun to manipulate the temper of the American film industry in 1947. Rising production expenses, declining domestic revenues, blocked foreign markets, and antitrust activity had made studio administrators more receptive than ever to independents with slender budgets. Despite the weaknesses of *Under Capricorn* and *Rope's End* as commercial properties, the shooting schedules impressively conformed to the economy wave sweeping Hollywood.

Hitchcock regarded the long-takes style as a technical challenge but promoted it as a revolutionary cost-cutting measure. Intrigued by these "new and exciting cost-saving procedures," RKO president Peter Rathvon believed that if *Rope's End* succeeded, the Hitchcock strategy would "be of great benefit to us in our own future pictures." Bernstein and Hitchcock had still more lures. Dollars advanced Transatlantic by RKO would be shipped abroad, converted into pounds, and used to pay expenses on the new company's first two films. With the cooperation of the British treasury, the pictures' box office earnings in the United Kingdom would be converted back into dollars and returned to the United States. Transatlantic could thaw frozen sterling. RKO listened with rapt attention.

The RKO response may have astonished Bernstein and Hitchcock. The studio demanded not only a 25 percent distribution fee and a third of the profits but a number of approvals: "Story, script, budget, schedule, performer, percentage deals, studio contracts, right to assign representative on production, no changes in script, schedule, etc. without approval, right to take over production under some conditions. Right to see rushes, to cut, to preview, to title choice." It also intended to countersign all Transatlantic checks. By tipping the balance of power away from the producers and toward themselves, the independents had unnerved Hollywood. Naturally the executives wanted as much control as they could negotiate.

As Hitchcock would learn, the studios never defined "independent" as "not subject to control by others." John Ford, Howard Hawks, and their peers enjoyed only the freedom given them by those who financed and distributed their films. Having been stung by Orson Welles, RKO reserved the final cut of the Transatlantic pictures for itself: Hitchcock had obviously established himself as a director but not altogether as a producer. Though Hitchcock may have been disturbed by the conditions, the Transatlantic partners seriously considered the RKO tender. Perhaps the steep terms approximated those offered by other major companies, or perhaps the director trusted RKO not to exercise its contractual controls. Whatever the case, Bernstein expressed guarded interest, then soon told reporters that Transatlantic would affiliate with RKO.

Although his organization, both the production and distribution arms, must have inspired little confidence by the late 1940s, Selznick hung on. The Hitchcock association meant more than his producer wished. Despite the cockney slang, Hitchcock had class, the critical cachet that Selznick himself had once enjoyed. The director was not an intellectual, but his superior wit and gnomic speech, as well as his "business and tricks," gave him the luster of a cinematic eminence. The image sufficed. Genius always dazzled moviemakers, and even exceptionally talented producers like Thalberg and Selznick courted men of intelligence (or presumed intelligence). Hunt Stromberg retained Aldous Huxley as his "kept intellectual," a role played by James M. Cain with producer Arthur Hornblow and by Bob Nathan with producer Arthur Freed. As early as 1940, Hitchcock represented a status symbol to his employer; as late as 1948, Selznick wished to lose neither Hitchcock nor his pictures.

Transatlantic had good reason for avoiding Selznick. The years since 1938 had demonstrated that the producer could not relinquish control. According to Hollywood rumor, Jock Whitney had not only tired of his friend's chronic disorganization, but had liquidated their company because of it. Not long before Bernstein and Hitchcock actively pursued RKO, Selznick raised an old bugbear with two associates: "I am going to have to stop being a producer otherwise in order to become an executive full time, because I am much too embarrassed by our present operation to let it go on uncorrected indefinitely. . . . We have to have pictures made by other people because I haven't the time, nor am I in the state of mind to make more pictures." Whitney and others had made the same observation nearly a decade before. Meanwhile, RKO again lost interest in Hitchcock. After considering the Transatlantic package, the studio decided that it wanted only product "of exceptional quality and saleability." Neither *Rope's End* nor *Under Capricorn* fit those criteria.

Rather than turn to the lame Selznick Releasing Organization, an increasingly problematic choice, Bernstein and Hitchcock arranged distribution through Warner Bros. The studio must have been pleased to sign Transatlantic, for the Hitchcock pictures would reduce overhead, generate product, yet involve minimal capital investment. The sixty-three-page contract gave the director some of the benefits that Selznick had begrudged him, including a two-week annual trip to New York; the contract also promised him an "office and secretary [paid for] in accordance with his standing and prestige." But Jack L. Warner had

271

not won power through concessions. He forced Hitchcock—by written agreement—to refrain from actions "that will tend to shock, insult or offend the community or ridicule public morals or decency." The fastidious Hitchcock loathed the "morals clause," however standard throughout Hollywood, and apparently even persuaded Selznick to strike it from a proffered contract. Warner also granted Hitchcock no "autonomous provisions as to cast, general artistic approval, story, script or editing." While the restrictions would compromise the director's independence, the distribution contract nonetheless made Transatlantic a reality. Officially the association of Alfred Hitchcock and David Selznick had ended.

Rope's End and *Under Capricorn* formally introduced the independent Hitchcock to filmgoers. Bernstein retained the "final say" in Transatlantic—"I have to, because otherwise we could find ourselves in a situation where nothing got done"—yet he also recognized "that the moment I exercise it, it's the end of our partnership." No longer compelled by Selznick to foreground narrative, to serve content through style, Hitchcock was free to experiment. Bernstein's carte blanche would prove more detrimental than Selznick's interference had ever been.

Working from a rented house in Bel Air, Sidney Bernstein followed the progress of *Rope's End.* Hume Cronyn wrote the prose adaptation, Arthur Laurents the script; they strengthened the resemblance to Leopold and Loeb. Both stage and screen versions focused on two young men (John Dall and Farley Granger in the film) who murder a colleague, then challenge their mentor (a miscast James Stewart) to discover the crime. The shooting script had no numbered scenes. As the camera would, it floated from one dialogue exchange to another. Hitchcock quickly abandoned an interest in characterization to concentrate on designing sets that would permit the anticipated ten-minute takes.

With Bernstein in attendance but characteristically silent, Hitchcock began shooting in early 1948. The strain of ten-minute camera runs wore down everyone. Each time the company neared the end of a take, Stewart recalled, the actors became "sort of glassy-eyed. All of us were thinking, 'Oh God, don't let me go up on my lines *now*! If I do we'll have to go back and do the whole thing again.' " Though few mishaps occurred, the fear of them, as well as the confusion of circles and pointers on the floor, sapped the concentration of the actors and frayed the nerves of the crew. Within three weeks, however, principal photography ended. Selznick would have admired the speed but not the screen values.

Rope's End, released as *Rope,* was the coldest picture Hitchcock ever made: its moving camera never paused long enough to discover the characters' humanity. Much later, Hitchcock called his experiment "quite nonsensical." Although Bernstein must have seen both the rushes and their implications, he maintained his silence. Would the confrontational style of David Selznick have helped the director dodge the bullet?

> Many people do their best when they work for me [Selznick said]. The talent is the same, but I bully them, harangue them, coach them into doing better. My constant struggle is to get people to raise their sights, even if I have to anger them into doing it. When they get angry with me they're always on their toes, if only to avoid my criticism. Then if I praise them, they feel they've really done a job.

According to his subordinates, Bernstein could scold. But he refused to play Selznick to Hitchcock. Audiences would tell both Bernstein and Hitchcock whether *Rope* succeeded.

Transatlantic and Warner poured $450,000 into a promotional campaign for *Rope,* which included passing out cigars at trade shows. Moviegoers quickly penetrated the smoke screen. By attempting to ban *Rope* in Chicago and Seattle, the censors momentarily stimulated box office sales, but ultimately audiences wanted pictures, not experiments. The reviews for *Rope* paled beside those of *Notorious* and even *The Paradine Case.* Bosley Crowther found *Rope* "dull," and Robert Hatch called it "more fidgety than thrilling." According to Dilys Powell, the respected critic of the London *Times* and Hitchcock's friend, *Rope* was "false to the strange, artificial truth of the cinema." As an aesthetic experiment and a commercial venture, the first American Hitchcock picture made outside the contract with David Selznick had failed.

Bernstein and Hitchcock followed *Rope* with an adaptation of *Under Capricorn,* a tale about a woman and her stableman-lover. Like *Rebecca, Spellbound, Shadow of a Doubt,* and *Notorious, Under Capricorn* involved confession and redemption, yet sin rather than salvation brought Hitchcock to the novel. "I don't think I would have made the

James Stewart, John Dall, and Farley Granger in *Rope*. It was Transatlantic Pictures' first release, and Hitchcock's first color film.

Michael Wilding and Ingrid Bergman in *Under Capricorn*, the second (and last) Transatlantic picture.

picture if it hadn't been for Ingrid Bergman," the director later said. Every American producer was competing for her, and "I made the mistake of thinking that to get Bergman would be a tremendous feat; it was a victory over the rest of the industry." The rest of the industry naturally included the producer whom Bergman—and Hitchcock himself—had recently abandoned, David Selznick.

Asked to script *Under Capricorn,* Arthur Laurents not only refused but questioned the wisdom of adapting the property for the screen. Bernstein shrugged: Hitchcock could turn dross into gold. Although Selznick believed that the Hitchcock alchemy could run the other direction, both Bernstein and Hitchcock revered Alfred Hitchcock. Bernstein might have applied his Grenada managerial style to Transatlantic and urged Hitchcock at least to test *Under Capricorn.* Bernstein had pioneered audience analysis in Great Britain; market research on the *Capricorn* story, even with the names Cotten and Bergman mentioned, might have affirmed Laurents's opinion. But Bernstein regarded Transatlantic as an indulgence for his friend. If the director of *Waltzes from Vienna* wanted to make another period picture, his partner would not interfere. The Selznick years were behind him.

Hume Cronyn again provided a treatment, then James Bridie (against *his* better judgment) produced most of the script. The cast included Bergman, Cotten, Michael Wilding, and Margaret Leighton. But the long take again starred. Experiencing marital problems, Bergman lost patience. "The camera was supposed to follow me around for eleven whole minutes," she wrote to a friend, "which meant we had to rehearse a whole day with the walls or furniture falling backwards as the camera went through, and of course that couldn't be done fast enough. So I told Hitch off. How I hate this new technique of his. . . . Little Hitch just left. Never said a word. Just went home . . . oh dear." The camera as conquerer, actors and fixtures swept aside by its power and motion: the technique was not new at all. Now, though, the things that dominated characters in Hitchcock's pictures had come to dominate actors.

Although Hitchcock hoped to approach the speed of his first independent picture, union strike meetings and four o'clock tea slowed progress. An amused Joseph Cotten wrote home from Elstree Studios in England that the repair of a "huge gap in the wall caused by the onrushing camera" also delayed the company. "Now what?" became the refrain of production manager Fred Ahern, who missed "the good old production-line methods at Selznick's." Almost ten weeks after it began, looking more overdressed than even Selznick's *Paradine Case,* the shooting of *Under Capricorn* ended. The picture required all of the Bankers Trust $2.5 million to complete; Bernstein, Hitchcock, and Bergman claimed well over a quarter of that figure in compensation alone. Shortly before the autumn 1949 premiere, Bergman decided to leave her daughter and husband for Roberto Rossellini, but the media circus that followed hurt *Capricorn* far less than Hitchcock had.

" 'Rope' and now 'Under Capricorn' are evidence enough that [Hitchcock's] new method (of long and uninterrupted 'takes') leads to intolerable dullness on the screen," wrote the critic for the *Manchester Guardian.* Even more damaging was the review in *The Hollywood Reporter,* which vindicated Selznick before his peers. Hitchcock's direction is "crude, obvious and frequently silly. If his opus draws chuckles where it should have impact it is his fault, for although no producer is listed, the company, Transatlantic Pictures, is a Hitchcock enterprise." *Capricorn* became Bergman and Hitchcock's last film together. Oddly enough, it opened a window for Selznick.

Scorned by Transatlantic, the Selznick Releasing Organization had won contracts from producers Mark Hellinger and M. J. Siegal, yet both died before delivering any pictures. SRO would soon expire. Although *Portrait of Jennie* opened to excellent reviews and earned two Academy Award nominations, the picture failed to return its $4 million investment, partially the victim of a box office slump. By summer 1949, Selznick had loaned nearly all of his contract stars to Warner, auctioned off his production equipment, and married Jennifer Jones. He then turned to film investment abroad. Happily, *The Third Man* (co-produced with Alexander Korda) became a popular hit both in England and America. And when Selznick later met Bergman in Rome, he sensed her warmth, perhaps even her desire to return to her former producer. Selznick told Jenia Reissar that he hoped Bergman's experience on *Under Capricorn* "demonstrated to her the difference in Hitchcock under our management and my supervision (*Spellbound,* and *Notorious*) and Hitchcock on his own." Chasing the past and the renown of *Gone With the Wind* occupied Selznick for much of the rest of his life.

Capricorn drew audiences only in London, Bernstein wrote Hitch-cock in October 1950. "I am not quite happy about Warners' method of booking but I suppose if the film had been a wow even they could have booked it properly." Had Bernstein finally blamed his associate for *Under Capricorn*? The two Transatlantic pictures certainly strained their friendship.

> Have at last got $25,000 of the Rope money—cheque on the way [Hitch-cock wrote to an associate in May 1951]. *Big difficulties* with B. over this—concerning my inferior financial participation in comparison with his (250,000). I had to insist however that this was salary—and belonged to agreements already made and if sacrifices were necessary, they should be made by arrangement in the future & not change what was in the past. All very embarrassing and uncomfortable.

The last blow came from the Transatlantic backers. Having lost their investment, Bankers Trust reclaimed the picture and licensed Daniel O'Shea to control its future. When the Museum of Modern Art in New York later staged a retrospective of Hitchcock's work, O'Shea denied MOMA permission to screen it. Hitchcock boiled. "With my long experience of Mr. O'Shea's business methods I, naturally, was not too surprised at this mean behavior," the director told a friend. "It is quite obvious that when he puts the film out he is going to try and cash in on the Hitchcock name." Fifteen years after their professional relation-ship ended, David Selznick still controlled Alfred Hitchcock.

Auteur critics regard the liberation of Hitchcock from Selznick as momentous. "A strong director like Hitchcock simply could not func-tion at his best under the kind of authority Selznick imposed," Peter Bogdanovich wrote in 1972. Hitchcock disliked all authority—except his own. Although his screen treatment of the police betrays his con-tempt for officialdom, his barbs often traveled much shorter distances. In *Suspicion,* he called an interior decorator "Depinet," an unflattering reference to an RKO executive; in MGM's *North by Northwest,* he and screenwriter Ernest Lehman named the villain after a prominent Loew's stockholder. In *Rear Window,* the stocky murderer with rimless glasses resembled David Selznick. Hitchcock may have sometimes thought Selznick a demon, yet the director of things, of negative acting and moving cameras, of stories as technical cinematic challenges functioned productively under him, far better than he functioned with Bernstein.

When Selznick produced pictures rather than deals, he could make valuable suggestions, especially to a director initially concerned more with cinematics than narrative. "I'm not sure that I like the fade-out of the sequence with the girl promising 'the surprise of their lives!'" Selznick told Hitchcock as the director worked on the shooting script for *Rebecca.* "Since she has nothing in mind at this moment, the line seems a device simply to give us a dissolve, rather than having any point in itself." The independent Hitchcock turned *Rope* and *Under Capricorn* into "device" pictures. Though he carried the Selznick gloss to extremes, he lacked the push from Selznick that had brought an unusual psychological and dramatic interest to their early work together, that had helped balance story and performance against eccentric composition, logic against "goddamn jigsaw cutting," drama against aestheticism. During the five years of Transatlantic, Hitchcock would struggle to justify his hard-earned independence. Except for one picture—*Strangers on a Train*—he would not succeed.

Collaborators mattered to Hitchcock. He did not depend on Selznick as Dietrich on von Sternberg or even Rogers on Astaire. Yet he depended on Selznick and others to provide the context or the aura that made the "business and tricks" resonate with meaning. "I need writers," Hitchcock conceded after leaving Selznick. "I am a visual man, but, unfortunately, I also must have delineation of character and dialogue. The plot I can depict, but I must have convincing characters and good dialogue." Talented screenwriters, cameramen, and actors stimulated Hitchcock; they *completed* him. During the early Transatlantic–Warner years, the director may have been too exhilarated by his independence to welcome others' contributions. He "wasn't much for asking advice," Carol Stevens said. "He wasn't much for anything but making pictures." Yet *Strangers on a Train*—his only commercial and critical hit of the period—demonstrated that a strong story along with the right chemistry between the director and his associates could make Hitchcock wonderfully "Hitchcockian."

Though *Strangers on a Train* triumphed, *Stage Fright, I Confess,* and the 3-D *Dial "M" for Murder* fizzled. Hitchcock and Bernstein finally acknowledged that "they were not getting anywhere in the corporation," Pat Hitchcock recalled, so they "disbanded it, but not for any break-up. They stayed very, very close friends." According to screenwriter John Michael Hayes, Hitchcock was not too salable after the Transatlantic years; his pictures did not return enough for the time and money invested in them. Hitchcock decided to "run for cover": he offered to make a picture for Paramount that could be scripted from a property the studio owned and shot economically on one set. *Rear Window* rewarded the faith of Paramount executives and became the first of the mature Hitchcock's timeless artistic achievements. *To Catch a Thief, The Man Who Knew Too Much*, and *Vertigo* followed.

By the mid-fifties, with help from collaborators like James Stewart, John Michael Hayes, and others, Hitchcock had been accepted within the industry as a great producer as well as a great director. He tested the limits of his authority when he moved from Paramount to Metro-Goldwyn-Mayer in 1958 for *North by Northwest.* Since Leo the Lion wanted Hitchcock under its corporate paw, the contract negotiations were prolonged. Metro fought a losing battle. "Over the last ten years in making deals with Hitchcock," a Paramount executive advised MGM attorney Floyd Hendrickson, "Hitchcock has been given increasingly greater control over every facet of the making of his pictures until now Paramount functions practically as a facility setup for him, and [MGM] should be prepared to give him everything." Metro granted the concessions, then prayed for box office absolution. Opening night promised a boon for the studio and the director. Fond of interposing the word *fucking* between the syllables of other words, Hitchcock sent Ernest Lehman an ecstatic wire after *North by Northwest* premiered in New York: "Reception e-blank-normous."

At Universal Studios in the 1960s, Hitchcock consolidated his independence and became a Hollywood Legend. When his television series, *Alfred Hitchcock Presents,* went international, the director toured the world. "There was not a day during our ten days stay [in Australia] without something in the papers," he boasted in a letter home. The train ride from Tokyo to Kyoto brought him "to the rail of the observation car at each of the 3 stops to receive fans and local exhibitors. You should see Alma receiving her flowers like the Pres. wife!" The maker of "little British thrillers" had finally arrived, imperious manner and all. One afternoon he entered Romanoff's for lunch and discovered a prominent Los Angeles attorney seated at Table One, customarily reserved for Hitchcock himself; the director left the restaurant and never returned. Even after he went into eclipse, with such Universal pictures as *Marnie, Torn Curtain,* and *Topaz,* Hitchcock could point to the masterpieces of his British and American periods as justification for his vanity.

Selznick had less to show. Although he threw himself into *A Farewell to Arms*—screenplay, photography, post-production, music, exploitation—neither reviewers nor audiences responded favorably to the 1957 release. "I take credit for my pictures when they are good, so I must take the blame when they are disappointing," he later said. "I frankly confess that while a lot of people thought extremely highly of *A Farewell to Arms,* it is not one of the jobs of which I am most proud." *Tender Is the Night* (1962) also involved Selznick and also failed. A motion picture career that had begun with such distinguished literary adaptations as *David Copperfield* and peaked with *Gone With the Wind* and *Rebecca* ended quietly, even sadly. Yet David Selznick's colleagues remembered him fondly. A director whom he once fired characterized him as "a generous man who would always go to any trouble for a friend, a tough businessman with a big streak of personal tenderness and loyalty." Hitchcock himself later claimed that he "got on very well with Selznick."

Throughout the early 1960s, Selznick and Hitchcock occasionally met; Selznick's daughter Mary Jennifer and Hitchcock's granddaughters were teen-age friends and saw one another on vacations with their families in Switzerland. The producer and his erstwhile contract director mellowed with age. Only months before his death in 1965, Selznick appeared at the Screen Producers Guild Milestone Dinner for Hitchcock. He affectionately recalled his early association with "Hitch, cool and imperturbable—undisturbed even by my memos—of which he received many."

Some years later, reminiscing about *Rebecca* and his producer, Hitchcock generously asked, "Are we missing some other stimulus that went with those earlier days—the great movie mogul, for example?" The answer must have kept the celestial Dictaphone humming for hours.

APPENDIX
The Films of Alfred Hitchcock and David O. Selznick

Although many persons worked on films produced by David Selznick and Alfred Hitchcock, studio traditions and Hollywood guilds often determined who received screen credit. Sometimes persons who contributed to a motion picture—even to such vital elements as the screenplay or the art direction—received no credit; often a supervisor or department head received credit for the creations of his assistant. Screen credits mask almost as much as they reveal.

Names pose another problem. The industry gradually changed the titles of tasks and personnel: the scenario became the screenplay, the cameraman became the director of photography, the art director became the production designer. For the collaborations of Selznick and Hitchcock, the author has taken the credits (task and personnel) from prints of the films. For work that Selznick and Hitchcock produced independent of each other, the author has used the term *scenario* in credits for the silent pictures, *screenplay* in credits for the sound pictures; *art direction* for the silent and early sound films, *production design* for pictures released after 1938; and *photography* for all pictures listed.

The matter of origins poses yet another problem. Since the early 1900s, the studios have looked to the publishing or theatrical worlds for the source of their screen stories. Identifying many of these earlier works has become practically impossible. When a writing credit listed below reads "from *a* novel/story/play by," the title of the original source material is unknown; unless otherwise indicated, the credit reading "from *the* novel/story/play by" means that the original work and the film share a common title.

For pictures that Selznick and Hitchcock produced independent of each other, the author has attempted to provide major production credits. Despite best efforts, however, some credits—especially for silent and early sound pictures—remained elusive. Dates provided are for initial release in country of origin.

Appendix

I. HITCHCOCK AND SELZNICK

REBECCA
Selznick International, 1940

Screenplay	ROBERT E. SHERWOOD AND JOAN HARRISON
from the novel by Daphne du Maurier	
Adaptation	PHILIP MACDONALD AND MICHAEL HOGAN
Photography by	GEORGE BARNES
Music by	FRANZ WAXMAN
Associate (Music)	LOU FORBES
Art Direction	LYLE WHEELER
Interiors Designed by	JOSEPH B. PLATT
Special Effects	JACK COSGROVE AND ARTHUR JOHNS
Interior Decoration	HOWARD BRISTOL
Supervising Film Editor	HAL C. KERN
Associate Film Editor	JAMES E. NEWCOM
Scenario Assistant	BARBARA KEON
Recorder	JACK NOYES
Assistant Director	EDMOND BERNOUDY

Cast:

Maxim de Winter	LAURENCE OLIVIER
The second Mrs. de Winter ("I")	JOAN FONTAINE
Jack Favell	GEORGE SANDERS
Mrs. Danvers	JUDITH ANDERSON
Beatrice Lacy	GLADYS COOPER
Giles Lacy	NIGEL BRUCE
Frank Crawley	REGINALD DENNY
Colonel Julyan	C. AUBREY SMITH
The Coroner	MELVILLE COOPER
Mrs. Van Hopper	FLORENCE BATES
Dr. Baker	LEO G. CARROLL
Frith	EDWARD FIELDING
Robert	PHILIP WINTER

SPELLBOUND
Selznick International, 1945

Screenplay	BEN HECHT
suggested by the novel The House of Dr. Edwardes *by*	
Francis Beeding	
Adaptation	ANGUS MACPHAIL
Photographed by	GEORGE BARNES
Music	MIKLÓS RÓZSA

283

Art Direction	JAMES BASEVI
Associate Art Director	JOHN EWING
Supervising Film Editor	HAL C. KERN
Associate Film Editor	WILLIAM H. ZIEGLER
Production Assistant	BARBARA KEON
Interior Direction by	EMILE KURI
Assistant Director	LOWELL J. FARRELL
Recorder	RICHARD DE WEESE
Dream Sequence Based on Designs by	SALVADOR DALI
Psychiatric Advisor	MAY E. ROMM, M.D.
Special Effects	JACK COSGROVE
Costumes	HOWARD GREER

Cast:

Dr. Constance Petersen	INGRID BERGMAN
John Ballantyne ("Edwards")	GREGORY PECK
Dr. Alex Brulov	MICHAEL CHEKHOV
Dr. Murchison	LEO G. CARROLL
Dr. Fleurot	JOHN EMERY
Mary Carmichael	RHONDA FLEMING
Garmes	NORMAN LLOYD
The Hotel Detective	BILL GOODWIN
The Matron	JEAN ACKER
Dr. Graff	STEVEN GERAY
Harry	DONALD CURTIS
The Stranger in the Lobby	WALLACE FORD
Lieutenant Cooley	ART BAKER
Sergeant Gillespie	FRANCIS TOOMEY
Dr. Hanish	PAUL HARVEY
Dr. Galt	ERSKINE SANFORD
The Sheriff	VICTOR KILIAN
The Bellboy	DAVE WILLOCK
The Police Captain	ADDISON RICHARDS
Norma	JANET SCOTT

NOTORIOUS
RKO, 1946

Screenplay	BEN HECHT
Production Assistant	BARBARA KEON
Director of Photography	TED TETZLAFF
Special Effects	VERNON L. WALKER AND PAUL EAGLER
Art Directors	ALBERT S. D'AGOSTINO AND CARROLL CLARK
Set Decorations	DARRELL SILVERA AND CLAUDE CARPENTER
Music	ROY WEBB
Musical Director	C. BAKALEINIKOFF
Orchestral Arrangements	GIL GRAU

Film Editor	THERON WARTH
Sound	JOHN E. TRIBBY AND TERRY KELLUM
Miss Bergman's Gowns	EDITH HEAD
Assistant Director	WILLIAM DORFMAN

Cast:

Alicia Huberman	INGRID BERGMAN
T. R. Devlin	CARY GRANT
Alex Sebastian	CLAUDE RAINS
Madame Sebastian	LEOPOLDINE KONSTANTIN
Paul Prescott	LOUIS CALHERN
Dr. Anderson	REINHOLD SCHUNZEL
Eric Mathis	IVAN TRIESAULT
Joseph	ALEX MINOTIS
Hupka	EBERHARD KRUMSCHMIDT
The Commodore	SIR CHARLES MENDL
Walter Beardsley	MORONI OLSEN
Dr. Barbosa	RICARDO COSTA

THE PARADINE CASE
Selznick International/Vanguard, 1947

Screenplay	DAVID O. SELZNICK
from the novel by Robert Hichens	
Adaptation	ALMA REVILLE
Photographed by	LEE GARMES
Music	FRANZ WAXMAN
Production Designer	J. MCMILLAN JOHNSON
Art Director	THOMAS MORAHAN
Gowns	TRAVIS BANTON
Supervising Film Editor	HAL C. KERN
Associate Editor	JOHN FAURE
Scenario Assistant	LYDIA SCHILLER
Sound Director	JAMES G. STEWART
Recorded by	RICHARD VAN HESSEN
Interiors by	JOSEPH B. PLATT
Set Decoration	EMILE KURI
Assistant Director	LOWELL J. FARRELL
Unit Manager	FRED AHERN
Special Effects	CLARENCE SLIFER
Hairstyles	LARRY GERMAIN

Cast:

Anthony Keane	GREGORY PECK
Gay Keane	ANN TODD

Lord Horfield	CHARLES LAUGHTON
Sir Simon Flaquer	CHARLES COBURN
Lady Horfield	ETHEL BARRYMORE
André Latour	LOUIS JOURDAN
Maddalena Paradine	[ALIDA] VALLI
Sir Joseph Farrell	LEO G. CARROLL
Judy Flaquer	JOAN TETZEL
The Innkeeper	ISOBEL ELSOM

286

II. Directed by Alfred Hitchcock

SILENT FEATURES

THE PLEASURE GARDEN
Gainsborough-Emelka, 1927

Producer	MICHAEL BALCON
Scenario	ELIOT STANNARD
from the novel by Oliver Sandys	
Photography	BARON [GIOVANNI] VENTIMIGLIA

Cast:

Patsy Brand	VIRGINIA VALLI
Jill Cheyne	CARMELITA GERAGHTY
Levett	MILES MANDER
Hugh Fielding	JOHN STUART
The Native Girl	NITA NALDI

THE MOUNTAIN EAGLE
Gainsborough-Emelka, 1927

Producer	MICHAEL BALCON
Scenario	ELIOT STANNARD
Photography	BARON [GIOVANNI] VENTIMIGLIA

Cast:

Pettigrew	BERNARD GOETZKE
Beatrice	NITA NALDI
Fear o' God	MALCOLM KEEN
Edward	JOHN HAMILTON

(Released in America as *Fear o' God.*)

THE LODGER: A STORY OF THE LONDON FOG
Gainsborough, 1927

Producer	MICHAEL BALCON
Scenario	ELIOT STANNARD
from the novel by Marie Belloc Lowndes	
Photography	BARON [GIOVANNI] VENTIMIGLIA

Editing   IVOR MONTAGUE

Cast:

The Landlady   MARIE AULT
Her Husband   ARTHUR CHESNEY
Daisy Bunting, a mannequin   JUNE
Joe, a police detective   MALCOLM KEEN
Jonathan Drew, the Lodger   IVOR NOVELLO

(Released in America as *The Case of Jonathan Drew.*)

DOWNHILL
Gainsborough, 1927

Producer   MICHAEL BALCON
Scenario   ELIOT STANNARD
    from the play by David LeStrange
Photography   CLAUDE McDONELL
Editing   IVOR MONTAGUE

Cast:

Roddy Berwick   IVOR NOVELLO
Tim Wakely   ROBIN IRVINE
Lady Berwick   LILLIAN BRAITHWAITE
Julia   ISABEL JEANS
Archie   IAN HUNTER

(Released in America as *When Boys Leave Home.*)

EASY VIRTUE
Gainsborough, 1927

Producer   MICHAEL BALCON
Scenario   ELIOT STANNARD
    from the play by Noël Coward
Photography   CLAUDE McDONELL
Editing   IVOR MONTAGUE

Cast:

Larita Filton   ISABEL JEANS
Her Husband   FRANKLYN DYALL
The Artist   ERIC BRANSBY WILLIAMS
The Counsel for the Plaintiff   IAN HUNTER
John Whittaker   ROBIN IRVINE

288

His Mother   VIOLET FAREBROTHER

THE RING
British International, 1927

Producer	JOHN MAXWELL
Scenario	ALFRED HITCHCOCK
Continuity	ALMA REVILLE
Photography	JACK COX

Cast:

Jack Sanders	CARL BRISSON
Mabel	LILIAN HALL DAVIS
The Champion	IAN HUNTER

THE FARMER'S WIFE
British International, 1928

Producer	JOHN MAXWELL
Scenario	ALFRED HITCHCOCK
from the play by Eden Phillpotts	
Photography	JACK COX
Editing	ALFRED BOOTH

Cast:

Farmer Sweetland	JAMESON THOMAS
Araminta Dench	LILIAN HALL DAVIS
Churdles Ash	GORDON HARKER
Thirza Tapper	MAUD GILL
Widow Windeat	LOUISE POUNDS

CHAMPAGNE
British International, 1928

Producer	JOHN MAXWELL
Scenario	ELIOT STANNARD
Adaptation	ALFRED HITCHCOCK
from a story by Walter C. Mycroft	
Photography	JACK COX

Cast:

The Girl	BETTY BALFOUR

The Boy	JEAN BRADIN
The Man	THEO VON ALTEN
The Father	GORDON HARKER

THE MANXMAN
British International, 1929

Producer	JOHN MAXWELL
Scenario	ELIOT STANNARD
from the novel by Hall Caine	
Photography	JACK COX

Cast:

Pete	CARL BRISSON
Philip	MALCOLM KEEN
Kate	ANNY ONDRA
Her Father	RANDLE AYRTON

SOUND FEATURES

BLACKMAIL
British International, 1929

Producer	JOHN MAXWELL
Screenplay	ALFRED HITCHCOCK AND BENN LEVY
from the play by Charles Bennett	
Photography	JACK COX
Art Direction	W. C. ARNOLD
Editing	EMILE DE RUELLE
Music	CAMPBELL AND CONNELLY

Cast:

Alice White	ANNY ONDRA (VOICE: JOAN BARRY)
Mrs. White	SARA ALLGOOD
Mr. White	CHARLES PATON
Detective Frank Webber	JOHN LONGDEN
Tracy, the Blackmailer	DONALD CALTHROP
The Artist	CYRIL RITCHARD
The Landlady	HANNAH JONES
The Neighbor	PHYLLIS MONKMAN
The Chief Inspector	HARVEY BRABAN

290

JUNO AND THE PAYCOCK
British International, 1930

Producer	JOHN MAXWELL
Screenplay	ALFRED HITCHCOCK AND ALMA REVILLE
from the play by Sean O'Casey	
Photography	JACK COX
Art Direction	NORMAN ARNOLD
Editing	EMILE DE RUELLE

Cast:

Juno Boyle	SARA ALLGOOD
Captain Boyle	EDWARD CHAPMAN
Maisie Madigan	MAIRE O'NEIL
Joxer Daly	SIDNEY MORGAN

MURDER!
British International, 1930

Producer	JOHN MAXWELL
Screenplay	ALMA REVILLE
Adaptation	ALFRED HITCHCOCK AND WALTER MYCROFT
from the novel and play Enter Sir John *by Clemence Dane and Helen Simpson*	
Photography	JACK COX
Art Direction	J. F. MEAD
Editing	RENÉ MARRISON AND EMILE DE RUELLE
Music	JOHN REYNDERS

Cast:

Diana Baring	NORAH BARING
Sir John Menier	HERBERT MARSHALL
Gordon Druce	MILES MANDER
Handel Fane	ESME PERCY

(Hitchcock also directed the German version, *Mary,* starring Walter Abel.)

THE SKIN GAME
British International, 1931

Producer	JOHN MAXWELL
Screenplay	ALMA REVILLE
from the play by John Galsworthy	
Adaptation	ALFRED HITCHCOCK
Photography	JACK COX

Art Direction   J. B. MAXWELL
Editing   RENÉ MARRISON AND A. GOBETT

Cast:

Mr. Hillcrest   C. V. FRANCE
Mrs. Hillcrest   HELEN HAYE
Mr. Hornblower   EDMUND GWENN
Jill Hillcrest   JILL ESMOND

NUMBER SEVENTEEN
British International, 1932

Producer   JOHN MAXWELL
Screenplay   ALMA REVILLE, ALFRED HITCHCOCK,
    AND RODNEY ACKLAND
   from the play by J. Jefferson Farjeon
Photography   JACK COX AND BYRAN LANGLEY
Art Direction   W. C. ARNOLD
Editing   A. C. HAMMOND
Music   A. HALLIS

Cast:

Ben   LEON M. LION
The Girl   ANNE GREY
The Detective   JOHN STUART

RICH AND STRANGE
British International, 1932

Producer   JOHN MAXWELL
Screenplay   ALMA REVILLE
   from a story by Dale Collins
Adaptation   ALFRED HITCHCOCK
Photography   JACK COX AND CHARLES MARTIN
Art Direction   W. C. ARNOLD
Editing   RENÉ MARRISON AND WINIFRED COOPER
Music   HAL DOLPHE

Cast:

Fred Hill   HENRY KENDALL
Emily Hill   JOAN BARRY
Commander Gordon   PERCY MARMONT
The "Princess"   BETTY AMANN

The Old Maid   ELSIE RANDOLPH

(Released in America as *East of Shanghai.*)

WALTZES FROM VIENNA
A Tom Arnold Production, 1933

Producer   TOM ARNOLD
Screenplay   ALMA REVILLE AND GUY BOLTON
  from the stage libretto by A. M. Willner, Heinz Reichert, and Ernst Marischka
Art Direction   ALFRED JUNGE AND PETER PROUD
Music   JOHANN STRAUSS

Cast:

Rasi   JESSIE MATTHEWS
Strauss the Younger   ESMOND KNIGHT
Strauss the Elder   EDMUND GWENN
The Prince   FRANK VOSPER
The Countess   FAY COMPTON

(Released in America as *Strauss's Great Waltz.*)

THE MAN WHO KNEW TOO MUCH
Gaumont-British, 1934

Producers   MICHAEL BALCON AND IVOR MONTAGUE
Screenplay   EDWIN GREENWOOD AND A. R. RAWLINSON
  from a story by Charles Bennett and D. B. Wyndham Lewis
Photography   CURT COURANT
Art Direction   ALFRED JUNGE
Editing   H. ST.C. STEWART
Music   ARTHUR BENJAMIN

Cast:

Bob Lawrence   LESLIE BANKS
Jill Lawrence   EDNA BEST
Betty Lawrence   NOVA PILBEAM
Abbott   PETER LORRE
Ramon   FRANK VOSPER
Clive   HUGH WAKEFIELD
Louis Bernard   PIERRE FRESNAY
Nurse Agnes   CICELY OATES

THE 39 STEPS
Gaumont-British, 1935

Producers	MICHAEL BALCON AND IVOR MONTAGUE
Screenplay	CHARLES BENNETT,
	WITH ADDITIONAL DIALOGUE BY IAN HAY
from the novel by John Buchan	
Continuity	ALMA REVILLE
Photography	BERNARD KNOWLES
Art Direction	O. WERNDORFF
Editing	D. N. TWIST
Music	LOUIS LEVY

Cast:

Richard Hannay	ROBERT DONAT
Pamela	MADELEINE CARROLL
Annabella Smith	LUCIE MANNHEIM
Professor Jordan	GODFREY TEARLE
The Crofter	JOHN LAURIE
His Wife	PEGGY ASHCROFT
Mrs. Jordan	HELEN HAYE
The Sheriff	FRANK CELLIER
Mr. Memory	WYLIE WATSON

SECRET AGENT
Gaumont-British, 1936

Producers	MICHAEL BALCON AND IVOR MONTAGUE
Screenplay	CHARLES BENNETT
from the play by Campbell Dixon and stories by W. Somerset Maugham	
Continuity	ALMA REVILLE
Photography	BERNARD KNOWLES
Art Direction	O. WERNDORFF
Editing	CHARLES FREND
Music	LOUIS LEVY

Cast:

Edgar Brodie ("Richard Ashenden")	JOHN GIELGUD
Elsa	MADELEINE CARROLL
The General	PETER LORRE
Marvin	ROBERT YOUNG
Caypor	PERCY MARMONT
Mrs. Caypor	FLORENCE KAHN

SABOTAGE
Gaumont-British, 1936

Producers	MICHAEL BALCON AND IVOR MONTAGUE
Screenplay	CHARLES BENNETT
from the novel The Secret Agent *by Joseph Conrad*	
Photography	BERNARD KNOWLES
Art Direction	O. WERNDORFF
Editing	CHARLES FREND
Music	LOUIS LEVY
Cartoon sequence from Walt Disney's *Who Killed Cock Robin?*	

Cast:

Mrs. Verloc	SYLVIA SIDNEY
Mr. Verloc	OSCAR HOMOLKA
Stevie	DESMOND TESTER
Ted Spenser	JOHN LODER
Renée	JOYCE BARBOUR

(Released in America as *The Woman Alone.*)

YOUNG AND INNOCENT
Gaumont-British, 1938

Producer	EDWARD BLACK
Screenplay	CHARLES BENNETT, EDWIN GREENWOOD,
	AND ANTHONY ARMSTRONG
from the novel A Shilling for Candles *by Josephine Tey*	
Continuity	ALMA REVILLE
Photography	BERNARD KNOWLES
Art Direction	ALFRED JUNGE
Editing	CHARLES FREND
Music	LOUIS LEVY

Cast:

Erica Burgoyne	NOVA PILBEAM
Robert Tisdall	DERRICK DE MARNEY
Colonel Burgoyne	PERCY MARMONT
Old Will	EDWARD RIGBY
Erica's aunt	MARY CLARE
Detective Inspector Kent	JOHN LONGDEN
Guy	GEORGE CURZON
Erica's uncle	BASIL RADFORD
Christine	PAMELA CARME

(Released in America as *The Girl Was Young.*)

THE LADY VANISHES
Gaumont-British, 1938

Producer	EDWARD BLACK
Screenplay	SIDNEY GILLIAT AND FRANK LAUNDER
from the novel The Wheel Spins *by Ethel Lina White*	
Continuity	ALMA REVILLE
Photography	JACK COX
Art Direction	ALEC VETCHINSKY, MAURICE CATER,
	AND ALBERT JULLION
Editing	R. E. DEARING
Music	LOUIS LEVY

Cast:

Iris Henderson	MARGARET LOCKWOOD
Gilbert	MICHAEL REDGRAVE
Miss Froy	DAME MAY WHITTY
Dr. Hartz	PAUL LUKAS
Mr. Todhunter	CECIL PARKER
"Mrs." Todhunter	LINDEN TRAVERS
Caldicott	NAUNTON WAYNE
Charters	BASIL RADFORD
The Baroness	MARY CLARE
The "Nun"	CATHERINE LACEY

JAMAICA INN
A Pommer-Laughton Production, 1939

Producer	ERICH POMMER
Screenplay	SIDNEY GILLIAT AND JOAN HARRISON
from the novel by Daphne du Maurier	
Continuity	ALMA REVILLE
Photography	HARRY STRADLING AND BERNARD KNOWLES
Production Design	TOM MORAHAN
Editing	ROBERT HAMER
Music	ERIC FENBY

Cast:

Sir Humphrey Pengallan	CHARLES LAUGHTON
Joss Merlyn	LESLIE BANKS
Patience, his wife	MARIE NEY
Mary, his niece	MAUREEN O'HARA
Harry	EMLYN WILLIAMS

Salvation Watkins	WYLIE WATSON
Thomas	MERVYN JOHNS

REBECCA
Selznick International, 1940

FOREIGN CORRESPONDENT
A Walter Wanger Production, 1940

Producer	WALTER WANGER
Screenplay	CHARLES BENNETT AND JOAN HARRISON
Photography	RUDOLPH MATÉ
Production Design	ALEXANDER GOLITZEN
Editing	OTHO LOVERING AND DOROTHY SPENCER
Music	ALFRED NEWMAN

Cast:

Johnny Jones ("Huntley Haverstock")	JOEL MCCREA
Carol Fisher	LARAINE DAY
Stephen Fisher	HERBERT MARSHALL
Ffolliott	GEORGE SANDERS
Van Meer	ALBERT BASSERMAN
Stebbins	ROBERT BENCHLEY
Rowley	EDMUND GWENN
Mr. Powers	HARRY DAVENPORT
Krug	EDUARDO CIANNELLI

MR. AND MRS. SMITH
RKO, 1941

Producer	HARRY E. EDINGTON
Screenplay	NORMAN KRASNA
Photography	HARRY STRADLING
Production Design	VAN NEST POLGLASE
Editing	WILLIAM HAMILTON
Music	EDWARD WAND

Cast:

Ann Krausheimer Smith	CAROLE LOMBARD
David Smith	ROBERT MONTGOMERY
Jeff Custer	GENE RAYMOND
Mr. Custer	PHILIP MERIVALE
Mrs. Custer	LUCILE WATSON
Chuck Benson	JACK CARSON

297

SUSPICION
RKO, 1941

Producer	HARRY E. EDINGTON
Screenplay	SAMSON RAPHAELSON, JOAN HARRISON, AND ALMA REVILLE

from the novel Before the Fact *by Francis Iles*

Photography	HARRY STRADLING
Production Design	VAN NEST POLGLASE
Editing	WILLIAM HAMILTON
Music	FRANZ WAXMAN

Cast:

Lina McLaidlaw	JOAN FONTAINE
Johnny Aysgarth	CARY GRANT
General McLaidlaw	SIR CEDRIC HARDWICKE
Mrs. McLaidlaw	DAME MAY WHITTY
Beaky	NIGEL BRUCE
Mrs. Newsham	ISABEL JEANS

SABOTEUR
A Frank Lloyd Production for Universal, 1942

Producer	FRANK LLOYD
Screenplay	PETER VIERTEL, JOAN HARRISON, AND DOROTHY PARKER
Photography	JOSEPH VALENTINE
Production Design	JACK OTTERSON AND ROBERT BOYLE
Editing	OTTO LUDWIG
Music	FRANK SKINNER

Cast:

Barry Kane	ROBERT CUMMINGS
Pat Martin	PRISCILLA LANE
Charles Tobin	OTTO KRUGER
Mrs. Van Sutton	ALMA KRUGER
Fry	NORMAN LLOYD

SHADOW OF A DOUBT
A Jack H. Skirball Production for Universal, 1943

Producer	JACK H. SKIRBALL
Screenplay	THORNTON WILDER, SALLY BENSON, AND ALMA REVILLE

from an original story by Gordon McDonell

Appendix

Photography	JOSEPH VALENTINE
Production Design	JOHN B. GOODMAN AND ROBERT BOYLE
Editing	MILTON CARRUTH
Music	DIMITRI TIOMKIN

Cast:

Uncle Charlie Oakley	JOSEPH COTTEN
Charlie Newton	TERESA WRIGHT
Jack Graham	MACDONALD CAREY
Emma Newton	PATRICIA COLLINGE
Joe Newton	HENRY TRAVERS
Herb Hawkins	HUME CRONYN
Ann Newton	EDNA MAY WONACOTT
Roger Newton	CHARLES BATES
Fred Saunders	WALLACE FORD

LIFEBOAT
Twentieth Century-Fox, 1944

Producer	KENNETH MACGOWAN
Screenplay	JO SWERLING
from a story by John Steinbeck	
Photography	GLEN MACWILLIAMS
Production Design	JAMES BASEVI AND MAURICE RANSFORD
Editing	DOROTHY SPENCER
Music	RENÉ HUBERT

Cast:

Constance Porter	TALLULAH BANKHEAD
Kovac	JOHN HODIAK
Gus Smith	WILLIAM BENDIX
Willi	WALTER SLEZAK
Alice MacKenzie	MARY ANDERSON
Stanley Garrett	HUME CRONYN
Charles J. Rittenhouse	HENRY HULL
Mrs. Higgins	HEATHER ANGEL
Joe Spencer	CANADA LEE

BON VOYAGE
British Ministry of Information, 1944

Producer	SIDNEY BERNSTEIN
Screenplay	J. O. C. ORTON AND ANGUS MACPHAIL
from an original subject by Arthur Calder-Marshall	

| Photography | GUNTHER KRAMPF |
| Sets | CHARLES GILBERT |

Cast: JOHN BLYTHE AND THE MOLIÈRE PLAYERERS

AVENTURE MALGACHE
British Ministry of Information, 1944

Producer	SIDNEY BERNSTEIN
Photography	GUNTHER KRAMPF
Sets	CHARLES GILBERT

Cast: THE MOLIÈRE PLAYERS

SPELLBOUND
Selznick International, 1945

NOTORIOUS
RKO, 1946

THE PARADINE CASE
Selznick International/Vanguard, 1947

ROPE
A Transatlantic Picture, 1948

| Producers | ALFRED HITCHCOCK AND SIDNEY BERNSTEIN |
| Screenplay | ARTHUR LAURENTS |

from the play Rope's End *by Patrick Hamilton*

Photography	JOSEPH VALENTINE AND WILLIAM V. SKALL
Production Design	PERRY FERGUSON
Editing	WILLIAM H. ZIEGLER
Music	FRANCIS POULENC AND LEO F. FORBSTEIN

Cast:

Rupert Cadell	JAMES STEWART
Brandon	JOHN DALL
Philip	FARLEY GRANGER
Mr. Kentley	SIR CEDRIC HARDWICKE
Mrs. Atwater	CONSTANCE COLLIER
Kenneth	DOUGLAS DICK
Mrs. Wilson	EDITH EVANSON

300

Janet	JOAN CHANDLER
David Kentley	DICK HOGAN

UNDER CAPRICORN
A Transatlantic Picture, 1949

Producers	ALFRED HITCHCOCK AND SIDNEY BERNSTEIN
Screenplay	JAMES BRIDIE
from the play by John Colton and Margaret Linden and the novel by Helen Simpson	
Photography	JACK CARDIFF
Production Design	TOM MORAHAN
Editing	A. S. BATES
Music	RICHARD ADDINSELL

Cast:

Sam Flusky	JOSEPH COTTEN
Lady Henrietta Flusky	INGRID BERGMAN
Charles Adare	MICHAEL WILDING
Milly	MARGARET LEIGHTON
The Governor	CECIL PARKER
Corrigan	DENIS O'DEA

STAGE FRIGHT
Warner Bros.-First National, 1950

Producer	ALFRED HITCHCOCK
Screenplay	WHITFIELD COOK
from the novel Man Running *by Selwyn Jepson*	
Photography	WILKIE COOPER
Production Design	TERENCE VERITY
Editing	E. B. JARVIS
Music	LEIGHTON LUCAS

Cast:

Charlotte Inwood	MARLENE DIETRICH
Eve Gill	JANE WYMAN
Wilfrid Smith	MICHAEL WILDING
Jonathan Cooper	RICHARD TODD
Commodore Gill	ALASTAIR SIM
Mrs. Gill	SYBIL THORNDIKE
Nellie Good	KAY WALSH
Chubby Bannister	PATRICIA HITCHCOCK

STRANGERS ON A TRAIN
Warner Bros.-First National, 1951

Producer	ALFRED HITCHCOCK
Screenplay	RAYMOND CHANDLER AND CZENZI ORMONDE
from the novel by Patricia Highsmith	
Photography	ROBERT BURKS
Production Design	EDWARD S. HAWORTH
Editing	WILLIAM ZIEGLER
Music	DIMITRI TIOMKIN

Cast:

Bruno Anthony	ROBERT WALKER
Guy Haines	FARLEY GRANGER
Miriam Haines	LAURA ELLIOTT
Ann Morton	RUTH ROMAN
Barbara Morton	PATRICIA HITCHCOCK
Senator Morton	LEO G. CARROLL
Mrs. Anthony	MARION LORNE

I CONFESS
Warner Bros.-First National, 1953

Producer	ALFRED HITCHCOCK
Screenplay	GEORGE TABORI AND WILLIAM ARCHIBALD
from the play Nos Deux Consciences *by Paul Anthelme*	
Photography	ROBERT BURKS
Production Design	EDWARD S. HAWORTH
Editing	RUDI FEHR
Music	DIMITRI TIOMKIN

Cast:

Father Michael Logan	MONTGOMERY CLIFT
Ruth Grandfort	ANNE BAXTER
Inspector Larrue	KARL MALDEN
Pierre Grandfort	ROGER DANN
Otto Keller	O. E. HASSE
Alma Keller	DOLLY HAAS
Willy Robertson	BRIAN AHERNE

DIAL "M" FOR MURDER
Warner Bros.-First National, 1954

Producer	ALFRED HITCHCOCK

Screenplay	FREDERICK KNOTT
from the play by Frederick Knott	
Photography	ROBERT BURKS
Production Design	EDWARD CARRERA
Editing	RUDI FEHR
Music	DIMITRI TIOMKIN

Cast:

Tony Wendice	RAY MILLAND
Margot Wendice	GRACE KELLY
Mark Halliday	ROBERT CUMMINGS
Lesgate	ANTHONY DAWSON
Inspector Hubbard	JOHN WILLIAMS

REAR WINDOW
Paramount, 1954

Producer	ALFRED HITCHCOCK
Screenplay	JOHN MICHAEL HAYES
from the short story by Cornell Woolrich	
Photography	ROBERT BURKS
Production Design	HAL PEREIRA AND JOSEPH MCMILLAN JOHNSON
Editing	GEORGE TOMASINI
Music	FRANZ WAXMAN

Cast:

L. B. Jeffries	JAMES STEWART
Lisa Carol Freemont	GRACE KELLY
Stella	THELMA RITTER
Tom Doyle	WENDELL COREY
Lars Thorwald	RAYMOND BURR
Mrs. Thorwald	IRENE WINSTON
Miss Lonelyhearts	JUDITH EVELYN
The Composer	ROSS BAGDASARIAN
Miss Torso	GEORGINE DARCY
The Sculptress	JESSLYN FAX

TO CATCH A THIEF
Paramount, 1955

Producer	ALFRED HITCHCOCK
Screenplay	JOHN MICHAEL HAYES
from the novel by David Dodge	
Photography	ROBERT BURKS

Production Design	HAL PEREIRA AND JOSEPH MCMILLAN JOHNSON
Editing	GEORGE TOMASINI
Music	LYNN MURRAY

Cast:

John Robie	CARY GRANT
Frances Stevens	GRACE KELLY
Mrs. Stevens	JESSIE ROYCE LANDIS
H. H. Hughson	JOHN WILLIAMS
Danielle Foussard	BRIGITTE AUBER
Bertani	CHARLES VANEL

THE TROUBLE WITH HARRY
Paramount, 1955

Producer	ALFRED HITCHCOCK
Screenplay	JOHN MICHAEL HAYES
from the novel by J. Trevor Story	
Photography	ROBERT BURKS
Production Design	HAL PEREIRA AND JOHN GOODMAN
Editing	ALMA MACRORIE
Music	BERNARD HERRMANN

Cast:

Captain Albert Wiles	EDMUND GWENN
Sam Marlowe	JOHN FORSYTHE
Jennifer Rogers	SHIRLEY MACLAINE
Miss Graveley	MILDRED NATWICK
Mrs. Wiggs	MILDRED DUNNOCK
Arnie Rogers	JERRY MATHERS
Calvin Wiggs	ROYAL DANO
The Millionaire	PARKER FENNELLY
Harry	PHILIP TRUEX

THE MAN WHO KNEW TOO MUCH
Paramount, 1956

Producer	ALFRED HITCHCOCK
Screenplay	JOHN MICHAEL HAYES
from a story by Charles Bennett and D. B. Wyndham Lewis	
Photography	ROBERT BURKS
Production Design	HAL PEREIRA AND HENRY BUMSTEAD
Editing	GEORGE TOMASINI
Music	BERNARD HERRMANN

Cast:

Dr. Ben McKenna	JAMES STEWART
Jo McKenna	DORIS DAY
Hank McKenna	CHRISTOPHER OLSEN
Mr. Drayton	BERNARD MILES
Mrs. Drayton	BRENDA DE BANZIE
Rien, the Assassin	REGGIE NALDER
Louis Bernard	DANIEL GELIN

THE WRONG MAN
Warner Bros.-First National, 1956

Producer	ALFRED HITCHCOCK
Screenplay	MAXWELL ANDERSON AND ANGUS MACPHAIL
from a story by Maxwell Anderson	
Photography	ROBERT BURKS
Production Design	PAUL SYLBERT
Editing	GEORGE TOMASINI
Music	BERNARD HERRMANN

Cast:

Christopher Emmanuel Balestrero	HENRY FONDA
Rose Balestrero	VERA MILES
Frank O'Connor	ANTHONY QUAYLE
Mrs. Balestrero	ESTHER MINCIOTTI
Lieutenant Bowers	HAROLD J. STONE
Tomasini	JOHN HELDABRAND
Mrs. James	DOREEN LANG
Detective Matthews	CHARLES COOPER
Daniell	RICHARD ROBBINS

VERTIGO
Paramount, 1958

Producer	ALFRED HITCHCOCK
Screenplay	ALEC COPPEL AND SAMUEL TAYLOR
from the novel D'Entre Les Morts *by Pierre Boileau and Thomas Narcejac*	
Photography	ROBERT BURKS
Production Design	HAL PEREIRA AND HENRY BUMSTEAD
Editing	GEORGE TOMASINI
Music	BERNARD HERRMANN

Cast:

John (Scottie) Ferguson	JAMES STEWART

Judy Barton ("Madeleine Elster")   KIM NOVAK
Midge Wood   BARBARA BEL GEDDES
Gavin Elster   TOM HELMORE
Pop Liebl   KONSTANTIN SHAYNE

NORTH BY NORTHWEST
Metro-Goldwyn-Mayer, 1959

Producer   ALFRED HITCHCOCK
Screenplay   ERNEST LEHMAN
Photography   ROBERT BURKS
Production Design   ROBERT BOYLE, WILLIAM A. HORNING,
                                      AND MERRILL PYE
Editing   GEORGE TOMASINI
Music   BERNARD HERRMANN

Cast:

Roger O. Thornhill   CARY GRANT
Eve Kendall   EVA MARIE SAINT
Philip Vandamm   JAMES MASON
Clara Thornhill   JESSIE ROYCE LANDIS
The Professor   LEO G. CARROLL
Lester Townsend   PHILIP OBER
Leonard   MARTIN LANDAU
Valerian   ADAM WILLIAMS
Licht   ROBERT ELLENSTEIN

PSYCHO
Paramount, 1960

Producer   ALFRED HITCHCOCK
Screenplay   JOSEPH STEFANO
  from the novel by Robert Bloch
Photography   JOHN L. RUSSELL
Production Design   JOSEPH HURLEY AND ROBERT CLATWORTHY
Editing   GEORGE TOMASINI
Music   BERNARD HERRMANN

Cast:

Norman Bates   ANTHONY PERKINS
Marion Crane   JANET LEIGH
Lila Crane   VERA MILES
Sam Loomis   JOHN GAVIN
Arbogast   MARTIN BALSAM

Al Chambers	JOHN MCINTIRE
Mrs. Chambers	LURENE TUTTLE
The Psychiatrist	SIMON OAKLAND
Cassidy	FRANK ALBERTSON
Caroline	PAT HITCHCOCK
Mr. Lowery	VAUGHN TAYLOR
The Highway Patrolman	MORT MILLS
"California Charlie"	JOHN ANDERSON

THE BIRDS
Universal, 1963

Producer	ALFRED HITCHCOCK
Screenplay	EVAN HUNTER
from the short story by Daphne du Maurier	
Photography	ROBERT BURKS
Production Design	ROBERT BOYLE
Editing	GEORGE TOMASINI
Electronic Sound Production and Composition	REMI GASSMAN AND OSKAR SALA
Consultant	BERNARD HERRMANN

Cast:

Melanie Daniels	TIPPI HEDREN
Mitch Brenner	ROD TAYLOR
Lydia Brenner	JESSICA TANDY
Annie Hayworth	SUZANNE PLESHETTE
Cathy Brenner	VERONICA CARTWRIGHT
Mrs. Bundy	ETHEL GRIFFIES
Sebastian Sholes	CHARLES MCGRAW
Mrs. MacGruder	RUTH MCDEVITT
Al Malone	MALCOLM ATTERBURY

MARNIE
Universal, 1964

Producer	ALFRED HITCHCOCK
Screenplay	JAY PRESSON ALLEN
from the novel by Winston Graham	
Photography	ROBERT BURKS
Production Design	ROBERT BOYLE
Editing	GEORGE TOMASINI
Music	BERNARD HERRMANN

Cast:

| Margaret (Marnie) Edgar | TIPPI HEDREN |

Mark Rutland	SEAN CONNERY
Lil Mainwaring	DIANE BAKER
Bernice Edgar	LOUISE LATHAM
Sidney Strutt	MARTIN GABEL
Cousin Bob	BOB SWEENEY
Mr. Rutland	ALAN NAPIER
Susan Clabon	MARIETTE HARTLEY
Rita	EDITH EVANSON
Sam Ward	S. JOHN LAUNER
The Sailor	BRUCE DERN

TORN CURTAIN
Universal, 1966

Producer	ALFRED HITCHCOCK
Screenplay	BRIAN MOORE
Photography	JOHN F. WARREN
Production Design	HEIN HECKROTH AND FRANK ARRIGO
Editing	BUD HOFFMAN
Music	JOHN ADDISON

Cast:

Michael Armstrong	PAUL NEWMAN
Sarah Sherman	JULIE ANDREWS
Countess Luchinska	LILA KEDROVA
Gromek	WOLFGANG KIELING
The Ballerina	TAMARA TOUMANOVA
Professor Lindt	LUDWIG DONATH
Jacobi	DAVID OPATOSHU

TOPAZ
Universal, 1969

Producer	ALFRED HITCHCOCK
Screenplay	SAMUEL TAYLOR
from the novel by Leon Uris	
Photography	JACK HILDYARD
Production Design	HENRY BUMSTEAD
Editing	WILLIAM ZIEGLER
Music	MAURICE JARRE

Cast:

André Devereaux	FREDERICK STAFFORD
Michael Nordstrom	JOHN FORSYTHE

Nicole Devereaux	DANY ROBIN
Rico Parra	JOHN VERNON
Juanita de Cordoba	KARIN DOR
Jacques Granville	MICHEL PICCOLI
Henri Jarré	PHILIPPE NOIRET
Michele Picard	CLAUDE JADE
Philippe Dubois	ROSCOE LEE BROWNE
Boris Kusenov	PER-AXEL AROSENIUS
François Picard	MICHEL SUBOR

FRENZY
Universal, 1972

Producer	ALFRED HITCHCOCK
Screenplay	ANTHONY SHAFFER

from the novel Goodbye Piccadilly, Farewell Leicester Square *by Arthur La Bern*

Photography	GIL TAYLOR
Production Design	SYD CAIN AND BOB LAING
Editing	JOHN JYMPSON
Music	RON GOODWIN

Cast:

Richard Blaney	JON FINCH
Bob Rusk	BARRY FOSTER
Brenda Blaney	BARBARA LEIGH-HUNT
Babs Milligan	ANNA MASSEY
Inspector Oxford	ALEC McCOWEN
Mrs. Oxford	VIVIEN MERCHANT
Hetty Porter	BILLIE WHITELAW
Johnny Porter	CLIVE SWIFT
Felix Forsythe	BERNARD CRIBBINS
Gladys	ELSIE RANDOLPH
Sergeant Spearman	MICHAEL BATES
Monica Barling	JEAN MARSH

FAMILY PLOT
Universal, 1976

Producer	ALFRED HITCHCOCK
Screenplay	ERNEST LEHMAN

from the novel The Rainbird Pattern *by Victor Canning*

Photography	LEONARD SOUTH
Production Design	HENRY BUMSTEAD
Editing	TERRY WILLIAMS
Music	JOHN WILLIAMS

Cast:

Fran	KAREN BLACK
Lumley	BRUCE DERN
Blanche	BARBARA HARRIS
Adamson	WILLIAM DEVANE
Maloney	ED LAUTER
Julia Rainbird	CATHLEEN NESBITT
Mrs. Maloney	KATHERINE HELMOND
Grandison	WARREN J. KEMMERLING
Mrs. Clay	EDITH ATWATER
The Bishop	WILLIAM PRINCE
Constantine	NICOLAS COLASANTO
Vera Hannagan	MARGE REDMOND

III. Produced by David Selznick

SILENT FEATURES

ROULETTE
Aetna Pictures, 1924

Director	S. E. V. TAYLOR
Scenario	GERALD C. DUFFY
Adaptation	GERALD C. DUFFY AND LEWIS ALLEN BROWNE

Cast:

Lois Carrington	EDITH ROBERTS
John Tralee	NORMAN TREVOR
Ben Corcoran	MAURICE COSTELLO
Mrs. Harris	MARY CARR
Peter Marineaux	WALTER BOOTH
Mrs. Marineaux	EFFIE SHANNON
Dan Carrington	MONTAGU LOVE

SPOILERS OF THE WEST
Metro-Goldwyn-Mayer, 1928

Director	W. S. VAN DYKE
Scenario	MADELEINE RUTHVEN AND ROSS B. WILLS
from a story by John Thomas Neville	
Photography	CLYDE DE VINNA
Editing	DAN SHARITS

Cast:

Lieutenant Lang	TIM MCCOY
The Girl	MARJORIE DAW
The Girl's Brother	WILLIAM FAIRBANKS
Red Cloud	CHIEF BIG TREE

WYOMING
Metro-Goldwyn-Mayer, 1928

Director	W. S. VAN DYKE
Scenario	MADELEINE RUTHVEN AND ROSS B. WILLS
Writer	W. S. VAN DYKE
Photography	CLYDE DE VINNA

Editing   WILLIAM LE VANWAY

Cast:

Lieutenant Jack Colter	TIM MCCOY
Samantha Jerusha Farrell	DOROTHY SEBASTIAN
Chief Big Cloud	CHARLES BELL
Buffalo Bill	WILLIAM FAIRBANKS
An Indian	CHIEF BIG TREE

FORGOTTEN FACES
Paramount-Famous-Lasky, 1928

Director	VICTOR SCHERTZINGER
Scenario	HOWARD ESTABROOK
from a story by Richard W. Child	
Adaptation	OLIVER H. P. GARRETT
Photography	J. ROY HUNT
Editing	GEORGE NICHOLS, JR.

Cast:

Heliotrope Harry Harlow	CLIVE BROOK
Alice Deane	MARY BRIAN
Lilly Harlow	[OLGA] BACLANOVA
Froggy	WILLIAM POWELL

SOUND FEATURES

CHINATOWN NIGHTS
Paramount-Famous-Lasky, 1929

Director	WILLIAM WELLMAN
Screenplay	BEN GRAUMAN KOHN AND OLIVER H. P. GARRETT
Photography	HENRY GERRARD
Art Direction	WIARD IHNEN
Editing	ALLYSON SHAFFER

Cast:

Chuck Riley	WALLACE BEERY
Joan Fry	FLORENCE VIDOR
Boston Charley	WARNER OLAND
The Shadow	JACK MCHUGH
The Reporter	JACK OAKIE

THE MAN I LOVE
Paramount-Famous-Lasky, 1929

Director	WILLIAM WELLMAN
Screenplay	HERMAN J. MANKIEWICZ
Photography	HENRY GERRARD
Editing	ALLYSON SHAFFER
Song	LEO ROBIN AND RICHARD WHITING

Cast:

Dum-Dum Brooks	RICHARD ARLEN
Celia Fields	MARY BRIAN
Sonia Barondoff	[OLGA] BACLANOVA
Curly Bloom	HARRY GREEN
Lew Layton	JACK OAKIE

THE FOUR FEATHERS
Paramount-Famous-Lasky, 1929

Directors	MERIAN C. COOPER, ERNEST B. SCHOEDSACK, AND LOTHAR MENDES
Screenplay	HOWARD ESTABROOK AND HOPE LORING
from the novel by A. E. W. Mason	
Photography	ROBERT KURRLE, MERIAN C. COOPER, AND ERNEST B. SCHOEDSACK
Editing	ERNEST B. SCHOEDSACK
Music	WILLIAM FREDERICK PETERS

Cast:

Harry Faversham	RICHARD ARLEN
Ethne Eustace	FAY WRAY
Lieutenant Durrance	CLIVE BROOK
Captain Trench	WILLIAM POWELL
The Slave Trader	NOAH BEERY

THE DANCE OF LIFE
Paramount-Famous-Lasky, 1929

Directors	JOHN CROMWELL AND EDWARD SUTHERLAND
Screenplay	BENJAMIN GLAZER
from the play Burlesque *by George Manker Watters*	
Photography	J. ROY HUNT
Art Direction	WIARD IHNEN
Editing	GEORGE NICHOLS, JR.

Songs   RICHARD WHITING, LEO ROBIN, AND SAM COSLOW

Cast:

Bonny Lee King	NANCY CARROLL
Ralph (Skid) Johnson	HAL SKELLY
Harvey Howell	RALPH THEODORE
Lefty	CHARLES BROWN
Sylvia Marco	DOROTHY REVIER
Bozo	AL ST. JOHN
Gussie	MAY BOLEY
Jerry	OSCAR LEVANT

STREET OF CHANCE
Paramount-Famous-Lasky, 1930

Director	JOHN CROMWELL
Screenplay	HOWARD ESTABROOK
Photography	CHARLES LANG
Art Direction	HANS DREIER
Editing	OTTO LEVERING

Cast:

John B. Marsden ("Natural Davis")	WILLIAM POWELL
Judith Marsden	JEAN ARTHUR
Alma Marsden	KAY FRANCIS
"Babe" Marsden	REGIS TOOMEY
Dorgan	STANLEY FIELDS
Al Mastick	BROOKS BENEDICT

SARAH AND SON
Paramount-Famous-Lasky, 1930

Director	DOROTHY ARZNER
Screenplay	ZOË AKINS
from the novel by Timothy Shea	
Photography	CHARLES LANG
Art Direction	VAN NEST POLGLASE
Editing	VERNA WILLIS
Music	NATHANIEL FINSTON

Cast:

Sarah Storm	RUTH CHATTERTON
Howard Vanning	FREDRIC MARCH

314

Jim Gray	FULLER MELLISH, JR.
John Ashmore	GILBERT EMERY
Mrs. Ashmore	DORIS LLOYD
Cyril Belloc	WILLIAM STACK
Bobby	PHILIPPE DE LACY

HONEY
Paramount-Famous-Lasky, 1930

| Director | WESLEY RUGGLES |
| Screenplay and Adaptation | HERMAN J. MANKIEWICZ |

from the novel and play Come Out of the Kitchen! *by Alice Duer Miller and A. E. Thomas*

| Photography | HENRY GERRARD |
| Songs | W. FRANKE HARLING AND SAM COSLOW |

Cast:

Olivia Dangerfield	NANCY CARROLL
Burton Crane	STANLEY SMITH
Charles Dangerfield	SKEETS GALLAGHER
Cora Faulkner	LILLIAN ROTH
J. William Burnstein	HARRY GREEN
Mayme	ZASU PITTS

THE TEXAN
Paramount-Publix, 1930

| Director | JOHN CROMWELL |
| Screenplay | DANIEL NATHAN RUBIN |

from the story "A Double-dyed Deceiver" by O. Henry

Adaptation	OLIVER H. P. GARRETT
Photography	VICTOR MILNER
Editing	VERNA WILLIS
Songs	L. WOLFE GILBERT AND ABEL BAER

Cast:

Enrique (The Llano Kid)	GARY COOPER
Conseulo	FAY WRAY
Señora Ibarra	EMMA DUNN
Thacker	OSCAR APFEL

FOR THE DEFENSE
Paramount-Publix, 1930

| Director | JOHN CROMWELL |

315

Screenplay	OLIVER H. P. GARRETT
Photography	CHARLES LANG
Editing	GEORGE NICHOLS, JR.

Cast:

William Foster	WILLIAM POWELL
Irene Manners	KAY FRANCIS
Defoe	SCOTT KOLK
District Attorney Stone	WILLIAM B. DAVIDSON

MANSLAUGHTER
Paramount-Publix, 1930

Director	GEORGE ABBOTT
Adaptation	GEORGE ABBOTT
from the film by Cecil B. De Mille	
Photography	ARCHIE J. STOUT
Editing	OTTO LEVERING

Cast:

Lydia Thorne	CLAUDETTE COLBERT
Dan O'Bannon	FREDRIC MARCH
Miss Bennett	EMMA DUNN
Eleanor	NATALIE MOORHEAD

LAUGHTER
Paramount-Publix, 1930

Director	HARRY D'ABBADIE D'ARRAST
Screenplay	DONALD OGDEN STEWART
from a story by Harry D'Abbadie D'Arrast and Douglas Doty	
Photography	GEORGE FOLSEY
Art Direction	WILLIAM SALTER AND VAN NEST POLGLASE
Editing	HELENE TURNER
Music	FRANK TOURS

Cast:

Peggy Gibson	NANCY CARROLL
Paul Lockridge	FREDRIC MARCH
G. Mortimer Gibson	DIANE ELLIS
Benham	LEONARD CAREY
Pearl	OLLIE BURGOYNE

THE LOST SQUADRON
RKO, 1932

Director   GEORGE ARCHAINBAUD
Screenplay   WALLACE SMITH, WITH ADDITIONAL DIALOGUE
BY HERMAN J. MANKIEWICZ AND ROBERT S. PRESNELL
Photography   ROB ROBINSON AND ELMER DYER
Art Direction   MAX REE
Music   MAX STEINER

Cast:

Captain Gibson   RICHARD DIX
Follette Marsh   MARY ASTOR
Von Furst   ERICH VON STROHEIM
The Pest   DOROTHY JORDAN
Red   JOEL McCREA
Woody   ROBERT ARMSTRONG
Fritz   HUGH HERBERT
The Detective   RALPH INCE
The Fliers   DICK GRACE, ART GOBEL, LEO NOMIS, AND FRANK CLARK

SYMPHONY OF SIX MILLION
RKO, 1932

Director   GREGORY LA CAVA
Screenplay   BERNARD SCHUBERT AND J. WALTER RUBEN
    from the novel by Fannie Hurst
Photography   LEO TOVER
Art Direction   CARROLL CLARK
Editing   ARCHIE F. MARSHEK
Music   MAX STEINER

Cast:

Dr. Felix Klauber   RICARDO CORTEZ
Jessica   IRENE DUNNE
Hannah   ANNA APPEL
Meyer Klauber   GREGORY RATOFF
Birdie Klauber   LITA CHEVRET
Magnus Klauber   NOEL MADISON
Miss Spencer   HELEN FREEMAN

STATE'S ATTORNEY
RKO, 1932

Director   GEORGE ARCHAINBAUD

Screenplay	GENE FOWLER AND ROWLAND BROWN
from a story by Louis Stevens	
Photography	LEO TOVER
Art Direction	CARROLL CLARK
Editing	CHARLES KIMBALL AND WILLIAM HAMILTON

Cast:

Tom Cardigan	JOHN BARRYMORE
June Perry	HELEN TWELVETREES
Vanny Powers	WILLIAM (STAGE) BOYD

WESTWARD PASSAGE
RKO, 1932

Director	ROBERT MILTON
Screenplay	BRADLEY KING, WITH DIALOGUE BY HUMPHREY PEARSON
from the novel by Margaret Ayer Barnes	
Photography	LUCIEN ANDRIOT
Editing	CHARLES CRAFT
Music	MAX STEINER

Cast:

Olivia	ANN HARDING
Nick Allen	LAURENCE OLIVIER
Harry Lanman	IRVING PICHEL
Henrietta	JULIETTE COMPTON
Mrs. Truesdale	ZASU PITTS
Little Olivia	BONITA GRANVILLE

WHAT PRICE HOLLYWOOD?
RKO, 1932

Director	GEORGE CUKOR
Screenplay	JANE MURFIN, BEN MARKSON, GENE FOWLER, AND ROWLAND BROWN
from a story by Adela Rogers St. John	
Photography	CHARLES ROSHER
Art Direction	CARROLL CLARK
Editing	JACK KITCHEN
Music	MAX STEINER

Cast:

Mary Evans	CONSTANCE BENNETT

Max Carey	LOWELL SHERMAN
Lenny Borden	NEIL HAMILTON
Julius Saxe	GREGORY RATOFF
Cassie	LOUISE BEAVERS
Butler	JAMES EDDIE ANDERSON

ROAR OF THE DRAGON
RKO, 1932

Director	WESLEY RUGGLES
Screenplay	HOWARD ESTABROOK

from the novella A Passage to Hong Kong *by George Kibbe Turner*

Photography	EDWARD CRONJAGER

Cast:

Captain Carson	RICHARD DIX
Natascha	GWILI ANDRÉ
Busby	EDWARD EVERETT HORTON
Helen	ARLINE JUDGE
The Gabby Tourist	ZASU PITTS

AGE OF CONSENT
RKO, 1932

Director	GREGORY LA CAVA
Screenplay	SARAH Y. MASON AND FRANCIS COCKRELL

from the play Cross Roads *by Martin Flavin*

Photography	ROY HUNT
Editing	JACK KITCHEN

Cast:

Betty Cameron	DOROTHY WILSON
Michael Harvey	RICHARD CROMWELL
Duke Galloway	ERIC LINDEN
Dora	ARLINE JUDGE

BIRD OF PARADISE
RKO, 1932

Director	KING VIDOR
Screenplay	WELLS ROOT, WANDA TUCHOCK, AND LEONARD PRASKINS

from the play by Richard Walton Tully

Photography	CLYDE DEVINNA, EDWARD CRONJAGER, AND LUCIEN ANDRIOT

319

Art Direction	CARROLL CLARK
Editing	ARCHIE MARSHEK
Music	MAX STEINER

Cast:

Luana	DOLORES DEL RIO
Johnny Baker	JOEL MCCREA
Mac	JOHN HALLIDAY
Thornton	CREIGHTON CHANEY
Chester	RICHARD GALLAGHER
Hector	BERT ROACH
The King	PUKUI
The Medicine Man	AGOSTINO BORGATO
The Old Native Woman	SOPHIE ORTEGO

A BILL OF DIVORCEMENT
RKO, 1932

Director	GEORGE CUKOR
Screenplay	HOWARD ESTABROOK AND HARRY WAGSTAFF GRIBBLE
from the play by Clemence Dane	
Photography	SID HICKOX
Art Direction	CARROLL CLARK
Editing	ARTHUR ROBERTS
Music	MAX STEINER

Cast:

Hilary Fairfield	JOHN BARRYMORE
Margaret Fairfield	BILLIE BURKE
Sydney Fairfield	KATHARINE HEPBURN
Kit Pumphrey	DAVID MANNERS
Gareth	BRAMWELL FLETCHER
Dr. Alliot	HENRY STEPHENSON
Gary Meredith	PAUL CAVANAGH

THE CONQUERORS
RKO, 1932

Director	WILLIAM WELLMAN
Screenplay	ROBERT LORD
from a story by Howard Estabrook	
Photography	EDWARD CRONJAGER
Art Direction	CARROLL CLARK
Editing	WILLIAM HAMILTON

Music   MAX STEINER

Cast:

Roger Standish	RICHARD DIX
Caroline Standish	ANN HARDING
Matilda Blake	EDNA MAY OLIVER
Dr. Daniel Blake	GUY KIBBEE
Frances Standish	JULIE HAYDON
Warren Lennox	DONALD COOK
Stubby	HARRY HOLMAN
Benson	RICHARD GALLAGHER

ROCKABYE
RKO-Pathé, 1932

Director	GEORGE CUKOR
Screenplay	JANE MURFIN AND KUBEC GLASMON
from the play by Lucia Bronder	
Photography	CHARLES ROSHER
Editing	GEORGE HIVELY
Music	MAX STEINER

Cast:

Judy Carroll	CONSTANCE BENNETT
Jake Pell	JOEL MCCREA
De Sola	PAUL LUKAS
Commissioner Howard	WALTER PIDGEON
The Man in the Night Club	STERLING HOLLOWAY

THE ANIMAL KINGDOM
RKO, 1932

Director	EDWARD H. GRIFFITH
Screenplay	HORACE JACKSON
from the play by Philip Barry	
Photography	GEORGE FOLSEY
Art Direction	VAN NEST POLGLASE
Editing	DANIEL MANDEL

Cast:

Tom Collier	LESLIE HOWARD
Daisy Sage	ANN HARDING
Cecelia Henry	MYRNA LOY

Owen   NEIL HAMILTON
Regan   WILLIAM GARGAN

THE HALF-NAKED TRUTH
RKO, 1932

Director   GREGORY LA CAVA
Screenplay   GREGORY LA CAVA AND COREY FORD
 from the autobiographical stories Phantom Fame *by Harry Reichenbach, as told*
 to David Freedman
Photography   BERT GLENNON
Editing   C. L. KIMBALL
Music   MAX STEINER

Cast:

Teresita   LUPE VELEZ
James Bates   LEE TRACY
Achilles   EUGENE PALLETTE
Farrell   FRANK MORGAN

TOPAZE
RKO, 1933

Director   HARRY D'ABBADIE D'ARRAST
Screenplay   BEN HECHT
 from Benn W. Levy's adaptation of the play by Marcel Pagnol
Photography   LUCIEN ANDRIOT
Art Direction   VAN NEST POLGLASE
Editing   WILLIAM HAMILTON
Music   MAX STEINER

Cast:

Auguste Topaze   JOHN BARRYMORE
Coco   MYRNA LOY
Henri   ALBERT CONTI
Dr. Bomb   LUIS ALBERNI
Baron de Latour-Latour   REGINALD MASON
Baroness de Latour-Latour   JOBYNA HOWLAND
Charlemagne de Latour-Latour   JACKIE SERLE
Dr. Stegg   FRANK REICHER

THE GREAT JASPER
RKO, 1933

Director   J. WALTER RUBEN

Screenplay   H. W. HANEMANN AND ROBERT TASKER
    from the novel by Fulton Oursler
Photography   LEO TOVER
Editing   ARTHUR ROBERTS

Cast:

Jasper Horn   RICHARD DIX
Jenny Horn   FLORENCE ELDRIDGE
Norma McGowd   WERA ENGELS
Madame Taime   EDNA MAY OLIVER
James Bush   BRUCE CABOT

OUR BETTERS
RKO, 1933

Director   GEORGE CUKOR
Screenplay   JANE MURFIN AND HARRY WAGSTAFF GRIBBLE
    from the play by W. Somerset Maugham
Photography   CHARLES ROSHER
Art Direction   VAN NEST POLGLASE AND HOBE ERWIN
Editing   JACK KITCHEN
Music   MAX STEINER

Cast:

Lady Pearl Grayston   CONSTANCE BENNETT
Pepi D'Costa   GILBERT ROLAND
Fleming Harvey   CHARLES STARRETT
Bessie   ANITA LOUISE
Thornton Clay   GRANT MITCHELL
The Duchess   VIOLET KEMBLE-COOPER

KING KONG
RKO, 1933

Directors   ERNEST B. SCHOEDSACK AND MERIAN C. COOPER
Screenplay   JAMES ASHMORE CREELMAN AND RUTH ROSE
    from a story by Merian C. Cooper and Edgar Wallace
Photography   EDWARD LINDON, VERNE WALKER, AND J. O. TAYLOR
Art Direction   CARROLL CLARK AND AL HERMAN
Editing   TED CHEESMAN
Music   MAX STEINER

Cast:

Ann Darrow   FAY WRAY

Carl Denham	ROBERT ARMSTRONG
Driscoll	BRUCE CABOT
Englehorn	FRANK REICHER
Weston	SAM HARDY
The Native Chief	NOBLE JOHNSON
The Second Mate	JAMES FLAVIN
The Witch Doctor	STEVE CLEMENTO
Charlie	VICTOR WONG

CHRISTOPHER STRONG
RKO, 1933

Director	DOROTHY ARZNER
Screenplay	ZOË AKINS
from the novel by Gilbert Frankau	
Photography	BERT GLENNON
Art Direction	VAN NEST POLGLASE
Editing	ARTHUR ROBERTS
Music	MAX STEINER

Cast:

Lady Cynthia Darrington	KATHARINE HEPBURN
Sir Christopher Strong	COLIN CLIVE
Elaine Strong	BILLIE BURKE
Monica Strong	HELEN CHANDLER
Harry Rawlinson	RALPH FORBES
Carlo	JACK LARUE

SWEEPINGS
RKO, 1933

Director	JOHN CROMWELL
Screenplay	LESTER COHEN, HOWARD ESTABROOK, AND H. W. HANEMANN
from the novel by Lester Cohen	
Photography	EDWARD CRONJAGER
Editing	GEORGE NICHOLS

Cast:

Daniel Pardway	LIONEL BARRYMORE
Thane Pardway	ALLAN DINEHART
Fred Pardway	ERIC LINDEN
Gene Pardway	WILLIAM GARGAN
Phoebe	GLORIA STUART

THE MONKEY'S PAW
RKO, 1933

Director	WESLEY RUGGLES
Screenplay	LOUISE M. PARKER AND GRAHAM JOHN
from the short story by W. W. Jacobs	
Photography	LEO TOVER
Editing	CHARLES L. KIMBALL

Cast: C. AUBREY SMITH, IVAN SIMPSON, LOUISE CARTER, AND BRAMWELL FLETCHER

DINNER AT EIGHT
Metro-Goldwyn-Mayer, 1933

Director	GEORGE CUKOR
Screenplay	HERMAN J. MANKIEWICZ AND FRANCES MARION
from the play by George S. Kaufman and Edna Ferber	
Photography	WILLIAM DANIELS
Art Direction	CEDRIC GIBBONS AND HOBE ERWIN
Editing	BEN LEWIS
Music	WILLIAM AXT

Cast:

Carlotta Vance	MARIE DRESSLER
Larry Renault	JOHN BARRYMORE
Dan Packard	WALLACE BEERY
Kitty Packard	JEAN HARLOW
Oliver Jordan	LIONEL BARRYMORE
Max Kane	LEE TRACY
Dr. Wayne Talbot	EDMUND LOWE
Mrs. Oliver Jordan	BILLIE BURKE
Paula Jordan	MADGE EVANS
Jo Stengel	JEAN HERSHOLT
Mrs. Talbot	KAREN MORLEY

NIGHT FLIGHT
Metro-Goldwyn-Mayer, 1933

Director	CLARENCE BROWN
Screenplay	OLIVER H. P. GARRETT
from the novel by Antoine de Saint-Exupéry	
Photography	OLIVER T. MARSH, ELMER DYER, AND CHARLES MARSHALL

Art Direction	ALEXANDER TOLUBOFF
Editing	HAL C. KERN

Cast:

Rivière	JOHN BARRYMORE
Madame Fabien	HELEN HAYES
Jules Fabien	CLARK GABLE
Robineau	LIONEL BARRYMORE
Auguste Pellerin	ROBERT MONTGOMERY
The Brazilian Pilot	WILLIAM GARGAN
The Brazilian Pilot's Wife	MYRNA LOY
Daudet	C. HENRY GORDON

MEET THE BARON
Metro-Goldwyn-Mayer, 1933

Director	WALTER LANG
Screenplay	ALLEN RIVKIN AND P. J. WOLFSON
from a story by Herman J. Mankiewicz and Norman Krasna	
Photography	ALLEN SIEGLER
Editing	JAMES E. NEWCOM
Songs	JIMMY MCHUGH AND DOROTHY FIELDS

Cast:

Baron	JACK PEARL
Joe McGoo	JIMMY DURANTE
Zasu	ZASU PITTS
Ted	TED HEALY
Dean Primrose	EDNA MAY OLIVER

DANCING LADY
Metro-Goldwyn-Mayer, 1933

Director	ROBERT Z. LEONARD
Screenplay	ALLEN RIVKIN AND P. J. WOLFSON
from the novel by James W. Bellah	
Photography	OLIVER T. MARSH
Art Direction	MERRILL PYE
Editing	MARGARET BOOTH
Songs BURTON LANE AND HAROLD ADAMSON, RICHARD RODGERS AND LORENZ HART, JIMMY MCHUGH, DOROTHY FIELDS, AND ARTHUR FREED	

Cast:

Janie Barlow	JOAN CRAWFORD

Patch Gallagher	CLARK GABLE
Tod Newton	FRANCHOT TONE
Mrs. Newton	MAY ROBSON
Fred Astaire	FRED ASTAIRE
Ward King	ROBERT BENCHLEY
Nelson Eddy	NELSON EDDY
Steve	TED HEALY
His Stooges	MOE HOWARD, JERRY HOWARD, AND LARRY FINE

VIVA VILLA!
Metro-Goldwyn-Mayer, 1934

Director	JACK CONWAY
Screenplay	BEN HECHT
suggested by the book by Edgcumb Pinchon and O. B. Stade	
Photography	JAMES WONG HOWE AND CHARLES G. CLARKE
Art Direction	HARRY OLIVER
Editing	ROBERT J. KERN
Music	HERBERT STOTHART

Cast:

Pancho Villa	WALLACE BEERY
Sierra	LEO CARRILLO
Teresa	FAY WRAY
Don Felipe del Castillo	DONALD COOK
Johnny Sykes	STUART ERWIN
Emilio Chavito	GEORGE E. STONE

MANHATTAN MELODRAMA
Metro-Goldwyn-Mayer, 1934

Director	W. S. VAN DYKE
Screenplay	OLIVER H. P. GARRETT AND JOSEPH L. MANKIEWICZ
from a story by Arthur Caesar	
Photography	JAMES WONG HOWE
Art Direction	CEDRIC GIBBONS
Editing	BEN LEWIS
Song	RICHARD RODGERS AND LORENZ HART

Cast:

Blackie Gallagher	CLARK GABLE
Jim Wade	WILLIAM POWELL
Eleanor	MYRNA LOY
Father Joe	LEO CARRILLO

Spud   NAT PENDLETON
Poppa Rosen   GEORGE SIDNEY
Annabelle   ISABEL JEWELL
Tootsie   MURIEL EVANS
Mr. Snow   THOMAS JACKSON

DAVID COPPERFIELD
Metro-Goldwyn-Mayer, 1935

Director   GEORGE CUKOR
Screenplay   HOWARD ESTABROOK AND HUGH WALPOLE
   from the novel by Charles Dickens
Photography   OLIVER T. MARSH
Art Direction   CEDRIC GIBBONS
Editing   ROBERT J. KERN
Music   HERBERT STOTHART

Cast:

Mr. Micawber   W. C. FIELDS
Dan Peggotty   LIONEL BARRYMORE
Dora   MAUREEN O'SULLIVAN
Agnes   MADGE EVANS
Aunt Betsey   EDNA MAY OLIVER
Mr. Wickfield   LEWIS STONE
David, the man   FRANK LAWTON
David, the child   FREDDIE BARTHOLOMEW
Mrs. Copperfield   ELIZABETH ALLAN
Uriah Heep   ROLAND YOUNG
Mr. Murdstone   BASIL RATHBONE
Clickett   ELSA LANCHESTER
Mrs. Micawber   JEAN CADELL
Nurse Peggotty   JESSIE RALPH
Mr. Dick   LENOX PAWLE
Jane Murdstone   VIOLET KEMBLE-COOPER

VANESSA: HER LOVE STORY
Metro-Goldwyn-Mayer, 1935

Director   WILLIAM K. HOWARD
Screenplay   HUGH WALPOLE AND LENORE COFFEE
   from the novel by Hugh Walpole
Photography   RAY JUNE
Editing   FRANK HULL

Cast:

Vanessa   HELEN HAYES

Benjie ROBERT MONTGOMERY
Ellis OTTO KRUGER
Judith MAY ROBSON
Adam LEWIS STONE

RECKLESS
Metro-Goldwyn-Mayer, 1935

Director VICTOR FLEMING
Screenplay P. J. WOLFSON
 from a story by Oliver Jeffries [pseudonym for David Selznick]
Photography GEORGE FOLSEY
Editing MARGARET BOOTH
Songs JEROME KERN AND DOROTHY FIELDS

Cast:

Mona JEAN HARLOW
Ned Riley WILLIAM POWELL
Bob Harrison FRANCHOT TONE
Granny MAY ROBSON
Smiley TED HEALY
Blossom NAT PENDLETON

ANNA KARENINA
Metro-Goldwyn-Mayer, 1935

Director CLARENCE BROWN
Screenplay CLEMENCE DANE AND SALKA VIERTEL
 from the novel by Leo Tolstoy
Photography WILLIAM DANIELS
Art Direction CEDRIC GIBBONS
Editing ROBERT J. KERN
Music HERBERT STOTHART

Cast:

Anna Karenina GRETA GARBO
Vronsky FREDRIC MARCH
Sergei FREDDIE BARTHOLOMEW
Kitty MAUREEN O'SULLIVAN
Countess Vronsky MAY ROBSON
Karenin BASIL RATHBONE
Stiva REGINALD OWEN
Yashvin REGINALD DENNY
Dolly PHOEBE FOSTER
Levin GYLES ISHAM

A TALE OF TWO CITIES
Metro-Goldwyn-Mayer, 1935

Director	JACK CONWAY
Screenplay	W. P. LIPSCOMB AND S. N. BEHRMAN
from the novel by Charles Dickens	
Photography	OLIVER T. MARSH
Art Direction	CEDRIC GIBBONS
Editing	CONRAD A. NERVIG
Music	HERBERT STOTHART

Cast:

Sydney Carton	RONALD COLMAN
Lucie Manette	ELIZABETH ALLAN
Miss Pross	EDNA MAY OLIVER
Stryver	REGINALD OWEN
Marquis St. Evrémonde	BASIL RATHBONE
Madame Defarge	BLANCHE YURKA
Dr. Manette	HENRY B. WALTHALL
Charles Darnay	DONALD WOODS

LITTLE LORD FAUNTLEROY
Selznick International, 1936

Director	JOHN CROMWELL
Screenplay	HUGH WALPOLE
from the novel by Frances Hodgson Burnett	
Photography	CHARLES ROSHER
Art Direction	STURGES CARNE
Editing	HAL C. KERN
Music	MAX STEINER

Cast:

Earl of Dorincourt	C. AUBREY SMITH
Ceddie	FREDDIE BARTHOLOMEW
Dearest (Mrs. Errol)	DOLORES COSTELLO BARRYMORE
Havisham	HENRY STEPHENSON
Mr. Hobbs	GUY KIBBEE
Dick	MICKEY ROONEY
Ben	ERIC ALDEN
The Claimant	JACKIE SEARL
Newick	REGINALD BARLOW
Rev. Mordaunt	IVAN SIMPSON
Sir Harry Lorridaile	E. E. CLIVE

Lady Lorridaile	CONSTANCE COLLIER
Mary	UNA O'CONNOR
Mrs. Mellon	MAY BEATTY
Dawson	JOAN STANDING
The Apple Woman	JESSIE RALPH
Higgins	LIONEL BELMORE

THE GARDEN OF ALLAH
Selznick International, 1936

Director	RICHARD BOLESLAWSKI
Screenplay	W. P. LIPSCOMB AND LYNN RIGGS
from the novel by Robert Hichens	
Photography	W. HOWARD GREENE AND HAROLD ROSSON
Art Direction	STURGES CARNE AND LYLE WHEELER
Editing	HAL C. KERN AND ANSON STEVENSON
Music	MAX STEINER

Cast:

Domini Enfilden	MARLENE DIETRICH
Boris Androvsky	CHARLES BOYER
Count Anteoni	BASIL RATHBONE
Father Roubier	C. AUBREY SMITH
Irena	TILLY LOSCH
Batouch	JOSEPH SCHILDKRAUT
The Sand Diviner	JOHN CARRADINE
De Trevignac	ALAN MARSHALL
Mother Superior	LUCILE WATSON
Hadj	HENRY BRANDON

A STAR IS BORN
Selznick International, 1937

Director	WILLIAM WELLMAN
Screenplay	DOROTHY PARKER, ALAN CAMPBELL, AND ROBERT CARSON
from a story by William Wellman and Robert Carson	
Photography	W. HOWARD GREENE
Art Direction	LYLE WHEELER
Editing	HAL C. KERN AND JAMES E. NEWCOM
Music	MAX STEINER

Cast:

Esther Blodgett ("Vicki Lester")	JANET GAYNOR

Norman Maine	FREDRIC MARCH
Oliver Niles	ADOLPHE MENJOU
Lettie	MAY ROBSON
Danny McGuire	ANDY DEVINE
Libby	LIONEL STANDER
Anita Regis	ELIZABETH JENNS
"Pop" Randall	EDGAR KENNEDY
Casey Burke	OWEN MOORE

THE PRISONER OF ZENDA
Selznick International, 1937

| Director | JOHN CROMWELL |
| Screenplay | JOHN L. BALDERSTON |

from Wells Root's adaptation of Edward Rose's dramatization of the novel by Anthony Hope

Photography	JAMES WONG HOWE
Art Direction	LYLE WHEELER
Editing	HAL C. KERN AND JAMES E. NEWCOM
Music	ALFRED NEWMAN

Cast:

Rudolf Rassendyll (King Rudolf V)	RONALD COLMAN
Princess Flavia	MADELEINE CARROLL
Rupert of Hentzau	DOUGLAS FAIRBANKS, JR.
Antoinette De Mauban	MARY ASTOR
Colonel Zapt	C. AUBREY SMITH
Black Michael	RAYMOND MASSEY
Captain Fritz von Tarlenheim	DAVID NIVEN
Cook	ELEANOR WESSELHOEFT
Johann	BYRON FOULGER
Detchard	MONTAGU LOVE

NOTHING SACRED
Selznick International, 1937

| Director | WILLIAM WELLMAN |
| Screenplay | BEN HECHT |

from the story by James Street

Photography	W. HOWARD GREENE
Art Direction	LYLE WHEELER
Editing	JAMES E. NEWCOM
Music	OSCAR LEVANT

Cast:

Hazel Flagg	CAROLE LOMBARD
Wally Cook	FREDRIC MARCH
Dr. Downer	CHARLES WINNINGER
Stone	WALTER CONNOLLY
Dr. Eggelhoffer	SIG RUMANN

THE ADVENTURES OF TOM SAWYER
Selznick International, 1938

Director	NORMAN TAUROG
Screenplay	JOHN V. A. WEAVER
from the novel by Mark Twain	
Photography	JAMES WONG HOWE AND WILFRED M. CLINE
Art Direction	LYLE WHEELER
Editing	HAL C. KERN AND MARGARET CLANCEY
Music	LOU FORBES

Cast:

Tom Sawyer	TOMMY KELLY
Aunt Polly	MAY ROBSON
Huck Finn	JACKIE MORAN
Muff Potter	WALTER BRENNAN
Injun Joe	VICTOR JORY
Mary Sawyer	MARCIA MAE JONES
The Sheriff	VICTOR KILIAN
Mrs. Thatcher	NANA BRYANT
Becky Thatcher	ANN GILLIS
Joe Harper	MICKEY RENTSCHLER
Amy Lawrence	CORA SUE COLLINS
Judge Thatcher	CHARLES RICHMAN
Widow Douglas	SPRING BYINGTON
Mrs. Harper	MARGARET HAMILTON

THE YOUNG IN HEART
Selznick International, 1938

Director	RICHARD WALLACE
Screenplay	PAUL OSBORN AND CHARLES BENNETT
from the novella The Gay Banditti *by I. A. R. Wylie*	
Photography	LEON SHAMROY
Art Direction	LYLE WHEELER
Editing	HAL C. KERN
Music	FRANZ WAXMAN

Cast:

George-Anne Carleton	JANET GAYNOR
Richard Carleton	DOUGLAS FAIRBANKS, JR.
Leslie Saunders	PAULETTE GODDARD
Colonel Anthony "Sahib" Carleton	ROLAND YOUNG
Marmy Carleton	BILLIE BURKE
Duncan MacCrae	RICHARD CARLSON
Miss Ellen Fortune	MINNIE DUPREE

MADE FOR EACH OTHER
Selznick International, 1939

Director	JOHN CROMWELL
Screenplay	JO SWERLING
Photography	LEON SHAMROY
Production Design	WILLIAM CAMERON MENZIES AND LYLE WHEELER
Editing	HAL C. KERN AND JAMES E. NEWCOM
Music	LOU FORBES

Cast:

Jane Mason	CAROLE LOMBARD
John Mason	JAMES STEWART
Judge Doolittle	CHARLES COBURN
Mrs. Mason	LUCILE WATSON
Conway	EDDIE QUINLAN
Sister Madeline	ALMA KRUGER
Eunice Doolittle	RUTH WESTON
Carter	DONALD BRIGGS
Dr. Healy	HARRY DAVENPORT
Cook	ESTHER DALE
Collins	RUSSELL HOPTON
Hatton	WARD BOND
The Farmer	OLIN HOWARD
The Farmer's Wife	FERN EMMETT
The Cook	LOUISE BEAVERS

INTERMEZZO: A LOVE STORY
Selznick International, 1939

Director	GREGORY RATOFF
Screenplay	GEORGE O'NEIL
from the original Swedish scenario by Gosta Stevens and Gustaf Molander	
Photography	GREGG TOLAND
Production Design	LYLE WHEELER
Editing	HAL C. KERN AND FRANCIS LYON

334

Music   LOU FORBES

Cast:

Holger Brandt   LESLIE HOWARD
Anita Hoffmann   INGRID BERGMAN
Margit Brandt   EDNA BEST
Thomas Stenborg   JOHN HALLIDAY
Charles   CECIL KELLAWAY
Greta   ENID BENNETT
Ann Marie   ANN TODD
Eric   DOUGLAS SCOTT

GONE WITH THE WIND
Selznick International, 1939

Director   VICTOR FLEMING
Screenplay   SIDNEY HOWARD
   from the novel by Margaret Mitchell
Photography   ERNEST HALLER, RAY RENNAHAN, AND
                                               WILFRED M. CLINE
Production Design   WILLIAM CAMERON MENZIES
Editing   HAL C. KERN AND JAMES E. NEWCOM
Music   MAX STEINER

Cast:

Scarlett O'Hara   VIVIEN LEIGH
Rhett Butler   CLARK GABLE
Melanie Hamilton   OLIVIA DE HAVILLAND
Ashley Wilkes   LESLIE HOWARD
Mammy   HATTIE MCDANIEL
Prissy   BUTTERFLY MCQUEEN
Gerald O'Hara   THOMAS MITCHELL
Jonas Wilkerson   VICTOR JORY
Suellen O'Hara   EVELYN KEYES
Carreen O'Hara   ANN RUTHERFORD
Charles Hamilton   RAND BROOKS
Aunt Pittypat Hamilton   LAURA HOPE CREWS
Dr. Meade   HARRY DAVENPORT
Belle Watling   ONA MUNSON
The Yankee Captain   WARD BOND
Bonnie Blue Butler   CAMMIE KING

REBECCA
Selznick International, 1940

SINCE YOU WENT AWAY
Selznick International, 1944

Director	JOHN CROMWELL
Screenplay	DAVID SELZNICK
from the book by Margaret Buell Wilder	
Photography	LEE GARMES AND STANLEY CORTEZ
Production Design	WILLIAM PEREIRA
Editing	HAL C. KERN AND JAMES E. NEWCOM
Music	MAX STEINER

Cast:

Anne Hilton	CLAUDETTE COLBERT
Jane Hilton	JENNIFER JONES
Lieutenant Tony Willett	JOSEPH COTTEN
Bridget (Brig) Hilton	SHIRLEY TEMPLE
Colonel Smollett	MONTY WOOLLEY
The Clergyman	LIONEL BARRYMORE
William G. Smollett II	ROBERT WALKER
Fidelia	HATTIE MCDANIEL
Emily Hawkins	AGNES MOOREHEAD
Zofia Koslowska	ALLA NAZIMOVA
Harold E. Smith	GUY MADISON

I'LL BE SEEING YOU
Selznick International, 1944

Producer	DORE SCHARY
Director	WILLIAM DIETERLE
Screenplay	MARION PARSONNET
from the novel Double Furlough *by Charles Martin*	
Photography	TONY GAUDIO
Production Design	MARK-LEE KIRK
Editing	WILLIAM H. ZIEGLER
Music	DANIELE AMFITHEATROF

Cast:

Mary Marshall	GINGER ROGERS
Zachary Morgan	JOSEPH COTTEN
Barbara Marshall	SHIRLEY TEMPLE
Mrs. Marshall	SPRING BYINGTON
Mr. Marshall	TOM TULLY
Swanson	CHILL WILLS

336

SPELLBOUND
Selznick International, 1945

DUEL IN THE SUN
Selznick Releasing Organization, 1946

Director	KING VIDOR
Screenplay	DAVID SELZNICK
from Oliver H. P. Garrett's adaptation of the novel	
by Niven Busch	
Photography	LEE GARMES, HAROLD ROSSON, AND RAY RENNAHAN
Production Design	J. MCMILLAN JOHNSON
Editing	HAL C. KERN, WILLIAM H. ZIEGLER, AND JOHN FAURE
Music	DIMITRI TIOMKIN

Cast:

Pearl Chavez	JENNIFER JONES
Lewt McCanles	GREGORY PECK
Jesse McCanles	JOSEPH COTTEN
Senator McCanles	LIONEL BARRYMORE
Laura Belle McCanles	LILLIAN GISH
Sam Pierce	CHARLES BICKFORD
Vashti	BUTTERFLY MCQUEEN
The Sinkiller	WALTER HUSTON
Scott Chavez	HERBERT MARSHALL
Mrs. Chavez	TILLY LOSCH

THE PARADINE CASE
Selznick International/Vanguard, 1947

PORTRAIT OF JENNIE
Selznick Releasing Organization, 1948

Director	WILLIAM DIETERLE
Screenplay	PAUL OSBORN AND PETER BERNEIS
from Leonardo Bercovici's adaptation of the novel by Robert Nathan	
Photography	JOSEPH AUGUST
Production Design	J. MCMILLAN JOHNSON
Editing	GERALD WILSON
Music	DIMITRI TIOMKIN

Cast:

Jennie Appleton	JENNIFER JONES

Eben Adams	JOSEPH COTTEN
Miss Spinney	ETHEL BARRYMORE
Mr. Matthews	CECIL KELLAWAY
Gus O'Toole	DAVID WAYNE
Mr. Moore	ALBERT SHARPE
Mrs. Jekes	FLORENCE BATES
Mother Mary of Mercy	LILLIAN GISH
Clare Morgan	MAUDE SIMMONS

THE THIRD MAN
British Lion/London Films/David O. Selznick, 1949

Producers	ALEXANDER KORDA AND DAVID SELZNICK
Director	CAROL REED
Screenplay	GRAHAM GREENE
Photography	ROBERT KRASKER
Production Design	VINCENT KORDA
Editing	OSWALD HOFENRICHTER
Music	ANTON KARAS

Cast:

Holly Martins	JOSEPH COTTEN
Anna Schmidt	[ALIDA] VALLI
Harry Lime	ORSON WELLES
Major Calloway	TREVOR HOWARD
Sergeant Paine	BERNARD LEE
Kurtz	ERNEST DEUTSCH
Dr. Winkel	ERICH PONTO
Popesco	SIEGFRIED BREUER
Professor Crabbin	WILFRED HYDE-WHITE
The Porter	PAUL HOERBIGER
Anna's Housekeeper	HEDWIG BLEIBTREU

THE WILD HEART
RKO, 1952

Producers	MICHAEL POWELL, EMERIC PRESSBURGER, AND DAVID SELZNICK
Directors	MICHAEL POWELL AND EMERIC PRESSBURGER; AND ROUBEN MAMOULIAN (UNCREDITED)
Screenplay	MICHAEL POWELL AND EMERIC PRESSBURGER
from the novel Gone to Earth *by Mary Webb Davis*	
Photography	CHRISTOPHER CHALLIS
Production Design	HEIN HECKROTH
Editing	REGINALD MILLS
Music	BRIAN EASDALE

Cast:

Hazel Woodus	JENNIFER JONES
Jack Reddin	DAVID FARRAR
Edward Marston	CYRIL CUSACK
Abel Woodus	ESMOND KNIGHT
Mrs. Marston	SYBIL THORNDIKE
Andrew Vessons	HUGH GRIFFITH

INDISCRETION OF AN AMERICAN WIFE
Columbia Pictures, 1954

Producers	VITTORIO DE SICA AND DAVID SELZNICK
Director	VITTORIO DE SICA
Screenplay	CESARE ZAVATTINI, LUIGI CHIARINI, AND GIORGIO PROSPERI
Photography	G. R. ALDO
Production Design	VIRGILIO MARCHI
Editing	ERALDO DE REMA AND JEAN BARKER
Music	ALESSANDRO CICOGNINI

Cast:

Mary	JENNIFER JONES
Giovanni	MONTGOMERY CLIFT
The Commissioner	GINO CERVI
Paul	DICK BEYMER

A FAREWELL TO ARMS
Twentieth Century-Fox, 1957

Director	CHARLES VIDOR
Screenplay	BEN HECHT

from the novel by Ernest Hemingway and the play by Laurence Stallings

Photography	PIERO PORTALUPI AND OSWALD MORRIS
Production Design	ALFRED JUNGE
Editing	JAMES E. NEWCOM, GERALD J. WILSON, AND JOHN M. FOLEY
Music	MARIO NASCIMBENE

Cast:

Lieutenant Frederic Henry	ROCK HUDSON
Catherine Barkley	JENNIFER JONES
Major Alessandro Rinaldi	VITTORIO DE SICA

Father Galli	ALBERTO SORDI
Bonello	KURT KASZNAR
Miss Van Campen	MERCEDES MCCAMBRIDGE
Dr. Emerich	OSCAR HOMOLKA
Helen Ferguson	ELAINE STRITCH

NOTES

Archival materials, personal interviews, contemporary newspapers, and other secondary works formed the research base for *Hitchcock and Selznick*. The following notes (many keyed to entries in the Selected Bibliography) provide sources for most quotations within the text. Unless otherwise indicated, quotations from correspondence between Selznick and his associates are from primary materials in the Selznick Collection at The University of Texas at Austin; quotations from correspondence between one member of the Selznick organization and another—including Katharine Brown, Richard Hungate, Barbara Keon, Val Lewton, Margaret McDonell, Daniel O'Shea, and Jenia Reissar—are also from the Collection.

The author has not cited—except within the text—quotations from his personal (P) or telephone (T) interviews: Judith Anderson (T), 11 January 1986; Pandro Berman (T), 19 January 1986; Robert Boyle (P), Los Angeles, 7 August 1981; Niven Busch (T), 8 December 1985; Olivia de Havilland (P), Paris, 9 July 1985; William Dozier (T), 11 May 1986;

Joan Fontaine (T), 5 January 1986; John Michael Hayes (P), Los Angeles, 24 May 1985; Raymond Klune (T), 6 November 1984; Arthur Laurents (T), 8 June 1986; Ernest Lehman (P), Los Angeles, 30 July 1981; Pat Hitchcock O'Connell (T), 30 September 1986; Marcella Rabwin (T), 20 July 1986 and 7 September 1986; Peggy Robertson (P), Los Angeles, 9 August 1981; Robert Saunders (P), Los Angeles, 7 August 1981; Lydia Schiller (P), Los Angeles, 12 May 1985; Irene Mayer Selznick (P), New York, 27 June 1985; Carol Stevens Shourds (P), Los Angeles, 27 June 1986; Leonard South (T), 13 July 1982; Ann Todd (P), London, 30 July 1985.

The author has also not cited quotations from treatments or screenplays whose authors and dates are noted within the text (all are from the Selznick Collection); quotations from contemporary reviews of motion pictures produced or directed by Selznick or Hitchcock; or paraphrased facts and opinions.

Preface

xi "I SNORE": David O. Selznick (DOS) to "Angel" [Irene Selznick], 9 August 1939; DOS to John Wharton, 16 December 1935, in Behlmer, *Memo*, 278, 100.
xii "CONTAINMENT WASN'T": Selznick, 157.
xii "A FUNDAMENTALLY": Hellman, 38.
xii "NEVER REVEAL": Wanger, 13.

I: Transatlantic Overtures

4 "I REMEMBER": quoted in Behlmer, *Memo*, 5.
4 "THE TROUBLE": quoted in Haver, 175.
5 "MARK MY": quoted in Selznick, 96.
5 DAVID WAS "PRECOCIOUSLY": Thomson, 42.
6 "SHOVELING FOOD": Bergman, 65.
6 "LIKE THEY'D BEEN": Myrick, 30.
6 "KNOWING HOW": William Paley to DOS, 8 December 1938, David O. Selznick Collection, Hoblitzelle Theatre Arts Library, Humanities Research Center, The University of Texas at Austin.
6 "IT NEVER": quoted in Haver, 174.
6 "WORK WAS": Selznick, 155.
8 "I DICTATE": quoted in Behlmer, *Memo*, xxiii.

8 "WOULD YOU": DOS to Richard Boleslawski, 17 June 1936, in Behlmer, *Memo,* 106.

9 "I WAS SHOCKED": DOS to Henry Luce, 7 December 1937, in Behlmer, *Memo,* 123–24.

10 "THE EVENING CONFESSION": quoted in Spoto, *Dark Side,* 18.

10 "I MUST HAVE BEEN": Truffaut, 25.

10 "I'VE ALWAYS": quoted in Thomas, "The German Years," 24.

10 "CINEMA IS": Samuels, 232.

12 "I AM VERY HAPPY": (London) *Sunday Observer,* 9 December 1934.

12 "THE REASON": Montague, 190.

13 "I DON'T": quoted in *New York Times,* 24 October 1972.

15 "THERE'S A": quoted in Spoto, *Dark Side,* 149.

16 EXPECTED "A LEAN, TOUGH": Lejeune, *Thank You For Having Me* (London: Hutchinson, 1964), 162.

16 HITCHCOCK INHERITED: quoted in *New York Times,* 14 December 1969.

16 "THREE UNIQUE": *New York Times,* 12 June 1938.

16 AN ORNAMENT: Selznick, 209.

16 SELZNICK INTERNATIONAL TREASURER: DOS to Wharton, 16 April 1937, in Behlmer, *Memo,* 112.

18 "MY CHASSIS": quoted in (London) *Daily Mirror,* 11 June 1936.

II: Signing Hitchcock

21 "USES HIS CAMERA": *New York Times,* 14 September 1935.

21 "PROBABLY THE BEST": *Variety,* 19 June 1935.

23 "MARRED BY INEXPERT": Bosley Crowther, *New York Times,* 13 June 1936.

23 CALLED A FACTORY: Taylor, *Hitch,* 41.

23 "A FEW PICTURES": Lillie Messinger to Pandro Berman, 31 August 1937, RKO Archive, Los Angeles.

24 "HOWARD HAS BEEN": DOS to Daniel O'Shea, 14 October 1937; "BUY HIM": 11 November 1938, in Behlmer, *Memo,* 157, 175.

24 "A NUMBER": Henry Ginsberg to DOS, 8 October 1937.

24 "UNDER ANY CIRCUMSTANCES": O'Shea to DOS, 26 November 1937.

25 "HOLLYWOOD REGARDED": Johnston, "300-Pound Prophet," 12.

25 "PSYCHOLOGICAL REACTIONS": quoted in Ryall, 107, 109.

26 "TYPICALLY ENGLISH": quoted in Yacowar, 217.

26 "IT IS LACKING": Katharine Brown to DOS, 6 December 1937.

26 "IF I AM RIGHT": John Hay Whitney to DOS, 12 January 1938.

26 "HAS CERTAINLY PROVEN": DOS to Whitney, 10 January 1938.

27 "THE GREATEST MASTER": DOS to Whitney, 1 March 1938.

27 "A VERY LONG TIME": Jenia Reissar to DOS, 10 May 1938.

28 "IN TERMS OF": DOS to Brown, 23 May 1938.

28 "BEING THE ONLY ONE": William Burnside, quoted in Marcella Rabwin to DOS, undated.

28 "TOUGH LITTLE": Thomson, 41.

29 HE MIGHT EVEN: Selznick, 208, 254.

29 "REALLY WAS KEEN": Alfred Hitchcock (AH) to Al Margolies, undated, Selznick Collection.

29 "IT LOOKS AS THOUGH": AH to Margolies, undated, Selznick Collection.

29 "ECONOMY WAVE": *New York Times,* 22 May 1938.

29 "TO CONSUMMATE": AH to Leo Mishkin, 3 April 1974, Alfred Hitchcock Collection, Margaret Herrick Library, Academy of Motion Picture Arts and Sciences, Beverly Hills, California.

29 "NOT GET BIDS": DOS to Frank Capra, 22 January 1940, in Behlmer, *Memo,* 252.

30 "I MADE": quoted in *New York Herald Tribune,* 19 March 1939.

30 "I AM PRACTICALLY": DOS to Sam Hirshfeld, 15 May 1937.

30 BUT SELZNICK: Harwell, 62.

30 "I HAVE": quoted in "Actual chopper," *Listener*, 8 May 1980: 610.

31 "TO MY MIND": quoted in Mary Benedetta, ". . . Film Stars of The Future" [clipping dated 14 July 1938, British Film Institute]; "THE RED FUNNELS": quoted in *New York Times,* 5 September 1937.

32 (photo) INCREASED PRESSURE: quoted in Russell Maloney, "Profiles: What Happens After That?" *The New Yorker,* 10 September 1938: 28.

33 "CAN HAVE": William Dover to George Stevens, 22 April 1940, George Stevens Collection, Academy of Motion Picture Arts and Sciences.

33 "THE SHOCKING": Charles Feldman to Stevens, 18 April 1940, Stevens Collection.

34 "I WANTED": quoted in Chris Hodenfield, "Muuuurder by the Babbling Brook," *Rolling Stone*, 29 July 1976: 56.

34 "HITCHCOCK'S FREE TIME": DOS to O'Shea, 9 January 1939.

35 "THE PUBLICITY ATTENDANT": O'Shea to DOS, 3 February 1939.

35 "REPLETE WITH PROVISIONS": "Memorandum Re: Certain Provisions of the Agreement Dated July 14, 1938 as Amended and Supplemented by Agreement Dated March 4, 1939, Between Selznick International Pictures, Inc. and Alfred Hitchcock Which Are Involved in Plan Under Discussion," undated, Hitchcock Collection.

35 "WHEN HE STARTS": "The Lady Vanishes," 29.

III: Rebecca

36 "THE MOST FASCINATING": Brown to DOS, 24 June 1938.

37 "PROBABLY EXEMPLIFIES": Val Lewton to DOS, 11 July 1938.

38 "OBVIOUSLY": DOS to Brown, 20 July 1938.

38 "THE AMERICANS": Hitchcock, "Films We *Could* Make," (London) *Evening News,* 16 November 1927.

38 "VASTLY AMAZED": Reissar to Brown, 2 September 1938.

39 "WELLES' GENERALLY": DOS to Myer Mermin, 22 November 1938.

39 "A CLEVER SHOWMAN": DOS to AH, 12 June 1939.

39 "THE ONLY SURE": DOS to AH, 12 June 1939, in Behlmer, *Memo,* 267.

39 "I BELIEVE": Hitchcock, "My Strangest Year," *Film Weekly,* 16 May 1936: 28.

40 "MERE PHOTOGRAPHIC": Hitchcock, "How I Make My Films," (London) *News Chronicle,* 5 March 1937.

40 "A DESCRIPTION OF": quoted in *The Observer,* 8 August 1976.

40 "I WOULD HAVE YOU": DOS to AH, 7 September 1938.

40 "PERFECTLY CHARMING": quoted in Doty, 21.

40 "TO USE AN ANALOGY": AH to DOS, 28 December 1938.

40 "THE WRITING": AH to DOS, 9 September 1938.

42 "PLEASE CABLE": Whitney to DOS, 9 November 1938.

42 "I HAVE NEVER HAD": DOS to Brown, 8 October 1936, in Behlmer, *Memo,* 145.

42 "ESPECIALLY NERVOUS": DOS to Whitney, 9 November 1938.

42 "SOMETHING MIGHT": AH to DOS, 18 November 1938.

43 "IS IT SUFFICIENT": AH to DOS, 18 November 1938.

43 "LOOK AFTER HORRIFIC": AH to DOS, 13 September 1938.

43 "IF I WERE DOING *REBECCA*": Notes, AH to Columbia University Department of Fine Arts History of Motion Pictures class, 30 March 1939, Hitchcock Collection.

44 "SANDALS": Ezra Goodman, "The Directorial Touch," *World Film News,* October 1938: 242.

44 "OBJECTED": quoted in *Brooklyn Daily Eagle,* 30 August 1937.

44 "THE LITTLE FEMININE THINGS": DOS to AH, 12 June 1939.

45 "HAS TO BE CHARMING": quoted in Lewton to O'Shea, 28 April 1939.

46 "EVERY LITTLE THING": DOS to AH, 12 June 1939.

46 "DECIDE WHAT": quoted in Freeman, 8–9.

47 "QUITE APART": quoted in Haver, 292.

47 "WEEPING BITTER TEARS": quoted in Brown to DOS, 19 June 1939; "I HAVE THROWN OUT": DOS to Brown, 21 June 1939.

47 "WILL SERVE AS A BASIS": AH to DOS, 26 June 1939.

47 "WE DID NOT": DOS to Brown, 18 July 1939, in Behlmer, *Memo,* 273.

48 "SAILING WAS THE RAGE": Huston, 60.

48 "I DON'T CARE FOR": DOS to AH, 12 July 1939.

48 A DIRECTOR AT ONE: Roddick, 43; Leff, "Hitchcock at Metro," in Deutelbaum, ed., 41–61.

48 "JUST WHO THE HELL": DOS to O'Shea, 23 June 1939.

49 "OF LEO GENN": AH to Rabwin, 19 April 1939.

49 OF JOHN MILLS: quoted in Rabwin to Brown, 6 June 1939.

49 OF GUY MIDDLETON: quoted in Bill Hebert to DOS, 18 July 1939.

49 BUT FROM THE BEGINNING: DOS to AH, 9 January 1938 in Behlmer, *Memo,* 260. (The memorandum was written 9 January 1939.)

49 SELZNICK ASKED HITCHCOCK: DOS to Brown, 18 August 1938.

49 "A LITTLE TOO SCHOLASTIC": AH to DOS, 10 January 1939.

49 "A FUND OF DISDAIN": Kyle Crichton, "Hollywood Doesn't Count," *Collier's,* 10 June 1939: 15.

49 "A VERY INTRIGUING": DOS to Whitney, 1 March 1938; "GAUCHE BEHAVIOR": DOS to Reissar, 10 October 1938, 4 October 1938.

49 PILBEAM WAS "CORRECT CASTING": AH to DOS, 10 October 1938.

51 DESPITE THE OBJECTIONS: Reissar to DOS, 17 October 1938.

51 "TOO IMMATURE": quoted in Reissar to DOS, 7 October 1938; AH to DOS, 18 November 1938, 10 January 1939.

51 "TESTED. POSSIBILITY": AH to DOS, 19 July 1939.

51 SHE HAS "A SINCERE": AH to DOS, 28 June 1939.

51 MIRIAM PATTY "SHOULD": AH to DOS, 19 July 1939.

52 "SECOND WIFE": quoted in Whitney to DOS, 9 November 1938.

53 "THE WHOLE STORY": DOS to Whitney, 6 September 1939, in Behlmer, *Memo,* 285.

54 "THIS IS A MELODRAMA": Basil Davenport, rev. of *Rebecca* by Daphne du Maurier, *Saturday Review of Literature,* 24 September 1938: 5.

55 "FILM BUSINESS HERE": AH to William J. Hitchcock, 23 September 1939, Selznick Collection.

55 "DEAR JACK": AH to Jack Saunders, 1 September 1939, Selznick Collection.

56 "HE SMILED": *New York Times,* 1 October 1939; Hellman, 34.

56 "SNIDE REMARKS": DOS to AH (unsent), 4 October 1939.

56 "A VERY SERIOUS PROBLEM": Whitney to DOS, 21 August 1939.

57 "COY AND SIMPERING": quoted in Haver, 319.

57 "THE LAST TEST": Whitney to DOS, 21 August 1939.

57 "YOUNG, PRETTY, GAY": Aherne, *A Proper Job* (Boston: Houghton Mifflin, 1969), 286.

57 "IN VIEW OF THE MANY SPEECHES": DOS to Ginsberg, 24 July 1939.

58 (photo) "DOING THE SAME THING": Transcript, Interview with Joan Fontaine, 12 April 1979, Oral History Collection, Southern Methodist University (SMU), Dallas, Texas.

59 "WE FELT BLIGHTED": Olivier, 110.

59 "AN ENORMOUS AMOUNT": DOS to Ginsberg, 18 September 1939.

59 "THE DESCRIPTIONS GIVEN": quoted in Barbara Keon to Lyle Wheeler, 4 September 1939, Selznick Collection.

60 BUT HITCHCOCK ALSO FILLED: *New York Herald Tribune,* 14 July 1940.

60 HITCHCOCK CONCEPTUALIZED: quoted in François Truffaut and Claude Chabrol, "Entretien avec Alfred Hitchcock," *Cahiers du Cinéma* 44 (1955): 28.

60 "AFTER ALL": quoted in John Wright, *Moviemaker*, August 1979: n.p. [clipping, British Film Institute].

62 "A HOLLYWOOD-WOMAN": Truffaut, 118.

62 "IT IS ALL": quoted in Benedetta, ". . . Film Stars Of The Future."

62 "IN OTHER WORDS": AH to DOS, 18 November 1938.

62 "TOO SLOW": quoted in "DeMarney Analyzes Director's Magic Spell" [clipping dated 5 February 1938, British Film Institute].

63 "THIS GIRL'S TERRIBLE": quoted in unedited transcript, Truffaut interview, Hitchcock Collection.

63 "EVEN IF": DOS to Raymond Klune, 13 September 1939.

64 "THE SLOWEST": DOS to Ginsberg, 19 September 1939.

64 "SPEED THE PACE": DOS to AH, 14 September 1939, in Behlmer, *Memo,* 286.

66 FACED WITH: Myron Selznick exacted a ten percent commission from his brother and from his client for arranging the Wanger loanout. Servant of two Selznicks, Hitchcock may have felt doubly exploited.

67 "THE BEAUTIFUL IRENE": Transcript, Interview with Joan Fontaine, Oral History Collection, SMU.

67 "MORE THAN EIGHT": quoted in Bergman, 138.

69 THE RESPONSE SUGGESTS: Curtis, 239.

69 "YOUR WORK WAS MONITORED": Huston, 83.

69 "A HANDSOMELY FRAMED PHOTO": DOS to Wheeler, undated.

70 AFTER READING A SYNOPSIS: quoted in Lewton to DOS, 15 July 1938.

70 "MRS. DANVERS' DESCRIPTION": Joseph Breen to DOS, 25 September 1939, Production Administration Code Collection, Academy of Motion Picture Arts and Sciences.

70 "OFFENDING PIECE OF FILM": quoted in Bob Thomas, "Those Good Old Bad Old Days," *Action*, March-April 1974: 20.

71 "YOU MEAN BREEN?" quoted in *New York Times,* 1 October 1939.

72 "WELL, MISS BATES": Notes from Alfred Hitchcock for *Reader's Digest* piece ("Unprintable Stories") undated, Hitchcock Collection.

72 "I THINK THERE IS": DOS to Hal Kern, 7 December 1939.

72 "IT WOULD BE": "Steffi" to George Sanders, 12 October 1939.

72 "TRY TO GET OLIVIER": DOS to AH, 15 November 1939.

72 SELZNICK WORRIED: DOS to AH, 23 October 1939, in Behlmer, *Memo,* 293.

74 "FOR GOD'S SAKE": DOS to AH, 13 October 1939.

74 "APPALLINGLY ROUGH": Olivier, 92.

74 "DURING THE FIFTH TAKE": quoted in *Photoplay* (Great Britain), September 1979: 57.

75 "I'D LIKE TO URGE": DOS to AH, 11 October 1939, in Behlmer, *Memo,* 292.

75 "I HAVE BEEN THINKING": DOS to Klune, 17 October 1939, in Behlmer, *Memo,* 229.

75 "MANY PEOPLE": quoted in Lane, 35.

75 "I THINK TODAY'S RUSHES": DOS to AH, 19 October 1939.

77 "WANTED TOTAL LOYALTY": Fontaine, 116.

77 "A TRIFLE SLOW": DOS to Klune, 14 November 1939, in Behlmer, *Memo,* 294.

78 "A PICTURE COULD BE RUINED": Kern, quoted in Haver, 292.

78 HIS FATHER'S "KNACK": Reynolds, 4 June 1938: 34.

78 "A CLOSE TWO-SHOT": DOS to AH, 25 October 1939.

80 "WE HAD SO MUCH": Klune to DOS, 14 January 1941.

80 "AFTER I GOT THROUGH": DOS to Brown, undated (circa March 1940).

80 "THE PICTURE LOOKS": DOS to AH, 24 January 1940.

80 "I KNOW THAT HITCHCOCK": DOS to O'Shea, 15 February 1940.

81 "IT IS WITH GREAT PLEASURE": DOS to Murray Silverstone, 28 December 1939, in Behlmer, *Memo,* 296.

81 "EXTREMELY NERVOUS": Pringle, 24.

81 ON *YOUR HOLLYWOOD PARADE*: Undated transcription of broadcast, Hitchcock Collection.

82 "OF COURSE, YOU CAN ALWAYS": quoted in *New York Herald Tribune,* 31 October 1959.

84 ALTHOUGH HE GAVE IT: DOS to Lowell Calvert, 11 December 1940.

84 "WELL, IT'S NOT": Truffaut, 127.

IV: Between Engagements

86 "OF THE HITCHCOCK VARIETY": quoted in Carringer, 13.

86 "AS SOON AS I WAS WORKING": Samuels, 234.

86 UNITED ARTISTS HAD ACCUSED: Balio, *United Artists,* 174; "IMPROPER SUPERVISION": O'Shea to DOS, 7 June 1940.

87 "A PECULIAR PERSON": Lewton to Brown, 4 May 1940.

87 "PHILANTHROPICALLY DONATE": quoted in O'Shea to AH (unsent), 14 May 1940.

87 SELZNICK CONSIDERED: O'Shea to Myron Selznick, 16 April 1940.

87 "FUND FOR STARVING HITCHCOCKS": AH to DOS, 20 January 1941.

88 "MR. SCHAEFER EVIDENTLY": quoted in Carringer, 2.

88 "IF [IT] TAKES": Harry Edington to J.J. Nolan, undated, RKO Archive.

88 HITCHCOCK WAS "VERY ANXIOUS": Nolan to George J. Schaefer, 26 June 1940; Dan Winkler to Nolan, 28 May 1940, RKO Archive.

88 THE PRODUCER WANTED: DOS to O'Shea, 17 June 1940.

88 "HE WAS SERIOUSLY THINKING": O'Shea to DOS, 21 June 1940.

90 "THE MORE WE CAN BUILD UP": DOS to O'Shea, 12 August 1940.

90 "I UNDERSTOOD IT WAS": O'Shea to DOS, 17 August 1940.

91 "AN IMPERIOUS YOUNG MAN": quoted in Spoto, *Dark Side,* 135.

91 "HAD THAT HABIT": cited in Brian McFarlane, "Joan Fontaine," *Cinema Papers* (Australia), June 1982: 234.

92 "HITCHCOCK HAS BEEN BEARING": quoted in Spoto, *Dark Side,* 237.

92 THE HITCHCOCK NAME: ARI Report XXXI, 15 October 1940, RKO Archive.

92 "A BEAUTIFUL SUITE": AH to Sid Rogell, 9 December 1940, RKO Archive.

92 YET RKO EXECUTIVE DAN WINKLER: Winkler to DOS, 16 September 1940, RKO Archive.

93 "YOU'LL NEVER HIDE": O'Shea to DOS, 13 September 1940.

93 "AM RETURNING 'BEFORE THE FACT' ": Fontaine to AH, dated "Saturday evening," Hitchcock Collection.

95 "REALLY LOOK DIVINE": quoted in Haver, 229; Doty, 51.

95 "I'D SAY 'CUT' ": quoted in Taylor, *Hitch,* 307.

95 "I HAVE NEVER IN MY 'PUFF' ": AH to Harry Edington, 2 May 1941, RKO Archive.

95 THE DIRECTOR MADE A LAST: AH to Schaefer, 18 August 1941, RKO Archive; Whitney Bolton to DOS, 16 September 1941.

96 (photo) "I PUT A LIGHT": Truffaut, 143.

97 "THE GIRL": Note from AH to Paramount, May 1941, Selznick Collection.

98 "HE WASN'T GETTING ENOUGH CREDIT": Selznick, 235.

98 "I AM TAKING ON": DOS to Irene Selznick, 26 April 1941, in Behlmer, *Memo,* 309.

98 "THE OLD-FASHIONED CHASE": Lewton to DOS, 7 May 1941.

99 "WE WHO ARE LEFT" . . . "THE BRITISH GOVERNMENT": Balcon and Hitchcock, quoted in *New York World-Telegram,* 27 August 1940.

99 "TRY TO GET SOMETHING": DOS Notes, 1 August 1941, Hitchcock Collection.

100 "WE RECOGNIZE": DOS to AH (unsent), 22 September 1941.

100 "RUSHING INTO DIFFERENT ROOMS": (Los Angeles) *Citizen News,* 6 November 1941.

100 "I THINK IT IS RIDICULOUS": DOS to O'Shea, 4 September 1941.

100 ONE SELZNICK READER: Elsa Neuberger to DOS, 20 October 1941; Lewton to DOS, 21 October 1941.

100 "FEELING RATHER LIKE A PIMP": Houseman, 480.

101 "DAVID WAS GOING": Selznick, 241.

101 "TO POINT OUT IMPORTANCE": DOS to Brown, 11 December 1941, in Behlmer, *Memo,* 317.

101 "THERE WAS A LOT OF FEAR": quoted in Haver, 329.

102 "HM," SAID HITCHCOCK: quoted in Taylor, *Hitch,* 183.

102 COMMENTING ON "A LACK OF VERSATILITY": *Variety,* 29 April 1942.

102 "ALL I NEED": "Hitchcock Brews Thrillers Here," 35; Wanger, 14.

104 "AFTER BEING HOME": DOS to Paley, 15 May 1942.

104 "I WARNED HIM": Selznick, 242.

104 "I HAVE MADE A NUMBER": DOS to Merian Cooper, 1 September 1942, in Behlmer, *Memo,* 319–20.

105 "IF POSSIBLE I AM": "Notes on Possible Development of Uncle Charlie Story for Screen Play, Alfred Hitchcock," 11 May 1942, Hitchcock Collection.

105 "AMAZING ADAPTABILITY": *New York Times,* 1 November 1942.

105 "NO DIRECTOR WAS EVER EASIER": quoted in Spoto, *Dark Side,* 259.

107 "DURING THE SHOOTING": quoted in Spoto, *Dark Side,* 258.

107 "I WEIGHED JUST UNDER": quoted in Spoto, *Dark Side,* 266.

107 "THE TRANSFER OF THESE ASSETS": *New York Times,* 16 November 1942.

109 "YOU RECENTLY HAVE SENT DIRECT": DOS to Samuel Goldwyn, 6 January 1943, in Behlmer, *Memo,* 327–28.

109 "I SEE THEY'RE SELLING": quoted in Johnston, "300-Pound Prophet," 56.

109 "MYRON WAS DRINKING": Thomson, 42.

111 "ONE OF THOSE INCREDIBLE": Steinbeck to Annie Laurie Williams, 21 February 1944, in *Steinbeck: A Life in Letters,* Elaine Steinbeck and Robert Wallsten eds. (New York: Viking, 1975), 267. Steinbeck painted Hitchcock unfairly. According to a member of the Twentieth

Century-Fox legal department, for example, Hitchcock wanted the "colored man" aboard the lifeboat treated "in dignified fashion and definitely not as a comic" (George Wasson to E. P. Kilroe, 14 February 1945, Hitchcock Collection).

111 "I HAVE JUST RECEIVED": AH to Darryl Zanuck, 20 August 1943, Hitchcock Collection.

112 "ONCE TALLULAH TRIED": quoted in Denis Brian, *Tallulah, Darling* (London: Sidgwick & Jackson, 1980), 137.

112 "ON THREE DIFFERENT DAYS": Zanuck to AH, 8 October 1943, Hitchcock Collection.

112 STEINBECK ASKED: Steinbeck to Williams, 19 February 1944, in *Steinbeck: A Life in Letters,* 267; Thompson, quoted in Truffaut, 156.

112 AN ARTISTIC EXPERIMENT: quoted in (Los Angeles) *Citizen News,* 4 July 1947.

113 (photo) "AN EXAGGERATED BOSOM": Notes for *Reader's Digest* piece, Hitchcock Collection.

114 "HE WAS MORE COMPULSIVE": Selznick, 243.

V: Spellbound

115 "HE CONFIDED TO ME": Selznick, 236.

116 "I'D LIKE TO STRESS": quoted in Spoto, *Dark Side,* 272.

116 "I DON'T THINK": quoted in Haver, 345.

116 "A SEQUENCE THAT I PERSONALLY": DOS to Karl Menninger, 22 September 1944.

117 IT "IS FILLED WITH DIABOLICAL": Comparative Analysis (The Novel Compared with our Treatments), undated, Selznick Collection.

119 "GAGS AND BITS OF BUSINESS": DOS to O'Shea, 26 November 1943.

120 "A WELL CONSTRUCTED": DOS to O'Shea, 26 November 1943.

120 "MR. ALFRED HITCHCOCK'S": (London) *Times,* 11 October 1943.

122 "TO TALK OVER": Philip H. Leonard to Carol Stevens, 3 January 1944, Hitchcock Collection.

122 "NO CONSISTENT FAITH": quoted in Brown, 38.

123 THE QUALITY AND AUTHORSHIP: Truffaut, 163; Spoto, *Dark Side,* 273n.

123 "ANY BETS": DOS to O'Shea, 3 May 1944.

123 THE ASSISTANT DIRECTOR: "The Mind of Dr. Edwards," Story Outline, 26 January 1944, Selznick Collection.

124 "IF THERE IS ANY HUMOR": DOS to AH, 12 June 1939, in Behlmer, *Memo,* 268.

124 "WORKED WITH EMINENT": *Variety,* 31 October 1945.

125 "SOMETIMES I FEEL LIKE": "The House of Doctor Edwardes," Second-Draft Treatment, 14 February 1944, Selznick Collection.

125 "CONSTANCE SAYS THAT A NEUROTIC": quoted in Doty, 203.

126 "I USED TO BE": quoted in unedited transcript, Truffaut interview, Hitchcock Collection.

126 HE ALSO "LONGED FOR": Taylor, *Hitch,* 194.

126 "MYRON IS GONE": quoted in Selznick, 256.

127 "GAVE OFF PLOT TURNS": Hecht, *Child,* 482.

127 "FOND AS I AM OF BEN": DOS to Ernest Scanlon, 12 July 1944.

127 "DON'T YOU THINK": DOS to O'Shea, 15 April 1944.

127 " 'WHAT DO THEY HAVE' ": Truffaut, 106–7.

127 "WITH THE IDEA": Truffaut, 134–35.

127 "HOW CAN YOU DO ANYTHING": quoted in Lambert, 160.

128 "SUBSTITUTED FREUD": Hecht, *Collected Stories* (New York: Crown, 1945), 159.

128 "GIVEN TO WANDERING": Hecht, *Collected Stories,* 206.

128 "THE MATING OF TWO": "The House of Dr. Edwardes," First-Draft Screenplay, 3 April 1944, Selznick Collection.

131 (photo) "AID THE CHARACTERIZATION": DOS to [Richard L.] Johnston and [Anita] Colby, 22 June 1944, in Behlmer, *Memo,* 355.

132 MARGARET MCDONELL ENJOYED: McDonell to Keon, 12 May 1944.

132 "THEY SAY PSYCHIATRICALLY": quoted in Bogdanovich, 9.

133 "TELLS ME THAT HITCH": DOS to O'Shea, 16 May 1944.

133 "BEN AND HITCH ARE BOTH LOADED": DOS to O'Shea, 16 May 1944.

133 "LESS ATTENTION": Conference Notes, 8 June 1944, Selznick Collection.

133 "AUDIENCE ACCEPTANCE": ARI Report, 12 June 1944, Selznick Collection.

134 A 1944 GALLUP POLL: DOS to Reeves Espy, 3 November 1944, in Behlmer, *Memo,* 356.

134 "HE PHOTOGRAPHS LIKE ABE LINCOLN": DOS to Brown, 11 March 1941, in Behlmer, *Memo,* 309.

135 "SHE HAD SO MUCH GO": Reissar to Brown, 22 September 1938.

135 "WE HAVE ENOUGH TROUBLE": quoted in Selznick, 225.

135 ("THE TERMS ARE"): Bergman, 112.

136 "PLUNGE AN ENGLISH ACTRESS": quoted in "What I'd Do to the Stars," *Film Weekly*, 4 March 1939: 12.

136 "DON'T POINT THOSE THINGS": Notes for *Reader's Digest* piece, Hitchcock Collection.

136 "HITCH TALKED TO EACH": Transcript, Interview with Kim Hunter, 2 January 1979, Oral History Collection, SMU.

137 "THE ARGUMENT THAT MURCHISON": Dr. Romm's Comments on the Second Temporary Shooting Script, summarized by Eileen Johnston, 6 July 1944, Selznick Collection.

137 BUT HECHT AND HITCHCOCK: Keon to DOS, 26 June 1944.

137 FREDRIC MARCH "INDIGNANTLY": DOS to AH, 23 June 1944.

137 "ROMANTIC RED HERRING": DOS to AH, 23 June 1944.

137 SELZNICK "PROBABLY THOUGHT": Truffaut, 165.

138 (photo) "AS A RESULT OF HAVING AN ACTOR": DOS to Ruth Burch, 14 July 1944.

139 "WHEN RKO RELEASED": "Gambling" folder, Selznick Collection.

139 "A PRONOUNCED VARIATION": ARI Report, 14 June 1944, Selznick Collection.

140 "DALI'S PHALLIC FRESCOES": Cameron Shipp to O'Shea, 19 July 1944.

140 "PRODUCERS AND WHAT THEY DO": quoted in Myrick, 14.

140 INGRID BERGMAN ASKED: Conference Notes, 21 June 1944, Selznick Collection.

142 BASED ON A FIRST READING: Breen to DOS, 19 May 1944; 19 June 1944.

142 "I HAVE NO FEARS": DOS to McDonell, 20 May 1944.

143 MEET PERSONALLY WITH BREEN: DOS to McDonell, 22 May 1944.

143 THE CHANGEOVER: McDonell to DOS, 19 June 1944.

143 ASKED TO SUPPLY SOME: Johnston to DOS, 23 June 1944.

143 "FOR GOD'S SAKE": Johnston to DOS, 16 June 1944.

143 "IS A SYMBOL": Johnston to DOS, 20 June 1944.

144 THE FACT THAT CONSTANCE USED: William F. Van Wert, "Compositional Psychoanalysis: Circles and Straight Lines in 'Spellbound,' " *Film Criticism* 3:3 (1979): 41–47.

144 "I CAN'T THINK OF ANY": DOS to Scanlon, 12 July 1944.

145 "AM I CORRECT": McDonell to DOS, 11 May 1944; 8 June 1944.

145 "ONE DAY": quoted in *The Observer,* 8 August 1976.

146 "SOME NOTABLY FINE WRITING": *New York Times,* 11 November 1945.

148 SHORT SCRIPT, "SUPERB AND": DOS to O'Shea, 11 July 1944.

148 "I WOULD MUCH RATHER": quoted in Haver, 345.

149 THE YOUNG SELZNICK HAD QUIT: Selznick, 103. "The scene they shot of the gals taking their afternoon naps at the barbeque is going to put you in bed when (or IF) you see it," Susan Myrick wrote to Margaret Mitchell from the set of *Gone With the Wind* in April 1939. "I told David the gals would have their hair loosened, their corset strings

unlaxed and there would be two to the bed or maybe three if he wanted them lying crosswise. He wanted their hair to look pretty and vowed that loosening the corsets would let the busts sag and I tried to argue him into my way of doing but he had his way. That was the day before we shot the scene. The day we did shoot it, AFTER it was finished in walked DOS, known as Pappy, and said to me 'Sue, was it all right for those girls to be lying down with their hair all done up and with their corsets on?' I was so dam mad I almost busted" (Margaret Mitchell Marsh Collection, Hargrett Rare Book and Manuscript Library, University of Georgia).

149 "STAND THOSE WOMEN": quoted in Spoto, *Dark Side,* 414.

149 "THE NEXT SHOT, NORMAN": quoted in Nugent, "Assignment," 13.

151 " 'YOU JUST BEHAVE' ": quoted in Nugent, "Assignment," 13.

151 "A FIGURE IN A STORY": Transcript, Interview with Norman Lloyd, 23 July 1979, Oral History Collection, SMU.

151 "FAKE IT": quoted in Kobal, 477.

151 "I FELT I NEEDED": quoted in Spoto, *Dark Side,* 276.

152 "MY DEAR BOY": quoted in Freedland, 68.

152 HITCHCOCK "LIKED HIS ACTORS": Transcript, Interview with Gregory Peck, 27 May 1977, Oral History Collection, SMU.

152 "SHALLOW": Truffaut, 167.

154 "I THINK HITCHCOCK": Kobal, 476.

154 "OF A DEAL PENDING": DOS to Reissar, 17 October 1944.

154 "SEX SUGGESTIVENESS": Breen to DOS, 19 June 1944.

156 "I HAVE SELDOM SEEN": quoted in Haver, 346.

156 "DAVID, IN THE DAYS": Hecht, *Child*, 482.

156 AFTER MYRON'S DEATH: Selznick, 258.

156 TO DISCOURAGE VISITORS: Bergman, 158; "Actual Chopper," 610.

156 "STORM" (FROM "STORM-AND-STRIFE"): *New York Times,* 5 September 1937.

157 SHE MUST BE "MORE COVERED": quoted in McDonell to AH, 21 August 1944.

157 THEY "MIGHT PREVENT": Johnston to DOS, 23 August 1944.

157 "THE PSYCHOANALYSTS IN THIS PICTURE": Leo H. Bartemeier to DOS, 26 September 1944.

157 THE NATIONAL CREAMERY: A. W. Rudnick to Will H. Hays, 25 March 1941, Production Code Administration Collection.

157 HITCHCOCK FOUGHT: Johnston to DOS, 23 August 1944.

157 "THE PHOTOGRAPHY, SETUPS": DOS to O'Shea, 25 October 1944, in Behlmer, *Memo,* 356.

158 (photo) "LONG SHADOWS": Truffaut, 165.

159 HITCHCOCK MAINTAINED: Truffaut, 165.

159 "THERE'S THE CONSTANT PRESSURE": quoted in Frank S. Nugent, "Mr. Hitchcock Discovers Love," *New York Times Magazine*, 3 November 1946: 13. According to *Variety,* the Little Carnegie was "a side-street sure-seater of around 300 capacity, playing to $1 top, with lounges, smoking and ping pong as bigger attractions for the people of the class neighborhood than its film. Clientele mostly *use house* for time killing" (30 June 1931).

159 "VERY ANXIOUS": Kern to Ruth Burch, 14 September 1945.

159 "FOUND NO TECHNICAL": Johnston to DOS, 21 August 1944.

159 "BECAUSE OF": William S. Cunningham to McDonald [sic], 8 August 1944.

160 " 'EDWARDS' PERSISTS": Lillian Deighton to DOS, 23 August 1944.

161 BESIDES, HITCHCOCK'S NAME: DOS to Brown, 28 August 1944.

161 "THE LOCATION WAS SUCH": DOS to Johnston, 20 October 1944.

161 SELZNICK CUT AROUND: Notes, 18 October 1944, Selznick Collection.

161 THE HITCHCOCK STRATEGY: Continuity Script Notes, 9 September 1944, Selznick Collection.

162 ALTHOUGH REACTION TO BERGMAN: Cards, Pasadena preview, 27 September 1944, Selznick Collection.

162 "THE END OF THE FILM": Truffaut, 320.

163 "IT TAKES TOO LONG": Schaefer to DOS, 23 May 1956.

163 "BRULOV HARD TO HEAR": Cards, 27 September 1944.

163 "UNTIL ALL HOURS": DOS to O'Shea, 6 January 1945.

164 "AS SOMEBODY SAID": DOS to AH, 19 September 1939 (unsent), in Behlmer, *Memo,* 286–87.

164 THE UNSETTLING COMPLEXITY: quoted in Truffaut, 194.

165 "IT WAS BEAUTIFUL": Kobal, 479.

165 "THE SO OFTEN DONE": cited in James Basevi to DOS, 14 December 1944.

165 "STRICTLY EFFECT PHOTOGRAPHY": Basevi to DOS, 29 November 1944.

165 "SCORE ENTIRE SEQ.": Notes on score, 11 September 1944, Selznick Collection.

165 HITCHCOCK AND SELZNICK NEVERTHELESS: Rózsa, 126.

166 HITCHCOCK "LEFT THE EDITING": quoted in Behlmer, *Memo,* 303.

166 ACCORDING TO ONE BIOGRAPHER: Taylor, *Hitch,* 197.

166 " 'ALFRED HITCHCOCK'S *SPELLBOUND*' ": DOS to George Volck, 10 November 1945, in Behlmer, *Memo,* 367.

166 NEARLY NINETY PERCENT: Cards, Huntington Park preview, 16 February 1945, Selznick Collection.

167 "BECAUSE I WOULD CONSIDER": DOS to Charles Glett, 1 February 1946.

167 "AT DOOR OF COTTAGE": Printing Notes, 1 December 1955, Selznick Collection.

167 ACCORDING TO POLLSTER: DOS to Don King, 2 April 1945.

168 BERGMAN'S 1944 ACADEMY AWARD: DOS to Neil Agnew, 26 April 1945, in Behlmer, *Memo,* 362.

168 "CRITICS AND PUBLIC ALREADY": Jack Goldstein to DOS, 14 November 1944.

168 "EXERT EXTRA PRESSURE": DOS to Paul MacNamara, 17 November 1945.

168 "MAY I SAY HERE": King to DOS, 27 March 1945.

169 THE INSTRUCTIONS, WHICH: DOS to Audray Granville, 29 October 1945.

170 "I DO NOT SEE": DOS to Levitt, 4 February 1946.

170 "IT IS ANOTHER": *Daily Oklahoman,* 17 February 1946.

171 (photo) "SO GOOD ALL THE TIME": Bergman, 132.

172 "EVEN A DRIVING RAIN": Mervin Houser to MacNamara, 21 May 1946, Selznick Collection.

172 "INCLUDING RECORDS FOR": Houser to Sidney Alex, 24 June 1946, Selznick Collection.

VI: Notorious

174 "WE CAN SEE THE WHOLE": AH to Hedda Hopper, 16 February 1961, Hedda Hopper Collection, Academy of Motion Picture Arts and Sciences.

174 "THE MORE I SEE": quoted in AH to Carol Stevens Shourds, undated letter.

174 "IF HITCH INVITED YOU": Laurents interview.

175 HITCHCOCK WOULD "VERY MUCH": McDonell to Neuberger, 7 August 1944.

177 THE DIRECTOR LUNCHED: Spoto, *Dark Side,* 283.

177 "IN ANY CASE," HITCHCOCK WROTE: AH to O'Shea, 20 November 1944.

177 "OLD-FASHIONED": Truffaut, 167.

179 "WE HAVE EVERYTHING": DOS to Scanlon, 15 December 1944.

179 "THERE ARE NO IDIOTS": Nugent, "Assignment," 12–13.

181 AUDIENCE RESEARCH SAMPLED: Haver, 353.

182 "PLEASE KEEP [*NOTORIOUS*]": DOS to Harriett Flagg, 26 January 1945.

182 "NOT TO DO ANYTHING": DOS to O'Shea, 26 January 1945.

182 "MORE HITCH": DOS annotations (undated) on Treatment, 9 January 1945.

186 (photo) "ALL CUSTOMARY CONDITIONS": Memorandum of Record, 22 May 1945, Selznick Collection.

187 "VASTLY OVERDRAWN": DOS to O'Shea, 6 March 1945.

187 "A COMPANY REPRESENTATIVE": DOS to O'Shea, 21 May 1945.

187 "MY REVOLT HAD BEEN SUDDEN": Selznick, 266.

187 BILLING "NOT LESS THAN 75%": Annotations (undated) on Hitchcock's Terms, October 1944, Selznick Collection.

188 (photo) "HE WOULD HAVE LIKED ME": Selznick, 164.

189 "A LIMIT TO THE EXPENSES": DOS to Richard Hungate, 19 December 1944.

189 "THE 'HUMILIATION CLAUSE' ": DOS to O'Shea, 2 February 1945.

190 "IF HITCH LIKED": Laurents interview.

190 HITCHCOCK WANTED: Annotations on Terms, October 1944, Selznick Collection.

190 "COMPLETELY UNTENABLE": DOS to Hungate, 2 February 1945.

191 "WE MAY HAVE WORKED": DOS to AH, 8 February 1945.

191 THE PRODUCER WANTED: DOS to O'Shea, 6 March 1945.

192 "IT MIGHT BE A SCOTTISH NAME": Truffaut, 138.

192 THE MACGUFFIN FOR *NOTORIOUS*: One Line Continuity, 30 March 1945, Selznick Collection.

192 "PLOTTED ALL DAY": Ben Hecht to Rose Hecht, 29 March 1945, Selznick Collection.

193 "GETTING A LITTLE THICK": DOS to O'Shea, 10 April 1945.

193 "DID NOT LIKE THE PART": Flagg to DOS, 23 March 1945.

193 "OUR ORIGINAL INTENTION": Truffaut, 167; Dialogue Treatment, 15 April 1945, Selznick Collection.

194 IN APRIL 1945, A MONTH BEFORE: Margaret Gowing, *Britain and Atomic Energy, 1939–1945* (London: Macmillan, 1964), 359.

194 "AUTOMATIC BOMB": "Comparison," 9 May 1945, Selznick Collection. Transcript of Telephone Conversation, DOS and Lou Nichols, 19 May 1945.

194 "WAS ALSO AWARE": Truffaut, 168.

194 "DEPOSITS OF MINERALS": Ann Harris to AH, 3 October 1945, referencing 15 June 1945 memorandum, Selznick Collection.

194 "SUCH A BOMB": Nugent, "Assignment," 12.

194 "THE LITTLE ATOMIC BOMB": Hecht to Rose Hecht, 29 March 1945, Selznick Collection.

194 "ABSURD TO USE": Truffaut, 168.

194 "A TREMENDOUS THING": DOS to Keon (carbon to AH), 26 May 1945.

195 "J. EDGAR HOOVER'S": McDonell to DOS, 22 March 1945.

195 "TICKLISH SUBJECT": Transcript of Telephone Conversation, DOS and Lou Nichols, 19 May 1945.

196 "WAS BEING WEPT OVER": Hecht, *Child,* 584.

196 "I PUT [PSYCHIATRIST MAY] ROMM": Selznick, 268.

196 HE LEFT IN THE WAKE: DOS annotations (undated) on Temporary Screenplay, 9 May 1945, Selznick Collection. On the Nazis, Selznick was correct. A January 1946 Audience Research poll for RKO tested the *Notorious* story with and without Nazis. One in three persons disliked the former, one in sixteen the latter (Hitchcock Collection).

197 FEARING THAT HIS SCENARIST: DOS to Keon (carbon to AH), 13 May 1945.

197 "NEARER AND NEARER THE CAMERA": "Hitchcock" script pages, 12 May 1945, Selznick Collection.

198 "PLEASE DON'T BE FAMOUS": Lucinda Ballard (Mrs. Howard Dietz) to author, 30 March 1983.

198 "I'M TRYING TO FIGURE OUT": DOS to Keon, 26 May 1945.

198 "THE MOST EXPENSIVE SCRIPT": DOS to Keon, 26 May 1945.

198 "JUST BECAUSE HITCHCOCK": DOS to Scanlon, 7 June 1945.

199 "BUT BOY, I CERTAINLY SEE": DOS to O'Shea, 6 January 1945.

200 "A BLOW TO MY EGO": DOS to O'Shea, 21 January 1945.

200 "A GODDAMN FOOLISH THING": quoted in Truffaut, 168.

200 "FAR FROM CLEAN": DOS to O'Shea, 21 May 1945.

200 "DEFINITELY UNACCEPTABLE": Breen to DOS, 25 May 1945.

200 "I THINK OF MOST OF": DOS to O'Shea, 31 May 1945.

200 "GET DOWN TO BUSINESS": DOS to O'Shea, 14 May 1945.

201 "DAVID SENT ME": Bergman, 132.

201 "WE CERTAINLY": DOS Notes on Temporary Screenplay, 9 May 1945.

203 "BERGMAN SHOULDN'T SAY": Notes (with "dialogue suggestions"), 2 June 1945, Selznick Collection.

203 "SUBJECT THE FBI": J. Edgar Hoover to DOS, 8 June 1945.

203 "THIS," THE OWI AGENT REITERATED: William Roberts to McDonell, 15 June 1945.

203 "WHAT AUTHORITY": DOS to Keon, 20 June 1945.

203 "SIMPLY THE STORY": Truffaut, 168–69.

205 THE COUPLE STILL ENTERTAINED: Spoto, *Dark Side,* 288.

205 "HE WOULD HAVE LIKED": Selznick, 269.

206 CLAUSE THIRTY-THREE: Robert Dann to Hungate, 7 August 1945.

207 "NOT ONLY WILL WE MISS": DOS to O'Shea, 8 August 1945.

208 "THIS IS REALLY": Hecht annotation (undated) on Final Script, 18 September 1945, Selznick Collection.

208 THE "CHARACTERS HAVE LOST": DOS Conference Notes, undated.

208 "HELP ROUSE": Davidson Taylor, Chief of Theatre at SHAEF, to Bernstein, quoted in Moorehead, 166.

208 "HITCH WAS VERY CAREFUL": Sussex, 96.

209 RAINS OFFERS "AN OPPORTUNITY": DOS to Hungate, 6 September 1945.

209 "TERRIBLE SIEGE": DOS to King Vidor, 16 August 1945, in Behlmer, *Memo,* 363.

209 "HE'D THOUGHT WE WOULD TALK": Selznick, 272.

210 "FAME, HIS MONEY": *Los Angeles Examiner,* 24 August 1945.

210 "VERY POOR": DOS to O'Shea, 25 September 1945.

210 "STAY WITH SEBASTIAN": Keon to Hecht, 19 October 1945.

210 "IT SHOULD BE": Hecht to AH, 21 October 1945.

211 "POMPOUS OR BOMBASTIC": Keon to Hecht, 26 October 1945.

211 HITCHCOCK BIOGRAPHER DONALD: Spoto, *Dark Side,* 288–89, 292.

213 "WE FEEL VERY *AWKWARD*": Hitchcock, quoted in *New York Times,* 18 June 1972.

213 "I WAS ON THE TRAIN": Truffaut, 262.

215 "WE COULDN'T HAVE ANY BOXES": Truffaut, 172.

215 "PULL BERGMAN": DOS to O'Shea ("Important, Immediate & Confidential"), 2 November 1945.

215 "WORKING AS I DO": Truffaut, 195.

216 ON *NOTORIOUS,* EDITOR THERON WARTH: Cutting Notes, beginning 26 November 1945, Selznick Collection.

218 "AS YOU KNOW," RKO EXECUTIVE: William Gordon to AH, 19 April 1946, Hitchcock Collection.

220 HITCHCOCK SHOULD "KNOW": DOS to O'Shea, 11 April 1946.

220 HE HAD CONCEIVED: Dann to DOS, 8 August 1946.

221 "HITCHCOCK HAS DIRECTED": *New York Times,* 16 August 1946; 25 August 1946.

221 "IN VIEW OF FACT": Ned Depinet to O'Shea, 19 August 1946.

221 "COST US ABOUT": Truffaut, 169.

221 "THAT YOUR GIVING OF THIS BONUS": O'Shea to Jack Skirball, 9 July 1942.

222 "COST US CONSIDERABLY": DOS to O'Shea, 24 July 1946.

222 "THEY SAY": quoted in Barber, 19.

222 "IT'S THE SAME OLD STORY": DOS to Hungate, 19 November 1945, in Behlmer, *Memo,* 374.

222 THE "FARCICAL NEGOTIATIONS": DOS to O'Shea, 24 July 1946.
222 "I'M NOT A HEAVY EATER": quoted in Barber, 19.
223 IS AMERICA YOUR PERMANENT: *PM,* 27 October 1946.

VII: The Paradine Case

225 "WE THOUGHT": quoted in Freeman, 48.
225 ACCORDING TO THE TERMS: Proffered Contract, DOS to AH, 11 February 1946.
225 " 'THE PARADINE CASE' IS BUILT ON": rev. of *The Paradine Case,* by Robert Hichens, *New Statesman*, 5 May 1933: 652.
227 "WHAT I WANTED": quoted in *New York Times,* 18 June 1971.
227 "FOR ME, SIDNEY": quoted in Moorehead, 171.
227 "A SOIGNÉE SOCIETY WOMAN": quoted in *New York Times,* 3 November 1946.
228 JOE BREEN TOLD LOUIS MAYER: Breen to Louis Mayer, 12 March 1935, Production Code Administration Collection.
228 "IF THERE ARE FAULTS": quoted in *New York Times,* 30 October 1938.
228 "I AM SURE": DOS to O'Shea, 15 March 1946.
229 "THE FLAVOR": AH, Notes on *The Paradine Case,* dictated 30 April 1946, Selznick Collection.
229 "WE ALL LIKE": A. C. Hayman, Cataract Theatre Corporation, to Depinet, 9 January 1942, RKO Archive.
229 THE "GRIM-FACED, HUMORLESS" KEANE: AH, Notes on *The Paradine Case,* dictated 30 April 1946, Selznick Collection.
230 "THE PICTURE STARTS OFF": Bart Sheridan (citing Jack Guenther and Stanley Gordon) to MacNamara, 10 October 1947, Selznick Collection.
230 "WHAT DOES IT MATTER?": Sarris, 251.
231 "HE IS NO ROMANTIC": DOS to O'Shea, 18 April 1946.
232 "MY FATHER": quoted in Leamer, 126.
232 "DISLIKED SELZNICK": quoted in Leamer, 125.
232 "COMPROMISE CAST": DOS to O'Shea, 23 April 1946.
233 "QUITE MY DISH": Rains to AH, 23 September 1946, Selznick Collection.
234 (photo) "I HAVEN'T YET MET ANYONE": Reissar to DOS, 20 April 1947.
235 "AS I WATCHED": quoted in Barber, 18.
236 BIOGRAPHER JOHN RUSSELL TAYLOR: Taylor, *Hitch,* 205; Spoto, *Dark Side*, 297.

237 ALTHOUGH HE LIKED: AH to James Bridie, 30 August 1946, Selznick Collection.

237 WE MUST "GET OUR CHARACTER": AH to Bridie, 5 September 1946, Selznick Collection.

238 "I AM ON THE VERGE": DOS to O'Shea, 6 December 1946, in Behlmer, *Memo*, 377.

239 HITCHCOCK CAUTIONED SELZNICK: DOS to Robert Ross, 29 July 1946; DOS to Argyle Nelson, 6 January 1947.

239 "COLDLY POLITE": T. D. Webb, "Guidance to Metropolitan Police Procedure in Lady Paradine Case," undated, Hitchcock Collection.

240 ON *INTERMEZZO*: Kobal, 470.

240 "I CHOSE MEDIUM SHOTS": quoted in (Los Angeles) *Citizen News,* 12 December 1947.

241 "UGLY AS TO COMPOSITION": DOS to Lee Garmes (carbon to AH), 23 December 1946.

241 "SLOWED DOWN": DOS to O'Shea, 28 December 1946.

243 "TWENTY YEARS BEHIND": quoted in DOS to O'Shea, 28 December 1946.

243 "SO PERVERSE!": quoted in Lambert, 128.

243 "REALLY BORED": quoted in Spoto, *Dark Side,* 298.

244 "HELL, I DON'T KNOW": quoted in *New York Times,* 19 July 1964.

245 "NEGATIVE ACTING IS WHAT": quoted in *Cue,* 1 November 1947.

245 "A LAUGHTON PICTURE": quoted in newspaper clipping [undated, Billy Rose Theatre Collection].

245 "CHARLIE, DO REMEMBER": quoted in Ann Todd interview.

247 "NONSENSE": quoted in Story #90, Press Releases, Selznick Collection.

247 THE PRODUCER CALLED: DOS to Louis Jourdan, 18 January 1947.

247 "FOR GOD'S SAKE": quoted in Todd interview.

247 "ONE OF THE MOST AWFUL": DOS to O'Shea, 1 May 1947, in Behlmer, *Memo,* 387.

248 HITCHCOCK WOULD "SEE": Transcript, Interview with Gregory Peck, Oral History Collection, SMU.

248 "A VERY POOR METHOD": Truffaut, 173.

248 "NOT A NEW JOB": DOS to Hecht, 15 January 1947.

250 "THERE IS NO SHADING": DOS to AH, 28 February 1947.

250 "WE CAN'T GO ON": DOS to AH, 23 January 1947.

251 "WHAT AM I TO DO?": quoted in Taylor, *Hitch,* 204.

251 "MR. HITCHCOCK'S INSISTENCE": quoted in DOS to Nelson, 19 December 1946; Ahern, quoted in DOS to O'Shea, 25 January 1947.

252 "THIS IS OF COURSE": Notes, 25 September 1946, Hitchcock Collection.

252 "CERTAINLY I HOPE": DOS to AH, 18 February 1947, in Behlmer, *Memo,* 384.

252 "WE KNOW THAT HITCHCOCK": DOS to O'Shea, 19 February 1947.

254 "WE MUST NOT FORGET": DOS to AH, 28 February 1947.

254 "I DO NOT WANT HIM": DOS to O'Shea, 27 March 1947.

255 "OH, IT'S WONDERFUL": quoted in *New York Times,* 16 November 1947.

255 "WHEN I THINK OF WHAT": DOS to O'Shea, 1 December 1947, in Behlmer, *Memo,* 392.

256 "YOU NEVER KNEW QUITE": Brown, 89.

256 "HITCHCOCK'S LIFELONG": Houseman, *Entertainers and the Entertained* (New York: Simon and Schuster, 1986), 158.

258 "MY DEAR JOE": AH to Joseph Levine, 28 November 1950, Hitchcock Collection.

258 "EXCESSIVELY CUTTY": DOS to O'Shea, 28 February 1947.

258 "TORTUROUS AND UNNATURAL": DOS to Lydia Schiller, March 1947.

259 "A LOT OF STUFF": DOS to O'Shea, 6 April 1947.

259 SINCE "HITCH'S SLOPPINESS": DOS to O'Shea, 6 April 1947.

259 "MY WORST SCENE": Peck to Schiller, 10 December 1947.

259 SELZNICK CONSIDERED: James Stewart to DOS, 9 May 1947.

260 IRENE "HAD A FLOATING": Bagnold, *Enid Bagnold's Autobiography* (Boston: Little, Brown, 1969), 288.

260 "IN VIEW OF WHAT HAPPENED": DOS to MacNamara, 13 August 1947, in Behlmer, *Memo,* 373.

261 "IT IS A JOY": DOS to Irene Selznick, 17 December 1947, in Behlmer, *Memo,* 392.

262 "HE IS SUPERB": DOS to Agnew, 5 November 1947.

262 "I HAPPENED TO WITNESS": Robert M. Gillham to Harold Ross, 7 January 1948, Selznick Collection. "I can't remember ever having seen 'The Paradine Case'—with or without John McCarten—and I couldn't have been 'fortified,' because I didn't drink in 1947 and don't drink now" (Lillian Ross to author, 20 October 1986).

263 THE "NEUTRAL" LINE: Lois [?] to DOS, 15 January 1948.

263 "I HAVE GOOSED": DOS to O'Shea, 24 January 1948.

263 A CONSOLATION OSCAR: DOS to MacNamara, 26 November 1947.

263 "HOW IRONIC": DOS to MacNamara, 25 February 1948.

263 PERSONS FROM TWELVE: Gillham to Agnew, 7 November 1947, Selznick Collection.

264 "WE SHOULD DEVISE": DOS to Milton Euzell, 9 August 1948.

VIII: Transatlantic Postlude

265 "WE TALKED": DOS to "Angel" [Irene Selznick], 9 August 1939, in Behlmer, *Memo,* 278.

266 "USUALLY THE WEEKEND": quoted in Spoto, *Dark Side,* 309.

266 "SINCE MY FATHER WASN'T ALIVE": Transcript, Interview with Kim Hunter, Oral History Collection, SMU.

266 "THE SUBJECT DOESN'T COUNT": Samuels, 233.

268 "PLEASE DON'T TELL HITCH": Brown to Taft Schreiber, 27 October 1947, Hitchcock Collection.

268 "FORGIVE MY SAYING SO": quoted in Moorehead, 172.

269 "WHAT A SLOW WORKER": Rathvon to Charles Koerner, 26 April 1944, RKO Archive.

269 SELZNICK HAD WORKED: DOS to O'Shea, 12 June 1947.

270 INTRIGUED BY THESE: Rathvon to Depinet, 24 October 1947, RKO Archive.

270 "STORY, SCRIPT, BUDGET": "Questions regarding RKO-Transatlantic association," undated, RKO Archive.

271 HUNT STROMBERG RETAINED: Roy Hoopes, *Cain* (New York: Holt, Rinehart and Winston, 1982), 353–54.

271 "I AM GOING TO HAVE TO STOP": DOS to O'Shea ("Extremely Confidential"), 20 August 1946, in Behlmer, *Memo,* 376.

271 "OF EXCEPTIONAL QUALITY": Depinet to Norman Freeman, 28 October 1947, RKO Archive.

271 THE SIXTY-THREE-PAGE CONTRACT: Notes, 20 May 1948, legal files, Warner Bros. Archive, University of Southern California, Los Angeles.

272 "THAT WILL TEND TO SHOCK": Contract, 13 October 1948, Warner Bros. Archive.

272 HITCHCOCK LOATHED THE "MORALS CLAUSE": The twenty-six-page contract that Selznick offered Hitchcock on 11 February 1946 does not contain the "morals clause" (Selznick Collection).

272 "AUTONOMOUS PROVISIONS": Floyd Hendrickson, Memorandum of Telephone Conversation with P. D. Knecht (Warner Bros.), 20 May 1958, Metro-Goldwyn-Mayer Archive, Culver City, California.

272 "I HAVE TO": quoted in Moorehead, 178.

272 LEOPOLD AND LOEB: After the release of the picture, the head of Paramount complained to Jack Warner that *Rope* would disturb the Loeb heirs and adversely affect American Jews. "Very confidentially," Warner replied, "had you or someone else called my attention to the resemblance between the [Leopold-Loeb] case and this picture before

the picture was made, Warner Bros. would not have made any deal to release the picture" (Warner to Barney Balaban, 5 March 1948, Warner Bros. Archive).

272 "SORT OF GLASSY-EYED": quoted in *New York Times,* 9 October 1983.

273 "QUITE NONSENSICAL": Truffaut, 180.

273 "MANY PEOPLE DO THEIR BEST": quoted in Lane, 35.

273 "I DON'T THINK": Truffaut, 185.

275 "THE CAMERA WAS SUPPOSED": Bergman, 191–92.

275 "HUGE GAP IN THE WALL": Joseph Cotten to O'Shea, 31 July 1948.

276 "DEMONSTRATED TO HER": DOS to Reissar, 13 June 1950, in Behlmer, *Memo,* 407.

277 "I AM NOT QUITE HAPPY": Sidney Bernstein to AH, 4 October 1950, Hitchcock Collection.

277 "HAVE AT LAST GOT $25,000": AH to Sherry Shourds, 15 May 1951, Hitchcock Collection.

277 "WITH MY LONG EXPERIENCE": AH to Sam Taylor, 8 November 1963.

277 "A STRONG DIRECTOR": Bogdanovich, "Hollywood," *Esquire*, October 1972: 87.

278 "I'M NOT SURE THAT I LIKE": DOS to AH, 12 July 1939.

278 "I NEED WRITERS": quoted in "A Talk with Alfred Hitchcock," *Action*, May–June 1968: 10.

279 "OVER THE LAST TEN YEARS": Hendrickson, Memorandum of Telephone Conversation with Max Raskoff (Paramount), 3 February 1958, MGM Archive.

279 "THERE WAS NOT A DAY": AH to Carol Stevens, letter dated "Sat May 21."

280 "I TAKE CREDIT": quoted in Behlmer, *Memo,* 441.

280 "A GENEROUS MAN": Cukor, quoted in Lambert, 90.

280 "GOT ON VERY WELL": quoted in Higham and Greenberg, *Celluloid Muse,* 97.

280 "HITCH, COOL AND IMPERTURBABLE": DOS "Remarks" (undated); see also *Variety,* 10 March 1965.

280 "ARE WE MISSING": AH, "In the hall of mogul kings," *Times* (London), 23 June 1969.

SELECTED BIBLIOGRAPHY

Allen, Jane. *I Lost My Girlish Laughter.* New York: Random House, 1938.

Balcon, Michael. *Michael Balcon Presents . . . A Lifetime of Films.* London: Hutchinson, 1969.

Balio, Tino, ed. *The American Film Industry.* Madison: University of Wisconsin Press, 1976.

———. *United Artists: The Company Built by the Stars.* Madison: University of Wisconsin Press, 1976.

Barber, John. "Hitchcockney from Hollywood: The Old Master Comes Back and Tells All." *Leader Magazine,* 25 May 1946: 18–19.

Beeding, Francis. *Spellbound* (originally published as *The House of Dr. Edwardes*). Cleveland: World Publishing Company, 1945.

Behlmer, Rudy, ed. *Memo from David O. Selznick.* New York: Viking, 1972.

———. *Inside Warner Bros. (1935–1951).* New York: Viking, 1985.

Belfrage, Cedric. "Alfred the Great." *The Picturegoer,* March 1926: 60.

Bergman, Ingrid, and Alan Burgess. *Ingrid Bergman: My Story.* New York: Delacorte, 1980.

Bernstein, Matthew. "Fritz Lang, Incorporated." *The Velvet Light Trap* 22 (1986): 33–52.

Betts, Ernest. *The Film Business: A History of British Cinema 1896–1972.* New York: Pitman, 1973.

Bogdanovich, Peter. *The Cinema of Alfred Hitchcock.* New York: Museum of Modern Art Film Library/Doubleday, 1963.

Bordwell, David, Kristin Thompson, and Janet Staiger. *The Classical Hollywood Cinema: Film Style and Production to 1960.* New York: Columbia University Press, 1985.

Brown, Geoff. *Launder and Gilliat.* London: British Film Institute, 1977.

Burdett, Winston. "Salute to Mr. Hitchcock: He Knows What to Do With a Movie Camera." *Brooklyn Daily Eagle,* 21 June 1936 [Billy Rose Theatre Collection, New York Public Library].

Capra, Frank. *The Name Above the Title: An Autobiography.* New York: Vintage, 1971.

Carey, Gary. *All the Stars in Heaven: Louis B. Mayer's M-G-M.* New York: Dutton, 1981.

Carringer, Robert L. *The Making of* Citizen Kane. Berkeley: University of California Press, 1985.

Crowther, Bosley. *Hollywood Rajah: The Life and Times of Louis B. Mayer.* New York: Holt, Rinehart and Winston, 1960.

———. *The Lion's Share: The Story of an Entertainment Empire.* New York: Dutton, 1957.

Curtis, James. *Between Flops: A Biography of Preston Sturges.* New York: Harcourt Brace Jovanovich, 1982.

Delehanty, Thornton. "A Liberated Hitchcock Dreams Gaudy Dreams in Technicolor." *New York Herald Tribune,* 22 April 1945 [Billy Rose Theatre Collection].

Deutelbaum, Marshall, and Leland Poague, eds. *A Hitchcock Reader.* Ames: Iowa State University Press, 1986.

Doty, Alexander. "Alfred Hitchcock's Films of the 1940s: The Emergence of Personal Style and Theme Within the American Studio System." Ph.D. diss., University of Illinois, 1984.

du Maurier, Daphne. *Rebecca.* New York: Doubleday, Doran, 1938.

Durgnat, Raymond. *The Strange Case of Alfred Hitchcock, or The Plain Man's Hitchcock.* Cambridge: MIT Press, 1974.

Fallaci, Oriana. "Alfred Hitchcock: Mr. Chastity." *The Egotists: Sixteen Surprising Interviews.* Chicago: Regnery, 1963, 239–56.

Fethering, Doug. *The Five Lives of Ben Hecht.* London: Lester & Orpen, 1977.

Fontaine, Joan. *No Bed of Roses: An Autobiography.* New York: Morrow, 1978.

366

Selected Bibliography

Foote, John Traintor. "The Song of the Dragon." *The Saturday Evening Post,* 12 November 1921: 3+, and 19 November 1921: 18+.

Freedland, Michael. *Gregory Peck.* New York: Morrow, 1980.

Freeman, David. *The Last Days of Alfred Hitchcock: A Memoir Featuring the Screenplay of 'Alfred Hitchcock's The Short Night.'* Woodstock, New York: Overlook, 1984.

"Gallup Looks at the Movies." *The Gallup Report* 195 (1981): 3–26.

Gomery, Douglas. *The Hollywood Studio System.* New York: St. Martin's, 1986.

Hagopian, Kevin. "Declarations of Independence: A History of Cagney Productions." *The Velvet Light Trap* 22 (1986): 16–32.

Haley, Michael. *The Alfred Hitchcock Album.* Englewood Cliffs, New Jersey: Prentice-Hall, 1981.

Handel, Leo. *Hollywood Looks at Its Audience: A Report of Film Audience Research.* Urbana: University of Illinois Press, 1950.

Harmetz, Aljean. *The Making of 'The Wizard of Oz.'* New York: Knopf, 1977.

Harris, Robert A., and Michael S. Lasky. *The Films of Alfred Hitchcock.* Secaucus, New Jersey: Citadel, 1976.

Harwell, Richard B., ed. "Technical Adviser: The Making of 'Gone With the Wind' The Hollywood Journals of Wilbur G. Kurtz." *The Atlanta Historical Journal* 27 (1978): 7–131.

Haver, Ronald. *David O. Selznick's Hollywood.* New York: Knopf, 1980.

Hecht, Ben. *A Child of the Century.* New York: Simon and Schuster, 1954.

———. *Spellbound. Best Film Plays—1945.* Edited by John Gassner and Dudley Nichols. New York: Crown, 1946, 57–113.

Hellman, Geoffrey T. "Alfred Hitchcock: England's Best and Biggest Director Goes to Hollywood." *Life,* 20 November 1939: 33–43.

Hichens, Robert. *The Paradine Case.* Garden City, New York: Doubleday, 1934.

Higham, Charles. *Hollywood Cameramen: Sources of Light.* Bloomington: Indiana University Press, 1970.

———. *Hollywood at Sunset.* New York: Saturday Review Press, 1972.

———, and Joel Greenberg. *The Celluloid Muse: Hollywood Directors Speak.* New York: Signet, 1969.

———. *Hollywood in the Forties.* Cranbury, New Jersey: A. S. Barnes, 1968.

"Hitchcock Brews Thrillers Here." *House and Garden,* August 1942: 34–35.

Hirsch, Foster. *Laurence Olivier.* Boston: Twayne, 1979.

Houseman, John. *Run Through: A Memoir.* New York: Simon and Schuster, 1972.

Huettig, Mae D. *Economic Control of The Motion Picture Industry: A Study in Industrial Organization.* Philadelphia: University of Pennsylvania Press, 1944.

Huston, John. *An Open Book.* New York: Knopf, 1980.

International Motion Picture Almanac. New York: Quigley Publishing Company, 1935–1961.

Jacobs, Lewis. "Film Directors at Work: I. Alfred Hitchcock." *Theatre Arts,* January 1941: 40–43.

Jewell, Richard B., with Vernon Harbin. *The RKO Story.* New York: Arlington House, 1982.

————. "How Howard Hawks Brought *Baby* Up: An *Apologia* for the Studio System." *Journal of Popular Film and Television* 11 (1984): 158–65.

Johnston, Alva. "The Great Dictator." *The Saturday Evening Post,* 16 May 1942: 9+.

————. "300-Pound Prophet Comes to Hollywood." *The Saturday Evening Post,* 22 May 1943: 4+.

Kobal, John. *People Will Talk.* New York: Knopf, 1986.

"The Lady Vanishes: and a British Trencherman Is Again Spotlighted." *Newsweek,* 17 October 1938: 28–29.

Lambert, Gavin. *On Cukor.* New York: Putnam's, 1972.

Lane, John Francis. "They Call It the Selznick Touch." *Films and Filming,* January 1958: 8+.

LaValley, Al, ed. *Focus on Hitchcock.* Englewood Cliffs, New Jersey: Prentice-Hall, 1972.

Leamer, Laurence. *As Time Goes By: The Life of Ingrid Bergman.* New York: Harper & Row, 1986.

Low, Rachael. *Film Making in 1930s Britain.* London: George Allen & Unwin, 1985.

Maloney, Russell. "Profiles: What Happens After That?" *The New Yorker,* 10 September 1938: 24–28.

McBride, Joseph, ed. *Hawks on Hawks.* Berkeley: University of California Press, 1981.

Montague, Ivor. "Working with Hitchcock." *Sight & Sound* 49 (1980): 189–93.

Moorehead, Caroline. *Sidney Bernstein: A Biography.* London: Jonathan Cape, 1984.

Myrick, Susan. *White Columns in Hollywood: Reports from the GWTW Sets.* Edited by Richard Harwell. Macon, Georgia: Mercer University Press, 1982.

Nelson, Donald M. "The Independent Producer." *The Annals of the American Academy of Political and Social Sciences* 254 (1947): 49–57.

Nugent, Frank S. "Assignment in Hollywood." *Good Housekeeping,* November 1945: 12–13, 290.

————. "Mr. Hitchcock Discovers Love." *The New York Times Magazine,* 3 November 1946: 13+.

Olivier, Laurence. *Confessions of an Actor: An Autobiography.* New York: Simon and Schuster, 1982.

Perry, George. *The Films of Alfred Hitchcock.* New York: Dutton, 1965.

Selected Bibliography

Phillips, Gene D. *Alfred Hitchcock.* Boston: Twayne, 1984.

Pringle, Henry F. "Hollywood's Selznick: The Man Who Made 'Gone With the Wind' Gambles $4,000,000 on a Smash Success." *Life,* 18 December 1939: 18+.

Reynolds, Quentin. "The Amazing Selznicks." *Collier's,* 28 May 1938: 11+, and 4 June 1938: 19+.

Roberts, Katharine. "Mystery Man." *Collier's,* 5 August 1939: 22.

Roddick, Nick. *A New Deal in Entertainment: Warner Brothers in the 1930s.* London: British Film Institute, 1980.

Rohmer, Eric, and Claude Chabrol. *Hitchcock: The First Forty-Four Films.* Translated by Stanley Hochman. New York: Ungar, 1979.

Ross, Murray. *Stars and Strikes: Unionization of Hollywood.* New York: AMS Press, Inc., 1967.

Rosten, Leo. *Hollywood: The Movie Colony, the Movie Makers.* New York: Harcourt, Brace and Company, 1941.

Rothman, William. *Hitchcock: The Murderous Gaze.* Cambridge: Harvard University Press, 1982.

Rózsa, Miklós. *Double Life: The Autobiography of Miklós Rózsa.* New York: Hippocrene Books, 1982.

Ryall, Tom. *Alfred Hitchcock & the British Cinema.* Urbana: University of Illinois Press, 1986.

Samuels, Charles Thomas. *Encountering Directors.* New York: Capricorn, 1972.

Sanders, George. *Memoirs of a Professional Cad.* New York: Putnam's, 1960.

Sanders, Terry B. "The Financing of Independent Feature Films." *Quarterly of Film Radio and Television* 9 (1955): 380–89.

Sarris, Andrew, ed. *Interviews with Film Directors.* New York: Avon, 1969.

Schickel, Richard. *The Men Who Made the Movies.* New York: Atheneum, 1975.

Selznick, Irene Mayer. *A Private View.* New York: Knopf, 1983.

Sherwood, Robert E., and Joan Harrison. *Rebecca. Twenty Best Film Plays.* Edited by John Gassner and Dudley Nichols. New York: Crown, 1943, 233–291.

Sklar, Robert. *Movie-Made America: A Social History of American Movies.* New York: Random House, 1975.

Spoto, Donald. *The Art of Alfred Hitchcock: Fifty Years of His Motion Pictures.* New York: Hopkinson and Blake, 1976.

———. *The Dark Side of Genius: The Life of Alfred Hitchcock.* Boston: Little, Brown and Company, 1983.

Sussex, Elizabeth. "The Fate of F3080." *Sight & Sound* 53 (1984): 92–97.

Taylor, John Russell. *Hitch: The Life and Times of Alfred Hitchcock.* New York: Pantheon, 1978.

———. *Strangers in Paradise: The Hollywood Emigrés 1933–1950.* New York: Holt, Rinehart and Winston, 1983.

Thomas, Bob. "Alfred Hitchcock: The German Years." *Action,* January–February 1973: 23–25.

———. *Selznick.* Garden City, New York: Doubleday, 1970.

Thomson, David. "Niven Busch: Sportsman: Niven Busch interviewed by David Thomson." *Film Comment,* July–August 1985: 40–49.

Thorp, Margaret. *America at the Movies.* New Haven: Yale University Press, 1939.

Todd, Ann. *The Eighth Veil.* New York: Putnam's, 1981.

Truffaut, François. *Hitchcock.* Revised edition. New York: Simon and Schuster, 1983.

Wanger, Walter. "Hitchcock—Hollywood Genius." *Current History,* 24 December 1940: 13–14.

Wasko, Janet. *Movies and Money: Financing the American Film Industry.* Norwood, New Jersey: Ablex Publishing Corp., 1982.

Weaver, John D. "The Man Behind the Body." *Holiday,* September 1964: 85+.

Weis, Elizabeth. *The Silent Scream: Hitchcock's Sound Track.* East Brunswick, New Jersey: Fairleigh Dickinson University Press, 1982.

Wood, Robin. *Hitchcock's Films.* London: Barnes, 1966.

Yacowar, Maurice. *Hitchcock's British Films.* Hamden, Connecticut: Archon Books, 1977.

INDEX

Bank of America, 56
Barnes, George, 60–62, 71, 82, 107, 145, 165
Barnes, Howard, 262
Barrymore, Ethel, 193, 207, 233, 263
Basevi, James, 140, 145, 164
Bates, Florence, 72, 79
Baxter, Anne, 57
Beeding, Francis, 117, 118, 123
Beery, Wallace, 25
Before the Fact, 87, 88, 93, 94
Bel Air Country Club, 102
Bellamy, Ralph, 137
Bendix, William, 111
Bennett, Charles, 13, 15, 21
Bennett, Joan, 135
Benson, Sally, 105
Bergman, Ingrid, 6, 37, 86, 87, 98, 107, 176, 179, 182, 191, 209, 224, 228, 232, 240, 255, 275, 276
  in *Notorious,* 175, 177, 199, 201, 203, 207, 211–213, 215, 218, 220
  in *Spellbound,* 117n, 135–136, 140, 146, 149, 151, 152, 154, 156, 159, 161, 162, 163, 165, 166, 168, 170, 172
Berle, Milton, 266
Berman, Pandro, 187
Bernstein, Sidney, 99, 118, 120–122, 123, 176, 177, 205, 208, 209, 218, 224, 227, 228, 233, 235, 236, 254, 256, 258, 261, 264, 268, 269, 270, 271, 272, 273, 275, 276, 277, 278
Best Years of Our Lives, The, 211
Beverly Hills High School, 51
Bill of Divorcement, A, 5, 40
Birds, The, 244
Blackmail, 10–11, 12, 45, 128, 162, 184, 227
Bogdanovich, Peter, 132, 277
Bon Voyage, 122
Boyle, Robert, 59, 101, 102, 105, 110
Brando, Marlon, 261

Breen, Joseph I., 70–71, 142–143, 154, 156–157, 159, 166, 200, 218, 228, 238, 248
Bridie, James, 230, 231, 233, 236, 237–238, 275
British Board of Censors, 142, 245
British Ministry of Information, 99, 120, 122
Brown, Kay, 23, 26, 36, 38, 42, 47, 48, 57, 101, 134, 255, 268
Buchan, John, 13, 39
Burbage, James, 151
Burns, Bob, 107
Burnside, William, 27, 28
Busch, Niven, 5, 28, 109

C

Cain, James M., 200, 271
Calhoun, Rory, 255
Canadian Forum, 221
Capra, Frank, 16, 18, 28, 29, 62, 90, 92, 97, 133, 206, 235
Carey, Macdonald, 105
Carroll, Leo G.:
  in *The Paradine Case,* 233, 252, 254, 258
  in *Spellbound,* 118n, 137, 162
Casablanca, 151, 191
Chaplin, Charlie, 12, 176, 220, 255
Charisse, Cyd, 48
Chekhov, Michael, 118n, 137, 159, 162, 163, 166, 172
Chirico, Giorgio de, 159
Churchill, Douglas, 56
Churchill, Winston, 194
Citizen Kane, 45, 88, 139
Claudia, 107, 176
Clipper, 86
Cohn, Harry, 6
Collier's, 55–56
Collinge, Patricia, 105
Colman, Ronald, 39, 49, 51, 84
Columbia Pictures, 33, 87

377